bo

All in the Blood

From Honor O Brolchain
to Brendan Ellis

All in The Blood

A Memoir by
Geraldine Plunkett Dillon

Edited by
Honor O Brolchain

A. & A. Farmar

British Library Cataloguing in Publication Data
A CIP catalogue record for this book is available from the British Library

ISBN-10: 1-899047-26-3
ISBN-13: 978-1-899047-26-0

First published in 2006
by
A. & A. Farmar Ltd
78 Ranelagh Village, Dublin 6, Ireland
Tel +353-1-496 3625 Fax +353-1-497 0107
Email afarmar@iol.ie

Printed and bound by ColourBooks
Typeset and designed by A. & A. Farmar
Cover designed by Kevin Gurry

Contents

Preface *Honor O Brolchain*

My grandmother, Geraldine Plunkett Dillon, who was born in 1891 and died in 1986, lived with us from the time I was very small. Our house was No. 13 Marlborough Road, Donnybrook. It must have been the most extensive tribal road in Ireland with eleven branches of the family living on it and about ten more houses belonging to them. All that is part of this story, her book, which I have compiled and edited from her voluminous writings, and from transcripts of interviews.

We called her 'Mamó', one of the Irish versions of 'Granny', and for 35 years of my life I lived with her stream of stories and memories. She talked about everything, from the appalling carry-on of her mother to the near misses with the Black-and-Tans in Galway, and wanted us and everybody else to know how awful it was at the time for herself and her siblings but even more for the people she saw in such great poverty and distress, often quoting the story of five families living in one room in a Georgian house, one family in each corner and one in the middle. She said she had almost total recall and disliked the notion of 'the good old days', which suggested that everyone in the past was virtuous and temperate, as she knew many people who drank themselves to death or out of a business, families ruined by violence and waste, and lives ruined by drugs. Her sense of humour rarely deserted her and she usually contrived to end even the most savage story with a chuckle. She also chuckled when she talked of her brother, Joe, whom she loved so dearly and referred to as a 'joker'.

After my mother died in 1998, my sisters, Barbara and Ester, and my brother, Fiacc, kindly gave me all the archival material from her house, including large plastic sacks of papers belonging to my grandmother which had been put away three years before she died. Among these were a set of ten spiral-back copybooks, telling the story of her ancestors, her family and her life from 1820 to the early 1920s with a wealth of description of her home and upbringing, life with her parents, Count and Countess Plunkett, and her six siblings, especially her brother, Joe (Joseph Mary Plunkett) and her own experiences in 1916 and in the War of Independence in Galway.

These copybooks date from the early 1950s and are the core of this book. When I went through them first I thought they read like a novel and her style and language made them roll along effortlessly but important information was difficult to decipher and, as my mother put it, my grandmother wrote as she talked, in knight's moves. My priority from the beginning was to make the text more linear and chronological and to check and confirm as much as possible. Along with these copybooks I used her research work from newspapers, commissions, legislation, reports and exhaustive correspondence with friends, historians and activists of the time. I also used the draft of a book on the 1913–1916 period she was working on for publication with Anvil Press for 1966, a project which fell through.

She wrote in her introduction to her unpublished book:

> I wrote all of this forty years ago when it was still fresh in my mind. Then I checked it with the newspapers of the time to make the dates as accurate as possible. I re-wrote it and got others to read it. It is, of course, possible for errors to have crept in but I am sure that I have represented the views and opinions of the principal actors correctly. Éamon de Valera, Seán T. O'Kelly and Cathal O'Shannon have read it and they allow me to say that I have stated correctly all that part of it that is within their personal knowledge.

And referring to 1916:

> I do not think that anyone who did not live in those times could realise how few our resources were or how small the material was out of which we had to build up a resistance. There is no comparison with the Ireland of today. The whole structure of living was organised against the Irish people in their own country . . .There was no possible choice of weapon, very small choice of plans; the leaders had nothing but their bare hands. There never was a prospect of success. The one certainty was that it was better to be dead than to be a slave. Because they were convinced of this, they did what they could and the ultimate result has been beyond their wildest dreams.

And in a 1980s newspaper interview she said:

> Anyone who says that nothing has been achieved since then has not the remotest idea of what conditions were like in Ireland. A terrific amount has been done and is being done every day and more would be done if people realised that they are free to do it.

My mother had pointed me to my grandmother's papers, dating from the 1980s, in the National Library in which she wrote the whole story again, although she was then in her nineties and battling illness. Along with the papers I have mentioned are transcriptions of a set of taped memoirs, her introduction to *The Poems of Joseph Mary Plunkett,* published in 1916, a series of articles for the 1950s *University Review,* statements for the Bureau of Military History on events leading to the 1916 Rising and on the War of Independence in Galway, 1920–1921, which included accounts she had collected to record both Black-and-Tan atrocities and Volunteer activities. She also wrote a series of seven talks for Radio Éireann entitled *The Years of Change* broadcast in 1958, articles for *The Capuchin Annual, The Connacht Tribune* and *The Dublin Magazine,* an article on her grandfather, Patrick J. Plunkett, and a lengthy letter to Professor Desmond Williams on Rory O'Connor and the Civil War.

From the Christmas after the 1916 Rising the men getting out of jail used to call on her to give her accounts of events and whenever 'the old comrades' met they would exchange anecdotes and information. She used all this and corresponded and checked her information with many people including Dan Nolan, Cathal O'Shannon, Frank Robbins, Bulmer Hobson, Hanna Sheehy-Skeffington, William O'Brien, Eamon Dore, Éamon de Valera, Seán T. O'Kelly, Edward Shields, Aidan McCabe, Donagh MacDonagh, Professor F. X. Martin, Professor Roger McHugh and Professor Desmond Williams. She was interviewed many times in all of the national newspapers and on radio and television, from the 1940s right up to her ninety-fourth birthday. Some of the radio and television interviews survive, the best being two unedited interviews in the Kilmainham Jail Archive for the 1966 commemorative programmes. There are many other small items of memorabilia which contribute to the picture, including the *Deed of Family Settlement* which tracks the legal origins, history and dispersion of the considerable family property.

In the construction of this book I have tried to combine these sources in such a way that each element will contain the best details and the best of my grandmother's voice which is so strong in flavour and conviction. For clarity, I reconstructed the text chronologically and inevitably this meant some stitching on my part. Because of the volume of material I had to make a selection, so my personal bias is there but influenced by my great friendship with her and I hope it serves her well enough. Accuracy had to be a primary consideration which meant constant background work to try to know and understand episodes in history. She was extremely accurate most of the time but I freely acknowledge that despite both our best efforts, inaccuracies are inevitable! Her papers in the National Library tend to have more mistakes than the other material as she was writing at speed, without reference material and already ill, but even these mistakes are usually minor.

There are some important elements here such as the account of the Castle Document which I hope will no longer be called 'bogus'. Her account is substantially confirmed by the Military Archive statement by Eugene Smith, who was responsible for smuggling out the information, and further confirmed by Paddy Little who published it. She also contributes more details to the accounts of the Connolly 'kidnap' and its real atmosphere, to the story of Galway's isolation and barbaric treatment by British Government forces in the War of Independence and she gives us the most complete picture of her brother, Joe Plunkett, ever printed.

Joe was not known to the public, or even to very many of the men he commanded in the GPO in 1916 because illness had kept him out of circulation so much. Roddy Connolly's view was typical: on Easter Monday when they had taken over the GPO and the dust had settled, he saw Joe lying on a mattress in front of the stamp counter, 'gorgeously apparelled' in his uniform, a silk scarf around his neck (to protect it after the operation on his glands the week before) and carrying a long sword. Roddy Connolly thought he looked out of place in a revolution and not much like a leader and asked his father who he was. James Connolly said 'That's Joe Plunkett and he has more courage in his little finger than all the other leaders combined.'

When she wrote, it was in order to provide a history of her times and an insight into what made her family so strange. Like many of her generation she did not write much about her own feelings but it is clear that her humourous and optimistic nature saved her sanity time and again. My grandmother did not write as much about her husband, Thomas Dillon, as one might expect. He was a great teacher of chemistry but in his personal life he could be flighty and irresponsible and one too many messy incidents meant that in her writings my grandmother did not give him the credit she might have done in the days when she loved and admired him so much.

When she was dying my grandmother gave me her brother, Joe's, copy of Wolfe Tone's *Autobiography*, which had been his bible. 'You'll understand about that,' she said, and although I knew what she meant, I knew I didn't understand, but I think I do, a little, now.

Acknowledgements

The generosity of my sisters, Barbara O Doherty and Ester O Brolchain Mazzetta, and my brother, Fiacc O Brolchain, was the key element to this book. They gave me all the archives from my mother's house after her death and continued to give and lend me material in the succeeding years. This is the core material of the book and they have my heartfelt thanks for that.

The second biggest element was the Geraldine Plunkett Dillon papers in the Manuscript Room of the National Library and my thanks are due to everyone there who helped me so much, especially Gerard Long and Elizabeth Kirwan of Manuscripts.

Statements from Geraldine Plunkett Dillon, her brother Jack and Máire Killeen O Brolcháin came from the invaluable collection at the Military Archive where Victor Laing and his staff could not have been more generous.

Niamh O'Sullivan at Kilmainham Jail gave me great inspiration and access to the RTE television series, *Portraits,* including the unedited interviews with Geraldine Plunkett Dillon and her sister, Fiona.

My thanks also to the RTE Radio Archive for access to the interviews by Donncha Ó Dulaing with Geraldine Plunkett Dillon.

At the National Museum Sandra McElroy supplied a copy of the photograph of Joe Plunkett working at wireless and an insight into the Plunkettabilia in the Museum. I am also indebted to Mairead Dunleavy for her copy of an interview with Geraldine Plunkett Dillon concerning the Dun Emer Guild.

I spent many happy hours in the Registry of Deeds checking the property manoeuverings of the Plunketts and Crannys and my thanks are due to a very kind and very patient staff.

The maps of Abbey Street and Larkfield are reproduced from maps in Trinity College Library, Dublin, with the kind permission of the Board of Trinity College. I was able to use this wonderful map library also to establish information on Plunkett and Cranny property and thank you to the very expert staff.

Tom Kenny of Kenny's Bookshop and Gallery, Galway supplied these important and sometimes dramatic images for the Galway section of the book: *The Model School, Séamus Quirke, The Funeral of Séamus Quirke and Seán Mulvoy, An Teach Beag Bán, Father Griffin's funeral, Ballinasloe House* and *Galway Jail* . He was kind, informative and very generous and I owe him a great debt of gratitude.

Special sources of information include Robert Mills of the Royal College of Physicians of Ireland for information on Dr John Joseph Cranny and Siobhan

O'Rafferty of the Royal Irish Academy on Geraldine Plunkett Dillon's paper to the Academy. Séamas Ó Maitiú and his excellent publications were a source of help and encouragement and I would also like to thank Seamus Fox for his website, *Chronology of Irish History 1919–1923* which proved essential. While on the subject of websites, I would like to thank all of those people who are so generous with information on the web and who so often prove to have some key element of confirmation.

It is impossible to praise librarians and archivists enough for what they do and how they do it but they have my humble thanks, especially the outstanding Gilbert Library, Boyle Library, Tralee Library and Rathmines Library.

Antique Prints (Hugh and Anne Iremonger) kindly allowed me to copy the postcard of the Imperial Hotel, 1916. My thanks to Taibhdhearc na Gaillimhe for access to masks made by Geraldine Plunkett Dillon and to the Royal Society of Antiquaries and the National College of Art and Design for additional information.

Special thanks to the nuns at Muckross Park Covent, especially the late Sister Maeve, for access to the house, information and the opportunity to photograph the interior. I am also grateful to Mary McEvaddy for allowing me to see the interior of No. 26, Upper Fitzwilliam Street. Thanks also to Father Carroll PP of Donnybrook Presbytery for information on the wedding of Count and Countess Plunkett and to the Rev. Patrick Comerford at Overseas House.

Many members of my extended family gave me information or images or both and first I'd like to mention Shivaun Gannon, grand-daughter of Patrick J. Plunkett, of Pender Island, Canada, who has been unstintingly generous and enthusiastic, giving me, among other things, the photograph of Patrick Plunkett taken in 1915 when he was ninety-eight. John and Dympna O'Donnell gave essential help in the Galway section, checking the text and giving me a tour of the sites. This meant a great deal to me. Art Ó Laoghaire generously gave me copies of documents and photographs relating to his grandmother, Mimi Plunkett. Of the many other relatives who helped in diverse ways, my special thanks are due to Norah Dillon, Rachel McNicholl, Michael O'Donnell, Ruth O'Donnell, Eiléan Ní Chuilleanáin and Phyllis Gaffney.

I owe much also to Tomás MacDonagh's descendants, Iseult McGuiness and Eithne McGuiness for many kinds of help over the years but especially for copies of Joe Plunkett's and Tomás MacDonagh's courts martial.

The historian, Sinéad McCoole, has been an enormous help to me both in terms of judgment and of encouragement and her knowledge of the women of my grandmother's time added reality to the compiling of the text.

Archivist Eibhlís Connaughton did some generous and valuable research work for me as did Gail Wolfe. Further insights and supportive information came through various events but particularly those run by the Society for the Study of Nineteenth-Century History in Ireland and the Rathmines, Ranelagh and Rathgar Historical Society.

ACKNOWLEDGMENTS

Mary McLoughney and Deirdre Corrigan provided help that was most important and valuable to me at a time when I needed it most, reading and taping documents. I cannot thank them enough and hope they know how much they are appreciated. In this context I would also like to thank Hilary Casey, Pauline Roche, Paul Fanning and the National Council for the Blind of Ireland and Jayne Husband and all the staff of Irish Guide Dogs for the Blind.

Donal O'Donovan was encouraging, helpful and supportive from the start, giving kindly of his journalistic and historical expertise all the way through and Susan Roundtree provided a large variety of ideas and solutions as well as entrées into hitherto unknown worlds.

Help, information, images and sundry services for which I am very grateful were provided by David Carmody, Jenny and Andrew Robinson, Dr Garrett FitzGerald and Mark FitzGerald, Helen Curtin, Dr Margaret MacCurtain, David Wilkes and Robert Wilkes.

My technological and psychological rescue team included my daughter, Isolde Carmody, my son, Mahon Carmody, Keith Brennan, Leena Tomukorpi, Michael O'Donnell and Ross Galbraith who all delivered me from gremlins and weebles, thus saving my sanity for another while.

It has been a privilege and a pleasure to work with an editor and historian of the calibre of Helen Litton, whose calm and direct judgment inspired confidence and I would especially like to thank Anna and Tony Farmar for their great interest and multiple layers of expertise, for their patient, painstaking and detailed work on editing and layout and for their ability to make the experience seem almost normal!

Brendan Ellis was in every part of the process from the beginning and undertook any and every task with his usual intelligence and humour. He read, taped, edited, re-read, researched, travelled, photographed, copied and checked references kindly and without fuss and was the core of support and reassurance all the way through. Thank you.

Honor O Brolchain
August 2006

Geraldine Plunkett Dillon's family tree

Note: Each new generation is represented by an indent.

Earlier ancestors

Great-great-grandparents include

George Plunkett (1750–1824) *m.* — ?
Daniel O'Sullivan *m.* Abigail —

Great-grandparents include

Walter Plunkett (1787–1844) *m.*— O'Daly
John Noble *m.* Abigail O'Sullivan
Black John Keane *m.* Elizabeth O'Sullivan
Patrick Cranny's antecedents are unknown.

George Noble, Count Plunkett's family
Patrick J. Plunkett (1817–1918) *m.* (1ˢᵗ) Elizabeth Noble (*d.* 1873)
    Mary Jane Plunkett (1848–1861)
    George Noble Plunkett (1851–1948) *(see below)*
    John Plunkett (*d.* in infancy)
m. (2ⁿᵈ) Helena O'Sullivan (1845–1925)
    Germaine, Helena, Oliver, Gerald

Mary Josephine Cranny, Countess Plunkett's family
Patrick Cranny (1820(?)–1888) *m.* Maria Keane 1824–1900
    John Joseph Cranny 'Jack' (1844–1904) *m.* Margaret Ellen Flanagan
    Francis Cranny 'Frank' (1848–1920?)
    Gerald Patrick Cranny 'Bob' (1852–1892)
    Mary Eliza (1854?–1869?)
    Mary Josephine 'Jo' (1858–1944) *m.* George Noble, Count Plunkett *(see below)*

George Noble Plunkett (1851–1948) *m.* Mary Josephine Cranny (1858–1944)

Philomena Josephine Mary 'Mimi' (1886–1926) *m.* Diarmuid O'Leary
    Colm *b.* 1919, Rory *b.* and *d.* 1925
Joseph Mary 'Joe' (1887–1916) *m.* Grace Gifford
Mary Josephine Patricia 'Moya' (1889–1928)
Geraldine Mary Germaine 'Gerry' (1891–1986) *m.* Thomas P. Dillon (1884–1971)
    Moya (1917–1992) *m.* Michael O'Donnell
        John, Moya, Ciarán, Michael, Ruth
    Blánaid (1918–1998) *m.* Eoin O Brolchain
        Barbara, Ester, Honor, Fiacc
    Eilís (1920–1994) *m.* (1st) Cormac Ó Cuilleanáin
        Eiléan, Máire, Cormac
    m. (2nd) Vivian Mercier
    Michael (1922–1992) *m.* Norah Curran
        Nuala, Margaret, Gráinne, Niall, Eamonn
    Rory (1925–1928)
    Eoin (1929–1997) *m.* Neans Stapleton
        Isoilde, Eoin, Mark
George Oliver Michael (1894–1944) *m.* Mary McCarthy
        Joseph, Eoghan, Seoirse, Máire, Siobhán
Josephine Mary 'Fiona' (1896–1976)
John Patrick Joseph 'Jack' (1897–1960)

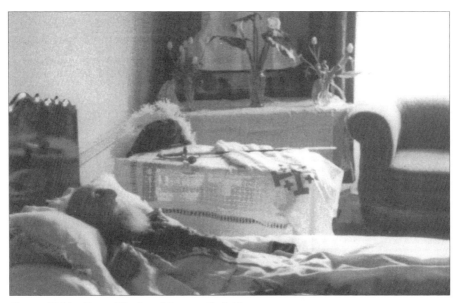

George Noble, Count Plunkett (1851–1948) laid out.

'Yesterday President Seán T. O'Kelly, the Taoiseach, Mr John A. Costello, members of the Oireachtas and prominent members of national, cultural and professional organisations were present at the obsequies of George Noble Plunkett, Count of the Holy Roman Empire and Knight Commander of the Holy Sepulchre. After Requiem Mass at St Andrew's Church, Westland Row, the funeral proceeded to Glasnevin Cemetery, where Count Plunkett was interred in the Republican Plot, beside Father Michael O'Flanagan. The coffin was draped in a Tricolour and on it were laid the sword, hat and cloak of a Knight of the Holy Sepulchre. Members of the National Graves Association, under Mr Seán Fitzpatrick, formed a guard of honour and detachments of Cumann na mBan and Cumann na Cailíní marched in the funeral procession. Flags were flown at half-mast on Government Buildings and the Last Post was sounded at the graveside by Mr W. Daly of St James' Band.'

Irish Press 16 March 1948

1 The Plunketts and the Crannys

IT WAS STRANGE AND QUITE BEAUTIFUL seeing Pa laid out in his white, gold-embroidered uniform, his hat and sword beside him, and all his troubles over. They gave him a State funeral; old comrades, ministers, bishops, priests and all sorts of artistic and academic people, not to mention a few blackguards, packed Westland Row Church and walked to Glasnevin for the oration at the grave. We buried him next to Father O'Flanagan, who had done so much to get him elected to the First Dáil in 1917. Pa was kind and courteous to the end, even about the stupidest things. He was ninety-six and he had lived too long but even in the last two years, when I tried to read to him, he never complained about being both blind and deaf and unable to get anything from any book, when books had always been his greatest joy. He was a funny old bird and I have cried for him every day since. We were always on good terms, friends from the beginning, at least from my first special memory of him, when I was two-and-a-half and I sat on his broad palm while he danced the Fandango in front of the long Adam mirror in the back drawing-room of our Fitzwilliam Street house in Dublin. That was the house where I was born in 1891. We could live in Fitzwilliam Street because my grandparents, through their hard work, had made us a wealthy family.

Both my grandfathers were extraordinary men. Oddly enough, they were both called Patrick, they both came up to Dublin from the country and they married first cousins who both had money and they had similar businesses a street away from each other. Out of those successes they made fortunes in building in the nineteenth century in Donnybrook, Rathmines and Ballsbridge on the south side of Dublin.

My father, George, was a Plunkett. Lords Fingall, Dunsany and Louth are all Plunketts, all related and all have* land in Louth and Meath, so the whole area is still full of big-nosed Plunketts called Henry, Walter, Luke and George and as like one another as peas in a pod. The Plunketts came to Ireland before the Normans and the name became exclusively Irish. They settled on rich land and prospered early, so there were many professionals, lawyers, soldiers, bishops and priests. Large castles are dotted over the two counties and they came to be known as one of the great families in Ireland. They were created barons in the fourteen and fifteen-hundreds, my ancestor being made Baron Killeen in 1463 by Edward IV, and in 1628 his descendant was created an earl, Lord Fingall. When the dissolution of the monasteries was ordered by King

* Or at least had when GPD was writing in the 1920s.

1

Henry VIII and Richard Plunkett, Abbott of Kells, had to surrender his monastery and all its possessions to the English Crown, he managed to hide the monastery's beautifully illuminated Bible, and it was quietly passed over decades from one Plunkett family to another until it reached Gerald Plunkett in Dublin. He gave it to Archbishop Ussher, and five years after he died Trinity College acquired part of his library including this Bible, the Book of Kells.

My grandfather, Pat Plunkett, was born in 1817 on a farm which he described to me as adjoining the demesne wall of Killeen, the castle of the Earls of Fingall, in County Meath. Pat's family and the Earl of Fingall were descended from two brothers who, after the Reformation, when the law in Ireland made it impossible for Catholics to own large amounts of land, had to choose between land, title and religion. The eldest brother opted to stay Catholic while the younger one became a Protestant, so keeping the land and the title. This was not an unusual arrangement as it served to keep the estate in the family. Later, the younger brother returned to Catholicism but retained the Fingall title, the land and Killeen Castle. My grandfather was even more closely related to Killeen through the O'Dalys of O'Dalys' Bridge in Virginia, County Cavan. An ancestor of his had married one of two O'Daly sisters and Lord Killeen had married the other. That particular Countess, a snob, never spoke to her sister again!

The last of the O'Daly family from Virginia, County Cavan, two old ladies, who were always old ladies as long as I knew them, were in and out of our house all our lives. These ladies were Jemima and Bedelia O'Daly, always called Jim and Dilly. They were highly valued by my father as friends and relations and they provided an amazing link with that lost Ireland which existed before the Famine. Their home was in O'Daly's Bridge and in front of the house was, and is, Rath an Dálaigh, a great mound in a field, a very old fort which must have been the family home from time immemorial. My sister Fiona and I spent a week with them in their house where not only traditions but many material objects formed ties with past history. There was an unlocked loft over a stable in which many of the family possessions were left to rot or be taken by any passer-by, including an illustrated thirteenth-century missal. This was just left there while something which was treasured was a candle which their father had brought back from Daniel O'Connell's funeral, at which he was an acolyte.

There was a strong contrast in character between the two ladies. Dilly was a bitter person but a good cook who resented the world and kept herself out of it, largely because her face had been badly scarred by a burn in early childhood. Jim, on the other hand, was a woman of great enterprise and when their brother, Willie, who had gone to Mexico to work as the manager of a silver mine, was killed by bandits she travelled to Mexico, hired a horse and a gun, found the killers, arrested them and brought them in to the Marshal. Once assured that they were jailed, she set out back for Ireland bringing with her

Willie's two sons to protect them from any revenge killing. She installed them in Blackrock College under the name of O'Neill and lived the rest of her life as a respectable spinster, later working in the Irish Sweepstakes, riding her high bicycle and having lunch every day in my parents' house.

Grandpa Plunkett's father, Walter, was educated at the end of the eighteenth century when education in Ireland was prohibited for Catholics, and it was also illegal for them to send their children abroad for it. However, many Catholic households like the Plunketts at Killeen secretly employed teachers who came to the house for weeks or months and taught not only the family but also children from the surrounding area. The teacher always stayed with Grandpa's people. Each teacher taught only his own subject. Grandpa's father, Walter, told him how strange it was to concentrate on nothing but French for months, and then on

Jemima (Jim) O'Daly, a Plunkett relation. Hearing that her brother had been shot by bandits in Mexico, Jim left her home in County Cavan, travelled to Mexico, hired a horse and a gun, arrested the bandits, turned them over to the law and came home again.

Greek or maybe mathematics. By Walter's time the laws had been relaxed, but for many Catholics, having tutors was still the only way to a decent education. Grandpa's parents were children during the French Revolution of 1789 and I could never get used to the way he spoke about it and about the 1798 Rebellion in Ireland—as though he had just heard about them by word of mouth. 'That woman,' he would say, talking of the French Revolution, 'that woman who killed that Frenchman in his bath . . .'

My grandfather's family were farmers and had lived alongside their Fingall relations for generations, but this relationship was not considered by Grandpa to mean that he himself was an aristocrat; it was not a very grand thing to be related to an impecunious Catholic peer. He was prouder of the fact that he was a lineal descendant of the brother of Archbishop Oliver Plunkett who, only four generations before, had been executed at Tyburn. Archbishop Plunkett was accused in 1678 of planning a French invasion of Ireland with the help of the Jesuits and organising 70,000 Catholics to rise in support of this. The case against him was thrown out of court in Dundalk. The witnesses against him were a Franciscan and some parishioners, whom the Lord Lieutenant dismissed saying, 'They find it more honourable to be the King's witness than cowstealers.' The case was taken to London instead and all the barristers in the family were in there fighting for him, but the witnesses perjured themselves and he was found guilty. He was hanged, drawn and quartered on 1st July 1681.

Walter Plunkett was not on close terms with his Fingall cousin and he had no lease on the land he farmed. The deer from the demesne, particularly one great stag, used to break out onto his farm and damage his crops. As a boy, my grandfather Pat resented this deeply and decided to lie in wait for the stag by a gap in the hedge. Every night for a week he waited in bright moonlight. When the stag came at last he jumped for its throat with his knife but the stag knocked him down with a sweep of its antlers and gored him on the temple. Grandpa Pat said he never hated any animal as much as that stag and the mark was on his temple until he died in 1918. About half the population of the district were Orangemen who were protected by police and government and Grandpa made us gasp with his account of how every 12th of July Orangemen used to attack the Catholic population. Once, when he lay in the heather near a stream when the battle was over, he watched the wounded Catholics crawl out of hiding to get a drink and saw, with horror, the women of the Orange faction waiting with great stones in their hands to beat out their brains.

Walter died in 1844 and was buried at the foot of the Fingall vault in Killeen where his father George (1750–1824) also lay. When the potato crop failed in 1845 and 1846, Grandpa Pat and his twelve brothers and one sister abandoned the farm. He did not tell me whether they could have survived on the wheat, which was such a wonderful crop both that year and the following year. The family scattered to other parts of Ireland and to England, but most of them, including Pat's sister, went to America. Pat came to Dublin and worked in one of the shops on O'Connell Street where Clery's now stands, and in the space of a year he had married my grandmother, Elizabeth Noble, who was always called Bess.

Her father was a leather merchant of Italian (and possibly Jewish) extraction who had moved to Dublin. He was a good painter (his self-portrait is still in the family) and his father had taught drawing in London. However, he would not allow Bess to study painting because he said it had caused him so much misery. John Noble was Protestant and his wife, Abigail O'Sullivan, one of the twenty-one children of Daniel and Abigail O'Sullivan of Tralee, was Catholic. Together they ran a leather shop at No. 11 Stephen Street. John wanted my grandmother, Bess, to marry a Protestant friend of his but her mother objected. She married Bess off to an old Catholic man named Murphy (whom Bess seems to have liked) while John was away on business and when he returned, he was so angry that he compelled Bess, who was still a minor, to return home. From 1840 the Stephen Street shop was in Bess' name and I believe she was now managing the business. When Murphy, her husband, died Bess was angry that she had not been allowed to look after him through his last illness and she quarrelled with her father about it, so she left Stephen Street and bought a shop with living space over it just around the corner at

Abigail O'Sullivan, mother of Bess Noble, and grandmother of Count Plunkett, was one of 21 children of a Tralee business family.

No. 1 Aungier Street with the money her husband had left her. Here she set up her own leather business and never spoke to her father again. This was in 1845. An Essex Street locksmith, whom I met in 1916, told me that she was always known as 'Bess-Noble-with-a-shop-of-her-own.'

Bess was clever with leather and already knew the business well, so she was successful and made plenty of money. She was artistic and a good critic and bought many pictures and objets d'art on her travels. She travelled Europe buying leather and in Italy she was often taken as Italian with her dark skin and good accent. Pa said that I looked like her. Bess was a friend of Anne Devlin, whose part in protecting Robert Emmet had not been forgotten by Dubliners but who now lived in a slum in Camden Street and worked cleaning pubs up and down Camden Street and Richmond Hill. She was poor and old when Bess got to know her, already dying with much suffering, a legacy of the torture inflicted on her when she was in jail. She told Bess about how Major Sirr had half-hanged her from the shafts of a cart to try to get information on Emmet from her. She was still considered dangerous to know in the 1840s and people were afraid to visit her in case they would be marked down as Nationalists by the watching police, but Bess continued to see her until Anne Devlin died in 1851.

Pat Plunkett and Bess Noble travelled in Europe after their marriage, stopping in Paris to collect the Frères Raingo clock and matching candlesticks which had been ordered for them. On their return they ran the shop, which was immensely successful, together and by the following year the name had been changed to *Patrick Plunkett, Irish, English and French Leather Merchant and Post Office Receiver*. They had three children: John, who died in infancy, Mary Jane, who lived until she was fifteen, and Pa, who was born on the 3rd of December, 1851 and, using both his parents' names, was called George Noble Plunkett.

Bess and Pat Plunkett's house was a well-known drop-in centre for Nationalists, and that December a neighbour brought two men to the house in Aungier Street. They said that they had heard there was a new baby in the house and asked that he be brought down to them. They, each in turn, held my father and then said to my grandparents, 'Now tell him when he grows up that the Big Drummer and the Little Drummer of Vinegar Hill held him when he was a baby.' My grandparents were proud to have this connection

Patrick J. Plunkett (1817–1918) with his children, George Noble and Mary Jane, in 1859. He came to Dublin from County Meath, married Bess Noble, who had a leather shop of her own, and, with profits from that, he built and developed redbrick houses, mainly in Rathmines.

with the 1798 Rebellion and promised they would. Twenty-one years later a young man called to the shop and told Pa that he was a nephew of one of the Drummers. He said they were both dead but that before his uncle died he had asked him to come to Dublin to remind that child, now grown to be a man, that the Big Drummer and the Little Drummer of Vinegar Hill had held him in their arms when he was a baby. No-one seems to know of drummers of any kind at Vinegar Hill but that was what they called themselves.

Pat Plunkett went into the building business in the 1850s, initially using his wife's money and, as he prospered, using his own. He already owned some yards and warehouses in the Werburgh Street area and he now bought a plot in Rathmines on what was to become Belgrave Road. He built three houses employing Edward Carson, an architect of Italian origin and the father of Lord Carson, but he suspected him of cheating and when he proved to his own satisfaction that he was right, he confronted Carson, made him refund the money and then sacked him. He was not the only builder to have this kind of trouble with Carson. He never employed an architect again, considering himself competent to do without them. He loved the work and the houses he built, and for every house he built for a client he built one for himself. Bathrooms were just becoming fashionable and he thought he was being very progressive in leaving space for them in the houses, but he didn't go to the extreme of actually installing them; after all, they might have just been a passing fad!

He and Bess kept on the shop in Aungier Street but moved house, first to No. 16 Upper Mount Pleasant Avenue while he and my other grandfather, Patrick Cranny, completed the building of Belgrave Road, then to No. 3 Belgrave Road, one of the Carson houses, in 1861. At this stage Pat Plunkett was building more houses on Belgrave Square and beginning the development of Palmerston Road. Blocking the vista on Belgrave Road is Holy Trinity, the Church of Ireland church in whose vestry the Rathmines Board of Commissioners held their meetings after Sunday services. This was illegal, but the Protestants of Rathmines continued to act as though the conduct of township business was still in the hands of the Vestry, as it had been in earlier times. Being held in a Protestant church, the meetings were effectively closed to the Catholic public and ratepayers, which meant they were not getting the services to which they were entitled. Pat Plunkett protested about this but without result. He put a ladder to the window of the vestry one Sunday and climbed in with a numerous company behind him, causing the meeting that was in progress to break up in disorder. The situation became a public matter, and after questions were asked in the House of Commons the Vestry system in Rathmines and elsewhere came to an end. This way of working was common at the time; the Unionists took all they could in any way they could and were allowed and encouraged to do so by the government. Rathmines had a strong Unionist population, and any Catholic becoming wealthy and successful was regarded with suspicion. This created many problems for my grandfather; for a time he couldn't get services for his Palmerston Road houses, and he resorted to putting gates across the end of the road, closing it to the public to make his point. Once again he succeeded. He did have a partner for a long time who was a Unionist, as were most of his clients, and many of them were honest men who did him plenty of favours.

In 1870, the Plunkett family moved to 14 Palmerston Road, built by
Pat Plunkett, along with many of the other houses on the road. The
leases for the houses mention a 'covenant for quiet lving'.

He was twelve years old in 1829 when the Catholic Emancipation Bill was passed and belonged to a generation that was all the time testing its liberty. Catholics like both my grandfathers, who as a result of their hard work and tenacity moved into the category of voters, changed the balance of power and fired the aspirations of those on the way up. Pat Plunkett lived through Daniel O'Connell's time, the Young Irelanders, the Fenians, Isaac Butt, Charles Stewart Parnell, the Home Rule agitation, the 1916 Rising, and even to see his son elected in 1917. He revered O'Connell but didn't like him, he respected Davis but not Davitt, and like the majority of Irishmen he was appalled and saddened at the outcome of the Fenian uprising in 1867.

He was an extraordinarily active man; he said it was better to wear out than to rust out. He took contracts for all kinds of building work, and lowered the whole ground floor of Arnott's in Henry Street by two feet in one night in order not to disrupt business. As well as the roads I have already mentioned, he built on Cowper Road, Palmerston Park, Windsor Road, Ormond Road and Killeen Road—these last in 1900, when he was eighty-three. When I knew him he was finishing up the last big jobs with his partner, a man named Smith, building the roads off Palmerston Road. He did all his repair work by direct labour, supervising it himself. He had rheumatic fever three times after he was forty but it never affected his heart and at ninety he was persuaded, with great difficulty, to come down from the roof of one of his houses. He was already over seventy when I first knew him, so he was always an old man to me, white-haired and with a short, white, fuzzy beard. He was about five foot seven with a pink, lined face, but photographs of him when he was younger, with my father and Mary Jane, show him to be a dark and handsome man and they also clearly show the affection he had for his children. The Plunketts, over generations, had a tradition of civilisation and learning; I don't know where or how Pat was educated but I remember him writing a fine hand and that he always expressed himself in a strong refined style. He had the air of a distinguished Victorian with a strong sense of his duty to the community. He also had a pretty bad temper and, as children, we had to be very quiet when he was cross. He was aloof but kind and at Christmas and Easter used to give us half-crowns and later half-sovereigns!

The family moved from Belgrave Road to 14 Palmerston Road in 1870; only seventeen houses had been built, but he was already planting trees on it. The leases for the houses mention 'a covenant for quiet living'. No. 14 was a good house, big, comfortable, even luxurious, well furnished and full of things which Bess, with her excellent taste, had bought—good pictures, fine china, mirrors, ornaments, clocks and candlesticks. Grandpa particularly loved it for the green space behind: a beautiful garden with a tennis court and two paddocks with stables where they kept a carriage, carriage horses and riding horses for the children. Because it backed on to the grounds of Rathmines Castle, the green view continued at the end of the garden and it was a great relief to him to have a feeling of countryside again after the noise of the city centre. Grandpa stayed in this house for the rest of his life.

I never knew my other grandfather, Patrick Cranny, as he died before I was born, but he was admired by his wife and children who talked to me about him. He left Borris in County Carlow in the 1830s to go to Tralee as a journeyman shoemaker, to learn the trade from Daniel O'Sullivan who had a business there (and twenty-one children). Patrick Cranny met one of the grandchildren, Maria Keane, daughter of Black John Keane and Elizabeth O'Sullivan, and they married and came to Dublin. He worked first in Lime Street, near the quays, and prospered so they bought a house with a shop at No. 72, South Great George's Street in 1842 and a couple of years later moved two doors down, to No. 74. With the help of Maria's dowry he was able to establish a good business in a very short time. All shoes were still being made by hand at this time and Patrick Cranny's was a high-class bespoke trade from which he made a good deal of money. Many of his customers had their own hand-carved wooden lasts kept for them in the shop so that they could order boots and shoes without having a fitting. The shoemaking tools and much of the leather were brought in from Florence and some of the workers were also Italian. In the back of the shop there was a forge on which were made the nails, and tips for the toes and heels of the strong boots. When the workers in the shop needed a meal, steaks were brought in from the local butcher and

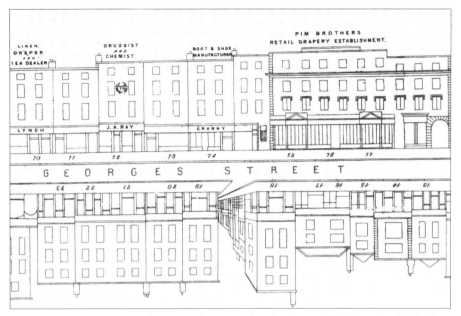

This George's Street streetscape shows Patrick Cranny's shoe shop (No. 74) beside Pim's. The Plunketts' shop at No. 1 Aungier Street, was only half a street away. From Shaw's Dublin Pictorial Guide and Directory *of 1850.*

cooked on the forge. The quality of the workmanship in the shop was re- markably good and in a few years they were able to add '*Bootmakers to the Lord Lieutenant*' underneath the name.

By now, Pat Plunkett and Patrick Cranny were each married to an O'Sullivan granddaughter, which made their wives first cousins, and each family had leather-related businesses in adjacent streets. They leased and loaned warehouses to each other and the Crannys gave the Plunketts a mort- gage on No. 1 Aungier Street, enabling Pat to begin his building. Patrick Cranny also began to invest in building houses as his shoemaking business grew. For both of them, the first building project was Belgrave Road in the 1850s, with Pat Plunkett working on the south side and Patrick Cranny on the north side. Patrick Cranny then had to face the problem of the shop's future, as shoemaking machinery had begun to appear. He would either have to bring in a completely mechanised system or sell up. My grandmother, Maria, who considered the shop as being somewhat beneath her, persuaded him to leave the business completely for building. I did not know any of this when I was growing up, as my mother was ashamed that she came from 'business people'. The Cranny shop was right next door to Pim's, '*wholesale & retail linen & woollen drapers, silk mercers, hosiers & haberdashers*', and after my grandfather had leased the shop to various clients it was sold to Pim's. They always kept the building separate, as it had been in his time, and used the window only for their shoe display; they told me much later that this was in honour of my grandfather and the excellence of his shop. Until I was about nine we all had our soft Morocco leather button boots made for us by an old man named Mahoney, the last of my grandfather's men. I remember being lifted up on to the table to be measured for the red boots he made for my fourth birthday. As always they were a perfect fit and impossible to wear out.

Since Maria Cranny's dowry had been used to set up the business, my grandfather, Patrick Cranny, was always concerned to provide well for her in return. He took a house for them out of town, 9 Serpentine Avenue, in the 1850s and leased land from the Lynches of Paris. This was first called Bushfield Avenue and afterwards Marlborough Road, in Donnybrook. On a site of just over two acres off the road he built Muckross Park, a house for himself and his family. They moved into it in 1861 and my grandmother could then begin to live in the style she thought she deserved. In 1875, when my grandfather was starting the building of Marlborough Road, he gave Maria the sole ownership of Muckross Park and the deeds. It was a lovely, villa-style house of good proportions with large glasshouses running down one side, a conservatory and walled gardens. Two-storeys over a basement, it had a short drive and a flight of steps to the front door with its Doric portico and there was an elegant balustrade on the roof. There were a couple of good drawing-rooms and a dining-room with high quality ceiling mouldings. The house was surrounded by fields, enough to keep riding and carriage horses, and each of the children had their own pony. Grandma Maria felt that the carriage was more fitting to her new position and she used to arrive at their shop in George's Street and demand that Patrick would join her to go for a drive in the carriage. He refused each time but she was putting him under constant pressure of this kind

Muckross Park, Donnybrook, Dublin, in 1900. Built by Patrick Cranny for his wife, Maria, in return for the use of her money to start his businesses, it was their family home from 1861 until his death in 1888.

Maria (Keane) Cranny (1824–1900), another member of the O'Sullivan family from Tralee, and Josephine (Cranny) Plunkett's mother. She was 'methodical, economical, competent, sharp-tongued, practical, domineering and religious'.

to leave the shoemaking business and move completely to the new suburbs. When he was building Muckross Park, there was a very inadequate chapel in Donnybrook village and he not only helped substantially in the building of the new church but in the meantime had Mass said at his own house. The Famine brought starving and destitute people to Dublin looking for relief and many of these called every day at the back door of Muckross Park where, on my grandfather's instructions, they would be given food. When it ran out, as it often did, he would send down his own dinner plate. If Grandma Maria protested, he said, 'Give it, I have enough.'

Grandma Maria Cranny was methodical, economical, competent, sharp-tongued, practical, domineering and religious. When she came in to the house, her thin, crêpe gloves were always put away in a drawer in the wrapping in which they were bought and the handles of her table-knives were always rolled in paper to keep them from discolouring. Nothing was ever done in any other way. She and Patrick had seventeen children, but only four survived into adulthood, John Joe (Jack), Gerald, Frank and Josephine (my mother), and none of them resembled their mother. Instead, they were flamboyant and extravagant both in physical appearance and character. There was another girl, my mother's older sister, Mary Eliza, who went to school for a time in the Dominican Convent, Sion Hill. She could speak five languages and play eight instruments and Grandma thought the light of Heaven shone from her eyes, but she died of tuberculosis when she was about sixteen.

The success of each of my grandfathers, first in one business and then in another, was remarkable. They had worked very hard for all those things that were made so difficult for Catholics to gain—wealth, rights and professions, and these were the things they wanted to give their sons. Between them they built houses on Belgrave Road, Belgrave Square, Palmerston Road, Palmerston Park, Ormond Road, Windsor Road, Killeen Road, Marlborough Road, Wellington Road, Elgin Road, Clyde Road, Raglan Road and Eglinton Road. Uncle Gerald Cranny was an architect and the guiding spirit behind his father's developments in Donnybrook and Ballsbridge. The ground landlord for many of the places where my grandfathers built was the Pembroke estate, which owned an enormous amount of Dublin (including a claim to own three miles out into Dublin Bay). Getting permission to build on Pembroke Estate land was exceptionally difficult for Catholics, but the Protestant Plunkett cousins helped out both my grandfathers in this respect. The Pembroke estate regulations were very strict; partly to keep standards high, but also, to keep the Imperial flavour, there was a stipulation that roads and streets must be named after eminent English statesmen. This was also the case with the Rathmines Commissioners. My grandfathers' response to this was to try to get away with names of people who were in disgrace or disreputable or, better still, sympathetic to Ireland and they often managed. One road which Pat Plunkett could name as he liked, because it was in the Cullenswood estate, he

Patrick Cranny (1820–1880) was a journeyman shoemaker from Carlow. His wife, Maria, had money of her own which they used to set up a highly successful shoe shop on George's Street before going into building in Rathmines, Ballsbridge and Donnybrook.

named Killeen after his home in County Meath.

The houses for which Gerald Cranny was responsible were particularly well designed and built and included bathrooms, and in this he was very much ahead of his time. On Elgin Road they had to battle with the cumbersome designs of the English architect for the Pembroke Estate, and these houses were always difficult to let, being the wrong size and shape for most people. The wealth from all these houses was in rents from middle-class, mostly business, people and from the ever-increasing number of colonial civil servants who were coming to Ireland at the time. My Plunkett grandfather sold many of his houses, but the Crannys tended to keep theirs and circulated them round the family. Uncle Gerald left the building business when the Marlborough Road houses were finished in the 1880s and went to Spain to set up a wine-exporting venture with a man named Woolworth.

Pa had far more love and affection from his parents than any of the Crannys had from theirs. He just remembered his brother as a baby, wearing baby clothes with flowers on them. He had not lived long enough to be a real brother, but Pa greatly loved his older sister, Mary Jane, and thought her charming and accomplished. However, by 1860 she was already in the grip of tuberculosis and as Pa was also thought to have a delicate constitution his mother, Bess, brought him with her on one of her buying trips and left him in a Marist school in Nice so that he would be protected by the better climate. There was a quarrel between Grandpa Pat and Bess about this but Grandpa told me that they quarrelled a lot. Pa enjoyed Nice, the climate suited him, he acquired excellent French and Italian and his time there marked the beginning of a lifelong love of Italy and art, passions he shared with his mother. Among many friendships made then was one with the great Provencal poet, Fréderic Mistral, with whom he corresponded until Mistral's death. Pa was there for three years, spending the summers in San Remo, until he was twelve and during this time Mary Jane died. He mourned her deeply all his life. I remember him often weeping when he spoke about her.

When he came back to Ireland he went to the Oblate Fathers School on Upper Mount Street, where he distinguished himself in Irish history among other things. At sixteen he went to Clongowes, emerging two years later with a good Jesuit education consisting of Latin, Greek, mathematics, natural sciences and philosophy. During all this time he and Grandpa kept up a constant and affectionate correspondence and Grandpa sent him any money he needed or asked for. Pa wrote to Grandpa when he was sixteen saying that he was determined that he would work for the good of the country. Grandpa wrote back saying that when he was older he would be able to make up his mind on this. They had very little in common but were always very close. Pa believed, partly because of the incident of the two Drummers of Vinegar Hill, that he was meant to do everything he could for Ireland, in any way he could.

George Noble Plunkett in 1872, aged twenty-one, when he fell in love with his second cousin, Josephine Cranny. After school he travelled the Continent, arriving in Paris in time for the 1870 siege. He entered Trinity College Dublin in 1873 where he met Bram Stoker, Oscar Wilde and others. He was made a Papal Count in 1884 for helping the Blue Nuns and presenting them with a villa as their house in Rome.

He decided that he wanted to work as a journalist with particular reference to Irish Nationalist affairs and by the time he left school, he had already had articles published in Nationalist journals. After he left he was published in many journals and newspapers on a variety of subjects but he also had a year of travel at his father's expense. Grandpa believed that his son deserved everything he could get from experience and education and was generous in providing for this, so Pa was able to continue studying the great love of his life, Renaissance art. He rented a palazzo in Venice for the winter of 1869 and arrived in Paris in 1870 in time to watch history being made as the Prussians put the city under siege. He spent so much time in Italy that, all his life, when exasperated he would say '*O per Bacco!*' (by Bacchus!) or 'Ye Heathens and Garibaldians!' Thanks to his father's wealth and affection, he had no financial worries. He was unrealistic about money but since he had no personal greed he was always generous with his own and careful with anyone else's.

Back in Dublin he continued to write for Nationalist papers such as the *Nation,* the *Freeman's Journal,* and the *Irishman* and to indulge his obsession with books. He lived in various furnished rooms and, since he bought books constantly, the rooms would fill up until there was no living space left. He would then lock them up, continue paying the rent and move somewhere else. He monitored catalogues for books or documents of Irish origin or interest, with a view to restoring them to the country, to contribute to its cultural stock. He bought everything he could find connected with Archbishop Oliver Plunkett including contemporary accounts of his trial, and the many pieces of Irish music he bought included the manuscripts of Beethoven's Irish songs, which he gave to the National Library. He was also buying china, silver, paintings, drawings, old prints and the never-ending and uncontrollable stream of books. He turned twenty-one on December 3rd 1872 and his mother gave him £100. She suggested that he might look at some paintings which were being auctioned in a house in Aungier Street, because she thought they were good. He took her advice and bought *The Adoration of the Magi.* It had no authenticating history but his studies led him to believe that it was by Rubens. He loved the painting which always dominated our dining-room at home, but Ma hated it because she found the naked infant indecent, although she acquired a sort of affection for the painting later on when she realised how valuable it was.

Bess Noble died the following year, 1873, and in the autumn Pa became a student at Trinity College, Dublin. He was now a tall, handsome man with a typical Plunkett head and face and he had grown a beard to keep his chest warm and free from tuberculosis. He read enormous amounts in French, Italian and Latin as well as English, with detective stories as light relief. He became fascinated by Christian symbolism and his favourite book was *The Lives of the Fathers of the Church* in French, in fifty-seven volumes. But he was neither deadly nor dull; he was full of wit and understanding. He had great kindness, no bigotry, in spite of being strongly religious and he was the perpetrator of terrible puns. Although ostensibly studying law he took very little interest in it at that time, taking the opportunity instead to expand his knowledge of art and literature. He gave papers on these in the Trinity College Philosophical Society and on Irish social, industrial and cultural areas. He was passionate about the Irish language (although he did not speak Irish well himself) and endowed a gold medal in Trinity College for spoken Irish. The first person to win it was his friend, Douglas Hyde, later the first President of

Ireland. He co-founded SPIL, the Society for the Preservation of the Irish Language, which among other things published three little beginner books for learning Irish by Father Eugene O'Growney, and translations of early Irish texts. He discovered, at this time, that since the death of Eugene O'Curry, author of *The Ancient Irish,* the Catholic University had stopped functioning and O'Curry's assistant, Brian O'Looney, was destitute. He gave him an annuity from his own income of £100 a year until O'Looney died, in 1913. This was only one example of his generosity.

Pa enjoyed the company at Trinity, making many friends, both there and outside, who had similar passions, including Charles Kickham, Isaac Butt, Katherine Tynan, Bram Stoker and Oscar Wilde. He and Wilde wrote regularly to each other for a long time after Wilde left Ireland, letters that Pa told me were brilliant and full of wit and speculation about his own Irishness and his feelings for Catholicism. Wilde was strongly drawn to the idea of Catholicism but considered that it would be death to any possibility of success as a playwright. Pa, for all his own strong religious convictions, sympathised with him. He knew Wilde's father, Sir William Wilde, and admired his scholarship but had no liking for him. Sir William Wilde told him that Oscar O'Flaherty, whose name was included in Oscar Wilde's name (Oscar Fingall O'Flaherty Wills Wilde) was a librarian to a sultan and a great scholar whom William Wilde had met on his travels.

When Pa went to London for extra law lectures he stayed with Wilde's mother, Speranza, who had moved there after Sir William's death in 1876. She also invited him to the soirées which she gave to try to help Oscar's career. Speranza, he said, was very tall and awkward, with large hands and feet; she wore voluminous robes, blue ribbons and lace and kept knocking things down, but she was extremely kind to everyone, especially to any of the Irish visiting London. Oscar Wilde wrote about fifty letters to Pa but, long after Wilde's scandal was already old, there was some discussion of the letters in our house and Ma took one of her fits: 'Oscar Wilde—that disgraceful man!' she said, and threw all the letters in the fire. She had only the vaguest notion of what the so-called scandal was about. Pa remained friends with Wilde to the end, and after his death his wife, Lady Wilde, gave him some bundles of letters which had been written to Oscar. She asked him to read them and destroy anything scandalous that he found. She must have had her fill of scandal by then. Pa, of course, agreed but he only found one letter he considered worth burning; the rest he put away safely. When I was sorting his papers after he died, I found them and gave them to the National Library.

Among Pa's frequent literary correspondents were Christina Rossetti, and the sister of the writers Michael and John Banim. He always kept these letters in bandboxes and would not let anyone go near them. Around this time he also started the Arts and Crafts Society and he supported anything which he considered genuine or scientific while in the university, distinguishing himself in French and French literature. He also owned and edited *Hibernia*, a literary journal which lasted eighteen months, in which he published many early poems of Katharine Tynan, Dora Sigerson, Rosa Mulholland and many other emerging writers. Katharine Tynan said that when she was starting her own library, Pa was one of the very first to make her a present of a book. That was typical of him.

My father fell in love with my mother when she was fourteen and he was twenty-one. She was born in 1858 and there was an age gap of thirteen years between her and her eldest brother, Jack, who was born in 1845; she was more or less forgotten about as she was growing up. Her father was working so hard he lost touch with his family and when Ma was four he met her on the stairs and, picking her up, said 'And what is the name of this little one?' Ma was allowed to sit in at her brothers' lessons with their French and mathematics tutors, she was taught piano by Jo Robinson, the widow of a celebrated piano teacher, and she had a master to teach her drawing and modelling. She had a good touch on the piano, a true soprano voice and played the flute, harp, violin, zither and cello but, although I always loved to listen to her, she did not like music and had no understanding of it. It was only a drawing-room accomplishment to her and she gave it all up later on. She was an heiress and considered an accomplished beauty—I have met men who told me that she was the most beautiful creature they had ever seen. She was tall with a lot of pretty light brown hair, regular features and grey eyes. In many ways she never lost the character of the wild Irish girl that she had when Pa first fell in love with her.

On my mother's sixteenth birthday in the spring of 1874, there was a party in Muckross Park to which her brother, Jack, now a doctor, brought some medical friends. Two of them asked her father for her hand in marriage the next day, as did my father. Patrick Cranny, shocked, sent them all away and sent her off to the Ursuline convent school in South Kensington in London where she spent a year upsetting the community with her unruly carry-on. Just as the Reverend Mother was writing to ask her parents to remove her (I found this letter after she died), they decided to bring her home. She spent the next eight years trying to behave like a lady. My grandmother was strict in her standards and never praised Ma for anything. She thought nothing of her, and expected less than nothing from her. Ma also had the task of travelling in attendance on Grandma to the spas and resorts of Europe and waiting on her hand and foot. She used to shake with fear whenever Grandma spoke to her or even came into the room.

Pa didn't give up his idea of marrying Ma in spite of her parents' opposition. My grandmother forbade the match because she did not consider Pa's profession, journalism, to be respectable for a gentleman. She believed that a gentleman should have a 'proper' profession regardless of his financial cir-

Mary Josephine Cranny (1858–1944), later Countess Plunkett, here aged fourteen when her second cousin, George Noble Plunkett, fell in love with her. She was an heiress and considered a great beauty, though not every photo catches this.

cumstances but she didn't lose all hope of Pa—after all he was a second cousin and came with plenty of property behind him. She gave him no peace about studying law and being called to the Bar but Pa's interests were everywhere else but the law. He was becoming increasingly involved in Irish politics, partly through knowing Isaac Butt. Pa told me that it was not easy for a young Catholic man to be a Nationalist at that time, particularly if he had intellectual interests or any education. Most cultural institutions were in the hands of the Unionists, and it was represented to young Catholics that it was

Helena, yet another of the O'Sullivans' of Tralee, aged about thirty, (1878) in the year she became Pat Plunkett's second wife. She and Pat said it was love at first sight but Josephine's mother, Maria Cranny, claimed the credit. Maria was not so happy when Pat Plunkett (aged sixty-one when he married again) and Helena produced four children but Pat Plunkett was scrupulously fair in distributing wealth through

merely ignorance that prevented them from taking a larger part in the affairs of the country, a silly patriotic ignorance, and that as soon as they gave it up and recognised England's greatness and their own menial position, they would have their reward.

Uncle Jack Cranny had fallen for a girl he knew and wanted to marry her but Grandma Maria, who was always far too involved in his life, selected Margaret Ellen Flanagan (Aunt Marie) instead. Grandma thought her much more suitable and properly endowed in terms of property and money—her family were Coat's Thread and so on. They were married in 1874 and Uncle Jack was given seven houses on Elgin Road as his marriage settlement, and his considerable debts were settled by an annuity from Aunt Marie's estate. Approval of Aunt Marie cooled however as the years went by and no children appeared.

In 1878 Grandpa Pat got married again. It was no coincidence that he chose yet another of the grandchildren of Daniel and Abigail O'Sullivan. This time it was Helena, daughter of William O'Sullivan. Maria Cranny had been pestering Pat for some time to re-marry, ostensibly in order to provide Pa with a more stable home so that he wouldn't be 'wandering all over Europe' which was what he loved doing most. She thought that her first cousin, Helena, was an excellent choice, being a woman of quiet elegance and independent wealth. She had been a governess in France for quite a while, acquiring a good deal of French culture; she kept a house really well and was a beautiful needlewoman. Helena was then about thirty years old, gentle, slight, dark and, although not thought handsome by the family, she was always dressed in stylish good taste. Helena's father had been a well-respected businessman in Dublin years before, but while he was acting as executor for a will, the beneficiaries accused him of making away with the money. He was so upset, he sold everything he had and retired into the workhouse. He was completely cleared and his good name restored, but he refused to take any benefit from his relations. However, every Saturday he would walk as far as Grandfather Cranny's shop on South Great George's Street where they would cook him a steak on the forge and give him a shilling for tobacco before he returned to the workhouse. This upset Helena very much, as she loved her father and knew him to be an honourable man.

George Noble, Count Plunkett and Mary Josephine Cranny were married in June 1884. This was the joining of two wealthy families and a considerable amount of house and ground rent property in the south side of Dublin. In this photograph, taken on the steps of the bride's family home, Muckross Park, are:

Back row, left to right: Gerald Cranny; Maria Cranny; Jack Cranny; the priest is probably the celebrant, Father Sylvester Bourke, the parish priest of Donnybrook; Pat Plunkett.

Centre, left to right: Patrick Cranny; George Noble, Count Plunkett; Mary Josephine Cranny (Countess Plunkett); Frank Cranny; Helena Plunkett.

Front: unidentified child and, on the right, Germaine Plunkett, eldest daughter of Pat and Helena Plunkett.

Pat Plunkett was already sixty-one when he married Helena (we called her Aunt Helena) and they had four children, Germaine, Helena, Gerald and Oliver. This did not suit Grandma Maria at all as she had her eye on Pa's inheritance for her own daughter, even if she had to wait until Pa became 'respectable' enough for her. In fact, both Grandpa and Aunt Helena always treated Pa exceptionally well and Grandpa went to great trouble to see that he got all the wealth that was created through his own mother, Bess's, money, and more besides.

In 1884 Pa became a Papal Count as a result of help he gave to an order of nuns with a convent in Nottingham, the Little Company of Mary, usually known as the Blue Nuns, dedicated to working with the sick and the dying. The Pope had asked them to set up a branch of the order in Rome for which they would need a house. Pa, who knew some Irish women in the order, was in Rome at the time and when he was told about their situation, he searched until he found a suitable house with a garden and a room that could be used as a chapel and he had it decorated throughout before presenting it to them in 1883. The business affairs of the order were also in some kind of a mess and at the request of one of his friends Pa sorted this out for them as well. This earned the Pope's gratitude, particularly as it coincided with threats of confiscation of Church property by Victor Emmanuel, and it was in recognition of his service that Pa was made a Papal Count on April 4th, 1884. He was now Count Plunkett but he had no interest in titles. Grandma Maria, however, did and her attitude to him as a suitor for her daughter changed completely. He might not have a 'respectable profession' but he did have a very interesting title, both aristocratic and Catholic, one that would certainly suit her daughter's position in society. Patrick and Maria Cranny granted permission for them to end their ten-year wait and marry.

My father and mother were married on June 25th, 1884 in the Church of the Sacred Heart, Donnybrook, by Father Sylvester Bourke PP. Germaine Plunkett, the eldest of Pat Plunkett's second family, was the bridesmaid and one of the witnesses, the other being Gerald Cranny. The whole company went back to Muckross Park for the reception and photographs. The wedding was a great occasion for the family, two sides of which were being united with two fortunes. My father was now thirty-three and my mother was twenty-six. They left for London to begin their long honeymoon and just after they left, Aunt Helena realised that my mother knew nothing at all about what was expected of a married woman. She got on the next boat and managed to catch up with them in London. She took my mother aside and simply told her that 'whatever George does is right'.

2 Family life in Fitzwilliam Street 1884–1899

M Y PARENTS' HONEYMOON LASTED TWO YEARS. They travelled from London through France to Rome, where Ma had a fever and Pa brought her to the small hospital run by his friends, the Blue Nuns, who looked after her until she recovered. In fact she had a miscarriage but she didn't tell him that. When she came out of the nursing home, they moved on to Naples where they took ship for New York. They had an excuse for going to America: Ma's uncle, George Keane, was due an inheritance from his father who had just died and my parents were trying to trace him. He had stayed on in America after a family trip there and disappeared somewhere along the Mississippi. My parents were given the task of finding him but their expedition was far more than just that search.

It took them to over twenty states and they were overpowered, everywhere, with Irish hospitality. In New York they met up with the Fenian exiles Jeremiah O'Donovan Rossa, who was already a great friend of Pa's, John Boyle O'Reilly and John Devoy, all of whom Pa admired politically and personally. Ma enjoyed the social side of New York where they met with various relations including Grandpa Pat Plunkett's sister Anne (O'Donoghue) who had also left Killeen in County Meath during the Famine. After New York they travelled to Maine, then on to Chicago and across to San Francisco. It was now 1885. They told me that when they went west, they travelled enormous distances, going through remote territories from town to town on horseback where there was no other means of transport, sometimes avoiding an Indian attack by a hairsbreadth. In San Francisco they stayed with Philip, a brother of Pat Plunkett, and with Bess Noble's brother-in-law, Dudley White, one of the city founders who had opened the first chemist shop there. Pa really loved it there, especially the Chinese theatre, and they bought Chinese ornaments, including four planters, and furniture to bring home with them. They were still hearing news of George Keane everywhere they went and his trail now brought them south towards the Mississippi. On their journey across the Texas prairie on mules, they came to a place where the only tree for miles was a single lemon tree that scented the air, and people came from hundreds of miles around to see it. Word of George Keane led them to New Orleans, but here they lost the trail and the family never heard of him again.

They continued on to Florida (where they seriously considered settling permanently to grow oranges) and the last part of the adventure took them to South America, visiting the Rio Grande on the way, but Ma thought it wasn't worth all the songs about it. In Rio de Janeiro Ma had another miscarriage. Again she did not tell Pa what it was, calling it a fever instead. They took the train back to San Francisco, across a desert, where the driver stopped the train to allow the passengers to eat the wild grapefruit which grew in abundance beside the tracks. Pa said that while they ate and drank there were prairie dogs all round them that 'sat up on their hind legs and barked'. They had now been away two years and travelled over 10,000 miles. It was time to go home.

When my parents married, considerable property was settled on them: from Pa's side Pat Plunkett gave them 6–13 Belgrave Road, Rathmines, (all houses built with Bess Noble's money) and the leasehold on three farms in County Clare (for which he paid £2,000, which was far too much) and he paid off my father's outstanding debts. From Ma's side came the odd numbers from 27 to 39 Marlborough Road, Donnybrook, and both of them were given money by their parents, more or less whenever they asked for it and in generous amounts. They were also given a house to live in, No. 26 Upper Fitzwilliam Street (an address considered suitable for a gentleman), bought for them by Pat Plunkett and Maria Cranny who decorated and furnished it before they arrived home from America. Pa had also bought some furniture before he left on his honeymoon, including a sideboard, table and chairs which had been commissioned by Arnott's for the World Exhibition. They were so large that nobody had wanted to buy them, so Scally's sold them to Pa for £70. They were of carved oak, the table very long when all the leaves were added and the sideboard with a mirror back and carvings of fruit, flowers and animals. We loved the whole set and years later I met the sons of the man who carved it and they said he was very proud of all his work but particularly of that set. Pa's pictures, including James Barry's *Lear and Cordelia* and the supposed Rubens *Adoration of the Magi*, and all his china, silver and glass, were installed in the house. Then there was the problem of his books. Aunt Helena and Dilly O'Daly went round to all the houses and lodgings my father had lived in, beginning in Nelson Street, his last address, and collected the books from the locked rooms, packed them in numerous sacks and filled the shelved walls of the study in Fitzwilliam Street with them. There was still an enormous number that wouldn't fit in the study, so they were put out in the stable loft. Sadly, that's where they stayed, and when the rain came, the roof leaked, completely destroying many, including a beautiful little medieval Bible.

The house on Fitzwilliam Street was one of those tall, narrow Georgian houses, four storeys over basement with a garden at the back giving on to Lad Lane, where the horses and carriage were kept in the livery yard. Essentially, there were only two rooms on each floor. Pa's study was at the front of the house on the hall door floor, with his research documents and books running up the walls on all sides from floor to ceiling and stacked in towers all over the floor like the remains of a prehistoric fort. It was always locked whether he was in it or not. Behind that at the back was the dining-room where *The*

Part of Count and Countess Plunkett's marriage settlement.

The settlement included Nos 6–13 Belgrave Road, Rathmines, (built 1855) from the Plunkett side and Nos 27–39 Marlborough Road, Donnybrook, (built 1880s) from the Cranny side. The houses were usually let to upper civil servants, many of them English, most of whom left after the founding of the Free State. One notable tenant was Captain Harold Kinsman, author of Tactical Notes *(London and Dublin 1912), a very detailed guide to infantry manoeuvres written for junior officers seeking promotion, which was later used by Joseph Plunkett as an indication of likely British tactics in 1916. It specifies the minutiae of practical infantry soldiering, such as the number of troops per yard needed to man a barricade, exactly how to destroy a bridge, and how far a platoon can be expected to march, with equipment, in a day. Among other general injunctions, Kinsman stresses the importance for the weaker force of not losing initiative by allowing itself to be pinned down to defensive positions.*

Belgrave Road, Rathmines, Dublin.

Marlborough Road, Donnybrook, Dublin.

The tall, inconvenient, but grand 26 Upper Fitzwilliam Street. This house was given to the newly-wedded Count and Countess Plunkett by Maria Cranny and Pat Plunkett. It was probably Maria Cranny's choice that her daughter should live in a Georgian house, at 'an address considered suitable for a gentleman' rather than in a family-owned redbrick in the suburbs.

Adoration of the Magi hung over the fireplace. This opened into the conservatory, full of Pa's treasures, including the four Chinese planters, his Italian fountain, and pieces of sculpture from all over Europe and Asia. He believed that everyone should have beautiful things to look at and he filled the house with pictures in every room, all the way up the stairs and even in the nursery. The first floor had two drawing-rooms: the front one, decorated mainly by Pa, had extremely good furniture and beautiful blue and yellow brocade curtains on the windows, complementing the curtains on the folding doors. The back drawing-room had a long Adam mirror and was often used as a schoolroom. On the second floor, where my parents slept, were two bedrooms, one for each of them and on the top floor the two rooms were designated as the nursery area.

The basement contained a kitchen and laundry room and was usually only peopled by staff but it also had a lavatory, exclusively for Pa's use, at the end of the passage leading to the kitchen. The cook used to wash the dinner china in the kitchen, but everything else was washed in that passageway. The pantry was kept locked and the rations dealt out once a week to the servants, a quarter-pound of tea, one pound of sugar, one pound of butter for between seven and ten staff, and they were also given charge of the daily rations for the family and sometimes guests as well. The house had been made ready in a hurry and over the next forty years, when it was finally sold, it was never really improved upon in comfort or appearance. As with the rest of the houses, around we had a water tank in the area at the front which was filled at night. The tank was made of 'Roman cement': brick clay mixed with bullocks' blood, which made it waterproof. After 1900 the water was piped up from the canal instead. We had a bath and lavatory on the top floor beside the nursery, for the use of everyone in the house. There was a copper cylinder in the top floor bathroom which gave plenty of hot water but it was later moved to the kitchen and then we all had fewer baths. Waste food went into a pit at the end of the garden, which was emptied once a year and smelt like hell.

It was 1886 when my parents returned from America and over the next eleven years we children arrived and were given our confusingly similar names: Philomena Mary Josephine Plunkett (1886), Joseph Mary Plunkett (1887), Mary Josephine Patricia Plunkett (1889), Geraldine Mary Germaine Plunkett (myself) in 1891, George Oliver Michael Plunkett (1894), Josephine Mary Plunkett (1896) and John Patrick Plunkett (1897). I don't know which of my parents was responsible for the fact that four of the seven of us had my mother's names, but it hardly mattered since we were mostly called Mimi, Joe, Moya, Gerry, George, Fiona and Jack. The top floor was prepared with great care when Ma was expecting the first of us, Mimi. The two rooms were arranged to accommodate a baby, a nurse and a nurse-

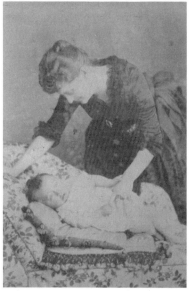

The Countess—Ma—with Mimi, who was born in 26 Upper Fitzwilliam Street in 1886.

maid, a large closet became a bathroom and as time went on the front room, which was the width of the house, was to be a day nursery and the back room, half that size, a night nursery. Mimi was born in the house, as we all were, and Ma was attended, as she always was, by her own maternity nurse. Mimi, who had her own nurse as was the style in well-off households, was brought down each evening for Ma to feed her, and the rest of the time she was bottle-fed by her nurse. Thirteen months after Mimi, in November of 1887, Joe arrived.

By 1897 there were seven of us children and two or three nurses and nurse-maids living in those same two rooms at the top of the house, originally set up for one baby and two nurses. We slept, ate, washed, dressed, played and quarrelled there, most of the days and all of the nights. We were cooped up with girls or women who were supposed to be nurses but very often were completely unqualified or ignorant or violent or all three. Ma hired them from the Irish Times Agency and, as she could not look her staff in the face, a habit acquired in her upbringing, she had no idea about their competence or value. As well as the nursery staff, she had the management of the downstairs staff, the cook, parlourmaid and housemaid, who all slept in the basement, and the gardener who also had charge of the pony and trap. They were given the minimum payment (she said it was wrong to pay more) and no justice. They had practically no time off or days off (never mind holidays) and she hired and fired frequently, usually on strange whims of her own. She believed that the 'lower classes' were made of 'a different clay' and therefore didn't feel pain

Frank Cranny (ca 1854–1918), the remittance man. The black sheep of the family, he was sent to Australia after embezzling funds and seducing a maid. He kept turning up in Dublin, making trouble and demanding money.

or unkindness as acutely as she did. When there was a proposal to distribute free beef to alleviate hunger she was firmly against it; she said that overfeeding the lower classes caused immorality, and she always said this in a scandalised whisper. She used to eat two dinners a day herself, meat with her breakfast and sometimes with supper. She said she had to eat to keep up her strength to bear and rear her family. I suppose she thought she was providing everything for the running of the household, in that she hired staff and gave them their instructions, but she had no skill, flair or interest in its supervision and the result was dishonesty, resentment and chaos.

When Joe was born my grandfather Patrick Cranny was already dying and Ma nursed him, something she was very good at, until he died in 1888. Ma admired him greatly, but I don't think she knew him very well. By the time he died he had acquired more houses and pieces of land yielding ground rents, in particular the houses and land on either side of Muckross Park, making himself and Maria owners of the complete site. He bequeathed to Maria five houses beside the gates of Muckross Park, Nos. 42–54 Marlborough Road, as well as houses on Eglinton and Wellington Roads. She also inherited 23–26 Belgrave Road, which she assigned to Ma, Uncle Jack and Uncle Gerald, and some ground rents including that of 74 George's Street, where they used to have the shoe shop. Ma already owned seven houses on Marlborough Road from her marriage settlement and my three uncles had one house each from the same time. Uncle Gerald now inherited the remaining twenty houses still in the family and Grandma Maria immediately bought three of these houses from him, Nos. 17, 19 and 21 Marlborough Road. Uncle Jack had seven houses on Elgin Road, Nos. 26, 28, 32, 34, 36, 38 and 40, part of the lot my grandfather had built in the 1860s. My grandfather did not intend to leave anything

Mimi and Moya Plunkett on a donkey and a distinctly mischievous-looking Joe on the ground (1892). Their boots which 'always fitted like a glove and never wore out' were made by a man named Mahoney, who worked for their grandfather, Patrick Cranny, in the George's Street shop.

to Frank, the 'black sheep' of the family. He had not only seduced one of the maids and made her pregnant when he was seventeen but at the same time, while keeping the books for his father's building business, he embezzled £1,700 from him—a huge amount of money in the 1870s. He was exported to Australia by the family and became what was known as a 'remittance man'. Patrick Cranny had said he owed Frank nothing but he relented and left him the value of his insurance policy and, in a codicil, stated that all Frank's debts to him were cancelled. The insurance policy was for £1,000 but somehow, I don't know how, this became only £500 so Frank was offered the £500 and this brought him to Dublin in a rage, looking for the rest of his money. All his life he was a drinker and a gambler and took money from anyone he could. On this occasion, Ma and Uncle Jack appeased him and sent him off again with some kind of settlement.

My sister Moya was born on March 3rd 1889 and in the following year Ma organised the first of her famous holidays. These were as much to get away from her children as to get away herself. This one was to Tuam in County Galway where she rented an unfurnished house, and she loved to tell how she had got all the luggage sent there by canal boat to Ballinasloe and from there in thirty carts to Tuam. She went there with Mimi, Joe and Moya, all under five years old, but she spent most of the time back in Dublin leaving the children in the care of their nursemaids and Miss Kelly, the owner of the

George Noble, Count Plunkett, in his barrister's wig and gown. He found that he was struck dumb doing court work and tried maritime work instead, in the office of a friend, Michael Dunne, but when Dunne died, he gave up the law altogether.

house, with whom she became very friendly. Ma knew nothing of country living, not even that it was the custom to give something to a child if they came into your house, and was shocked when Mimi came running in to her with an egg which she had been given. The holiday was supposed to last a few months, but Mimi saw Miss Kelly wearing Ma's rings while she was away and told her about it. There was a big scene; everything was packed up again in a hurry and they left for Dublin with the furniture following behind them. Pa stayed outside the argument and a short time later gave Miss Kelly's nephew help to get to America; his contribution to any situation usually took the form of helping somebody out.

Pa's title of Papal Count (Knight Commander of the Holy Sepulchre) was a source of embarrassment and annoyance to him. (Ma had no problem being called Countess, she demanded it from the servants and expected it from others). He did not use the title in the beginning but a request came from the Vatican for him to do so, and out of courtesy he did, although he nearly always used George Noble Plunkett or GNP as his signature. As an ardent Nationalist he did not like being mistaken for some kind of English or Continental aristocrat and because of his title, he was constantly begged for every kind of favour from a great variety of people. Being generous he usually gave and usually too much, until Ma stopped him. He was also frequently charged the maximum for goods and services by those who didn't know him.

From the time of his marriage my mother and grandmother started persecuting Pa into becoming a lawyer. The Bar was 'a profession for a gentleman' and they were also hoping it would keep him out of politics. He gave in and was called to the Bar in 1886. He was a sound and intelligent lawyer but was struck dumb when he went into court, so he confined himself to work in chambers. His days were spent writing and reading, usually in his study in Fitzwilliam Street. He wrote letters to friends all over the world and to learned societies in many countries, and a great number of articles on various subjects for newspapers and journals, lectures and books, primarily about art, politics and literature. He was a respected expert and guest speaker at societies in Britain, Europe, North and South America as well as founder and co-founder of many such societies. In spite of his mother-in-law's views he never did abandon journalism and founded a benevolent fund for journalists.

Like Charles Lamb, Pa would read anything that could be called a book and nearly all his waking hours were spent reading, even by moonlight or by the light of the street lamp outside, marking passages that he wished to remember with small pieces of paper sticking out at the top between the pages. When he was an old man his Bible was marked in this way at the top of nearly every page, and he had started marking it at the bottom. Next to the Bible the book he read most often was Dante's *Divina Commedia*. His morning post contained booksellers' catalogues and parcels along with the journals of learned societies. Every day he went to the bookshops and bookstalls and brought home two or three volumes, and he went to auctions and bought books by the shelf-full. The books overflowed out of the study into the return and into several of the smaller rooms and any empty cupboards.

Pa met Isaac Butt in the 1870s and from that time on was committed to the Home Rule movement. He admired Butt greatly and thought he had been underestimated, but believed that he was not in touch with the ordinary people here in Ireland. He said Butt was responsible for the link with the Radicals in the British Liberal Party, a group that was regarded with great fear and suspicion here. Butt lost control of the Home Rule Party as Charles Stewart Parnell rose to power, and when he died in 1879 Pa commissioned his friend, Thaddeus Jones, to paint a portrait of him to honour his memory. Pa had complete faith in Parnell and was his friend and advisor, and, as time went on, became as close to him as it was possible to be. He stood as a Parnellite in several elections, in constituencies where there was no chance of winning, because, unlike most candidates, he could afford to lose his deposit. When Parnell was cited as the co-respondent in the divorce between Captain William O'Shea and his wife Katharine, there was a public outcry, despite the fact that it had been a liaison of long and honourable standing and that her husband did not care until he thought that there was some political capital to be made from making a fuss. Parnell stood his ground and married Katharine O'Shea after the divorce. This lost him the support of the majority of the party, which, led by the churches, went into moral fits. When the *Freeman's Journal*, which was so essential to Parnell's cause, became anti-Parnellite, Pa and some other like-minded men started the *Irish Daily Independent* as a Parnellite newspaper. It was run by a board of management, and after Parnell died they sold it to William Martin Murphy, the owner of both Clery's and the Dublin Tramway Company.

In spite of his friendship with O'Donovan Rossa, Pa was thought by those who didn't know him to be a Clericalist rather than a Nationalist, but he spoke out for Parnell against the priests who condemned him.

Katharine Tynan wrote in her memoirs:

Mr Parnell had a great fascination for women, but he fascinated men almost as much. There is one of these who stood by him for whose action I have always had the greatest admiration, and that is Count Plunkett. Count Plunkett belonged to what one might call the official Catholics of Dublin. I mean he was one of those trusted Catholic laymen who represented the best and most orthodox Catholic feeling in Dublin. He had entertained the Papal Legate, Monsignor Persico, when he was in Dublin. He was a Papal Count. In all things he was of the most orthodox. Yet he came out to stand by Parnell and bore with the rest of us the obloquy, the unjust condemnation, the wrongs that even yet have left their iron in the soul.

In 1891, before Parnell left Ireland for the last time, he called to our house in Fitzwilliam Street with a cab full of papers. He was looking for Pa, who was out at the time. Parnell waited for him for a long time but in the end he left, saying sadly, 'perhaps it is just as well'. Pa was terribly upset when he returned and heard he had missed him. Parnell, who was still fighting hard for his leadership, went to England and died suddenly in Brighton in October of the same year. Pa talked a lot about him; he had seen and regretted the whole O'Shea plot and was heartbroken at the miserable end to Parnell's career. He

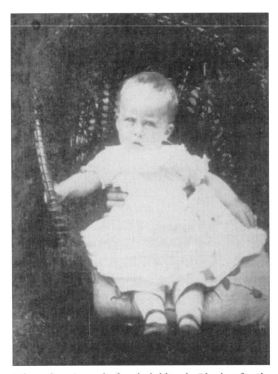

The author, Gerry, the fourth child in the Plunkett family, at one year old, in 1892. She always said she was 'born the year of Parnell's funeral'. She had almost total recall and saw people and events complete in her mind's eye, which often made it difficult for her to put them into order.

mourned him deeply, and when they auctioned the contents of Parnell's house, Avondale, he bought a pearwood walking stick and a stool which became our piano stool. It was always called 'Parnell', although as children we didn't know why. Eventually we just killed it with affection. For some years there was a commemorative procession on the anniversary of his death and I remember looking out the nursery window one year, when I was quite small, to see it pass as it turned the corner from Baggot Street to go down to Merrion Square. There were some carriages and traps and a float full of wreaths and flowers with a sort of pillar in the middle covered in beautiful purple flowers. I remember being disappointed the following year when there was no pillar and no purple flowers.

After Parnell died Pa continued his association with the Irish Party. He stood for election again in the general election of 1892, as a Parnellite stalking horse for Mid-Tyrone, but withdrew from the three-handed fight in order to prevent the Unionist from winning the seat. He then began work on the reform of the St Stephen's Green electoral register (this electoral district covered a large part of the city and extended nearly to Blackrock). The United Irish League believed that there was a real Nationalist majority in the area and that the voters' list was fraudulent. There were various forms of malpractice going on but the problem was that on appeal to the revision judges, Unionist families were always granted rights when Catholic families were not. Whole families who had moved from the area would come back to vote, while whole families living in the area were completely disenfranchised. Pa worked on this, using his own money and his own employees; he was promised reimbursement but it never happened. The work, involving investigation and legal challenges, took several years and cost about £2,000. We got a bonus out of all this; Pa brought home the office equipment when it was all finished and this included the first typewriter we had ever seen. It was a source of endless joy for us children.

In the 1895 general election, before the reform of the register was complete, Pa stood in the St Stephen's Green area as the only Nationalist candidate. During the election campaign he held several enormous outdoor meetings, and when he held one in Mount Street the terrified Unionist population of Fitzwilliam Street and Fitzwilliam Square barricaded themselves into their houses in the belief that he was going to lead a mob against them. At one of these meetings Pa's watch was stolen, but the thief returned it the next day saying that if he had known whose it was he would not have taken it. This incident became the running gag at the Christmas pantomimes that year: 'Who stole Count Plunkett's watch?' and so on. I remember when I was three-and-a-half passing one of his meetings at Donnybrook Green, now the football ground. Pa was speaking from a waggonette and we were in the pony and trap and I really wanted to go closer to hear what he was saying. He also had meetings in halls around the town, the Antient Concert Rooms in Brunswick Street, in York

The Plunkett family and nurse (holding Gerry) in a carriage at Powerscourt, County Wicklow (1892). This is the only photo to include one of their servants. She is probably the maternity nurse (un-named) who delivered them all in 26 Upper Fitzwilliam Street.

Street, and at the Royal Dublin Society Horse Show. The newspaper reports commented on the consistently courteous tone of his delivery and his gentle manners and style to all alike but his rhetoric was Nationalist: '*Do we vote for the country that crushes us, or for the beginning of our liberty?*' to resounding cheers in York Street. He was defeated by the Unionist candidate, William 'Placehunter' Kenny, by 2,000 votes. He did far better in the 1898 by-election. His speeches then were about the establishment of a Catholic university and freeing political prisoners and he asked his voters to vote, not for themselves, but in support of those who had died for Nationalist causes.

He was defeated this time also but this time by only 138 votes, thanks to the reform of the register, and this enabled the Nationalists to win the seat in 1900 after the Parnellites and anti-Parnellites finally got back together as the Irish Parliamentary Party and elected John Redmond as their leader. Pa never liked Redmond and said that the only reason he was elected leader was that he happened to be in the chair at that meeting. Redmond would not allow Pa to stand for the 1900 election, in spite of the work he had done on the register; he wanted his own candidate, P. J. Brady, to stand. The official reason for this was that Pa had started a Tariff Reform League for the protection of Irish industry. The British Liberal Party, to which the Irish Party was officially linked, was committed to a free trade policy so the Irish Party could not support tariff reform. Pa disliked the way that Redmond and the Irish Party were going; he felt that their interest was more in London than here in Ireland, that there was no genuine interest in the problems of real people here and that Redmond treated Ireland as his back garden. Ma put her foot down and said that there were to be no more elections and she held the purse strings, so Pa became discouraged and turned away from politics for the time being.

I was born on November 27th 1891, the year of Parnell's funeral. I remember being born: a slimy tube, choking, hearing talk and then nothing. This was a nightmare to me all my life until I realised what it was. I was christened Geraldine Mary Germaine; Germaine Plunkett, Pat Plunkett's daughter, was my godmother as well as my half-aunt, and of course the Geraldine was for Uncle Gerald, who was my godfather. My next memory is of sitting on the floor on the landing between the day and the night nurseries, while hairbrushes, combs, shoes and other solid objects were flying back and forth over my head, accompanied by screams and screaming. Then Biddy Lynch rushing into the fray, ignoring the howling row, picking me up and whisking me to safety; I was one-and-a-half years old and Biddy was my nursemaid. The howling row was a battle between Mimi and Joe and the horrible head nurse. Mimi and Joe told me in later years that they were just trying to draw attention to what was going on there—they were at the mercy of this nurse and her threats. On this occasion the woman was sacked and left the next day. Joe told me that one of the nurses used to heat the poker until it was glowing red and threaten to shove it down his throat when he cried. Another trick was to push the go-car out over the edge of the canal and threaten to let go; this was supposed to be for 'fun'. Biddy Lynch was different. We each had a nurse brought in for us when we were born and she was mine. She stayed with us until I was nine, bringing order, affection and pleasure into our lives. Biddy was an angel; she was kind, sensible, just, clever, intelligent, patriotic (a Parnellite), absolutely reliable, religious, scrupulously exact and honest. She taught us to read and to write and to sing Irish songs, she taught us our religion, she washed us and dressed us, she made our clothes and hats and, in her spare time, knitted stockings for her mother at home in County Meath. She saved me from the worst fights in the nursery area and gave me a deep sense of security. Biddy's only defect was her soft heart; her love-affairs were always hopeless. She kept everything spotless and when she left, she handed Ma a box containing every collar and hair-ribbon that had been given into her charge.

Ma visited the nursery about once a day for half an hour, when everything was tidied up for her inspection. The nurses were supposed to have us washed and dressed and give an impression of control; they were also expected to address us as 'Master Joseph' and 'Miss Geraldine' even when we were babies. Ma, of course was 'Countess'. On one of her visits she saw that George, who was being bathed, was black and blue all over. She asked about this and the nurse said that he must have fallen. I shouted out that she had beaten and pinched him. Ma sent the nurse to fetch a towel and as she passed me the

The Plunkett family in 1894. Left to right: Moya, Joe, the Count, George on the Countess' knee, Mimi and Gerry.

nurse said, 'Wait till I get you later.' I screamed as loudly as I could and Ma came running. I was glad that that one was sacked. From time to time we would be brought down to take breakfast with our parents in the back drawing-room on the second floor. We were expected to have beautiful manners and to be able to talk freely and intelligently to them but since we were quite unused to their company, and spent most of our time with ignorant and often ill-natured women, these occasions usually produced disappointment and bad temper from Ma, and tears and misery from us. These breakfast sessions were the closest thing to family life during our nursery years and they never lasted for long. There were only 30 steps between us on the nursery floor and the drawing-room floor where our parents lived but we could not go down to see them without permission. Once or twice a week there was a formal expedition and we were washed and stuffed into our best pinafores and brought down to the dining-room for a little dessert after dinner, or we would be brought down to be shown off to visitors. Pa would take each of us in turn on his lap and give us a '*canard*', a lump of sugar soaked in a teaspoon of coffee, which softened as we sucked it.

The nursery food was pretty awful and always the same couple of things: two meals a day of potatoes and gravy or an egg but no meat. All our meals were brought on trays to the accompaniment of the complaints of the maids between whom and ourselves there was constant war. Since it was 84 steps from the nursery to the basement, nobody wanted to run down and back up again if the food ran out or something else was needed. The first Monday in the New Year was known as Hansel Monday and you could have a small present of your choice for good luck by saying 'My hansel on you for . . .' When I was five I asked for a pound of unsalted butter as my hansel. I was given it and I ate it, and the incident woke Ma up to the lack of food in the nursery; a third meal was added to our day, so now we had the same midday meal as the servants, which certainly helped. Some of the maids lived in but those who didn't used to finish work at about seven o'clock in the evening. As this was the usual time in all the houses around, they would meet up with their friends outside, often standing and chatting and making lots of noise, so Joe and George dropped light bulbs from the nursery window on the fourth floor on to the basement area and the maids thought the explosions were revolvers. They complained next day, saying that they knew they had been noisy, but they didn't think it justified being shot at. There was a lot of waste in our house, of people as well as food. None of the staff stayed very long, apart from Biddy Lynch, and as we got older we became very aware and increasingly disturbed by how badly they were treated.

In 1892 my godfather, Gerald Cranny, died. I and several of my generation were named for him and I was always sad that I never met him. He was greatly loved by everybody who knew him. Of all the houses in the family the ones that he worked on and built were by far the best in both design and building, and they gave less trouble than any of the rest. After he left Dublin to set up the wine business with Woolworth in Spain, Woolworth embezzled the partnership funds and then shot himself. Gerald, who was engaged to be married, returned to London where he got pneumonia. Tom Gurrin, a friend of the family and a handwriting expert in the British Foreign Office, stayed with Gerald and looked after him. He told the family that at the end Gerald sat up in the bed, said 'Adios Senoras', then lay back and died. There was now another family reshuffle. Gerald had simply assigned all his property to his brother, Jack, who consequently now owned most of the Cranny houses on Marlborough Road and houses on Elgin Road, Eglinton Road and Wel-

Gerald Cranny (ca 1848–1892), son of Patrick and Maria Cranny, and Gerry's godfather, was the architect for many of his father's houses and built some of his own. He gave this up to become a wine importer and died in London at just over forty years old.

lington Road. He and Ma, however, used to pass these back and forth be-tween them in such a casual way as to cause plenty of trouble for solicitors later on. Although all my parents' property was held jointly, Pa was not al-lowed any say in its management or disposition. He made a few attempts at being involved but was summarily dismissed by Ma. This really suited him as he only needed houses as storage places for books and he was not a good property manager, but then neither was Ma.

In 1893 Grandma Maria, who was finding Muckross too big for her now that she was on her own, arranged for the Dominican nuns to buy it for £4,000; they had a house with a university centre for girls in Merrion Square. The arrangements took a few years to complete and they didn't move in until 1900 when they began their primary and secondary schools. In the meantime, Grandma let the house to Mrs Verschoyle for £200 a year. Two thousand pounds of the selling price went to pay off Ma's debts. I think that if Uncle Jack had had any children, Grandma would have made Muckross over to him and I think the reason she didn't make it over to Ma was that she didn't trust her. Grandma moved in with us in 1893 while she was setting up No. 17 Marlborough Road for herself. We spent that summer in a house called King-ston near Kilternan, County Dublin.

When George (who was born in 1894) was a year old and I was three-and-a-half we all—Ma and Pa, Grandma Maria, the five children, Mimi, Joe, Moya, George and I, Biddy Lynch, and the nurse—went to Brittany for three months. I remember the train to Southampton and the velvet-covered seats on the boat from St Malo to St Quay, the wonderful sunny sands, the old ladies with their baskets of cakes for sale, the nuns who kept the guesthouse, Pierre, the gardener, who gave me almonds, and the horses in the town gathering their four feet together to slide down the cobbled street. There was lots of trouble about the language; Pa spoke it but he was not expected to be concerned in domestic or catering matters. Ma certainly spoke and wrote good French but did not bother herself with anything she thought of as the servants' work, nor did she think of asking whether any of the servants had French. I did have some (there was a notion in our house that you always spoke French at the dinner-table) but Biddy had never seen or heard French before. Resourceful as ever, she tackled and mastered the laundry list on the first day and the grocery list the second day and went on from there to acquire all she needed. She had no trouble ticking off some women who she thought were being disrespectful to us: 'These are a gentleman's children,' she said. Pa took Mimi on his back and swam with her far out into the sea and he brought me on his back through a field with snakes in it, telling me a story about a snake who thought that his skin was another snake. The story was to keep me from being afraid, but I was never afraid when he was around. On the way back Ma, Grandma, Biddy and the nursemaids got left behind at a station and poor Pa had to mind us children. He had no idea what we ate and decided that bread and milk were probably safe. We, of course, didn't think much of this as a diet for two days and were very relieved when the others caught up with us.

I was four when I was solemnly brought downstairs from the nursery on one particular morning, to the back drawing-room, which was being used as a schoolroom. Ma was there, and the governess who was teaching Mimi, Joe and Moya. Each time a new governess was appointed (which was fairly often) Ma presided over the lessons. She would pretend to be one of us children and show off how clever she was, but she always got bored after a short time, especially with the younger ones. On this occasion I was handed a book which I began to read—slowly. A hell of a row broke out immediately. Apparently there had been a huge discussion between Ma and the governess about the correct way to teach reading and methods were going to be demonstrated and argued using me as the example. Unfortunately, Ma hadn't bothered to find out what was going on in the nursery at the time, so she didn't know that Biddy had taught me to read and write. She was raging at being shown up; I was told I wouldn't have lessons with the others until a much later time, and I was sent back upstairs to the nursery.

Fiona, christened Josephine Mary, was born on January 12th 1896. When she was a year-and-a-half we went to Rhyl in Wales, which I loved for the sandy beaches. That winter Mimi was sent to Mount Anville School to make her First Holy Communion, and Moya and I went to live with Grandma in 17 Marlborough Road. We went to school in the Sacred Heart Convent, Leeson Street, which I liked but I remember being aware of how isolated we were as a family. I saw children going to the National School when we were on our way to school. I envied them their freedom and thought they must be happy, because they came from poor families. I knew we were rich and unhappy so those who were poor must be happy. We girls were sent to school for, at most, a term at a time, and then Ma would take us away. She didn't provide us with the things we needed for school, such as uniforms, shoes, copybooks, pencils or money to buy any of these. If we were in any kind of disgrace with her, she would confiscate our books, or keep us from school, usually threatening to stop paying all our fees. The boys fared somewhat better (Joe was in CUS— Catholic University School, Leeson Street—at that time) as she believed that they needed education, but supplies and conditions were still very difficult for them. At the same time, Ma had no problem hiring very expensive costumes for a children's fancy dress party in the Mansion House given by the Lord Mayor. The four of us were dressed up, Mimi, wearing an 'Irish' costume, Moya in a Kate Greenaway dress, Joe as a Gallowglass and I was dressed as the Duchess of Savoy. As far as I was concerned it was just an excuse for being stuffed, poked, pinned and pushed into something I hated for a party I didn't want to go to and having it done all over again the next day, to have our photographs taken, for hours on end, in the Lafayette Studio in Dame Street. It was all for adult taste and adult pleasure and nothing to do with giving us

The Plunkett children were sent to the Lord Mayor's fancy dress party for children in the Mansion House, Dublin, in 1896. Left to right: Gerry as the Duchess of Savoy, Moya in a Kate Greenaway dress, Mimi in old Irish costume and Joe as a Gallowglass. Next day they were dressed up again (to Gerry's disgust) for this photograph.

children something we would like.

After Grandma left the big house she sometimes lived with us but mostly she lived in 17 Marlborough Road which she furnished and decorated in the dreadful style she liked so much. The front drawing-room had black chintz curtains and wallpaper with huge birds and flowers on it. It was infested with enormous solid alabaster vases of the crudest kind on brackets on the walls, literally solid, so they could not even take any flowers. She was very proud of these, showing them off to Pa because 'dear George will appreciate them, as he has that Italian alabaster fountain of his own'. Pa, of course, was too polite to point out the difference between his elegant little fountain and her great lumps of vases. On her dining-room mantelpiece she had a row of china dogs and vases with a clock in the middle and this was the mantelpiece we, as children, always drew rather than the beautiful one we had at home in our drawing-room, which Pa had arranged. There was a bathroom upstairs in the house, which had been built by Patrick Cranny and Uncle Gerald in the 1880s. This was rather an innovation at the time as bathrooms usually had to be added by converting a small bedroom. The circulating system of heating water by a boiler in the range had not yet come in, so all hot water for this bathroom had to be brought up from the kitchen. The range, which used one ton of coal a month, was always kept red-hot and never allowed to go out. Huge pots of water were heated on it and, after every step of the stairs had been covered with newspaper, the unfortunate maid had to drag each of these pots up to the bathroom. Our presence in the house meant much more of this kind of work for them, as my grandmother very seldom had a bath.

We used to help her to dress in the morning after she had put on her corset. Over the corset there was first an under-petticoat, then a petticoat of pink wool and on top of that a large black cotton one, on which the bustle was tied. I was fascinated by this archaic object; it was almost incredible that anyone should wear such a thing. A fat little cushion made of horsehair hung at the back around her waist so as to make quite certain that nobody thought that she had a division at the back of her legs. Over this came the skirt, then a bodice, hooked or buttoned down the front and trimmed with jet or velvet. Round the neck of this she wore a little sort of bow on elastic and she wore a cap of stiffened buckram, the same kind as Queen Victoria's; she always kept a new one of these in a bandbox upstairs to wear when anyone came to see her. She wore only black after Grandpa died, as all widows did at the time, and long plain cloaks that were really driving cloaks, usually worn going out in the trap. We got great use out of those cloaks for years afterwards. One of them was her Sunday cloak for going to twelve o'clock Mass in the Pro-Cathedral. She went to Mass and Holy Communion very frequently, often fasting from the night before until noon the next day to do so. She made coats for us girls, all three out of the same rather ugly yellow-grey wool, each with a different colour satin lining. Ma jeered when she saw them but we had begun to appreciate what some of our relations did for us when they saw how she neglected us, and we badly needed warm coats. Aunt Helena was really good to us in this way and a very fine dressmaker. Several years in a row she made us two sailor suits each, one of serge and one of white piqué.

Grandma was very prim and rigid, with plenty of business ability and practical sense. She loved good workmanship and taught me how to do some house repairs and to mix house paints. When she got a new muslin cap, her oldest one was carefully unpicked to make a strainer for the paint which she mixed herself and used to decorate her houses. I suppose we were alike in our enjoyment of these things, but she rarely showed enjoyment, and if she was ever young, she had forgotten it. She was a plain woman who didn't really like children but tried to do her best by them, believing that they should be completely controlled; she always gave us very small chocolate creams on our birthdays. Her view of the world was as organised as my mother's was chaotic, and she helped me with my reading and writing and taught me prayers, including the English translation of *Anima Christi*. When Ma heard me saying it, she said 'Who taught you that?' 'Grandma,' I said, and Ma said, 'She shouldn't have, it is most unsuitable,' and had a frightful row with her mother about it. I loved the prayer, but talk of body, blood or passion would embarrass Ma dreadfully.

Grandma was very fond of my sister Moya but always very hard on her,

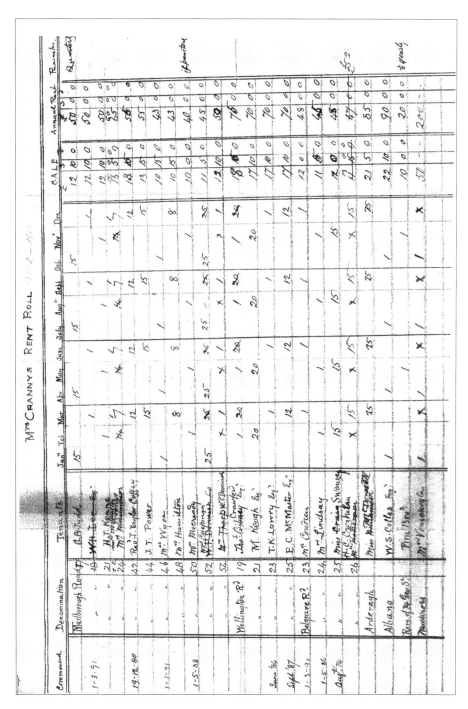

Maria Cranny's rent rolls (1891) show ten houses on Marlborough Road, four on Wellington Road, four on Belgrave Road, and two (now gone) on Eglinton Road; also ground rent for the George's Street shop and rent for Muckross Park (to Mrs Verschoyle) at £200 p.a.

and the slightest bit of nonsense from Moya and she banished her to the kitchen. Moya loved this because she could get plenty of buttered toast there, whereas there was never any in the dining-room. However, Grandma took too much of an interest in her; Moya was very attractive when she was two, with a lovely mop of curls, but Grandma, without a word to anyone, least of all Ma, took her out one day and had her head shaved. Curiously enough, when Moya's hair grew again, it was no longer curly, but straight and fine, and the whole thing had a very shocking effect on her. On another occasion, Moya was punished for something by being told that her grandmother would not be giving her a birthday present and then told that Grandma had relented and was giving her a ham. Not only was a ham no good to a six-year-old, but Moya couldn't eat salt meat as it made her come out in spots. When Moya was six and I was four we found ourselves one day walking up the stairs carrying silver salt cellars; we didn't know how or why we came to be doing this and we didn't know what to do about the salt, so we put it under the carpet, in the way that any child might. The maid found it and, although she usually covered up for our troubles, something was upsetting her and she told Grandma. It was made into a most tremendous sin, as though we had done something particularly malicious and we were punished for it in some way that I don't remember. We could never understand the moral system; we were rarely punished for doing wrong and never rewarded for doing right. Apart from going to school Grandma didn't let us out of the house as she was afraid that we would be stolen by agents for Mrs Smyllie's Bird's Nest children's home in Kingstown. There used to be many scare stories around Dublin about Mrs Smyllie stealing Catholic children to have them adopted by Protestant homes. This really used to happen but the practice ended when support for it in England stopped. As far as I could make out Mrs Smyllie was very sincere but a silly ass.

The year my youngest brother, Jack, was born, 1897, the family rented a house called Charleville in Templeogue on the outskirts of Dublin. We children were sent there with Biddy. At first it was only for the spring and summer, but then we were left there for over a year, although most of us were supposed to have started school. Pa came to stay with us quite often, Ma very seldom. Across from Charleville was Cherryfield, a horse breeding and dealing stud where we got Black Bess, a four-year-old with such excellent manners that we older ones could all drive her straight away. It was the beginning of great freedom for us: we could do everything from standing at the gate to shout 'Boo!' at the woman who used to drive past in a trap whipping her two ponies unmercifully, to harnessing Black Bess to the small round trap and driving with Biddy all over the countryside. We had a saddle and could all ride her. I got a loan of Joe's pants and rode her astride and this made it rather awful when Ma made me ride side-saddle afterwards on a bad-natured horse named Bob. Our freedom was curtailed, however, when a governess was brought in for us.

She was small and dark, a wild creature and a terrible tyrant, and she always abandoned us if possible. She was supposedly French, Mademoiselle Ditter, but in fact she came from Alsace and had a strong hatred of the French. She used to teach us how to curse the French with appropriate gestures and to sing anti-French songs. She did also teach us to recite real French poetry and sing more conventional songs and to sew and make paper flowers. She took a fancy to Moya and kept her locked in her own bedroom, teaching her to sew, but Moya climbed out the window and escaped up a tree with Ditter climbing up after her. Ditter locked her up again without her dinner but we smuggled food into her. When Moya got out again, she and I went in to the stallion's field but he began sniffing around us so we ran for the edge of the field; Moya wasn't looking where she was going and ran into a stick which went straight into her eye. She was in terrible pain and Grandma, who was there at the time, wanted to leave it to heal itself, but Biddy insisted on bringing Moya into town to Fitzwilliam Street. Finding no-one there she went out and found an eye-doctor, Dr Maxwell, who operated on her eye, but it never recovered fully and Moya was always self-conscious about its appearance. Mademoisellel Ditter gave up trying to teach her to sew after this.

Food was supposed to be sent from town on a regular basis but Ma used to forget fairly often and we could get badly stuck. She had bought a Black Minorca cock and five hens to provide eggs (she believed that better quality fowl produced better quality eggs) but the henhouse was kept locked and she had the key in town. When we ran out of food, Moya was delegated to break in to the henhouse to provide us with something to eat, which she did by squeezing through the hens' door. Ditter had her own supply of dandelion and rice and she also ate the beef liver that was meant for the prime Minorca fowl. The cook hated her but we loved her wonderful fruit toffee.

Jack was born that October and afterwards Ma came out to visit us. There was a new nurse for Jack, Nurse O'Grady, who went out one night and got very drunk. She was severely incapacitated by a hangover the next day and Ma fired her. Ma told us all to stand outside the door and sing 'Sweet Rosie O'Grady' as she was leaving but I didn't; I thought it was too silly. After that, sewage got into the well and both Biddy and the other nurse got scarlatina. Biddy was in hospital and we were all brought back in to Fitzwilliam Street where Ma cooked for us and looked after us. She was an excellent cook but, as with everything she was good at, she got bored very quickly. The night before we left Charleville she called me to her bedroom, as she had each of the others, to kiss her goodnight. After the kiss, I turned away and wiped my mouth. She screamed loudly and suddenly, 'You unnatural child—wiping away my kiss!' I didn't know that it was possible to wipe away a kiss. This was the beginning of the misery of knowing that my mother did not want me and wanted to blame me for it, the same way she did with Mimi. It was a month before my sixth birthday and I made a decision then that was to be my safeguard all my life: I decided to hate my mother.

In Fitzwilliam Street we were always on the outside, surrounded by people who didn't like us, Unionists and bootlickers to the administration, and, mainly because of Pa's political activities, we were regarded with deep suspicion. Most of the children there were not allowed to play with us. Some of them spat at us or called us names when we passed by and to cap it all Ma froze out anyone who might have been a friend, including poor Pa's friends. We did not like playing in Fitzwilliam Square, which was free to residents but otherwise cost £2 2s for a key. Dublin was much sootier then and all the trees and shrubs were blackened. The local children were taught to hate us; some of them put out their tongues at us as we passed which did not add to our happiness. Christo and Baba Hennessey were the first to speak to us but the young Campbells, James and his sister, Maggie, tied Christo and his dumb sister to holly trees and pelted them with stones. In Upper Fitzwilliam Street there were no Nationalists and I do not think any Catholics except ourselves until Jim Hogan, the dentist, and his family rented No. 16 over the way, but this was not until about 1909. Sir Valentine Blake of Galway, an old soak, had No. 9 on the Square. In Galway he used to be taken home in a wheelbarrow by his manservant every night when he was on the tear. I was in school with his daughter but she was not allowed to play with me. Lady Atkinson had a house on the Square; her husband lived in London. She had been a celebrated beauty and had once ridden from Navan to Kells on a pennyfarthing high bicycle, dressed only in pantalettes frilled from waist to ankles, for a bet. She liked entertaining young people but not us. She would come out into the Square on a fine evening in a pink negligée with a companion and a maid to fan her, while she sat in a special chair.

Behind our house was Lad Lane, which led to an inner court, and that court led to another. This inside court had been the site of a gallows but I didn't know that for years. Had I known, it would have explained the horrible atmosphere in the whole place. Along our side of the lane were the stables belonging to each house; some of these were let to cabbies who lived in the lofts with their families, often in the greatest squalor, others were let to pigkeepers, some were just used as dwelling-houses and coachmen slept in some of them in the lofts over the horses. On the other side of the lane were courts within courts of slums, always wrapped in a strong stench, and there was the B Division Metropolitan Police Station. On most nights the whole lane was pandemonium but on bank holidays it was real murder. I often lay awake listening to the sound of women being beaten with belts for hours, to men roaring and fighting, to girls being dragged off to the police station. Later on, as students, we used to see the girls with great welts on their necks where their mothers had cut off their sores with a penknife. We used to try to persuade them to get it done properly, but we usually failed. I don't know why nothing was ever done about Lad Lane; Gordon, the lawyer who lived

Joe Plunkett, aged eight (ca 1895).

just next door to us, was the Attorney-General and had the power to do something about it but didn't. He was typical of the neighbours we had on Fitzwilliam Street—he used to thrash his son and daughter up and down the stairs every day and you wouldn't expect much after that.

With Jack's arrival in 1897 we were seven children usually treated as two groups, the older and the younger ones. As I was in the middle, I was sometimes the youngest of the senior group, sometimes the oldest of the juniors, sometimes left out of everything altogether, but mostly it suited me very well. I had awful tonsils and adenoids which made it impossible to breathe. I used to be told all the time to shut my mouth but I had to keep a corner of it open to breathe at all. I must have looked a fool and most unattractive, in spite of my wavy hair, but Uncle Jack, who was our family doctor, was against any interference so nothing was done about it. One or two of the nursemaids used to bring all of us children for a walk every day but before we could leave there were seventy little buttons to be done up on my clothes. The walk was always the same, from Fitzwilliam Street along Leeson Street and Morehampton Road to Donnybrook Church and a little way on to the Stillorgan Road, with Jack in the pram and the two small ones, George and Fiona, in a mailcar which was a back-to-back go-car made mostly of bamboo. I had to walk with Joe and Mimi and Moya. Once in Donnybrook, when the nursemaids had stopped for a chat with a couple of friends, they were so involved that they didn't see an old man come up to me, take me by the hand and lead me away. It was not until he had reached the corner and was about to turn it that they woke up to what was happening and rushed to rescue me.

After we got the pony and trap in Charleville and brought them back into town with us, things improved greatly. Best of all was when Biddy took us out. We went to all sorts of places, to the sea at Dalkey, to Blackrock and out to Kingstown and to countryside places around Dublin. Bess was so quiet we could harness her and drive her ourselves and she would stand tied, but the traction engines that went in front of the sand lorries made her go quite wild. The first motor van she saw was Pim's; it was bright red and she shot into the ditch and then bolted. On our trips to Kingstown the drivers of the electric trams tried to make her bolt by ringing the bell suddenly but she was too clever for that one. Years later, when we started riding bicycles, the cabbies used to chase us with whips. We went horse-riding in different places, Ma usually went to a stables at Baker's Corner, but we went to the Phoenix Park, or Sandymount strand which was notorious for falls and accidents. The sight and smell of the sea there always made the horses skittish and for the unprepared it meant trouble. I fell off on my very first time out there and Ma was completely unsympathetic; she was an excellent horsewoman, could drive a coach-and-four, and never saw the problem for anyone else. Horses were used for everything then, and they gave us plenty of excitement, particularly runaways, tripping over their reins and breaking their necks, or finishing up impaled on railings.

Pa used to bring us out, mostly on Sundays, to the Zoo, the pantomime, the opera, plays, circus, anything at all he deemed worth seeing. He had no ideas about things being suitable or unsuitable for children, he simply thought of us as people. He treated everybody that way. On one of our outings with him, we saw a man on the pavement kicking his young son to death, with a crowd standing around them doing nothing about it. Pa stopped the pony and trap, got out and punched the man, knocking him out cold. It was an extraordinary thing to see from such a gentle man, someone who would apologise for causing the slightest inconvenience, but he never could bear mindless cruelty.

In 1898 Pa went round the house celebrating the 1798 Rebellion by singing 'Who fears to speak of '98', and Biddy had lots more songs to add. That was the year he stood for election again and nearly got in and at the same time was working on his book on the painter, Sandro Botticelli. It was commissioned by the English publishers George Bell and Sons and was to be the most comprehensive study of the artist ever written in the English language. Joe was in school in CUS again and we girls were back in the Sacred Heart, having missed half the year. I didn't enjoy it so much this time; at the end of the year I got three second places and Ma told me off for not getting a first prize. She went off to France again on one of her trips, so we had lunch with Pa on most days in Fitzwilliam Street, and always on Saturdays, when he gave us our pocket money: Mimi and Joe got twopence, Moya and I got a penny and the others were still too small for any. Pa was looked after by Bessie, a professed cook, and at lunch we clustered around one end of the long dining-room table because the rest of it was covered with the galleys of *Sandro Botticelli* which my father was proofing. I remember it, neatly and carefully laid out, each chapter with its illustrations.

We children spent that summer of 1898 on a big farm called Coolawinna, near Ashford, County Wicklow, and the following summer Mimi, Moya, myself and Biddy went to Llandudno in Wales for a couple of months. I didn't like it as much as Rhyl, but the freedom and comfort of just having Biddy in charge made it much more fun. We swam as often as we could in a little cove that was shingle rather than sand and went to the concert parties given by The White

Coons in Happy Valley, beside Great Orme's Head, or in the town hall on wet days. There was a wonderful afternoon thunderstorm with two huge balls of fire; one travelled roof height along Mostyn Street to the town hall and set it on fire, the other went along the pier and exploded against the pavilion. Ma had struck such a hard bargain with the hotel that although she thought she had arranged for us to eat in the dining-room we were not allowed to by the proprietor, who said that our bill didn't cover it. Instead we ate (quite happily) in the public restaurant downstairs. Ma didn't visit at all but Pa did. When he discovered the eating arrangements he was quite annoyed that we were being cheated. The proprietor was impressed at having a Count staying in his hotel, so when Pa said that we should be eating in the dining-room, he instantly gave in, and that's where we ate while Pa stayed. When he left however, the hotel guests objected (we were told) to Biddy, a servant, eating there with us, as they said it was improper. We went back to eating downstairs as we had no intention of being so rude to her or being parted from her.

3 Going wild in Kilternan 1900–1903

GRANDMA MARIA CRANNY DIED in 1900 aged seventy-six. I was jumping on a bed in the front nursery when the hearse arrived at 26 Fitzwilliam Street, and I continued jumping, wondering why I was doing it. There was an important fuss made and we all got horrible little black suits, a skirt and jacket made of cheap, solid cloth, chosen by our nurses. Even Fiona, who was only four, had a black jacket over her white dress. Ma had been staying in Grandma's house, so we hadn't seen her for a while. She looked quite different; she had had a shock right enough! She was wearing a bonnet and cape that even I knew were very out of fashion, but I supposed it must be all right for a funeral. We wore those black suits for a year afterwards and that year stretched when Ma, as usual, forgot to buy new clothes for us.

The whole property reshuffle had to begin again but now there were only my mother and Uncle Jack as beneficiaries. The Marlborough Road houses were divided up between them as life interests, and they were to go to their children on their respective deaths. If Uncle Jack died childless his share was to come to the seven of us. Grandma's will did not mention Frank, so he arrived in the country making all sorts of threats of court actions and plans to disgrace his brother's name by hiring a monkey and a barrel-organ to play outside Uncle Jack's club. Uncle Jack sent money to Frank's family and his eldest son wrote back gratefully, describing how badly they had been treated by their father. Uncle Frank signed himself into the South Dublin Union as a charity case, hoping to embarrass everyone, and while he was laying down the law about politics, someone stole his breakfast. He left again saying that it was no place for a gentleman.

Straight after Grandma's funeral was over all of us children, except Joe, were sent to live in No. 17 Marlborough Road. Joe had pneumonia and pleurisy and was not expected to live, but Ma nursed him for months and he started to recover. We were in the care of Biddy and Jack's nurse, Lizzie. Lizzie loved Jack but hated Fiona and used to torment her and beat her and Biddy had no authority to interfere. Moya and I either got the tram to school, getting off at the Fitzwilliam Street stop, or, if it was fine enough, walked all the way, which I much preferred. The nuns had not yet taken over Muckross so we used to go and play in the gardens and in and out of the greenhouse, which was full of roses. I once saw over the whole house and thought it very fine, particularly the sets of deep drawers on rollers set into the side of the big staircase. That must have been Grandma's idea. That April I was brought into

49

George, Fiona and Jack in 1900. Count and Countess Plunkett had seven children in eleven years who all lived on the top floor of the Fitzwilliam Street house with nurses and nursemaids, only seeing their parents a few times a week. Thanks to their mother's strange arrangements, food, clothes and schooling were erratic and unpredictable.

town by two of the nursemaids to see that old so-and-so Queen Victoria and her entourage drive through the streets. I saw her pass by in College Green, which was lit and decorated and packed with people; I was lifted off my feet by the crush. The women all around me were wearing enormous hats held on with huge hatpins with fancy tops and I saw a small boy holding a big bundle of these pins of all colours, which he had picked out of the hats. Mimi was at Mount Anville at the time where they were taught 'God Save the Queen' and how to cheer. As far as I know it was the only school Victoria visited when she was here and Mimi told me that John Redmond's two daughters were taken home from the school for the duration. When Victoria died the following January, it caused fear and shock among a surprising number of people.

At Easter we all got chicken-pox and whooping-cough. There was stuff called Vepo Cresolene (I think) that you heated over a tiny lamp and it gave some relief from coughing. Ma came to see us now and again, but all the real work of looking after us was done by Biddy and Lizzie. As our doctor, Uncle Jack was greatly concerned about Mimi, who was so ill that he thought she would not live. It took her a long time to recover. When Moya was better she was sent to Mount Anville school to make her First Holy Communion, and when the rest of us recovered we were put in a house called Parknasilogue, in Enniskerry, County Wicklow. It was cut out of the side of the hill and had a bridge from one of the top bedrooms to the garden; it was gloomy and badly furnished. The two sitting-rooms were horrible and smelt of cats, but since we didn't use them except when Ma was there we didn't care. Ma was angry because the rooms weren't nicer and she took it out on Biddy, who wept, but Biddy couldn't have done anything about it because Ma had given orders beforehand that nothing was to be done to the house without her explicit instructions. The farmer employed by the owner lived in a two-storey house in the farmyard where there was also a dairy with a separator, big cowhouses, pigsties, lofts, storehouses, and a yard kitchen with a big hearth on which the pigfood was boiled. Mimi, who was still recovering from illness, mostly stayed in the house, Moya was left in Fitzwilliam Street running messages for Ma up and down all those eighty-four steps of the stairs and Joe was also there, recovering from pneumonia, although I thought he would have been better off with us.

I had a lovely time, I think the three younger ones did too. We spent all our time on the farm with the farmer's younger children. We helped in all the work, fed the calves, carried buckets of pollard, bound oats, snagged turnips and when we gathered potatoes we would make a bonfire of their stalks and roast them on the ashes. I was nine and must have been the only one old enough to be able for all these jobs, but I brought the others along with me. There was a threshing machine with a horse turning it on a circle and Georgie, now six and a half, was old enough to sit on the beam and drive the horse for a bit. When we arrived in Enniskerry we were all weak and very underweight so Uncle Jack, concerned about this, ordered that we should have cream on our porridge every morning and this, combined with regular, good quality food, very quickly began to make a difference to all of us. Biddy was in charge of us and we had the pony and trap for outings. Biddy, as usual, lost her heart to one of the men working on the farm. She was a tiny little woman with curly hair and enormous black eyes but she was so clever and determined that she tended to put men off. On this occasion she gave me a letter in a pink envelope to give to the man she had her eye on. He took out her letter and replaced it with a handful of baby fieldmice he had just found, and told me to bring it back to her. She was delighted when I handed it to her, but when she opened it she screamed and the poor mice fell on the floor and died. I could not understand why she didn't love the beautiful little mice. She was insulted and it was the end of the affair.

Ma decided to take Joe to Rome for the winter to recover as he was still terribly weak and susceptible after his long illness, but when they got to Paris, one of the international exhibitions was on and Ma changed her mind and put Joe in the Marist school in Passy as a boarder. He learned to speak French very well and got to know all the children's games. Joe was in need of a warm climate but Passy's climate tended to be cold and wet and severely detrimental to his health. He developed an enlarged gland in his neck for the first time. The reason Ma gave for staying in Paris was that she had fallen very ill there, and she signed herself into a nursing home, where she managed to live and go to parties and social events. The climax of her illness, which she described in dramatic terms, was when she nearly passed out in her bedroom and she boasted that she had the presence of mind to grab the open bottle of champagne beside her bed and drink from it. 'Do you not think, doctor, that in this way, I saved my own life?' she said to her doctor, months later when she came home. 'I'm sure you did,' he said.

Pa's book on Botticelli was published in the autumn of 1900 and was immediately praised on all sides. It is very readable and for many years was the authority on Botticelli. Pa's passionate enthusiasm for both the painter and the Renaissance comes across all the way through. When he travelled in Europe his journeys were always from one art gallery or museum to another, and he bought and studied every available book on Renaissance Art.

Part of the Preface reads:

> I have endeavoured to illustrate the motive and purpose of his principal compositions by reverting to his sources of knowledge and interpreting the feeling of his age. If I have erred on the side of enthusiasm it has been owing to my anxiety to realise the character and capacity of the man . . . The man of letters, no less than the artist should be grateful to him for the beautiful unfettered fancy . . . of which he has made them his heirs.

With the £300 he was paid for the book, Pa took a house in the country because he said we all looked 'peaky' and he was a great believer in fresh air. The house was Kilternan Abbey in Kilternan, County Dublin and Pa concluded the deal in November, just before my mother arrived back from Paris with Joe. She was annoyed at first as she usually made all the family decisions without reference to him, and did not like him doing the same. She was not keen on the peace and quiet of the countryside but after a while the best side of her came out. She had an ability to deal with whatever situation she found herself in and really liked the idea of 'a place in the country' as a social asset,

Published in 1900, Count Plunkett's book on Botticcelli was filled with his passionate enthusiasm for the painter and Renaissance art. It was an immediate success.

fancying the thought of visitors arriving out to envy her in her position.

Kilternan Abbey was a big house at the top of the Glenamuck Road with 120 acres of land, mostly let to local farmers, with a pillared entrance between Willis' shop and the Golden Ball pub and a gatelodge at the beginning of the quarter-of-a-mile long avenue with its tree-topped double bank. The two lambs we hand-raised used to gallop along these banks beside the pony and trap. The avenue had a sharp bend and a steep hill, and ended in a gravel sweep with very old evergreen shrubs on either side, backed with trees, including Scots pine and Arbutus. These were heavenly for us as we could make great treehouses in them. The house was four storeys with about twenty wide steps up to the hall door and its design was like a suburban house and not a bit like a real, large country house. There was a glassed veranda around two sides at hall-door level and a gazebo on the gravel sweep that we called the bandstand. We had a marvellous view of Dublin Bay from the front of the house and on very clear days we could see from Howth to Killiney and a shadow beyond that we thought was Wales. Right out at the back, between us and the hills, we had the ruins of the Abbey. There was a tiny church outside the back gate supposed to be a very early one. It was sinking a bit, but you could still get inside it and it was not destroyed. When I went to try and trace it, not so many years ago, it had been crushed to the ground by the weight of the ivy which had been growing over it all those years.

Kilternan Abbey, County Dublin. In 1900 Count Plunkett bought the last seven years of the lease with the £300 paid to him for his book on Botticelli to give his children fresh air. This dark photo, taken between 1900 and 1908, gives only a slight idea of the house which backed on to the Dublin mountains. With many rooms, outhouses, glasshouses and fields outside, it was ideal for children.

A big sitting-room built on the side of the house had a conservatory off it and another one had a billiard table that was Joe's and my delight; there was also a dining-room on this floor. Ma and Joe each had a bedroom on the first floor; Joe's had a bath, but the water pressure was only a trickle so it was unusable, and there was a spare room with black figured wallpaper hung on canvas which used to move whenever there was a storm and which terrified us. The nursery was the big back bedroom on the top floor and housed George, Fiona and Jack with Biddy and Lizzie. The rooms at the back of the house were nearly uninhabitable because the wind blowing straight off Two Rock Mountain got in everywhere and it was impossible to protect or heat any room against it. In fact, the house rocked in the frequent gales and one of the rooms had to be permanently boarded up for this reason. The top floor also had two front rooms; the smaller one was Mimi's and the big one Moya's and mine. The kitchen was under the sitting-rooms with a big range and a coalhole with rats in it. The coal store was about fifty yards from the house but a ton or so could be kept in the kitchen. It was re-stocked about once a year with coal which came from Kingstown on terribly heavy and cumbersome coalcarts which, for some reason, always came up the front avenue where there was a bad hill, instead of in the back way where there was none. There was every conceivable kind of laundry, pantry and cupboard in the basement, all made very dark by the veranda overhead, and a really black, dark, maid's room. The back stairs led to a bathroom and a lavatory and the bedrooms. There were dozens of superfluous windows and there was glass wherever it could be, often coloured. The whole thing had been built or rebuilt, I'm not sure which, by a man named Joyce who was rather mad and was tried and convicted for poisoning his mother.

Cellars led to a yard sunk ten feet below the level of the house with an office, outhouses, stables and the bungalow, where Pa lived most of the time, and which he filled to the ears with books. Beside the coachman's gatelodge at the back gate there was a big shed, a haggard and a walled space that looked like the remains of a house. A long wall beside the kitchen had rambler roses and a fig tree, whose roots ran under the range so the fruit always ripened very early. There were two orchards, one walled-in, with dead apple trees in it but on its north wall there was a line of Morello cherries which were used for cooking and jam. The second orchard had some good greengages and plum trees in it. All this was insignificant beside what became Ma's pride and joy. At right angles to the front of the house were unheated glasshouses, the central one a hundred feet long and in the shape of an E. In the centre it had peaches, nectarines and passion fruit and there were vines in the arms of the E. One little cross house had Muscat vines, which we liked the most. The vines needed more heat than they ever got, they weren't really the right type for the situation. Only one house, which was near the furnace, was heated, and it was kept for flowers, ferns and mushrooms.

We had about five acres of land for our use, including a pond-field (the pond was the overflow from the excellent water-supply, which came complete with filter beds) and a field with a couple of cows. Horses made all the difference to the freedom of living somewhere like that, and ours included Uncle Jack's seventeen-hands, dark bay ex-hunter called Gerry (like myself), who was overfed and vicious. Because he was so big, it was very hard to get another horse to match him for the heavier carriage so we had two ponies for it instead. This carriage could be turned into a waggonette and we used it like that in the summer, with the top off and in the winter with the top on to go to Mass in Sandyford Church. The other horses included a cob, a farmer hunter and of course our favourite, Black Bess. She could go up and down the steps of the house, drink out of a cup and learned to peel a peach with her teeth and spit out the stone. She gave us the use of the countryside for gallivanting (this included the run of the Powerscourt demesne, which was open to local residents), and we could go to Bray for both necessary and unnecessary trips.

Ma, after her initial misgivings, decided that she was the best and most original farmer-gardener. She threw herself with gusto into the whole business of running the place. There was quite a number of staff still there from the time the house had been lived in by the L'Estrange family, who had been very successful with both growing and marketing the fruit. Ma, in her usual style, did not allow for anyone else's expertise, and when the first crop of peaches was ready and the gardener, who was excellent, prepared a number of them to send to the Dublin market, she ordered him to put all the rest of the peaches in, bringing it to a total of about 1,000. She flooded the market and was offered a penny each for them. She took them home in great indignation and said she would make jam instead. For this she bought grosses of jamjars and hundredweights of sugar and started into the job herself. She had never done it before, knew nothing about the principle or quantities and, of course, would not consult anyone or accept advice. It never got as far as being jam: she had economised on the sugar so it turned musty with inch high green and orange fuzz on top while the bottom ran all over the place. Just the thought of peach jam was enough to make any of us sick after that. Ma's version of all this was different: she used to boast of it for the rest of her life to anyone who would listen, as though it was all a complete success—she had taken the market by storm and made the best peach jam ever. This often happened with her family sitting round, embarrassed to the ears with the nonsense of it. Actually the peaches were won-derful but they required a lot of care. They were badly infested with scale and if they were neglected, as they often were, the production was very low. For a couple of years Ma took a tremendous interest in them and saw that they were cleaned and so on, but when she ran into the difficulties of marketing them, she neglected them completely.

Young Plunketts in Kilternan with their favourite horse, Black Bess. She could go up and down the steps of the house, drink out of a cup and learned to peel a peach with her teeth.

I really liked the gardener, he was an old man, very expert and taught me a lot. He allowed me to help him with potting and other jobs but when Ma found him making up a box of flowers and holly to send to the L'Estrange family, the previous owners, she accused him of dishonesty and sacked him. The man she employed to replace him didn't know as much about the fruit; the vines grew musty and the scale on the peaches got very bad. The horticultural inspector for the district was horrified and Ma dragged all of us in for a rush operation to try to save them but it wasn't really any good. I did learn things from the new gardener but never as much as from the first man. Ma went round making derogatory remarks about the previous owners because they had allowed local people to call at the house for fruit and jam; she did not see that they had run the business as a success for a long time whereas she had managed to destroy it in just a couple of years.

In the meantime she turned her energies to 'improvements' and farming. She started with the Morello cherries, all of which she cut down to the level of the top of the wall; they never fruited again. She cut down all the greengage and plum trees; Mimi began to think she was a complete fool and said that it was terrible to be at the mercy of a forty-three-year-old child. Ma now brought in a ploughman to make over the one-and-a-half acre field. She gave orders to plough, harrow and cross harrow, clear it of scutch and plant potatoes, then oats. The ploughman's name was Mick Aherne, a Tipperary man, over six foot tall with a red face and broad shoulders; he was very kind and had a great sense of humour. He ploughed the field and sowed it with oats and harvested and thrashed it. We sometimes helped and sometimes just sat and watched this enormous man, strong as a horse, hammering the grain out of the straw with a big flail he had made himself. Once Mick and his men were ploughing the orchard and they came across a flagged entrance to an underground passage. They were frightened and closed it up again at once and of course we wanted to know where it was, but they wouldn't say and Ma would not pursue it; I think she was frightened too.

We all helped Mick Aherne and liked him but Ma was getting over her enthusiasm and had to think up a reason to get rid of him. She used the excuse that he had been seen escorting one of the maids down the avenue and this was enough to cast him as immoral. She sacked him and the girl just like that. He was a good man.

We had a yardman there named Johnny Doherty whom we all loved and who was great with the horses. We used to go round with him when he was looking after the horses and he would entertain us and play games with us. The youngest three were particularly fond of him. He took a bad chance by ordering some stuff for himself from Clery's shop and charging it to Ma's account. The shop checked up on the order and Johnny was sacked and George, Jack and Fiona were broken-hearted. Ma went off to the agency immediately and hired a replacement and when Jack and Fiona, who were five and six at

The seven Plunkett children at Kilternan. Back, left to right: Mimi, Gerry, Joe, Moya; front, left to right: Jack, George, Fiona.

the time, saw the new man they rushed up to Ma in great excitement and delight shouting 'Johnny Doherty is back!' Ma said 'Nonsense, he was sacked.' It took them some time to persuade her that they were right. She had employed the same man again. She was furious with them for showing her up, but if she had ever looked at the man's face, it wouldn't have happened. That was her way with servants. It was one of the things that we hated about home.

It was in the first year of Kilternan that Lizzie was sacked and my wonderful Biddy Lynch left. She had been allowed to do all the housekeeping as long as it suited Ma who then without warning gave the maid the position of housekeeper over Biddy, and this was too much. Biddy protested and Ma said she was getting above herself, so Biddy left. For nine years she had been a life-saver for all of us, keeping our lives in some kind of order, looking after our clothes and food, entertaining us and giving us real and intelligent care. Ma didn't know the value she was getting from Biddy nor how much she was doing that was outside her job. I was very close to Biddy. She was originally brought in as my nurse when I was born and she was the person I loved most in the world. It was the end of the cottonwool time of my childhood.

In spite of Ma's carry-on we loved Kilternan Abbey. When we went there first, it had been about a year since we had lived with our parents (Jack didn't recognise Ma at first when he saw her) and we were delighted to have them back with us again. It was a great place to live. We were no longer cooped up on the top storey of a house in town, we had all the peaches and grapes we wanted, and we had complete freedom to roam all over the countryside. Outside our door were shrubberies, glasshouses and beyond our fields, the wild hillsides, mountainy streams, cattle, goats and our own cromlech. Seven children can make great use of all this. Joe and I in particular went wild whenever we could, roaming all over the hills behind. We would get up at fantastic hours of the morning, usually somewhere around five o'clock, to have the whole world to ourselves. We would find something to eat in the kitchen, and since the doors were always locked and the keys on Ma's table, we got out a window onto the shed roof or down the fig tree by the kitchen wall. We made a house in one of the evergreen trees in front of the house and we had a whole series of complicated stories for every corner of the place. Out the back, beyond the house, there was a large wild place, which was used for grazing by a local farmer and some way up from it was a wonderful cromlech where we went most days. It was a huge thing with a kind of sacrificial hollow in the top with the word 'Repeal' scratched deep into the stone.

Now that Biddy was gone Ma was in charge of us and I loved the way she read to us. For a while she read every night, mostly Uncle Remus stories which we all enjoyed and she was really good at it. She was not coy or arch as she so often was on social occasions. On the other hand, she hadn't a clue about providing us with clothes; she didn't seem to realise that we were all growing all the time and that hand-me-downs might keep the younger ones dressed but didn't do anything for the older ones. She had funny notions about economics and, in a bid to outdo the shop at the gate, bought a large tin of rather nasty sweets and proposed to sell them to us. Joe pointed out to her that we couldn't buy them unless she gave us the money, as we had none of our own. She was stymied by this, but rather than give us the sweets, she threw them away.

It was about that time that Ma started thrashing us. Up to then she had often been very pleasant. She could be the life and soul of a picnic or a Christmas party and on any occasion when strangers were present. She had a sense of fun, often silly or cruel, but it was genuine; unfortunately she had no wit at all. She did not even understand Pa's lovely puns which were so awful that he made a rule against them himself. She was slow and her humour, which was often some form of jeering, was for her own enjoyment. If you didn't join in it, even if it was against yourself, you were mean and a spoilsport. She was unable to read a real book and make an estimate of its worth and this applied to lots of other things. Without Biddy she was in direct control, but she had no system and she did not know us, so when she found that what she wanted was not done, she used violence. In this she was not unusual for her time but she gave us no guidelines, no moral code and her orders varied from day to day and from hour to hour. We were supposed to be totally obedient to her; she told me for instance, that I must realise that she was the will of God. I was already learning Christian Doctrine and knew this wasn't so. I analysed her orders and decided they were impossible; Mimi agreed with me on this. Joe felt a duty to her all his life because she had nursed him through such illness but he still could see that things were wrong. Poor Moya tried all the time to get everything right.

When we did anything against Ma's (unspecified) wishes, we were beaten. It was very often for a mistake or an accident and she always said 'I will not punish the person who did it if they confess' but then she always did. Who-ever was the guilty party had to grovel in contrition, then stand still while she shook them and lectured them. Once, in the middle of this, I asked her what I was supposed to have done. She took this as impertinence and working herself up into a rage, thumped me with her closed fist, then rushed to the hall-stand for her riding cane, with which she thrashed me until she was too tired to continue. Then she stood there, panting and shouting that I would kill her, my good mother, with my ingratitude. Later that day I said to Moya that if Ma did that again I would run away. Moya said where would I go and being nine, I hadn't really worked that out so I said, 'Well, as far as Bray first anyway.' Moya, frightened by this, told Ma who subjected me to the scene in which she was the hurt, affectionate mother and I the ungrateful daughter (Mimi always said that she would sooner be beaten than lectured like this). I had frightened her a bit, but it was by no means the last time she beat me. She also used a horsewhip on us a few times; she tried this on Joe, but he fainted and she never did it again. I have no memory of being hurt, except in my mind, by all this, but I still see this big, fat woman, her face all blown up with rage, screaming 'Defy me, would you?' and thumping my little sister with her fists while six-year-old Fiona looked up at her with defiance, which made it much worse, as Ma was determined to 'break her spirit'.

At the time that Ma took charge in Kilternan we had lots of dogs (one of them called Sandro Botticelli) and mine was a standard poodle called Maisie, a wonderful dog. All the dogs had mongrel pups which Ma allowed us to keep until they were quite big and then she had them all drowned. We had thir-teen cats, one each and some spares, and Ma lost her temper one day and gave orders for them all to be drowned. Lots of them were but my cat, Squallrag, was drowned three times and still came up alive. The poor coachman who had been given the dirty work said she was a witch and refused to try again, so I got my cat back. She was a great cat and a fine rabbiter.

Pa was rarely around to see what domestic life was like and in any case he regarded that as Ma's province and believed that she knew what she was do-ing. When he was in the country he more or less retreated to the bungalow in Kilternan and worked on books, prepared lectures and acted as one of the local magistrates at the Petty Sessions. He had gained a considerable reputa-tion after the publication of *Sandro Botticelli* and was travelling all over Europe to various societies and institutes, giving lectures and seminars and publishing pamphlets and articles. He was also a member (usually an honorary member) of the principal art and literature societies of most European countries and those in North and South America. We didn't think of it as working for a living but in fact he never stopped working all his life. He never minded what physical conditions he lived in, hot, cold, wet, or dry and he didn't mind what he ate, but he loved wine with his dinner, although the quality of it didn't much concern him. In Fitzwilliam Street he ordered barrels from France every year and when the barrels arrived the wine was bottled by a local publican in the house. In Kilternan he enquired about wine at the Golden Ball and found that the owner had a hundred dozen claret on the premises. Pa bought the lot at a shilling a bottle which even then was cheap.

The Countess—Ma—aged about forty. She was capricious and neglectful of her children. The eldest daughter, Mimi, once remarked how terrible it was to be 'in the care of a forty-year-old child'.

When Joe had come back from the school in Passy, he had a swollen gland in his neck and was frequently too ill to go anywhere. Ma used to look at his neck and say 'I must get some goose grease for that. I'm sure if it was rubbed with goose grease it would go away'. I don't know whether she knew nothing about tuberculosis or was trying to ignore it. Joe was supposed to be going to Belvedere College whenever he was able for it. To do this, he had to cycle the one-and-a-quarter miles to Carrickmines station, put his bicycle on the train to Harcourt Street and cycle across to the north side of town to the school. He always had a shilling in his pocket for his lunch but he spent it on pet mice or curios or books from the shops on the quays. He came back at about half-past three and we met him at the station with the pony and trap as often as we could but if we couldn't, he had to walk back as the hill was too steep for cycling most of the way. He would have his dinner and do his homework which often took until as late as half-past ten. Even for a healthy boy of thirteen this would have been a tough day and Joe certainly wasn't that.

Joe had started asking questions about science and was getting more and more upset at his own ignorance, until he realised that the people he was asking for information knew nothing either so he started looking elsewhere. On his way to school he found some chemistry books in Webb's bookshop on the quays and went crazy about it. He took over a half cellar in the basement known as Johnny Adair's kitchen; it was supposed to be the kitchen of the old house when Johnny Adair, Robin Adair's father, lived there before he went to Puckstown (the song says 'You're welcome to Puckstown, Johnny Adair'). This was Joe's laboratory and he persuaded Ma to buy him some basic apparatus like flasks and condensers after he had bought the books with his lunch money. Some of his experiments were disappointing at first but then he found Emerson Reynold's *Elementary Chemistry* and had some great fun, as indeed I had helping him. Pa had a similar passion when he was young and nearly blew himself up. Joe had two big problems—there was no gas supply to run a Bunsen burner (methylated spirit was no substitute) and Ma started taking an interest. She had no idea what he was doing but she brought visitors around and asked silly patronising questions. Joe said she seriously expected him, at the age of thirteen, to make important and original discoveries. He was so appalled by this that it put him back years in his confidence in himself and he gave up on it. He had also been fascinated by Marconi's wireless from the start. The information was being published in weeklies and Joe made a collection of them and started building his own sets, first in Fitzwilliam Street and then in Kilternan. He kept updating them right through his life. By the time Joe was fourteen the glands on his neck had to be lanced for the first time. They were done at home by Uncle Jack, and Ma's old maternity nurse was brought out to nurse him.

In 1901 Mimi was still in Mount Anville and Moya was sent to join her. Mimi was obviously very clever, and Mount Anville then was not a good school academically, but Uncle Jack insisted on our being sent there because the food was better there than anywhere else. I was sent there for the summer term to make my First Communion and found the whole thing quite a contrast to life at home. It was very grand and the food was indeed extremely good. I was prepared to be happy there but the place was half empty which made it odd enough. My Communion was made with great ceremony, with candles and flowers and incense and relations, and it was overpowering and not spiritual. Grandpa Pat Plunkett and Aunt Helena came to the Mass. Aunt Helena gave me a gold watch on a long gold chain and a copy of the *Imitation of Christ*, a little book of prayer and contemplation that I have always been fond of, and Pa gave me a lovely ivory crucifix. It was about a month later when we were back in Kilternan that we got a telegram from Ma, who was in Fitzwilliam Street, saying 'Go to Mount Anville Fête tomorrow. Bring Fiona properly dressed.' Fiona was only four and had nothing decent to wear, so Moya, who was really frightened by these orders, took the pony and trap into Bray and bought a piece of white muslin with the very few shillings she had of her own. She sat up until one o'clock in the morning making a dress for Fiona, thinking that Ma would give her the credit for it. Mimi had said that she shouldn't do anything but Moya was not prepared to face the fury that would be roaring up the next day. At the fête we met Ma almost immediately and she said 'Where did you get that disgraceful dress?' Moya was terribly upset. She was reduced to tears, to pulp and to not knowing what to do next. She was still only twelve.

Ma really liked being the grand lady in her country house and frequently invited guests out for lunch or afternoon tea. We suffered a lot from these

Gerry's First Holy Communion (1901) aged nine. She was sent to Mount Anville school for the summer term to be prepared for it. She found the ceremony, which was held at the school, 'overpowering and not spiritual'.

guests as they inevitably said 'I hope you appreciate your good mother' or 'Do you know how good your mother is to you?' because Ma used to tell them what a good mother she was and how much she had sacrificed for us. We were too young and inexperienced with people to know whether they were even being serious. On one of these occasions, a Sunday lunch in Kilternan, Ma looked at the torn pink dress I was wearing, which had been Mimi's four years before, and told me to go and change it. I said I didn't have anything else. 'Nonsense,' she said with one of her little deprecating laughs and sent me away. I was beaten afterwards 'for lying', but we did get some clothes as a result. She brought us back blouses from France and found a cheap dress-maker to make school uniforms and other bits and pieces. Aunt Helena made each of us girls two sets of blouses and skirts with tops. They lasted until Fiona grew into (and out of) Mimi's. One of the maids stole Mimi's skirt, and Jack and Fiona, who used to see everything, told Ma about it. Her response was that Mimi should take more care of her clothes; Jack and Fiona made up a song about it and sang it all over the house.

Ma was very fond of sending telegrams, and one arrived from her when we four girls were in Kilternan ordering us into town at once, so we tidied and closed up Kilternan (we were used to this now as we were frequently there without either parents or servants), took out the pony and trap and headed into town. We found Ma in Fitzwilliam Street in an awful tear but couldn't find out why. She packed us off to Mount Anville that same day without proper clothes or uniforms, and when we arrived there we found that the school was not due to open for ten days. We had to stay in Dargan's guest-house, which was usually used by the nuns' relatives. It was a beautiful old house, with a huge drawing room that had mirrors on all the shutters reflect-ing the countryside all the way to the sea. As far as we could make out when we did get to the school, the nuns had been told that we were in some kind of disgrace but I don't think they believed it. Because we had no money for copybooks, or anything else, we wrote to Ma asking for some but got no reply, so Mère Econome had to give them to us for nothing. Fiona was only four and could read but she was the only girl there who was that young and there was no real provision for her. She was put in the care of an elderly blind nun and I don't know what they did, except that one day I was sent with a message and found her scrubbing the floor with a toothbrush. We were only allowed to play with her for twenty minutes on Sundays. After six weeks we were told that Ma was waiting to see us in the parlour. Before we went down, we con-sulted with each other about how we would take it and Mimi said, 'Ignore it'. Ma received us with frigid coldness and seemed to presume that we would be overwhelmed with sorrow but she still didn't tell us why. She had brought Pa along and seemed to have told him some fancy story—poor man! Long after-wards Ma told me, as the youngest and therefore least responsible, that all this was a punishment for leaving soiled articles (sanitary towels) and under-

*Kitty McCormack (left) and Phyllis Kelly. Kitty,
who worked in the Dun Emer Guild with Evelyn
Gleeson, was Gerry's lifelong friend.*

clothing in a cupboard in Kilternan. To her prurient mind, this was the worst crime, socially or morally, that a woman could commit, but the story wasn't even true as she had not been out to Kilternan until after we had been dispatched to school in disgrace.

The nearest house to ours on the Dublin side in Kilternan was the Glebe House, the Church of Ireland rectory. Pa and the rector, Mr O'Morchoe, were friends (they were both book people) so we got to know the O'Morchoe boys from the time we moved out there. They were the same age as ourselves and we roamed all over the countryside, playing complicated games with them. They were good people and we liked and respected them. These friendships lasted into adulthood, although being from different religions and traditions, we went into different schools, universities and armies. The O'Morchoes joined the British Army before the First World War at the same time as we were becoming deeply involved in Nationalism.

About the year 1902, when I was eleven years old, my parents brought us to meet Miss Evelyn Gleeson, who had just moved to Dundrum, near Kilternan. Miss Gleeson's arrival with her sister, Mrs McCormack and the McCormack children, Kitty, Gracie and Eddie, brought great changes in our lives. They were just settling in to their house which was then called Runnemede on the Sandyford Road outside Dundrum, and the carpets were not even on the floor when we first called on them. It was a beautiful big house with a large garden and field but very close to the road. We were immediately on good terms with all the family and Ma took to them at once, remaining their friend ever afterwards, doing everything she could for them. The enthusiastic local curate arrived while we were at the house, to commandeer us to dance a four-hand reel at the inaugural concert of the Gaelic League's Enniskerry branch. Kitty and Gracie McCormack, Moya and myself were the four, and it was the beginning of a lifelong friendship for myself and Kitty. A young man taught us the four-hand reel and we danced at the concert. We were delighted to have done so, as it was our first contact with anything of that kind. Kitty and Gracie used to come up to Kilternan all the time; we used to fetch them in our pony and trap as they had no transport of their own. We were also continually in and out of their house and Miss Gleeson was the soul of hospitality and kindness in every way.

Miss Gleeson had been a friend of the English artist and designer, William Morris, and believed completely in William Morris' ideals of handcraft; she was determined to start a similar industry here. She had been a painter and designer, and trained in carpet making. She had no money of her own, but her brother, Jim, was a very wealthy man, and provided her with a personal income of £2,000 a year, with another £2,000 for whatever enterprise she was creating. This indeed he owed her, as she had always been the head of their very difficult family and looked after them. She came to Ireland from London to start the Dun Emer Guild with the Yeats sisters, Lily and Lolly. Lily was a designer and embroiderer and Lolly was already a printer. Their brother, Jack Yeats, had been advising them and designing for them and they were already printing some of the poems of their other brother, Willie Yeats. They set up the printing press in the upstairs rooms and the carpet looms in some of the large rooms downstairs. Gracie McCormack was a trained weaver and Kitty was already a designer although she was still very young, about my own age. The last member of the guild was Nora Fitzpatrick, a bookbinder, who beautifully bound the books that the Yeats sisters were already producing.

Evelyn Gleeson's very open house meant that all sorts of marvellous people were in and out. It was always full of writers, painters, thinkers and talkers. On the wall of the studio George Russell had drawn an enormous picture of fairies and angels in chalk. We joined a brush painting class given by Lily and Lolly and enjoyed ourselves very much at it. It was the first time anyone had given us any indication about how these things should be done. Joe and I got Nora Fitzpatrick to show us something about bookbinding but since we were so afraid of our own ineptness, the things we bound were not worth keeping. The paper we chose to use in the books was of such poor quality that it fell out, even though the bindings were excellent! The whole house was such a centre of intelligence, culture and art that we loved it and we spent as much time there as we could.

After some time the Yeats sisters decided to leave the Dun Emer Guild and set up the Cuala Press in Dundrum village on their own. They took with them all the materials Miss Gleeson had provided and paid for and said that they were under no obligation to pay her for any of it. On the other hand, Nora Fitzpatrick remained with Miss Gleeson for a long time afterwards and she was the life and soul of all the theatrical entertainment and nonsense that was going on there. When Miss Gleeson's brother died unexpectedly some years later, she found that he had not made any provision for her and both her own and the business income disappeared. Even the house was in his name and the result was she had to leave it and come in to live in 10 Pembroke Road. Ma brought all their looms, materials and equipment to the Hardwicke Hall in Hardwicke Street, which she had just bought, and set up studio spaces for them. The looms went into one of the big rooms there and the small rooms were used for storage and embroidery.

Ma got the Archbishop of San Francisco, who was rebuilding the cathedral lost in the fire, to give the order for vestments to Dun Emer. They were wonderful, gold poplin from Atkinson's for the cope, embroidered with gold. The beautiful thing about poplin was that it was always embroidered right down to the ends. The Archbishop took so long to pay that the loan Dun Emer had to get was so swollen with interest that they lost money. It was a small concern and terribly expensive to run. The workers were very young, all under twenty years of age, about ten of them at the most and all local girls. The girls did not get paid much and they did not have regular hours but there was a good spirit between all of them because they were getting training and they knew they would get a job afterwards, which they did, going on to work in other well-known places. Miss Gleeson did all the fine work herself.

Mimi had the idea of a family magazine, just for us children. We called it *The Morning Jumper* and everyone had to write or draw something, then we kept it concealed until it was finished. I did the decorations as well and Mimi illustrated the advertisements. The first two numbers were fine and then Mimi was invited to Italy. A friend of Pa's, Mrs Mulhall, the widow of a celebrated mathematician and another relation of ours, had lived in Italy for some time. She wanted to give Pa's eldest daughter a social season in Rome when she was eighteen and made the offer when Mimi was still only sixteen, and, like the rest of us, very inexperienced socially. We might have been quite wealthy as a family, but comparatively little money was spent on us children. Ma's socialising was sporadic and whimsical and she didn't like us being friendly with any contemporaries who were not relations. Mimi was always sensitive to what was going on and was well aware of the fact that she wasn't ready for the kind of season Mrs Mulhall had in mind and said that she would love to go another year, but not now.

But Ma was excited by the whole idea and said, 'Nonsense! she must go'. She made Mimi some skirts and blouses, which even I could see were not right, and sent her off to Rome straight away. Mrs Mulhall was a kind woman

Pages from The Morning Jumper, *a family magazine started by Mimi. The Countess decided to 'improve' it in Mimi's absence in Rome, and killed it.*

and saw at once that Mimi was only a schoolgirl and that it wouldn't work, so she sent her instead to the Sacred Heart school at Trinita del Monte at the top of the Spanish Steps. This suited Mimi much better and she managed at the same time to get to some life drawing classes in an art college. Mimi said very little about the whole thing when she came back, except that Betty Colleran had said she would have thirty pink evening dresses when she married. Later on Betty did, and she had!

While Mimi was away, Ma got hold of *The Morning Jumper* and decided she was going to 'improve' our magazine. She drew pictures and stuck them in, wrote stories, did a lot of messy copying on the Roneo duplicating machine and added in a lot of very adult and unsuitable limericks. She did eventually realise that she had gone too far and killed it. She said 'Perhaps I should not have tried to improve it', meaning that we were not capable of appreciating the value of her additions.

Ma eventually began to get bored with Kilternan. She now had several failing fruit crops, a cold and windy country house, a very limited social life and seven children who refused to be her mindless and obedient slaves. The Fitzwilliam Street house had been kept on and she and Pa went in there every day, taking the train from Carrickmines to Harcourt Street station each day, buying sixpenny novels and magazines to read on the journey. These were the only reading matter in the house in Kilternan (Pa had all the good books locked up in the bungalow) and it filled up with them until they were all over the place. We devoured them, I think I read every one of them. The books, yellow-covered paperbacks, were mostly detective stories, including a lot of Sherlock Holmes, and bad novels. The magazines often had useful scientific articles, and I particularly remember photographs analysing the movements of horses. The first couple of winters we spent some time back in Fitzwilliam Street and furniture was brought in and out between the two houses as it was needed; but as our parents came out less and less, Ma stopped this and just left a minimum of requirements in Kilternan for us children.

Pa had given up court work some time back but continued his subscriptions to the Law Library. A friend of his, Michael Dunne, another barrister, asked him to come and work in his chambers at 42, Lower Mount Street, where they specialised in maritime cases. Pa was very interested in the work and Dunne was showing him how to make use of his talents at the Bar, but he was drowned in a yachting accident in Dublin Bay not long afterwards and the business came to an end. It was also the end of Pa's career in law; his wig and gown came back from the Four Courts and we used them for dressing up.

The Irish Party was campaigning for Catholics to apply for the higher level jobs, from which they had been excluded up to now, and this took Ma's fancy. Edward Ennis became Under Secretary and shortly afterwards was killed falling off an outside car and Ma wanted Pa to apply for the job. She called on poor Mrs Ennis to find out more. She then called on our cousin, Dudley

White, to ask for his help but he refused her, saying that she was hard-hearted to be asking when the poor man wasn't yet cold in his grave. She didn't know that the position of Under Secretary was a political one, reserved for those in the Irish Party. Pa applied for and secured the position of Secretary of the 1903 Cork International Exhibition. He lived in Cork for most of the year before the exhibition and enjoyed the whole thing very much, making quite a few friends, including the man we called Mr Hadji Bey, owner (to our joy) of the Turkish Delight factory. King Edward VII and Queen Alexandra visited the exhibition in the summer and Pa presented the Queen with a little bell with an amethyst clapper, which he had had made in Kinsale. Kilternan was let to the Aliaga Kellys for most of this year and we missed it very much. Whatever the difficulties of living there, it was infinitely preferable to living in Fitzwilliam Street. We now had a French governess called Germaine Cavalier, whose family had had vineyards that were ruined by the phylloxera epidemic. She was very young and pleasant and we had a good time going on cycling expeditions and picnics. We had to put a binding on the hems of our skirts to stop them from ravelling when they got caught in the bicycles. We were appalled when Ma summarily dismissed Germaine, without any consideration and barely with a character. Ma stayed in Dublin while Pa was in Cork and he wrote to her frequently, as he always did when he was away, but in one of his letters he mentioned that his secretary had acquired a gold bracelet and was telling everyone that he had given it to her. That got Ma going all right! She went down and stayed with him in Cork after that.

Sometime that year Ma took Mimi and Moya on a trip to Hove in England, and came across St George's school for boys. She had a horror of Irish boys' schools, because she had heard of a boy being expelled from Clongowes for something 'unmentionable', and she had heard Aunt Helena extol the virtues of English schools. When she came home she took the three boys off to St George's, left them there and returned home delighted with herself. Joe was fifteen, George was nine and poor Jack was only six. There was no provision for anyone so young, not even a version of the school uniform he could wear, so he wore a tunic and pants, as he did at home. A few weeks later Ma received a telegram from the school saying that there was an outbreak of scarlatina (though none of my brothers had it) and would she please take the boys home. She collected them and brought them to the bungalow in Kilternan, keeping them in quarantine there for weeks, without telling any of us where they were. While they were there, Joe managed to persuade her that the school was very unsuitable because of what went on there. She was horrified, 'Surely the English couldn't allow such things in their schools' and said she would write to the government about it. The school was closed down by the government two years later. Poor Ma! It was not fair, she was doing her best. Pa was back from Cork while this quarantine was going on (he had been asked to stay

Some of the young Plunketts and their cousins on the steps of Kilternan Abbey.

on in Cork but wanted to come home) and we girls were in Mount Anville where he often came to see us.

Joe's glands were very swollen again and were operated on by a friend of Uncle Jack's, an old army surgeon. He hacked poor Joe about savagely, referred to the healing tissue on Joe's neck as 'proud flesh', a very old-fashioned term, and burned it off with copper-sulphate crystals without an anaesthetic. This was done in the orthopaedic hospital near Fitzwilliam Street, and Joe was sent to convalesce in Delaford, on the Firhouse Road. Ma decided she needed a holiday after the shock of Joe's operation and since she believed a travelling companion was essential, brought Moya with her. She thought it wasn't proper for her to travel alone but in fact, there was no social problem, she was a very good traveller and she enjoyed herself much more when she didn't have one of us with her. It was a three month cruise to the Canaries via Lisbon and as Mimi was in Mount Anville, she decided that I was to be the housekeeper in Kilternan. I was twelve. The household I was to look after consisted of Pa, Joe, who was still bedridden, George, Fiona, Jack, Nurse Keating (there to nurse Joe), two maids, a coachman and a gardener. This was not a joke of Ma's or a learning exercise, it was simply that she saw nothing odd about leaving a twelve-year-old in charge of a large household. The arrangement didn't surprise Pa either, he always had a touching faith in my competence.

I went into Fitzwilliam Street with Pa about twice a week in either the trap or the carriage; the house was looking dirty and miserable. They had let it the year before when we were all in Kilternan, and nobody had fixed it up after the tenants left. Pa had refused to allow any letting until the books in his study were fitted with wire doors over every shelf. I loved travelling and being with Pa; we had the same sense of humour and I was just beginning my discovery of books about which he knew everything there was to be known, and of course he was so kind. He looked at what I was reading one day (it might have been a detective story or a romantic novel) and was obviously a bit worried that it was rubbish. He said that for himself, he didn't mind what he read, as long as it was clever enough and I quoted Charles Lamb back at him, when he said his sisters' reading would make them excellent old maids. He was delighted with this and the fact that we understood each other. He was a very sophisticated old bird and no matter what I read there was no allusion I could make that he could not cap. Sometimes he forgot who he was talking to and quoted from books that I was not supposed to have read. When I recognised them he either gave me a funny look or burst out laughing and said no more. When we arrived in Fitzwilliam Street we would call at local shops to buy groceries and meat. We didn't normally buy these in Willis' in Kilternan becuse they were too dear. I had £1 a week to spend but Pa used to warn me frequently not to spend too much. Ma was spending money like water and writing back for more all the time. I told him that all I could do was buy whatever the servants told me was needed and they never asked for anything unreasonable.

I was growing like mad and had nothing to wear. There was no budget for clothes so I bought myself three pieces of cotton and a *Weldon's Ladies' Journal* which had blouse patterns. I made myself three blouses which were quite passable, with leg-of-mutton sleeves and buttons down the back, on the old chain stitch Wheeler and Willcox machine. Although Mimi was very uncomplimentary when she saw these first, she was happy enough when I made summer dresses for her and for Moya later. The boys were just as badly off and I decided to take a look at their suits to see if there was anything I could do. I tried making trousers from a pattern I made up myself, but they were really awful so I decided to take one of their suits apart (probably Joe's) to see if I could work out the construction. I learned a lot from that suit. The first time I tried to set a sleeve in a jacket, I got it wrong seven times before I got it right. Over the years I learned a lot more about tailoring, enough to know what those suits lacked, but they were much better than nothing and from then on I knew that I was capable of providing clothes whenever they were needed.

Mimi, who was at Mount Anville, told Pa it was disgraceful that I was not at school and that he should send me there straight away. He agreed to this and I had to organise myself to go. I was very aware that Mimi had laughed at the blouses I had made for myself but I had no school uniform and no other clothes so I had to bring them. The only shoes I owned had big holes in the soles so I put pieces of cardboard, which I painted with black ink, in them.

The problem was that Ma held the purse strings and she insisted that nobody should spend money without her authorisation. Pa came to see us twice every week without fail with a bag of sweets in his pocket and a smile even when he was not feeling well. If he was sick, he apologised for it. He asked us how much money we needed and we told him the exact amount, and since he trusted us, that's what he gave us. He was always like that when Ma wasn't around.

This time, when it came to the end of the term, I had a sore throat and could not go to the prizegiving. I was put into a room on the top floor and no-one came to see me except when my prizes were brought up, all six of them rubbish, *Aytound's Lays*, ballad stuff, a history of the Indian Mutiny, and a history of the mutiny of certain Scottish regiments when they were ordered to wear trews instead of kilts! Then I was simply left behind in the school while all the other pupils, including my sisters, went home. I was only told they had gone home when I asked the nun who brought me my meals. I had heard that Ma was back but nothing else, and nobody explained why I had been left. Nothing was ever explained to children at that time, they were simply sent here and there and told to do things without reasons being offered. I spent the time reading any books I could find and wandering by myself around the grounds where I found the redcurrants in the garden. Nobody ever spoke to me except on one occasion when I had picked some purple flowers and put them on a small altar. A nun passing by told me that purple was an emperor's colour and not suitable for a martyr, and she told me to take the flowers away. Another nun once smiled at me—once in three weeks! It taught me not to depend on anyone. After three weeks I was brought home. I was not told why I had been left there but years later I concluded that it was probably thought that I had diphtheria and was very infectious. The Mount Anville water was polluted and there had been several cases of diphtheria in the previous year. The water supply was from a spring behind the building pumped up by a horse working in a circle like an old-fashioned churn. The place was too high for the town water supply and there was no pressure. An engine had to be brought in to bring the water up. I don't think I really had diphtheria. No doctor saw me and I got no treatment. Ma was apt to think that her daughters' illnesses were their own fault like Job's comforters.

Ma and Moya came home from the Canary Islands with Ma in a temper. Moya, then a very lively fourteen-year-old, had always been her favourite in the family, so much so that we used to ask her to negotiate for us when we needed anything. Moya always took this seriously and tried hard to get us clothes, extra food, pocket money, lessons, or even medical attention. On the cruise, members of the crew and particularly the ship's doctor took a particular interest in Moya and played deck games with her. Ma went into one of her spins of outrage. She accused Moya of immoral conduct (always a favourite with her) and flirting. Mimi and I were sure that Ma was madly jealous. She was no longer the beautiful Countess, she was forty-five and very fat from eating and drinking far too much. In her mind and her language she was at the same time prudish and coarse, whereas Moya was extremely innocent, more than any of the rest of us older ones, and desperately anxious to do right and to please. Moya was now in disgrace; there was nothing we could do about it and she never regained her position with Ma.

That was also the year of the hurricane, one of the times we saw the other side of Ma. It was September 10th, we were out in Kilternan and I woke up in the middle of the night thinking I was in a boat because the whole house was swaying in the wind. Ma was going round sprinkling holy water everywhere; there wasn't very much else she could do at that stage. I did manage to go back to sleep eventually and in the morning there were reports of whole lines of trees down, of stacks of hay being blown away and of the little river flooding and carrying off cattle. Just as we were starting our breakfast, an enormous beech beside the house came down with a crash that sounded like the end of everything. Ma loved a crisis and she took charge of everything, rebuilding walls, cutting up logs and blowing up stumps with dynamite with a team of men. We learnt a lot about trees that time, and a lot about dynamite.

Joe was still not well enough to go to school, so it was arranged that Mr Greenan, the teacher in the Sandyford school, would come in to teach us. He came to the house after dinner in the evenings, twice a week, and stayed until about ten p.m. Here at last was so much of what we wanted. He was a lovely man and a wonderful teacher. Joe and I loved mathematics and we worked on it more than anything else. Joe was particularly good at it and delighted to have such a good teacher. Moya sometimes joined us and Mr Greenan would work through a rule, explain it all and work with it, then say, 'Now, will we do that rule again or go on to the next one?' and we would say 'Go on!' and on we went. The maths I did with him at that time got me into college four years later. He did teach us other things, he taught the younger ones reading and writing and in fact he was a genius at teaching three or four subjects to three or four different ages. We were all so deprived of learning that we jumped at the chance of learning anything at all. At no stage in our education in any school did we learn Irish or Irish history and we were beginning to feel the need of it. We had the benefit of Pa's information and experience, but our understanding of it was very haphazard.

During our next term in Mount Anville Moya and I, now in the same class, were so well armed with Mr Greenan's teaching that we were able to help out the mathematics teacher. She, like many other teachers there, had been sent from the mother house in Roehampton to convalesce, but in fact she was dying with a tubercular throat. She was a first-class mathematician but, because she lost her voice every so often, she would ask Moya and me to take over the running of the class. After this had been reported to Reverend Mother, she walked into our classroom one day to check up on it. There was the usual initial silence and then she said, 'We will now continue the lesson'. Moya took up the lesson where she had left off. We were both taken out of that class and sent to the senior one instead. That only lasted a few days as it would have looked like rewarding us, so we were sent back to our original class. We always either knew too much or too little! We were taken out of school early again that time, and forty years later, going through Ma's papers, I discovered that on that occasion, and on nearly all the others when we were taken out of school at odd times, it was because Ma had not paid the fees. In fact, she never paid the fees for us in any school; she simply ignored the bills.

4 We grow up, Ma gets worse 1904–1907

WHEN UNCLE JACK DIED IN 1904 it was a terrible shock to Ma, who idolised him. Born in 1845 and christened John Joseph, he was the eldest of the Crannys and always his mother's favourite. His father's prosperity enabled him to qualify as a doctor from Trinity College, Dublin. He worked in the Rotunda Hospital and was subsequently made surgeon to Jervis Street Hospital. He had a general practice, first at his home in Muckross Park, then in 82 Harcourt Street and, from the 1880s, in 17 Merrion Square, being one of the first Catholic doctors to live and practice on the Square. Professionally, he was highly thought of and considered advanced in his ideas; he was one of the first in Dublin to adopt Lister's theories on anti-septic agents, which many of his colleagues thought a joke, and he tried to clean up the wards in Jervis Street Hospital. He was made a Fellow of the College of Surgeons and as a member of the Council stood for election as Vice-President. He had every expectation of success but was not elected and was very put out about it. He felt there must be a reason of which he was unaware and was afraid that it would throw doubt on his professional competence. He got word from Dublin Castle later on in his career that there was a black mark against him because when he was a student he had treated some Fenian prisoners in Mountjoy Jail after the uprising in 1867.

He was a big, good-looking, bearded man who kept two carriage horses and a riding horse. I remember seeing him on his rounds, most of which he used to do on horseback, but he became far too fat and had to make do with the much less spectacular brougham. He was not as fat as the doctor who lived a few doors away from us who had to have a big curve cut out of his dining table to fit his stomach at it. Uncle Jack smoked the best cigars, had a yacht in Kingstown and travelled in France, Spain and Morocco. He brought Ma with him to Morocco before she was married and taught her to shoot with a revolver and with miniature rifles. She was always furiously jealous of his wife, Marie, sneering at her and treating her as an interloper in the family. Aunt Marie was an heiress with shares in various businesses and she held the £5,000 mortgage on the Elgin Road property.

In 1902 Uncle Jack took a country house, Rockfield, in Dundrum, a nice house, with a long avenue and a bridge over the railway where it intersected the land. He commuted from there to the Merrion Square house and his work, but Aunt Marie stayed in Dundrum most of the time. He was a good doctor but he drank like a fish and broke down every so often. He and Aunt

Uncle Jack, Ma's favourite brother, and the family doctor, died in 1904. His obituary in the British Medical Journal, *August 1904 ran:* Dr Cranny graduated in the University of Dublin in 1869 and began his professional life by acting as Assistant Master at the Rotunda Lying-in Hospital. Soon after he became Surgeon to Jervis Street Hospital, where he was highly esteemed as a conscientious and painstaking surgeon. For some years he was a member of Council of the Royal College of Surgeons and on one occasion offered himself as a candidate for the Vice-Presidency but was not successful.

Marie were staying in Rockfield in 1904 when he insisted on taking the pony out one night after he had been drinking. The coachman was also drunk and had overfed the pony and given it no exercise. Both the trap and the pony were very small and Uncle Jack lashed the poor pony down the drive, making it bolt and smash into the bridge over the railway, overturning the trap. The pony broke a leg and had to be put down and Uncle Jack broke several ribs. He was haemorrhaging and they brought him in and put him to bed in Merrion Square. Westland Row station was being re-roofed with iron girders at the time and the building and hammering noises went on all day and through the night. Uncle Jack had a message sent to the builders asking them to stop at night but of course this was impossible. His ribs had started to repair when he had a stroke and between the noise, the pain and the relapse, he couldn't take any more. He went downstairs in the middle of the night and took an overdose of morphia which killed him. He was buried in the purple velvet of the College of Surgeons.

Aunt Marie, Uncle Jack's widow. 'She went in for being the complete widow and her mourning clothes were of the most tremendous and expensive kind.'

Each of us girls was sent in turn to stay with Aunt Marie in Merrion Square to keep her company. Moya was first, being Uncle Jack's god-daughter, and I went there after her. Aunt Marie went in for being the com-

Uncle Jack left two of his houses on Elgin Road to his god-daughter, Moya, and the other five of those houses jointly to the remaining six Plunkett children, but their mother prevented them inheriting and they only managed to do so after her death in 1944.

plete widow and her mourning clothes were of the most tremendous and expensive kind. It is impossible to imagine what the old-fashioned crêpe was like. There was no way it could be washed or cleaned, it was a very crimped-up silk material, speckled sometimes with very glossy little dots of something or another, I couldn't make out what. She had a poplin skirt with a large coat over it and the skirt had about fifteen inches or more of crêpe around the end. It must have weighed a ton, and of course one was supposed to admire the weight of it. They used to hand you the thing and say, 'Feel the weight of that!' The coat over it all had a kind of collar and crêpe on the sleeves and round the hem. There was no end to it; she must have been weighed right down. I remember that the coat alone cost £40; what it would cost now, I have not the slightest idea. It was all the best silk poplin and was completed with a little bonnet and veil. She had always loved clothes. Ma objected strongly to her taste in evening dress, which she considered far too décolleté and shocking.

Uncle Jack left all his movable possessions to Aunt Marie together with a life interest in all his houses, except for those he had inherited from Uncle Gerald, which he bequeathed to Ma. He left two Elgin Road houses to Moya, his god-daughter, and the other five on that road jointly to the rest of us children, to be inherited at our coming-of-age. In the meantime, they were to be used to pay for his funeral expenses. These provisions meant nothing to Ma, her children could not possibly own property! It was automatically hers and any other notion was outrageous. When we did come of age she kept our inheritance from us, using the excuse that she had had to mortgage one of her own houses to pay Uncle Jack's debts. His debts were quite large all right and rather peculiar. He had given my sister Moya a violin and a bicycle a few years previously which had never been paid for, he had not even paid the bills for furniture and equipment from the time when he had set up practice as a doctor in the 1860s. Aunt Marie was supposed to have an annuity from her husband's estate and it was part of my parents' duty as executors to make sure that it was paid, but Ma said Aunt Marie didn't need it and she used to 'forget' it. On paper my parents were the joint executors of Uncle Jack's will but, as usual, Pa left all the business to Ma. He believed everything she told him about how things were arranged and knew that she would not allow him a hand in it anyway.

Frank Cranny arrived for the funeral and the reading of the will, this time with one of his sons, Fred, who got himself a job singing in Messager's operetta *Véronique* in a touring company. I realised for the first time that Uncle Jack and Frank and Ma all had the same piercing grey eyes, which gave the impression that they could see everything that was in your mind. This was often the reason for their surprising influence over those around them. This time around, Ma made a deal with Frank that she would give him ten shillings a week if he stayed out of Ireland. He accepted the deal and left. Ma herself now had life interests in houses and land from her father, her mother and two of her brothers, Gerald and Jack, and consequently was in control of a considerable amount of property on Marlborough Road, Elgin Road, Eglinton Road, Wellington Road and Belgrave Road in Rathmines, Donnybrook and Ballsbridge. As she was acquisitive and always on the lookout for a quick way to a fortune (the one she had was never enough), she was constantly buying bits and pieces of property in other parts of the city as well. In spite of her desire for wealth and houses, none of it was properly looked after or maintained.

Although she had heard Mr Denning, the solicitor, read Uncle Jack's will, Ma chose to disregard its provisions. She put all of us in Uncle Jack's Dundrum house, Rockfield, while she and Aunt Marie discussed arrangements. My mother told Aunt Marie that we would mind the place for her, but in fact Ma was taking things out of it all the time and disposing of them for herself. It was also very convenient for her to have us there as the Aliaga Kellys were still living in Kilternan. Mimi's health had been very bad with a succession of tooth infections and she took to her bed when we arrived in the house. A Nurse Harris was looking after us and Fiona, who was about seven at the time, amused herself by persecuting her. Nurse Harris sat on a slug on a bench in the garden and Fiona had an elaborate funeral for it. She buried it and put a tombstone over it inscribed 'Here lies Mary-Ann slug, sat on by Nurse Harris' with the date underneath. It was the last straw for Nurse Harris who, to our delight, left in a huff. On our own now, we had a great time in that house. There were lots of good books and it was there that I discovered Sir Thomas

Browne's *Religio Medici* and decided that this was a friend for life. There was a Great Dane who lived in a stable in the yard, barking and jumping up on the door all day long, and a telephone in the house, which was a novelty to us; we didn't have one in Fitzwilliam Street until 1908.

We had no idea that Ma had no right to Rockfield or its contents, and we ate everything in sight including an incredible number of pots of Scott's jam that we found in kitchen cupboards. Mimi was not well enough to take control and six children between seven and seventeen can cause a lot of havoc in a strange house. On top of all this, there were some animals on the property including Aunt Marie's pet, a little white cow, that Ma had ordered to be driven off and sold. Finally, Aunt Marie began to realise that she was not getting a fair deal over Rockfield and one day she and Ma arrived in the house at the same time. There was a gorgeous row, with Aunt Marie raging about her cow and her jam while the husband and wife from the gatelodge were denouncing Ma for having taken Uncle Jack's things and he hardly cold in his grave, and Ma throwing a magnificent fit of hysterics, saying that they were all accusing her of burying Uncle Jack alive and she kept on at such a rate that it put an end to the whole thing. Aunt Marie and Ma parted brass rags for ever. Ma left, taking us with her, and removed as much as she could, including a basket-work chaise-longue which she said was for Joe. Months later, Joe was sitting on it outside the house in Kilternan, but he went in to the house for something and when he came back, it was gone. My brother Jack was the only one who saw Aunt Marie drive up, see the chaise-longue and instruct her coachman to strap it to the top of the carriage and drive off. When Jack told Ma, she would not believe him.

We children were sent back to Kilternan, this time with no furniture, only mattresses on the floor to sleep on. Mimi was so angry and disheartened about the way we lived that she spent all the time lying on one of the mattresses reading sixpenny novels. She refused to do anything because she had found before that no matter what she did Ma used it to hurt her, so Moya and I had to spend the whole time looking after the three young ones, trying to keep them fed and clothed. When we went out there first we brought some meat and groceries with us and milk was bought locally. After that the meat was sent out in a round basket by train on Fridays. Ma used to send a telegram to us to say it was coming and we would collect it from the station in the pony and trap. Groceries came the same way but at different times. Sometimes what was in the basket wasn't even suitable to cook. Tallons, the Enniskerry bakers, called twice a week with a lovely bread they made with potatoes that lasted for days. When the meat didn't arrive we didn't know what to do. When the groceries didn't arrive we were really stuck. Moya and I were fifteen and thirteen and we were cooking any way we could, lighting one of the little fires in an upstairs room. We could not have tackled the range, I had tried it before and found it unmanageable and anyway there wasn't enough coal for it. When the food ran out we approached Willis' shop in fear and trembling and asked for credit. We were taken aback when they willingly gave it to us and we were able to buy some basic supplies. We told Ma later about this, terrified that we had been wrong to do it, but she just looked surprised and gave us one of her false laughs.

The house was so big, with the glasshouses and outhouses, and the grounds so extensive, that we were afraid to go around it all after dark so we tried to get the locking up done while it was still daylight. If we did not, it meant carrying a lamp and on a wild night, the wind used to blow it out, no matter what care we took. The chimney of the light was then too hot to take off to relight the lamp. When Joe was there he used to take charge of things, including lights and locking up, but that year he wasn't there so it was something else for Moya and me to worry about. Even when the thirteen outer doors were locked, there were still five ways to get in to the house, so at night we were usually huddled together in the billiard room. I don't know what we would have done without the dogs, especially Nellie and my standard poodle, Maisie, who kept the rats down and gave us a sense of security.

The house might have been rattling empty and the gardens neglected, but there were always the lovely pond and the heron coming to stand beside it every night to fish for trout. I had always loved him and I used to watch him whenever he appeared at the pond; he seemed more important than ever now. He came by himself as his mate had been shot years before and was stuffed and in a house in the village. We also used to watch the trout in the evening, rising to the fly and once a trout jumped right out of the water onto the path. Ma decided to drain the pond, to clean it she said. It was not dirty, it was not even muddy. She had all the trout taken out and put in a tank. The pond was drained and refilled but in the meantime someone had stolen all the fish. We never had trout in the pond again and the heron never came back.

The lease Pa had taken on Kilternan was for seven years and due to expire in 1907. Nearly all the 120 acres was let to local farmers, which suited Ma as it paid the ground rent, but in 1905 she decided to make a claim for the whole acreage to the Land Commission, set up under the Wyndham Act of 1903. She claimed that she had been farming all of it herself and she tried to get the local farmers to back her up. Since it was not at all true, and she had done them no favours, they wouldn't and she lost her case. We did get an extra year out of it while the case went on so we had it until 1908 instead of 1907 although we hardly ever used it in those years. When the Land Commission would not give Ma the land she wanted she left the country in a temper. She went to London where she stayed with the Gurrins, friends of Uncle Gerald's, and from there to Florence to stay with the Dunnes. She spent far too much money and when she came home and saw the size of her overdraft, she was even more furious. She was still in a temper about it when we left the place for good. Black Bess, our wonderful pony, then about fourteen, was sold for a milk-cart, which was not right, but I did hear that she was not badly treated. Ma denuded Kilternan of everything movable which included taking all the glass from the conservatory and the glasshouses and the whole length of the peach houses and selling it. The glasshouses were left to rot like that for years and as far as I know, never functioned again. The house itself accidentally burned down afterwards and was never rebuilt.

It must have been when Ma was in London that Tom Gurrin told her about Stonyhurst, the Jesuit school in Lancashire. His sons had gone there and one of them had entered the order. She brought Joe, who was now eighteen, over to see the school and he was accepted for the Philosophers' class. He would not have been strong enough for ordinary school so this was ideal. It was mostly intended for foreign students going on to, or already

Joe, aged twenty, and his father, Count Plunkett, in 1907.

in, university and they were mainly from Spain, France, Austria, Germany, Malta and the Americas. A lot of them were foreign aristocrats using it to learn enough English to pass. I remember Marc Antonio Colonna and an Austrian with thirty-two quarterings and Alfred (Taffy) Asphar from Malta who stayed with us, as did some of the others. Joe was the only Irish person in the class and very happy there as he could study as much as he liked; it had a splendid library and it gave him access to all the ideas and information he had wanted for so long. He also had complete independence for the two years he was there. He holidayed with Taffy Asphar in Malta, which worked very well as they had a lot in common. Joe was given a £5 prize when he was leaving and with it he bought all the poetry he could.

George was sent to the ordinary Stonyhurst school at the same time, for five years. In the first year he worked very hard and won the class prize. I came back from school just before George with six small prizes for different things and my mother looked at George's prize, a beautifully bound book with the Stonyhurst arms engraved on it, and she said 'Only one prize?' although there was no comparison between the value of his and mine. She expected him to bring back at least six and refused to accept that his was more important for being the overall prize and to my fury demeaned George about it and made

Mimi, aged eighteen, wearing the dress made for her by Mrs Clancy. 'For once she looked like the daughter of a wealthy family.'

him miserable. He was upset by this and came back each year more disorganised and resentful. He was a good mathematician but the school gave him no opportunity to develop this (I was told that they thought the Irish were always good at maths and needed no improvement in it) and all the concentration in his class was on Classics, which he hated. Up to this time he had been a funny combination of great innocence and bad temper so he tended to get left out a lot at home. Ma alternated her usual forms of ill-treatment with 'spoiling' him, but since this included giving him a Shetland pony that was so bad-tempered he couldn't manage it and it broke its knees, her indulgence was no help. George had to join the officers' training corps and train for three weeks of every year at Aldershot. He really hated this at first and tried to get out of it, but couldn't because Ma liked the idea of it. When he came home the first time, he brought his khaki uniform with him and we were shocked when we saw it. That didn't help his sense of confusion, because he had begun to like the actual soldiering. Jack told me later that Joe told him to stay in it, to learn as much as possible about the army and get as much training as he could.

In September of 1905 I went to Mount Anville again and began the only full year of school I ever had, but nearly all my teachers were young uneducated nuns, who should not have been asked to teach at all. It was not too bad but I found the only thing I could do was to keep ahead as much as I could and try to avoid boredom. I must have been asking too many questions or making comments too often because eventually the nun who was the class teacher appealed to me not to be making such a mess of her class and said that she could not carry on if I did. We had a confrontation about it and both finished up in tears. After we had stopped crying at each other I agreed to leave her alone and she let me pretend I had something wrong with my back and had to lie down for hours at a time. She allowed me to go upstairs to an empty classroom, where I spent my time sewing and managed to cut out and put together a blouse to bring home with me. The moment I always loved most in Mount Anville was the day before each holiday, when we stood in the study hall and sang the plainchant *Magnificat* in Latin at the tops of our voices. Finally I said to Ma that it was nonsense to go back to this school. Not only was the teaching standard very low at the time, but the water was bad as well. Ma got very indignant and said they were not honest people if they were doing this to me, but she allowed me to leave. I was fourteen.

Most of us were back living in Fitzwilliam Street and Mimi, now eighteen, was very pretty, a good dancer, slim, popular but not happy. She had taken her matriculation at Mount Anville and wanted to do an arts degree. This was before the National University was founded and you could study for a degree, either at school or with a tutor, for the Royal University exams. Mimi could have gone to either the Loreto Convent on Stephen's Green or the Dominican Convent, now at Muckross Park, but Ma knew nothing about education and the means of acquiring it. She found a tutor for Mimi and one day, while he was teaching her, Ma was listening through the half-open door and heard him reading a very famous speech of Lady Macbeth's. In horror, Ma marched in and threw the unfortunate young man out. Mimi knew of no other way of tackling the problem of working for a degree and gave up the whole idea. She had learned the piano for a number of years, but Kilternan had made it impossible to keep it up. She decided to start again with Miss Hynes, who was impressed by her potential and proposed that she should take it seriously. She said she should practise at least three hours a day and have two lessons a week. Ma said 'No' immediately, that Miss Hynes was only looking for more money. Mimi gave up the piano there and then and although she kept the instrument all her life, she never played again. She enrolled for art classes at the United Arts Club and at the School of Art with William Orpen and continued with these for a couple of years.

After Mimi was 'presented' she was invited to large and small parties and dances and the invitation cards were stuck up on the frame of the mantelpiece mirror. Dances went on until five or six o'clock in the morning. She was supposed to dress herself for these on an allowance from Ma (which Ma rarely gave her). Ma hoped that Mimi would marry very well but had no intention of providing the money to make this happen, or a dowry when it did. Pa had a friend, Mrs Clancy, a high-class dressmaker whom he helped with legal affairs when she moved here from Rome. She met Mimi at a party, when Mimi was wearing an old blouse of Ma's which went around her twice and a huge, black skirt, also of Ma's, fixed at the waist with a safety pin. Mrs Clancy, who was quite wealthy, asked if she could make some dresses for Mimi; it was meant as a kindness to Pa, but of course Ma thought it was a tribute to herself. Mrs Clancy made a lovely afternoon dress and two skirts and asked a tailor to make a coat, and in each case she only charged the price of a very ordinary version of these. She also made a really beautiful white satin evening dress that Mimi wore to her next party. For once Mimi looked like the daughter of a wealthy family. At the party Pa met the Italian consul, Signor Salazar, who brought with him an introduction from Mrs Mulhall, the woman who had invited Mimi to Rome in 1902. This was when Mimi met the consul's son, Demetrio, a delinquent with patent leather hair who could dance the Boston. Mimi danced with him, he proposed, she accepted and she gave him the little forget-me-not ring she was wearing, which had belonged to Pa's sister, Mary Jane. At a party a month later, she saw her best friend was wearing the forget-me-not ring as an engagement ring. There was a hell of a row, during which poor Mrs Mulhall got some of the blame, but she had never said anything about the consul having a son!

I think Dan Doyle was next to propose to Mimi. Ma was in some kind of conspiracy with him and invited his sister, Alice, to stay with us. Alice used to go riding in the Phoenix Park, where she was trying to catch some fellow's eye and I was told to go with her to keep her company. Ma lent her the cream-coloured cob and her good habit and she sent me, in an old habit, on Bob, the other cob. He was an ill-tempered brute who used to try to brush me off on the low branches of trees. I hated side-saddles and so did the cobs; they were more used to shafts than saddles of any kind and they showed it by stopping at every pub on the way to the park. For all that, we had lots of good gallops on the Fifteen Acres and I got to like Alice. She never caught her man, though, and she eventually went home in despair. Ma, however, liked the idea of sending me out riding and continued to send me out alone. The brutish Bob bucked me off on Ailesbury Road but I was helped up and looked after by the head of the fiire brigade, Captain Purcell. Then Ma sent me out on Diana, her own mare, but when Hickey, the owner of the Lad Lane livery stables, saw this he sent his own son after me to keep an eye on me because, he said, Diana was a killer. She didn't give Ma any trouble, she had always been good with horses, but even Ma couldn't touch her with a whip when driving her. Diana was a clever horse, though, and talked all the time with her ears.

Mimi persuaded Ma to give a children's party and a dance once a year, to repay all the hospitality we owed. Most of the houses in the area gave these and dates were usually agreed on in advance, so as not to clash with each

Count and Countess Plunkett with Mimi, 1907.

other. Before our parties we had to clean the whole house thoroughly. We used the front and back drawing-rooms on the first floor for dancing, so we covered the carpets by tacking dancing cloths of unbleached linen damask on them. We hadn't enough for such a big area so Aunt Helena lent us hers as well. We four girls worked in the kitchen with the cook and the maids to prepare the supper of cold meats, galantines, more cold dishes, fruit salads, cream and ice-cream. Some of this was also brought in by outside caterers. We used to lay the food out in the dining-room and the study on the hall floor and this meant that I had to persuade Pa to let me in to clear his desk, which was always piled high with papers. He allowed me to do this for special occa-sions, like Christmas or parties. I always took it as a compliment that he trusted my understanding of his work that much. The children's party took place in the afternoon and when they had all gone the first floor was re-arranged for dancing. Miss Gasparro and her violinist played for this and if the violinist did anything out of order Miss Gasparro kicked him on the an-kle. While the professional musicians had their supper a friend of Pa's played the piano, but only if he was provided with whiskey. We usually had about 120 guests and the guest list always put Ma in a bad temper, but she was very good at presenting a table and if the whole thing went well she would be in good humour for weeks. We danced two-steps and waltzes—we all loved the tune 'Ach du liebe Augustin'—and, of course, the Boston after Demetrio Salazar had been here. This was a version of the two-step with an added heel click between steps. At the end of the night there were Galops and Lancers and we had wine and supper at midnight in relays. We went on dancing until six in the morning, finishing up with more of the supper. If there was still too much of it left we had a small dance again the next day.

Mimi wanted to put order on the housekeeping in Fitzwilliam Street and to introduce some organisation. She tried to start a housekeeping rota among us girls but it was impossible to make it work without Ma's co-operation and Ma didn't like the idea at all. The system of a nursery dinner and a grown-ups' dinner had coalesced into two dinners a day, which we found too much, and whenever Ma was away, we had lunches of eggs and tea instead. Ma would have none of this as it deprived her of half of her meat ration. Mimi and I took over the catering on alternate days but we had no control over the cook, who stole as much as she could and was drunk every night. It was no use telling Ma about the cook, she just laughed at us and when she felt like it would add something like two legs of mutton onto the menu at the last minute in spite of our protests. What we hated most was that we always had to order rabbit for the servants when we were ordering good meat for the family. In spite of all this, Ma did come to rely on us to a limited extent, and Mimi aimed to increase that reliance.

Ma never got up before noon except on Sunday and she kept her bedroom curtains shut until then, from excessive modesty. Before electric light was installed she had a special candlestick with a glass cylinder on it and lay in bed reading letters, newspapers and novels in the otherwise dark room. She was supposed to be resting and was not to be disturbed. When the electric light came it was the worst and most inefficient wiring I've ever seen. Before that we had gas, first fishtail burners and then incandescent mantles. There were leaks all over the place and once I was half gassed. Ma had one of the earliest telephones in Dublin installed by Bell Telephone before the Post Office took them over. She had it beside her bed and could transact most of her business without getting up; even workmen who repaired the houses would be sent up to her bedroom for orders and although she was very prudish she could see nothing improper in this. She came downstairs for lunch and afterwards the horses would be harnessed and whatever carriage she was using at the time brought to the front door so that she could go into town to see about her affairs. These outings were often a trial to us as, even when there was a coachman, one of us would have to go with her and stand holding the horse outside a shop or an office or a house while she was away, sometimes for hours at a time.

Before dinner she rested again, this time on a sofa pulled across in front of the dining-room fire. She often warned us solemnly to be very quiet when she was resting as she said that if she were wakened by a sudden noise she would die. She had had rheumatic fever about twenty years before and had been immobilised for six months so she had cultivated the legend that if she was wakened suddenly she would drop dead. The dining-room was the only usable sitting-room in the house, as fires were never lit in the two large drawing-rooms, making them bitterly cold for most of the year. Heat of any kind in our bedrooms was unthinkable so we were supposed to lead a Spartan life, in penance for our many crimes and, perhaps, to harden us for the rigours of the bad ends to which Ma was sure we were all bound to come. She was an expert idler, really very fat, and took no exercise. Here again, Victorian convention encouraged her to indulge her natural taste. Women of childbearing age were not supposed to exert themselves in any way and were supposed to eat enormously to keep up their strength. It was supposed that exercise of any kind would endanger the lives of future children. They were constipated all the time and talked constantly about their health, their labours, their pills and their operations.

In spite of practising endless economies on us and not paying her bills, Ma was still spending too much on such things as servants, horses, carriages, food and frequent cruises and holidays. Her income was quite good, but she was under the impression that she could not dispose of her house property except by will or deed or by appointment to her children. She used to threaten that if we did not please her she would leave us nothing, but some of us didn't care and Mimi used to say that there would be nothing left anyway. Most well-off households had accounts in all the businesses they dealt with, from groceries to building materials, and you only paid everything you owed if you were going to close the account, and Ma said it was impossible to check items so long after they had been purchased. We used to think there was enough dishonesty about already, but she didn't care. Ma's version of paying a bill was to mark each one she received 'Account rendered' and put it away in a huge file. She enjoyed trading on being a Countess and knew that most places would be too glad to have her as a customer to bother her for payment. She was always on the lookout for quick moneymaking schemes and she was frequently conned by people who saw her as an easy mark. Her version of divine intervention was to ask us to pray that she would find £400 by next Tuesday or else, she said, we would all be in the workhouse. We believed this until Mimi told us not to worry. She made no provision for costs relating to her houses, such as ground rents, rates increases, head rents, repairs. She did sell one house and a piece of land, but she found the whole business of it too tiring and expensive. She heard of people making fortunes on the Stock Exchange and decided to try that. She even invited the two stockbrokers who were 'helping' her to Sunday dinner, but they got very drunk and turned nasty. She had fallen among thieves and they cheated her out of as much as they could.

A lot of her problems were due to nervousness; she was afraid of asking questions, even about the price of eggs, she was terrified of people, with the result that she repulsed ordinary people rudely and welcomed chancers. She used to say that friends were a bad thing, one was better off without them. She managed to cut Pa off from most of his friends and at the same time made friends herself with the most extraordinary women, some of whom turned out to be spies for Dublin Castle (they told her this themselves later). Pa used to go for a walk every night, twice around Fitzwilliam Square and if, as he often did, he met a friend, such as the painter Thaddeus Jones or Sir Roger Casement, he would bring them back for a glass of wine. After Ma's freezing reception, few of them ever came again. She could not distinguish rogues from honest men, and her meanness was of a kind that I have only found in wealthy women. When I needed an evening dress for a special party, she went out and bought me a horrible piece of cloth that she got as a real bargain and gave it to me as my birthday present. On Joe's twenty-first birthday she made a tremendous fuss and public display and then presented him with a cheap and nasty gold-coloured cigarette case. She could, however, be extremely charming; to strangers she must have seemed humorous, attractive, lively and sometimes very clever and she was very proficient at close needlework and embroidery.

During 1907, when I was going on sixteen, my parents made the rather unsuccessful experiment of a European trip together, something they hadn't done for a long time, and Pa brought me back my Dürer etching *St Eustace and the Stag*. That summer I went to Belfast and Portadown with both of them and at a party we met a doctor who told Ma that she should get something done about my nose problem immediately and told her who she should see about it. To my delight and surprise, she organised it straight away. We went to Dr Dempsey and the only problem was that Ma sat in on it and talked such snobby rubbish, non-stop, that he rushed into the job before the injection had really taken, so it was hell, but worth it. He took away a piece of the turbinate bone with the growth on it and all that breathing trouble I had had all my life was gone.

Pa was made Director of the National Museum in 1907. This was one of the most wonderful things that happened to him and to us and we were immensely proud of him, particularly since it was widely acknowledged that he made a great job of the whole thing. He had a curious start in it. In September of that year the then Director of the Museum, Colonel G. T. Plunkett, retired. He was an English civil servant, with long service in the colonies, who did not even know that his name was Irish until I told him. Since the Liberals had come to power in 1905 Home Rule had been looked on as a certainty and John Redmond MP had been telling Irishmen that they should apply for such positions. My father, while he would not have taken any job he saw as political, did not consider an educational institution such as the museum in the same way. Although Lord Aberdeen was the Viceroy, his wife took care of

A cartoon by Fitzpatrick of Count Plunkett with Mimi as Art *on the right, and Gerry as* Architecture, *on the left. The caption on the original read:* How happy could I be with either, Were t'other dear charmer away. *—a well-known quote from Gay's* Beggar's Opera.

most of the business, so it was from her that Pa got a letter saying that he had been appointed. The news of his appointment was in all the papers and the Department of Agriculture and Technical Instruction in Ireland, which controlled the museum, immediately contradicted the report saying that no appointment had yet been made. Someone had already painted out Colonel Plunkett's name on the notice boards and replaced it with Pa's. The department had this painted out and Colonel Plunkett's name put back. Pa wrote for clarification to Lady Aberdeen, who stuck to her guns and replied stating that he had been properly appointed. His name went back on the noticeboards and he began as Director of the Museum on October 16th. In spite of the controversy over his appointment he was accepted by the Board of Visitors as 'a gentleman already well and favourably known in Dublin for his scholarly and artistic achievements' when they praised his improvements and innovations a few months later.

Pa was familiar with the museums in most of the countries in Europe as well as some in North and South America and had strong ideas about what should be done here. He had an open and enthusiastic attitude to the whole place and whereas when he started there were no two members of staff on speaking terms by the time he left they were all friends. The employees were ex-English soldiers, several of them men of great ability, notably Mr Duffy. Pa was determined to employ as many staff as possible who understood the Irish language. He wanted people, particularly young people, to see and experience everything from ancient artefacts to specimens and bones. The front hall, the rotunda, was ideal for display, but it was full of enormous coaches. Moving them elsewhere caused a major argument with the department, who regarded any change as appalling. Eventually Pa got his way and re-organised both the rotunda and the central hall into real exhibition spaces. He created a lecture room for talks and discussions. He brought in schoolchildren, gave them introductions to everything and devised competitions for everyone based on the museum. He also brought out a series of popular guides to the museum and a reprint, revised by himself, of Margaret Stokes's *Early Christian Art in Ireland*. Dr Sharpe was in charge of the natural history side before Pa arrived, with no money at all for improving it as far as I could make out, but it had beautiful things in it, such as a set of blown-glass models of mainly single cell marine creatures magnified about two hundred times, made by two Italians, father and son, named Blaschka. They were lovely to look at as well as being invaluable for study. Dr Sharpe, showing what a gifted person he was, added lots more, including a marvellous rock pool and a set of birds showing their actual colourings. Pa wanted to do something with the furniture section so he acquired a complete room from Old Bawn House in Tallaght, County Dublin, which was being demolished at the time. The room, complete with panelling, was then reconstructed in the museum. There was terrific opposition from the department to this scheme and he had endless trouble getting funding for it.

Pa's biggest concern was with showing the collection of Irish antiquities. This had originally been the Royal Irish Academy collection and included the Cross of Cong. Sir William Wilde catalogued it in 1873 and the RIA gave it into the care of the museum in 1890. Before Pa started in the museum, Dr George Coffey had done trojan work on this, single-handed and with little or no money, but he had to leave because of ill-health after a stroke. Pa was the first director who was also a member of the Academy and he used that to the advantage of the museum. Over his years there he succeeded in taking many beautiful and ancient things out of their protective storage and showing them to a rapidly increasing public. He was told about five miniature gold axes and a gold torque which had been found on the shores of Strangford Lough but had gone out of the country to Mr Samuel Fenton of the Old Curiosity Shop, 33 Cranbourn Street, London, who was asking for £150 for them. Pa wrote to Lord Iveagh telling him about the gold axes and the torque and saying that such objects should be secured for Ireland and that he was starting a society similar to that of the National Art Collections Fund for the assistance of the National Museum. Lord Iveagh sent the £150 by return of post and Pa was able to buy the objects for the museum. One of his best ideas had to do with the Society of Antiquarians in Ireland—at that time it was only an ordinary society and as such had no special powers to acquire or publish anything. His great idea was to organise a Charter for them and hold a party, a 'conversazione', in the museum to celebrate. This was a real success and there was general delight with the use being made of the museum and its welcoming atmosphere.

Some people in the department never forgave Pa for the fact that he was not appointed by them and obstructed him in various civil service ways. At one stage they brought in the Board of Visitors to exercise control over him, but he told them they couldn't do that as the board was only an advisory body. They cut his grant for books and personnel and objected to lectures being given in the evenings, on the grounds that people would have to 'go through rooms full of objects of inestimable value to get to them.' They closed the lecture room a couple of times and finally closed it completely in 1914, using 'war economy' as the excuse. They closed the student room that he had opened for biology students and tried to prevent him displaying the Irish antiquities in the main hall. This was a major bone of contention; they thought that things of such great value and beauty as the gold ornaments should be kept locked up in a strong room since they were too precious to be shown to the public. Pa not only wanted to show everything of the collection that he could, but also caused consternation by sometimes taking items out of their cases and allowing students to handle them. He was absolutely happy as director for the nine years he was there in spite of all the difficulties he had. I have often heard since, particularly from staff who worked there with him, that he was the best director they ever had. He certainly changed the number of visitors from hundreds to thousands while he was there. His salary was £700 a year, nearly all of which went on books.

Redmond and the Irish Parliamentary Party also made it known that they approved of Nationalists attending the Viceregal Court as a goodwill gesture to those who promised us justice. By the time Lord Aberdeen (who was very much in favour of Home Rule) was appointed Viceroy in 1906, most professional men already attended the levees at Dublin Castle. Nationalists, who had never thought of such a thing before, threw themselves into the new Castle season. Women, including Ma, being presented at a 'drawing-room' wore three little ostrich feathers perched on their heads, with a flowing veil and a train several yards long. They practised the 'correct' curtsy for weeks with an instructor and sat for hours in carriages, waiting for admittance to the Presence. This meant spending a lot of money and led to an awful lot of snobbery. At the same time it was all very shabby-genteel; the Aberdeens were very economical and managed to refurbish their castles in Scotland on the

Count Plunkett wearing the uniform prescribed for lawyers to wear to Castle functions. When he became Director of the National Museum he had to buy another uniform—gold-embroidered with white knee-breeches.

Viceregal salary and expenses. Catering, for instance, was done by a Glasgow firm and at the tea-parties the ration per person was one half-a-farthing bun. Pa had never liked this Dublin Castle socialising business, he had political reservations about it and it bored him dreadfully, but he did it to please Ma who had simple ideas about success and prosperity, and it was expected of him as a higher civil servant. As director of the museum he had to buy the appropriate uniform to go to the Castle functions. Instead of his lawyer's suit of black velvet and cut steel, the new uniform was gold-embroidered with white knee-breeches and a sword whose tassel contained £1's worth of bullion. It cost plenty but he did look better in it than most of them. Ma had a dress with a train and, to her delight, was presented in Dublin Castle. There was a queue all the way down College Green and Dame Street and all the 'roughs' gawking at the ladies in their finery and jeering at them. Ma got a special entrance ticket kept for important people and that put the cap on her pleasure.

Lady Aberdeen had a lot of good ideas and got a lot of very good work done. She started the Women's Health Association, which was a whole campaign against tuberculosis, Irish ignorance of which was colossal. She also encouraged Irish industry and gave patronage to Irish lace, even wearing highly elaborate Irish lace gowns to London social occasion. She gave an Irish Industries Ball on St Patrick's Day at which she staged sixteen-hand-reels with each set representing a different industry—poultry, linen and so on. Lady Aberdeen asked Ma to get up the poultry set with Mimi in it, so Mimi had wings made of scraps of coloured linen all stuck onto wing shapes and she carried a rod with a chicken on top. The 'poplin' set wore cloth-of-gold costing a small fortune. There were all sorts of hangers-on who had to be taught to dance the reel and they hated it because it was not English dancing. Ma offered her daughters' services to teach the reels and we had a most unpleasant time with as ill-mannered a set of toffee-nosed chancers as I have ever met. The Viceregal staff were very polite and badly treated, the food was bad, men from each of the regiments were ordered to act as partners and their full dress uniform had spurs which tore the ladies' dresses. If I had had any wish to go to Castle functions, I would have been well cured by this, but I had already decided, with Joe, that the whole thing was a fraud, as well as a stupid waste of our own and public money. When I was offered to be presented I said I had no time for it and to my surprise and pleasure the rest of the family agreed with me.

Joe came back from Stonyhurst that same year, 1907, in poor health, but full of ideas and arguments on all subjects. He was fiercely interested in everything intellectual—philosophy, mysticism, physics, poetry—and in chemistry, wireless and aeronautics. He had long been interested in photography, having started with a little pin-hole camera which cost five shillings and was surprisingly good. When the news came out in June 1907 about the Lumière brothers and their colour photography, he wrote to them and got materials and instructions. At this stage they

COUNTESS PLUNKETT.

In 1906, the Countess, to her delight, was 'presented' at a Castle 'drawing-room'. Women being presented wore three little ostrich feathers perched on their heads.

were very complicated and used eight different baths, each plate having to be washed between the developer and the firing. It was most exciting and there might still be a plate somewhere of Jack against a fuchsia hedge. It had three primary colours—of rice flour, I think! Joe was far too logical for ordinary life and at first did not understand the family atmosphere, the continual awful rows, upset tempers and natural reactions, always defensive. The house was full of hairsplitting arguments which got worse when he got home. He had quite enjoyed his time in Stonyhurst and in between terms had had pleasant holidays, and the changes home life brought were very hard on him. Ma had given him plenty of independence when he was away and he thought that Mimi's attempts to put some order on the household, and her efforts to get Ma to accept that order, were exaggerated.

Joe said casually he was thinking of putting up some pictures in his room and Ma went off and found a lot of faded photographs of classical buildings, had them framed in a schoolroom manner and presented them to him as being exactly what he would like. He was very annoyed, as he realised that it was going to be very difficult to live in the way that he wanted. Instead, he covered his shabby bedroom with vivid posters and painted a copy of a poster by H. B. Irving on the wall in oils and some Egyptian figures on the door. He was fascinated by Egyptian stuff and claimed he was a reincarnation of Rameses the Second because the outline of the back of his head was the same as that of Rameses's skull. Ma made little of his bad health to the servants and, as there were several kinds of food he couldn't manage, he sometimes went hungry. Any weakness like this produced an onset of his tubercular symptoms but either Ma couldn't see this or she didn't care. He was back less than three months when Ma picked a quarrel with him and left him without a penny for a tram for as long as it pleased her.

This was a method she developed that she used on all of us at different times. She would become displeased with us but never disclose the reason (I don't think she had one)—we were just supposed to know what it was. She would work herself into a screaming temper and at this stage, Mimi would go and stand in front of the sideboard drawer in which the carving knives were kept. I asked Mimi did she really think Ma would go that far and Mimi said 'You never know'. Sometimes we were accused of 'bringing her grey hairs in sorrow to the grave' or 'turning her blood to gall'. On the few occasions Pa was there, he sat saying nothing and looking grieved. Sometimes she would finish by knocking you down, dragging you out of the room and up the stairs, punching you all the time with her closed fists, and stuffing you into bed. One of the times this happened to me, it was because I had forgotten to speak French at the table. My sisters came and got me out of the bed almost immediately afterwards and told me that if I stayed there, it would be giving in to her. She kept the quarrel going by not speaking to any of us, keeping us waiting for her at mealtimes and then, when she arrived, serving us rudely and abruptly. She sat at the top of the table with a 'puss' on her and all she would say was 'Pass that to so-and-so' and nothing else. Our ages now ranged from ten-year-old Jack to Mimi, who was twenty-one, and we were all trying to do different things, like getting an education, so this was serious because as long as it went on you couldn't get money for anything, books, stationery, clothes or trams, so it was a useful economy for Ma. Mimi had tried to introduce regular pocket money days to prevent some of this but Ma would have nothing to do with it. Ma's sulk would last for one to three weeks and while it lasted the atmosphere in the house was quite sulphurous. We found that the only way to deal with it was to be absolutely silent, so there we would sit, a party in a parlour, all silent and all damned!

After a year or two, when we were all at home, we found a way of making it more bearable and sometimes ending it. We would start a quiet conversation about something of general interest or a metaphysical argument and go on from that to a discussion on everything happening. All the time, we had to pretend to be having a happy, normal conversation and be very careful not to make any reference to the head of the table. We got quite good at it and were able to talk about many things she knew nothing about, as she had no intellectual interests at all. After this had gone on for some time, perhaps a week or two, she couldn't resist it any longer; she would say when we laughed 'Won't somebody tell me the joke?' or join in the conversation and forget the sulks. What was Pa doing? He was ignoring the whole thing; he answered politely when spoken to but obviously did not want to let her down. He pretended she had some reason for it and it would not be fair to involve him. She used to give him stories about us conspiring against her and behaving immorally and I think he half believed her sometimes, or didn't want to disbelieve her. Once, when I was the one out of favour, he put his hand on my head afterwards and said 'I'm sorry to see my little one under a cloud' and I thought my heart would break, but later on, when I complained to him about some of her dreadful carry-on, he said 'You must remember that Mammy is only a little girl!' That was the way he always thought of her.

At our ages the everyday results of all this were shocking. An arrangement for any one of us which had to be made in advance, such as schools, colleges, courses, would probably have to be cancelled. We were not even sure of what we could do from day to day. This left us, when we were younger, absolutely at Ma's mercy and even when we were grown-up we did not dare tell anyone about it as we knew we would not be believed. When I did tell people they thought I was lying or inventing it. Strangers just thought we weren't much good. In spite of our interesting conversation we were badly dressed, looked peculiar and it seemed as though none of us would ever come to anything.

5 Opening minds 1908–1912

IN NOVEMBER 1908 THE NATIONAL UNIVERSITY OF IRELAND ACT was passed, but it did not take effect until the following year. I decided that I wanted to study Medicine. Ma was delighted because she liked the idea of a doctor in the family and had had great respect for her brother Jack who had been a doctor. When I checked, I discovered that I knew most of what was needed for the Matriculation exams already but my Latin was inadequate, and I hadn't done any of the experiments in the course which was then called natural philosophy, approximating to what was later elementary physics. My cousin, Mary White, helped me with the Latin and she suggested that I should go to Loreto College on Stephen's Green for anything else I needed. Sister Stanislaus (Mary Jo Ryan, the first of that great family that I met) very kindly allowed me the use of their experimental laboratory and I worked my way through the textbook doing all the experiments there. I sat the exams in June 1908 and when the notice arrived in the post, I couldn't believe I had passed. Best of all, I got 66 per cent in mathematics almost entirely due to the wonderful Mr Greenan seven years before in Kilternan.

That summer of 1908, Ma sent all of us to Howth for three months and in the autumn I enrolled in Loreto College to study for First Arts, which was compulsory for Medicine, as Sister Stanislaus had told me that I could come back there. My fees were very moderate and Ma paid up for them like a lamb. The teaching was wonderful, Patrick Semple for Latin, James Macken, English, George Ebrill, physics, Miss Byrne, French and Frank Ward, maths, a fine teacher with a first class honours degree from Cambridge. I met him again later in Galway under strange circumstances in Black-and-Tan times. Sister Stanislaus ran the First Arts class extremely well and prepared us for the whole exam. I spent all my time either in Loreto College or in the National Library. I read every book mentioned in Stephen Gwynn's *Masters of English Literature*. The other girls used to just memorise the *Masters* and they told me I would fail by wasting my time reading all the books themselves, but I had too much to make up. In addition I was reading many of the books in their original editions because I was studying in the National Library. I already knew enough French to pass the exam, but my mathematics was now behind the others so I was given extra teaching to bring it up to standard. Irish was not required and up to then I had had no opportunity to learn it, but the students' campaign to make it compulsory was just beginning. I made a rake of new friends in my class and the degree class ahead, Agnes and Chris Ryan,

Lily Grant (afterwards Mother Attracta), a descendant of the musician Michael Balfe, Kathleen Phelan, Jane Kissane, Berthe Browne, Sally Cross, Marie and Nancy Wyse-Power and Eibhlín Nicholls. Eibhlín was very large and very fine looking. Tomás MacDonagh told us later that Pádraig Pearse was in love with her but she refused him when he proposed to her. She was drowned in the Blaskets trying to save a boy's life. In June 1909 I passed my First Arts. My average was 48 per cent, which was low enough, but passing it at all made me feel relatively independent for the first time in my life. I was having a gaudy time but I didn't talk to anyone at home about it.

Other members of the family were not doing so well. Moya's engagement to Frank Cotton had been announced. Frank and his family were old friends of ours, but Moya had a strong feeling that the whole thing was not right. She tried to make a go of it and did a bit of courting but it was not very successful and produced an immediate reaction from Ma who accused her, most unfairly, of immorality. Moya had lots of boyfriends—we used to say she had seven Berties, but Frank Cotton's mother had told him that Moya expected him to propose and she told Moya the same about Frank. He wanted to work as a gas engineer and managed to find some relevant training here, although the training seemed very short to me. As he could find no opening for himself in this country it was decided that he should go to America and Grandpa Plunkett wrote to his brother in New York who had large shares in gas and power. Frank was sent over to this brother, who gave him a job immediately. His letters to Moya seemed very unsatisfactory and after he had been there for a year and a half, he wrote home to tell her that he had found someone else.

Moya was being kept in a state of total dependence, forced to ask for every single thing. She had not a penny in her pocket, she could not buy her clothes and she had no occupation. It was all part of the usual mess at home. Ma brought two Limerick sisters, who were expert lace makers, to Dublin. She found a designer and installed the sisters in No. 27 Marlborough Road. She put Moya in charge of the scheme, unpaid of course, and poor Moya and the unfortunate girls had to live there in an unheated house on nothing but potatoes and margarine. The girls produced a considerable quantity of the most beautiful lace and Ma thought she was showing everyone how to set up a lace industry. She accumulated a large amount of lace but there was no market here for it and she didn't know what to do with it. At that stage one of the girls developed tuberculosis and her sister took her away down to Limerick to die. Ma didn't succeed in selling any of the lace and Moya had had a miserable time with it. When the scheme ended she was back where she started—at home doing nothing.

The year 1908 was a turning point for us older ones in the house. We had at last managed to pin Ma down and nearly had her agreement to a more orderly kind of life. We wanted to be able to say, 'This is pocket money day', or 'I need some clothes' but Ma wanted to do these things whenever she felt like it or ignore them if she didn't. Now we had her in a corner and she could see she was going to have to give in but as usual, she found a way out. This time it was by bringing in someone else, Cousin Sarah Ferrall from Duluth, Minnesota, in the United States. Sarah's mother was a sister of Grandma Maria's and when she died Ma wrote and invited Sarah to 'come for a holiday at home here in Ireland for six months' with the suggestion that it might be permanent. When she was writing Ma painted a colourful picture of our wonderful social life in Dublin and the hardships of raising a family and suggested that Sarah would be of great assistance to her. Poor Sarah had lost track of the generations and ages and arrived in Dublin expecting to help 'dear cousin Josephine with her seven little children'.

She had a terrible shock when she met us, as we had with her, and of course Ma hadn't bothered to stay around to meet her so we didn't know what to do with her. She was

Sarah Ferrall, an American cousin of Countess Plunkett's, who came to live in the Plunkett household in Fitzwilliam Street in 1908. She returned to the US in 1915 and died suddenly in 1916—from the shock, it was said, of hearing of Joe's execution.

about fifty, her mother had just died, she was skinny, had obviously been ill, and her hair was falling out. Moya did her best to make her at home and comfortable, which is more than I can say for any of the rest of us. Sarah was dried-up, middle-aged, haggard and high-voiced, uneducated and opinionated. She often used German terms for food and knew the meaning of American Indian place-names, which really impressed us. She had rarely come across fresh fish and preferred her salmon tinned. She was supposed to be in charge of us but we were now aged from eleven to twenty-two and, unlike us, she had never read a book at all and couldn't understand a word we said. At the dinner table she would insist on her opinions, which were of the most conservative and, while we had the habit of speaking almost in an undertone, she spoke in a loud voice which got louder as she went on trying to make Pa listen to what she had to say, until she had us all deafened. When Roger Casement came to dinner and talked to Pa of the plantations and the treatment of native workers in the Belgian Congo, Sarah made it clear that they might as well have been

Springfield, the Raffertys' house in Kilternan, County Dublin. The Raffertty family befriended the young Plunketts, who found peace and quiet and order in the house, and spent long happy periods there.

talking Chinese. She was similarly lost when Pa had to entertain such people as curators of European or American museums. Pa found her an intolerable bore and Joe found her opinions appalling, so it was the young women of the house, Mimi, Moya, myself and Fiona, who had to put up with her for the next seven years. Sarah had worked as a book-keeper and was a good dress-maker and she was given a small bedroom in the return on the second floor. Since she used this also for dressmaking it became the clothes centre of the house and my room, which was in front of it, was the passageway to it for most of the household as they traipsed back and forth for new clothes or repairs; I found this very difficult when I was trying to study. Sarah's voice might have been loud but she moved like a ghost and only seemed real when she was dressmaking in her own room.

In the beginning Ma made quite a fuss of Sarah, trying to live up to her original invitation and talking a lot about parties and dances, Dublin Castle and the Viceregal Court, as though these were a constant part of our lives. In fact, these events were rare, each being no more than once or twice a year. Poor Sarah believed all this and spent far too much of her little store of cash on two beautiful poplin evening dresses, one blue, one white, and a beige afternoon one. Ma brought her to Dublin Castle and presented her at the Viceregal Court but then had no other social events for her. When Sarah started run-ning out of money, Ma suggested that she could keep the rent books for her. This Sarah did conscientiously and more efficiently than had ever been done before and she understood that Ma was going to pay her for this but Ma never did. Sarah started in to make a whole lot of clothes that were badly needed at the time and co-operated with Ma in making nightdresses for all of us girls. I had mine made of heavy sheeting and when I was making clothes myself Sarah allowed me to use her irons, which was an enormous help. Sarah liked Moya, who was always kind to her, but she had a very sensitive streak and complained once to Ma about some way in which she thought Moya had slighted her. She was quite shocked when the result was that Moya was beaten for it. Moya was eighteen at the time.

Ma decided to send us to Achill for three months in the summer of 1909. I don't really know why she picked Achill but it must have been recommended to her because she had apparently heard of a lodging house in Dugort and she sent five of us to stay there, Joe, myself, George, Fiona and Jack, with Sarah as a kind of chaperone; our friend, Theo McWeeney, joined us. The lodging house was run by the sister of the Mission agent and the atmosphere in the place was dreadful. He was a most extraordinary, unpleasant old fish and I think he was out to convert us or something, but he left us alone when he discovered that we would have nothing to do with him. The other guests in the house were the wife and children of the inspector in the local police. The wife behaved like Lady Muck and never spoke a single word to us, not at dinner or passing in the hall or outside on the street, and the children were obviously forbidden to speak to us either, but she had the brass neck to send a note down the table during a meal to ask if one of her children could have an orange from our bowl of fruit. We found the atmosphere in the place so nasty that we wrote to Ma to ask could we change but she wrote back saying no.

We wandered all over the island, exploring and swimming, and Joe and Theo amused themselves with the big waves on the north strand but myself and the younger ones found it too rough so we used to go down to a little harbour just beyond it. Even there I found I had great difficulty bringing the younger ones in because of the stormy weather. We went to Irish classes given by the Gaelic League teacher, John Langan, a fine man whom we all liked. The local group of Evangelicals lay in wait for him and beat him up because of his Irish teaching and broke the window of the room where he taught Irish dancing. He brought us on the big July annual pilgrimage to Croagh Patrick. The heavy climb took its toll on Joe who collapsed and was bedridden again. It was on Achill that I met Muriel Gahan for the first time—the most wonderful and marvellous person—and we became close friends. She did many things in her life but the greatest was the founding of the Irish Countrywomen's Association which had so many excellent consequences. Of all the individuals I have ever come across, I don't think anyone could beat her for steadfast community service and amiability of character.

On Achill we began to see something we had never seen before, the frightful poverty in the Irish countryside. We had never seen anything remotely like

Joe and George and one of the Cronin cousins on the steps of Springfield where Joe spent most of 1909–1910, trying to improve his health and being minded with kindness by the Raffertys.

it, huts that must have been hell to live in, children with starved bodies, and women who reminded me of the woman I saw in Dublin when I was out in the brougham with Uncle Jack. She came rushing after us as we drove down the street, screaming for money. Uncle Jack took all the money he could find from his pockets and threw it to her. As we drove away from her, I realised that she was wearing nothing at all but a skirt and a tattered shawl. Achill made us think. It was obvious to us that nobody in power cared and nobody was doing anything about it.

Back in Dublin, Joe was not very well; he had no glands problems at that time but he was never quite right. Several years earlier he had overheard a conversation referring to him as 'not strong'. He confused this at the time with muscular strength and thought that he ought to develop his muscles. He bought several kinds of Sandow exercisers such as weights with elastic cords and so on and exercised with these until muscles stuck out in lumps all over him. It didn't do him any good and may even have done him some harm but he found the lack of exercise when he had to stay in bed very tedious. He was sent to Sir Almroth Wright in London who gave directions to a Dublin doctor to give Joe certain injections and take his 'opsonic index', a system which Sir Almroth Wright rejected completely later on. It certainly did Joe no good at all and at that stage the Raffertys invited him to come for a long stay in their house, Springfield, in Kilternan. He stayed for most of a year, only

Moya (left) and Gerry, August 1908.

coming in to Fitzwilliam Street for special occasions like Christmas, and the mountain air and the care and kindness he got from the Raffertys did him a lot of good.

William Arthur Rafferty, Pa's great friend, was a remarkable man and very important in our lives. He was the son of a journalist, born in Marseilles in 1843, but the family moved to Paris and at the age of eighteen William ran away to London to the 1861 Great Exhibition which was full of mechanical marvels. He achieved his great ambition, getting a job as an engine driver driving the London to Dover train. He used to get up at five every morning to put order on his beloved engine, bringing his dinner with him in a tommy can. He got to know Pa in London and they became firm friends. William Rafferty inherited the family farm in Kilternan from his great-uncle and, although his heart was with the railways and he was then and always a Frenchman, he followed what he believed to be his duty and moved to Ireland. Springfield is a beautiful big house on the side of the mountain facing the Scalp and to begin with Mr Rafferty lived there on his own, building up the farm in the careful way that he had so that it was run in an orderly and productive manner. Sometime in those early days he found the Flemings, an abandoned family of nine children. Their mother was dead and their father, who had been a stonemason, had suddenly gone totally blind and, as was the savage custom of the time, he took to the roads as a beggar. He had a donkey which acted as his guide and he travelled great distances with the donkey grazing the 'long acre'—the grass borders of the roads. Mr Rafferty took all the nine children in to live with him and fed them, he told me, on porridge until, one by one, he found them homes with families. One of them, Michael Fleming, stayed with him all his life as his coachman and gardener. Michael loved all children and had a big family himself.

Mr Rafferty wanted to marry Miss Carew, a young Englishwoman with Spanish ancestors, but he was not deemed respectable enough by her maiden aunts. Pa was able to stand as Mr Rafferty's guarantor and this gained the maiden aunts' permission and William Rafferty's gratitude to Pa for life. He and Pa worked together when they were Coroner and local Magistrate respectively in Kilternan, and they helped in the stocking of local Carnegie libraries. I am sure that it was because of Mr Rafferty that Pa took the lease on Kilternan Abbey in 1900. Mr Rafferty. had his two sisters, Tante Em and Tante Lou, living with him and his daughter, Lena, who was the apple of his eye. She went to Mount Anville, did a degree in Mental and Moral Philosophy, and joined the French Sisters of Charity, finishing up in the top administration in Paris. She was tremendously kind to Joe when he stayed in Springfield, making him comfortable, giving him good food, being good company, and she was a great friend to me all my life.

Mr Rafferty's income was moderate but as Johnson said of his Quaker friend, 'There was no want and no meanness—all was reason.' Mr Rafferty had a heart as well. Every man he employed as a farm labourer was taught a second trade, such as carpentry, laying concrete, running a thresher or repairing machinery. The accounts were always in order and it was a lovely place to be. There was a pond with a boat on it and the house itself was full of clocks, so many that we used to call Mr Rafferty 'Mr Clockwork'.

He taught us to think, to reason and to organise, which we found wonderful. He did not approve of young people being kept from adult talk. We used to ask him what we should do and he would answer that it was our own business and we must make up our own minds. After leading us through a logical sequence, he would tell us what he would do in our position—and it would be a severe judgment. We were a badly brought-up and undisciplined lot. Our manners were bad, we were immature and we were as ignorant of social conventions as a kish of brogues. We learned in Springfield that order and freedom were not incompatible and the discovery was a great relief. Mr Rafferty was the Coroner for South Dublin and the local Royal Irish Constabulary would bring the police reports on any violent death in the area to the house. Based on these, he would have to decide whether to hold an inquest or not. He would give us the reports to read and watch us absorbing the sordid details. Then he would ask us if we thought he should have an inquest and when we had given our opinions, he would give his own. When he came back from an inquest, he would describe the setting, the evidence and the verdict and discuss with us whether he had been right in his conclusions and especially the social implications. The great thing was the way everyone in his

Members of the Plunkett and Cronin families, and Sarah Ferrall, at Springfield. Mr Rafferty, who had worked as a train driver before coming to Dublin, owned one of the first cars in Ireland.

house spoke so openly about everything; at home we always spoke under our breath, as though we were in jail.

Mr Rafferty did special things for several of us around this time. Jack was twelve and going to school in Belvedere and whenever he had a free day he would cycle the ten miles out to Kilternan where Mr Rafferty would have the tools ready and waiting. The big man and the small boy would set out solemnly across the fields to carry out a repair, or to make a new gate for the field with the mare and foal, or check the engine of some machine. Jack already had a feel for engineering and I'm sure it was Mr Rafferty's recognition of this that led him to go on with it later. The letter from Frank Cotton breaking off his engagement with Moya arrived while we were staying in Springfield. She was in a pretty bad state of mind until Mr Rafferty took her aside and talked to her for a couple of hours. He managed to produce a much more reasoned reaction from her when he argued that she could not possibly go on with an engagement that was unsatisfactory on both sides. The whole point about this story is that Mr Rafferty was the only person we knew with common sense and judgement about affairs in general to whom you could speak properly and who could be relied on.

Joe's year living in Springfield was very important to him. He and Mr Rafferty became great friends and although they did not agree on politics, Joe valued highly all their detailed discussion on moral issues. I think that the kindness and consideration he received there, both intellectually and physically, gave his confidence a great boost and allowed him to follow his strongest belief, that no intellectual decision should be made lightly. For me, it was a mixture of all these things. I loved the Raffertys and Springfield dearly and went there as often as I could, often to stay overnight. Like the others, I made the decision to have a new method of living based on what I found there, but the decision and the method had to be secret because if they were suspected by Ma, they would have been smashed to pieces. It was the most beautiful place in the world to us and when I think of it now, it is in those memories of sitting on the porch steps on wet days, watching the rain drift through the Scalp mountain pass.

I registered at the Medical School in Cecilia Street in the autumn of 1909 and Ma paid the fees. I started off trying to do Second Arts with First Medical, because I loved Latin and didn't want to give it up, but although I had been told it was possible, there just wasn't enough time. There were very good preliminary lectures for the medicals by Ebrill and McLaughlin and then the First Medicals were moved out of Cecilia Street. We had physics and biology in Nos. 86 and 85 St Stephen's Green, and chemistry in Earlsfort Terrace. There were six or eight girls in the class and a few girls in the class above us who were kind and encouraging to us and I met my second cousin, Evelyn Noble, for the first time. She was a grand-daughter of Bess Noble's brother but I had never met her, because the family was not well off so Ma had actually stopped Joe from bringing Evelyn's brother, Jack, into our house. Evelyn and I became close friends straight off. We resembled each other in so many ways that when we met it was like suddenly recognising an old friend. We remained friends always; she married Louis Flannery of Tubercurry later on. By the end of the year I had made a lot of friends with boys as well, Louis Courtenay, Eugene Coyne, P. J. Smyth, the two Maguires, Seán Ford and so on. We used to meet sometimes in the Botanic Gardens and one of them took a trip out to Kingstown and brought me back a love-offering of a dogfish to dissect. There was a hangover of chronics as well, starting, failing, starting again, but most of them got through eventually.

I thoroughly enjoyed the whole year's lectures. I had the great privilege of being taught zoology by George Sigerson. He was a poet, a patriot and a scientist and although he was already an old man then, he became a great friend and was very good to me. Our class was very big and at the back of his class there was a riot every day, but at the front there were people like me who loved his teaching. He was especially good on bones and development and used to identify specimens of beetles and butterflies for me after I had left college. He had a kind of open house and I was there on a number of occasions and met all kinds of scholars, talkers and writers, including his daughter, Dora Sigerson Shorter. I went to a lecture he gave for the National Literary Society on the famine of 1880 and the investigating commission, of which he had been a member. He gave a harrowing account of going into one house after another and finding everyone dead. All the time, as he talked, the tears poured down his face and splashed on to the page on the table.

I was finding it tough at home. There was the usual unpleasant atmosphere in the house, my brothers and sisters trying to get things they wanted and not succeeding and having things they didn't want forced on them. I tried studying in the room I shared with Moya but the traffic to and from Sarah's room, Ma's new toy, a very loud electric bell, just outside our door and Ma sending Fiona and Jack up to torment me and stop me from working made it impossible. (Fiona told me later she had no idea what was going on. How could she? They were only eleven and twelve.) I gave up and spent all my time in the National Library instead.

One of my lecturers, James Bailey Butler, had a tank full of water beasts and used to bring us on field trips, although they were slightly marred as his wife tended to come along and when she did, she scolded him all the time. He was good to all of us but I was particularly indebted to him as he encouraged me to go for a scholarship and gave me books to study for it. When it came to the end of year exams only sixteen out of forty-eight passed. P. J. Smith got first place and I got second. I was flabbergasted! I had not expected to be placed at all. I got first in chemistry and my scholarship, along with an 'exhibition' for overall second place of £12 10s—that put a gleam in Ma's eye while she thought about how she could take it from me. I had been listening to blowers and boasters in my class and believed them. Those ones had all done badly. Under a new rule, I was awarded Second Year Arts as well, even though I had stopped studying for it during the year and didn't sit the exams.

In the same year, Jack began secondary school in Belvedere College and Joe spent the winter in Springfield with the Raffertys so between that and my hectic college life I didn't see that much of him. He decided to do the University College Dublin Matriculation in June with a view to studying either Medicine or Science. He wanted to include Irish in his Matric subjects and he asked Ma to help him to find an Irish teacher. Ma put an advertisement in the paper and it was answered by Tomás MacDonagh. It was an instant friendship. They were both poets, loved theatre, read history, argued fiercely about politics and were full of humour and wit. There were nine years between them but from the beginning it was a deep, personal and important relationship for both. They haunted each other—if Tomás didn't come in to see Joe, Joe went out to see him. As soon as Tomás came into our house everybody was a friend of his. He had a pleasant, intelligent face and was always smiling and you had the impression that he was always thinking about what you were saying. Joe up to that time had not had a friend who was a poet and could criticise the work he was doing. Tomás encouraged him in every possible way and was not at all as critical of Joe's work as he was of his own.

Tomás told me all sorts of things about his earlier life. He was a native of

Cloughjordan in Tipperary and was educated at Rockwell College where I don't think any fees were paid for him; he was there on some kind of personal recommendation by a friend or schoolmaster, as being exceptionally bright, with the idea that he might even enter the order when he grew up. He was a very good musician and spent his last year in Rockwell only on music, all kinds of music, and playing the organ for every occasion. At eighteen he decided that he had no vocation and went to Paris to study art. He was intensely artistic and was already writing poetry by this time. After two years in Paris he realised he was not a painter but while there he enjoyed himself in his openhearted way, mixing in all kinds of company, enjoying everything that came along and acquiring a thorough knowledge of French literature and theatre and becoming a splendid actor and producer. He even found himself the guardian of a young lady in the Comédie

Tomás MacDonagh answered an advertisement placed by Countess Plunkett for an Irish teacher for Joe. He and Joe became inseparable friends, seeing each other nearly every day and arguing and agreeing about poetry, literature and politics.

Française when an old man who was a friend of his died. However, he managed to get himself out of that. While in Paris he also acquired a solid taste for scholarship and discovered that he was an Irishman.

He came home and met Pádraig Pearse and began working in St Enda's school in Oakley Road with him. He could teach anything, even mathematics which he didn't like—he was the best geometry teacher I ever came across. He published about four books of poetry at that time (I remember one was called *The Ivory Gate*) and was completely dissatisfied with all of them. He burnt them all and in the process, discovered how difficult it is to burn a whole book, especially in a small grate. That was terrible. He was happier with *Songs of Myself* (1910) and *Lyrical Poems* (1913). It was not until 1910 that he took his BA in English and Irish and Donagh (his son) told me that when a student informed the Professor of English that Tomás couldn't attend the lecture that day, the Professor said 'Oh, I'm so sorry, I do enjoy his lectures!' Tomás was a great talker and characteristically contributed more than any other student to the classes. In the oral Irish exam for his finals, he and Douglas Hyde got so involved in a discussion on Irish folklore that everyone else's exam was delayed! He was very critical of his poetry and decided to give it up to concentrate on prose and that was when he wrote *Campion and the Art of English*

Poetry, and he was appointed assistant to the Professor of English in UCD shortly after that. It was then he began his book *Literature in Ireland*; this was intended as his thesis for his doctorate but the Rising interfered and it was not published until after his death. When he wrote poetry, which he did with great facility, he could change every word in every line in a way which seemed to me incredible, with synonyms and new ideas or new forms, without altering the original idea at all. Row after row of words cut out and put in until you had a pile of alterations going up the page.

Joe went off to spend summer at the Irish College in Gortahork, County Donegal, which he enjoyed immensely. While he was there, there was an outbreak of foot and mouth in the country so he wrote a ballad, a take-off of the old topical ballad with all its beautiful badnesses. I love this because it shows the side of Joe that made him so entertaining to live with.

FOOT AND MOUTH

As I walked over to Magheraroarty
On a summer's evening not long ago,
I met a maiden most sadly weeping,
Her cheeks down streaming with the signs of woe.
I asked what ailed her, as sure became me
In manner decent with never a smile
She said 'I'll tell thee, O youthful stranger,
What is my danger at the present time.
On my father's lands there are many mansions
With sheep and cattle and pigs go leor,
Until the Saxon came over the border
With detention orders that raked him sore.
His herds they plundered and killed five hundred,
And the rest they sundered North, East and South,
Saying, keep the hides and the woolly fleeces
For the beasts have diseases of the foot and mouth.
With these words deceitful, sure he was cheated,
Not a mouth was dropping nor a foot was sprung,
But the only disease came over from England,
The Cloven Hoof and the Dirty Tongue.
Now what can avail me, O youthful stranger,
To save the beasts and my father's life
And my marriage portion that's my only fortune
For the lad that's courting me to be his wife.'

Joe fell in love with Columba O'Carroll while he was in Donegal. We had all known Columba and her family forever. Her father was one of the three young men who had proposed to my mother after her sixteenth birthday party and my mother had stayed friends with him ever since so we had grown up with his children as close friends. Columba was a medical student and her family had a house in Donegal. I liked her—she was a lovely person, pale faced with black eyes, tiny, very beautiful and graceful with dark skin and dark hair but while she was generally thought glamorous I could not see it, though I tried my best. Joe's love for her was quite unreal and got no response from her though she was fond of him and kind to him. I don't think she liked sick people and he had no money so he couldn't bring her around. He bought and offered her a little amethyst ring but it looked like a cheap toy and she refused it. He wrote poems for her but she didn't want rings or poetry, she needed an adult type to give her freedom from her father. A few years later she brought home Dudley Heathcote; her father didn't like him, and he beat her around the room with his walking stick. Columba's reaction was to walk straight out and marry Heathcote, but it turned out that he was already married three times and not divorced! Poor Columba did eventually get her life sorted out and qualified as a doctor. Joe, who was not the only one of our crowd who was in love with Columba, remained faithful to this hopeless cause for the next five years. To make matters worse he failed the Matric and, since he had already left for Donegal by the time the notification arrived, I had to write and let him know. He sent me back a postcard of the enormous Cloughaneely stone:

Falcarragh, Co. Donegal.
Fri. 21 July 1910
Thanks for letter. Don't know what I'm going to do. Find out will you. I've tried thinking and gave it up. This isn't a bad little stone. I'd like to chuck it at some futile persons positioned in a recent National Institution! When are you going off? And where? Let me know.
Joseph

Mimi, Jack, Fiona and I were off to Knokke in Belgium for a couple of months. George, who had been ill, came later. Sarah was supposedly in charge. Pa and Ma didn't come over until September when the Festival was on. It was an extraordinarily cheap holiday. When I looked at the figures afterwards, I could hardly believe that we could have had such a nice little hotel for practically nothing. We had a very good time and enjoyed ourselves thoroughly; the only problem was that Sarah thought that she was there to economise. We went swimming and Sarah was appalled when she found that we had to pay for it; she thought this was quite wrong. However, she had to give in. We also went for picnics and canal expeditions and found ourselves brown and healthy and hungry and sleepy. We went to art galleries, exhibitions, churches and buildings. Sarah's economy here was to refuse to pay in for the young ones so we couldn't bring them. She couldn't understand galleries and museums as anything but tourist attractions and she only went to them herself in order to be able to write home to her sisters and say that she had been there. Mimi left us in September to go to London to start in the Slade School of Art. The rest of us left Knokke and were back in Dublin by October when I was to begin my second year in Medicine.

I got some decent clothes for the first time that year. Thanks to my scholarship and exhibition, being given some work as a demonstrator in chemistry and giving 'grinds' in Latin, mathematics and chemistry, I was now pretty independent financially. I still had some fees and I started paying them myself when Ma went into a sulk about it. She had a row with me first and said she wouldn't pay them, then when it was too late and I had paid them already, she said she would pay them after all. She got a real shock when I said they were already paid. It did not suit her at all that I had moved so far out of her control. Even after all this, she told the younger ones that she was paying my fees and she couldn't buy them stuff because of that. There was one final break. Ma was still giving me lunch money but Moya found out that part of it was going on cigarettes and although Moya was smoking herself, she told Ma and Ma stopped my lunch money completely. This was a nuisance because I then had to get from Earlsfort Terrace to Fitzwilliam Street for lunch and on down to Cecilia Street in one hour, but I felt freer than I had ever done before.

I had to smoke! We were now in the official Medical School, Cardinal Newman's decrepit building in Cecilia Street, and the smells in there were really foul. The building was much too small and completely inadequate for its purpose and to cap it all, the Catholic bishops had expressed their disapproval of having students of both sexes in the same room for dissection, so all the women from three classes were stuffed into the one tiny room which had absolutely no ventilation. Smoking was the only way to survive the stink of chemicals and dissection. The women's room in Cecilia Street was small and dirty. It had two cubicles with WCs. The two windows which gave onto the street were filthy and had no curtains. One of the senior women told all this to Dr Coffey who was president of the university and he told her to buy some curtains for them. She got two pairs for £1 7s 6d and he said they were much too dear and told her to bring them back. We collected money and gave it to a porter to clean the room but he wouldn't do it for us. Our classes in Cecilia Street were unstructured, badly organised and sometimes even absurd as, for example, when in physiology we were given jars with solutions, not told their contents and instructed to pour one into the other and to observe whether they turned red or blue. McPolin, a classmate, and I wanted to do a science course in chemistry and physiology along with the Second Medical and Coffey assured us that this was possible, but the timetabling and logistics made it impossible so, since it was so disorganised, we gave up Medicine and transferred to Science where we knew there was more order.

I was having a great time! I had many friends and I got involved in the

Gerry, wearing her silk dress; she was persuaded to give the opening lecture to the revived UCD Medical Society (1910). She was nervous about it but 'I had an orange tussore silk dress with a Maltese lace yoke and that helped.'

beginnings of the Students' Union. I was made secretary of the Musical Society for which I had no claim at all but I was available and so I had to get up a concert. There was of course the Literary and Historical Society where we had a great fight over getting the girls in because some of the boys (not by any means all of them) wanted to keep the girls out and keep the society as it was in the old Jesuit University College days. Finally, there was a ruling made that the girls were to be allowed into everything except the boys' Swimming Club and the Boxing Club. The tiny Scientific Society had a little room in which we would meet, have tea and brack and someone would give a paper. Since we also had keys to the side door we used to come in on Sundays as well until Coffey stopped us, saying that the building was not insured after six o'clock. I think the only thing he wanted from the college was to see a line of doctors' plates on Merrion Square. The first general religious lectures were given in Cecilia Street and the place was crammed each time with students anxious for factual lectures. The first was an historical examination of the Scriptures and was good, but the Church was afraid of 'modernism' and the clergy were afraid that someone would find out it was all lies. The lectures were moved to Earlsfort Terrace and then few of the ordinary students went to them; it was mostly clerical students who were a rowdy lot, always breaking benches and causing trouble. There were extra-mural activities as well; we used to go to football matches, particularly medical matches between the Mater Hospital and St Vincent's Hospital, and there was the students' National Literary Society which was also a cover for the Irish Republican Brotherhood (IRB). I used to go to the céilídhe they held in No. 25 Parnell Square and this was the first time that I heard of the IRB. The President that year was Paddy McCartan. It was at these céilídhes that you could meet people who were interested in ideas and in the future of Ireland and most of us who went there became comrades.

Harry Barnville (Barney) told me that he wanted to re-start the Medical Society which had lapsed. Before the National University there had been a hooley every year in the men's common room which was now infested with bookmakers. The hooley was rowdy, the ladies were the local tarts and the cake was cut with a brain knife, so Harry wanted to have a respectable kind of society with a respectable opening meeting and proper tea, sandwiches and cake. So he asked me to do the tea and tell him what it would cost. I went to it and made estimates of how many people and how much food but when Barney told Dr Coffey of the plan, he approved of it and said he would provide the tea. This was dreadful. Mill's of Merrion Row did these bad teas for Dr Coffey and Barney could not afford to offend Coffey as he was in his final year. Then he insisted that I would have to give the opening lecture. He said it need only be twenty minutes. He said he had gone over all the other possibilities and I would give the least offence to the different hospital factions. I thought the idea was awful and what would I talk about to the top medics? He said it didn't matter and it could always be about something chemical which they wouldn't understand anyway. I wanted to help Barney so I said I would talk. It took a hard neck to do it but I knew a lot of them and knew they would be kind to me, and besides, I had an orange tussore silk dress with a Maltese lace yoke and that helped. There was a blackboard and chalk and I gave a twenty-minute talk on sugars and starches with illustrations. When I was counting the numbers of carbon atoms there was a giggle from the audience so I turned round and said 'Did I do something wrong?' 'No,' they said, 'not at all', and I finished up in the knowledge that I had got away with it. The tea, as expected, was dreadful and the 'cake' was made of stale cake crumbs. Someone saw me home. I was exhausted.

Barney and Harry Meade were first cousins and they were always kind to me. Harry Meade took out my appendix and didn't charge me for it so when Ma got him to take out Moya's appendix, she tried to get him to do it for nothing. She also proposed that he should marry Mimi. Fortunately for him, he had a very useful protective engagement with his girlfriend. George got appendicitis and our doctor was on the booze and did not diagnose it until the abscess burst. He was blown up with peritonitis when Johnny MacArdle operated on him at ten o'clock at night in our house. Johnny asked me to assist and during the operation, while I was holding the artery forceps, Ma was hammering on the locked door, raging that I was in there and she was kept out. Three weeks later George was dying and a cable arrived from Moya, who was away, wanting to know what was wrong with Georgie. Nobody had yet informed her about George's condition. She was often telepathic like this and you could sometimes even send her messages by telepathy when she was away. It took a full year for George to recover and all through that time Ma nursed him well and treated his nurses well. She was very grateful to Johnny Mac at first and wanted to give him large sums of money but when she got his bill for £50 she was mad.

George seemed to me to live inside a bubble and to be annoyed if he was forced to break out of it. He was two-and-a-half years younger than me but always included with the younger ones and kept in the nursery where he was isolated from real life. He had not walked until he was over two years old but there was no defect, and then he just picked up a box and walked around the nursery with it and we all cheered. He was now sixteen and when he was getting over the peritonitis he told me that the nurse had told him some facts about his development in the womb. He would not believe that there had been any development in the structure of his throat and nose. When I confirmed that this was true and tried to tell him more, he would not accept it. He thought he had come into the world 'whole, alive and with the fur on'. He was always like this, which explains how he accepted that it was morally wrong to oppose his mother's slightest whim and he felt he had to do everything to carry out her wishes. This was impossible as she changed her mind every minute and he was blamed instead of praised for his pains. He wanted to do engineering in UCD and I taught him geometry and maths and he passed all right. I got to know him better as a result and he told me that in his second year in Stonyhurst he found himself going around in a daze for quite a long time and that he was put in charge of the pet animals to get him over it. He discovered that he particularly liked snakes.

Joe had spent most of the winter in Springfield with the Raffertys, so I only saw him when I had a break from college and could go out to Kilternan to visit and sometimes stay. In the spring he went to Malta to stay with Taffy Asphar and met up with Ma in Sicily. They stayed in Messina and in Naples at the beginning of April. Ma went to Pompeii on her own as Joe was sick again and they met up again in Naples. They went on to Florence where they visited Pa's friends, the Dunnes. Ma went to see Botticelli's *Primavera* in the Academia delle Arte and Joe bought a copy of *Mireio*, Provencal poems by Pa's old friend, Fréderic Mistral. Michael Dunne brought Ma out on expeditions to visit chapels and palazzos and they toured several other towns in the area—Ma was capable of travelling more than a hundred miles in a day on sightseeing trips. Joe and Ma went to Orvieto, Venice, and Bologna, touring galleries and cathedrals before coming home somewhere around the end of April.

In June, Joe did the College of Surgeons Matric, which he passed, and had a poem published for the first time in *The Irish Review*. 'White Dove of the Wild Dark Eyes' appears along with poems by David Houston (Professor of

Bacteriology in the College of Science, co-founder and editor of the magazine in its first years), Tomás MacDonagh (co-founder), Pádraic Colum, Pádraig Pearse, William Butler Yeats and Standish O'Grady.

> White Dove of the wild dark eyes
> Faint silver flutes are calling
> From the night where the star-mists rise
> And fire-flies falling
> Tremble in starry wise,
> Is it you they are calling?
>
> White Dove of the beating heart
> Shrill golden reeds are thrilling
> In the woods where the shadows start,
> While moonbeams filling
> With dreams the floweret's heart
> Its dreams are thrilling.
>
> White Dove of the folded wings,
> Soft purple night is crying
> With the voice of fairy things
> For you, lest dying
> They miss your flashing wings,
> Your splendorous flying.

I think this poem would be difficult to surpass on its own ground.

The new king of England, George V, made a State visit here in July 1911 and Ma went into her Castle stage. There was the usual sort of parties and events and Ma went to the races at Punchestown for the first time. There was a garden party in the Viceregal Lodge to which anybody and everybody was asked. This resulted in two cards for our family, one addressed to The Plunkett Family and the other to Mr George Plunkett and Mrs Plunkett, it apparently not being the Royal Practice to recognise foreign titles except in the case of diplomats. Ma, the Countess, was furious but Pa, who as director of the museum, had to attend, didn't think it mattered so he went as Mr Plunkett. I said that I would not have anything to do with the garden party, that the whole thing was a fake, but Moya said to me that it was her only chance to get Ma to pay for some clothes; for Moya there was always a real problem as to whether she even had a pair of shoes on her feet. Ma, in a grudging manner, did produce money for a suit in white tweed, I made Moya a chiffon blouse to go with it and fixed up my own clothes. Ma had her dress made in London, the only time that she did this. It seemed an odd system to me, you sent your measurements to London and they sent you back a perfectly made dress! If it didn't fit, you couldn't get your money back as it would be your fault for not giving the correct measurements.

The day of the garden party we dressed and came down the stairs where Ma was waiting. She looked up and said, 'You can take off your finery and stay at home,' then went into the study where we saw her take her own invitation and leave ours on the mantelpiece. She then locked the door, pocketed the key and we just sat down on the stairs while she whisked herself off in the carriage to the Viceregal Lodge. I said, 'This is too much, I've had enough,' so we put a kitchen table in the basement area below the study window and a chair on top and thirteen-year-old Jack on top of that and he prised the heavy window open with his jack-knife, took our invitation card and came down, shutting the window behind him. We replaced the table and chair and since I had enough money for both of us we were able to call an outside car from the hazard and off we went to the Phoenix Park in our finery and in fits of giggles. They had opened the side-gate of the lodge so that one went straight into the big garden. Some people took the trouble to go to see his humble majesty but most just walked about and looked for tea tents. Luckily we met some of Grandpa Plunkett's family, Helena, Germaine and Oliver, and we made sure Ma saw us. By that time we were fed up and our cabby had kindly waited for us so we were home well ahead of our parents. They came in quietly and nothing was said on either side.

Ma never mentioned this incident afterwards but I think it must have had a lot to do with her giving in to Moya and agreeing to send her to Cromwell Road School of Physiotherapy in London for training as a masseuse. When Moya came home a year later, she proposed taking an occasional client into the house, but Ma put her foot down. Moya had no money and no resources to set herself up so that was the end of that. Ma's whole policy towards her was humiliation and degradation. She reduced what had been a high-spirited girl with lots of fun in her, into a wretched shuddering female, who could not possibly have any judgement or make up her mind. Mimi had been having her year at the Slade School of Art in London. She had a nice eye and had brought home some good watercolours at Christmas. In London she stayed with Frank Cotton's aunts, the O'Connell Fitzsimons, in their grace-and-favour flat in Kensington Palace (Moya also stayed there while in London) and she wanted to stay a second year in the Slade but Ma said, 'No, come home at once'. Mimi was raging and refused.

Joe wasn't well again. Ma resented his need for special food (she should be the only one to get special care) and threw it at him in such a way as to put him off eating it. Anyway, she was advised either by Dr James Meenan or my friend, Harry Meade, that Joe should be sent to a warmer climate for the winter. Egypt (which would have been ideal) was rejected as being too dear but I don't know why she chose Algiers, perhaps because Uncle Jack had been

there. She made no arrangements for Joe. She went to London or Paris or somewhere and told Pa to bring Joe as far as Marseilles. Pa was going to the south of France on a sort of busman's holiday, visiting museums. By this time he had been elected President of the Royal Society of Antiquaries in Ireland, made an honorary member of the Academy of Fine Arts in Florence for his work on Botticelli and was a judge in the Nobel Prize for Idealistic Literature. His French trip was to start in Arles where Fréderic Mistral and the Felibrige Society had started a folk museum, an area which greatly interested him. Joe and Pa left in October, travelling together as far as Marseilles. Pa went on to spend the next six weeks going from Arles to Lyon, visiting every museum on the way, and Joe took the boat to Algiers where he found himself a small hotel and sent a card to Ma:

> ALGER Hotel de la Regeuse Oct. 15th 1911
> Here at last. Beautiful place, very lively crowd in all sorts of costumes and faces and attitudes. Arrived last night after a perfectly smooth passage, not a bit tired and quite well.
> Love Joe

Ma wasn't back yet when this card arrived but Moya was and Pa got home about the same time.

I had thought that proper arrangements had been made for Joe but I was worried about the whole thing. Moya discovered very quickly what had really happened and was absolutely raging. She demanded money from Pa and set out for Algiers herself to look after Joe. He was by now very unwell and very unwelcome in the hotel as no more money had been sent since the beginning. Moya found a small flat for them and searched Algiers for fresh eggs and nourishing food for him. When Ma got home she made Moya's action an excuse for temper and she took advantage of it to keep them without money, always sending too little, always a fortnight too late so they were always a fortnight in debt. Joe found someone to teach him Arabic and studied and transcribed Arab texts and poetry while at the same time keeping his Irish going. He also amused himself trying to confuse archaeologists by getting an Arab silversmith to make a brooch with the crown of Osiris on the cross pin, and Celtic patterns on the rest made in the Arab way with silver and turquoise. He made Moya carry a gun which she had to

Joe in Arab costume in Algiers. He went to Algeria in October 1911 for the sake of his health, and stayed for about six months but the spring of 1912 was the worst in living memory.

use as a threat one day when she had gone outside the town to visit the black statue of Our Lady of Africa. He wrote this for Moya at this time:

MURDER
The clatter of blades and the clear
Cold shiver of steel in the night—
Blood spurts in the strange moonlight—
The pattering footsteps of fear,
A little thud and a sigh—
The babbling whispers are still,
Clouds come over the hill
Silence comes over the sky.

Joe was writing poetry constantly by now and, while he was in Algiers, Tomás MacDonagh organised and edited the first volume of his poetry to be officially published. Tomás made the selection himself, approached George Roberts of Maunsell, and saw the book through the press. You had to pay a few pounds to do this and it was typical of Ma that she paid for this quite happily (it gave her something to boast about) while at the same time refusing to pay for what Joe needed to keep him alive and healthy. Tomás, who by this time we all loved for his sweetness, his gentleness and his fascinating talk, got engaged to Muriel Gifford (who had glorious red hair), sister of Sydney, Nellie, Grace and the other eight Giffords, and they were married on January 3rd, 1912 while Joe was still in Algiers. Tomás did a lovely job on the book, *The Circle and the Sword*, the title taken from the mystical idea of the eternal circle and the destroying sword.

Joe was profoundly critical of his own work, partly because continual bad health from babyhood had cut him off from his contemporaries and compelled him to rely on his own judgment. He continued to be diffident even when he was adult and where another man would have managed to haunt the shadow of AE or Yeats, he had not the courage to try. He was perhaps fifteen when he wrote his first poem. Before this he had, of course, written funny schoolboy verse and filled exercise books with nonsense but his first serious poems, written in 1908 when he was twenty, were patriotic and mystical. He continued to write nonsense for relaxation whenever he was too depressed and tired to do anything serious. He did not write easily, and between 1908 and 1911 he produced only enough to fill this one small book. He would have rejected much of its contents, but the publisher demanded a certain bulk. *The Circle and the Sword* came out at Easter.

Joe read very quickly and I think he must have read everything available of English poetry. Crashaw and Donne left the strongest mark for a long time. He revered AE, the poets' poet, and was delighted to hear him talk of the Persian and Indian mystics. In lyric poetry he tried to follow Yeats's unemphasised song speech, but it was difficult to talk about Yeats in our home as Pa had known him as a young man and disliked him intensely. *The Circle and the Sword* includes the sonnet 'I saw the sun at midnight, rising red', and the poems '1867', 'My soul is sick with longing' and 'The stars sang in God's garden', which are all above the level of first books. I know Joe wished only these few of his early pieces to be considered as part of his mature work as well as his best known poem, 'I see his blood upon the rose':

> I see his blood upon the rose
> And in the stars the glory of his eyes,
> His body gleams amid eternal snows,
> His tears fall from the skies.
>
> I see his face in every flower;
> The thunder and the singing of the birds
> Are but his voice—and carven by his power
> Rocks are his written words.
>
> All pathways by his feet are worn,
> His strong heart stirs the ever-beating sea,
> His crown of thorns is twined with every thorn,
> His cross is every tree

Joe and Moya spent a lot of time at the skating rink in Algiers where Joe,

Joe and Moya, dressed for a fancy dress party in Algiers. Moya followed Joe out there to look after him. They took up skating and Joe was offered the job of manager of the skating rink, which he nearly took for the glamorous white suit that went with it.

who loved exercise when he could take it, became so proficient that, when the manager eloped with the owner's wife, he was offered his job. He was sorely tempted, particularly since a very dashing white suit came with the position! However, things were changing by then and his health was really suffering from the fact that it was the worst spring weather in Algiers in living memory. It snowed so heavily that the reservoir burst and Moya, who had been trying to work out what she should do, was told that the place to go was Egypt as it was both cheaper and healthier. She had even been given directions to accommodation at a reasonable rent. She wrote a very careful letter home to Ma, explained the problems, told her she had found them a place in Egypt and asked Ma to send the money for their fares. She got a cable by return—'Come home at once'. Ma sent them enough for their fares but not enough to discharge their bills, so more cables had to go back and forth before they could organise their affairs and arrange the journey back. Ma chose to be offended by the whole thing and she sneered at the little presents they brought back and threw them away, then cut Moya and Joe off completely.

6 A measure of independence 1912–1913

IT WAS A RAW COLD EASTER and we all got 'flu. Joe hadn't a penny and the only overcoat he owned was very thin and light. He asked Ma if he could have a heavier coat but she would not even answer him. Dr James Meenan found him walking home in the rain because he hadn't the money to pay for a tram, soaked through and with a temperature of 103°. Meenan had a fair idea of Ma by this time but he was afraid of her and thought her hopeless. Still, he must have frightened her because Joe was put in a nursing home almost at once and it was here that he had his first really big lung haemorrhage. We got Dr Crofton to look after him; this was a concerted plan between Harry Meade, James Meenan and myself. Dr Crofton had one really good point: he treated his patients as being ill. He put them to bed and fed and nursed them instead of the usual procedure then, which was to treat them harshly and make them take too much exercise. Joe was in the nursing home for several months and had another haemorrhage, then Ma complained so much of the expense that Crofton said he might be taken home. Sarah Ferrall was moved out of her room in the return and moved into Moya's and my bedroom, which was awful for us, and Joe was installed in Sarah's room. Joe and I had become very good friends and I found it heartbreaking to see him in this state. While he was in the nursing home he had been visited by all sorts of people, newly acquired friends from the literary crowd and friends from my crowd but especially his greatest friend, Tomás MacDonagh, but when Joe came home to Fitzwilliam Street, Tomás didn't come around so much. Even he, for all his kindness and good humour, found Ma difficult to deal with.

By this time I had a complete life outside the house, spending all day in the chemical laboratory and all evening in the National Library. I was also going to dances and meetings in UCD so the complete answer to 'Where have you been?' was 'in college'. When I came in one evening, annoyed by men trying to pick me up, Ma said it must be my own fault, she had never been spoken to by men in the street. I should have been sitting my degree exams that October but that was when I got the appendicitis that Harry Meade operated on. When I was well enough to go back to college Professor Hugh Ryan installed myself and Joe Algar and Father Fitzgerald in a small laboratory doing research. Initially it was very unsatisfactory as Ryan had already done most of the work on the project he gave us, and then he asked me to do an analysis on a bomb but it exploded, as I had told him it would!

I got engaged to my chemistry lecturer, Tommy Dillon! Though Ma liked

Tommy Dillon in 1912 when he became engaged to Gerry. He was seven years older than her and an outstanding teacher of chemistry. Later in life she lost respect for him and even left him for a while but they survived to have a 56-year marriage.

Tommy personally and actually invited him to dinner in Fitzwilliam Street, she treated the engagement as some rather objectionable business of mine which she had nothing to do with. She was already making preparations for giving me no dowry and no trousseau, not that I ever asked her for either. In the event, I paid for my own trousseau, such as it was.

Tommy was born on 15th January, 1884, in Enniscrone, County Sligo. The family then moved to Ballina in County Mayo. His father, John Blake Dillon, a nephew of John Blake Dillon, the United Irelander, was a student of the Catholic University of Ireland and an engineer and contractor who built, among other things, the Ballina waterworks. Tommy's uncle, Valentine Dillon, was Parnell's solicitor and Lord Mayor of Dublin; his mother, Elizabeth Sullivan, was a daughter of William Kirby Sullivan, founder of the College of Science in Dublin, the second President of Queen's College Cork and an enterprising scientist and innovator. Tommy had three brothers, William, Jack, and Andrew, and his sister, Kathleen, was one of the earliest women medical graduates in Ireland and for many years on the staff of Mullingar Mental Hospital. The condition of the National Schools at the time was so unhygienic as to be avoided if possible, so his mother gave him his earliest education, with help from the National School's teachers. Tommy then went to the local Diocesan College for two years. These secondary schools had been founded in each diocese on orders from Maynooth but there was no provision for staffing or equipping them. They were hopelessly bad and Tommy and his fellow pupils were left literally without any teaching.

After two years he was sent to St Nathy's in Ballaghaderreen in the hope that it would be better but if anything it was worse. He lived there with his father's cousin, Mrs Deane, who had inherited the business of Duff and Co. from her mother, and after two years Mrs Deane sent him to Clongowes Wood College. He was now fourteen and his education seemed so defective that he was put into the pass class, but he managed to get a scholarship all the same, to the surprise of the school.

In 1900 he got a scholarship to Royal University (formerly Queen's College) Cork, arriving there aged sixteen to live in lodgings by himself, not knowing what he wanted to do and carrying gold sovereigns for his fees. He thought he would try Medicine, which required passing First Arts before the professional exams. After also passing his First Medical he decided, inspired by Professor Dixon's teaching, that the only thing he wanted to do was chemistry. With a Bachelor of Arts (BA) degree in chemistry and physics (there were no Science degrees as such) Tommy came up to the Royal College of Science, 51 St Stephen's Green, Dublin, to begin work for a Master's in Chemistry.

Professor Hugh Ryan at that time was Professor of Chemistry in the School of Medicine of the Catholic University

Gerry, in 1912, when she became engaged to Tommy Dillon, her lecturer in chemistry.

in Cecilia Street. He took Tommy on as an unpaid assistant in his entirely inadequate department and when the National University came into existence in 1908, Tommy and George Ebrill were appointed as assistants in the Chemistry Department. Tommy's pay averaged £6 a month, being £10 a month from October to June with no pay in the holidays. It was a meagre enough income, so he and George Ebrill had to supplement it by working in other places as well. Tommy taught in CUS and in the Loreto Convent, Dalkey, and George had a long list of secondary schools, exhausting himself going from one to the other. George also gave brilliant pre-Medical lectures in Cecilia Street. Professor Ryan proposed to divide up the work of the department between himself and his assistants but, owing to a ridiculous piece of legal advice given to Dr Coffey, he was told that he would have to give all the lectures himself and that no lectures could be given by his assistants, they could only demonstrate. In addition, Dr Coffey was advised that if in any examination he asked a question which he had not specifically mentioned in his lectures, a student could take an action against him and the College. This trouble lasted for years; Ryan was a bad lecturer already but this was the last drop. By the time I came across Tommy first he already had his MA and in 1912, the year we got engaged, he was awarded his doctorate.

Ma had designated my sister, Fiona, as 'the beauty' but it didn't make her treat her any better. She just fussed more about people Fiona might meet and expected all young men to prey on her. She thought she would make 'the great marriage' but did nothing to make it happen. She wouldn't buy decent clothes for her or give her money to go anywhere so Fiona had no chance of meeting this imaginary rich suitor of Ma's. When Fiona decided that she wanted to do the UCD Matriculation Ma said 'no' and sent her to the Bon Secours school in Holyhead instead. This was the autumn of 1912 and Moya, concerned about Fiona's lack of warm clothes, asked Ma to give her a winter coat. Ma began to scream at her that there was no necessity for a winter coat as the convent Fiona was going to was French (as though the nuns brought the climate with them) and as she screamed and worked herself into hysterics she started hitting Moya, who was standing on the stairs, with her walking stick. Pa, hearing the racket, came out of his study, saw Moya with her hands over her head and thought that she was attacking Ma so he also began to hit Moya with his walking stick. Joe arrived in the hall to this appalling scene, took the stick from Pa and broke it over his knee. Ma took this as a personal insult and redoubled her screaming. Joe comforted Moya while Pa, realising his mistake, stood helplessly patting her on the head to show he was sorry. By the time I came in, Pa had retreated to the study, Ma to the dining-room, and Joe was still trying to soothe poor Moya.

Joe, as always happened after an affair like this, was boycotted by Ma but she did give Fiona the coat. It was a cloth one, lined with rat fur, and just the right size for Fiona. Ma had bought it for herself in the Shelbourne House in Merrion Row, which was one of her favourite haunts and where Maguire was always offering her bargains like this one. She paid about 14 shillings for it, stuffed herself into it leaving the front open since it wouldn't close and per-suaded herself it was just right for her. She came into the dining-room one day and threw it at Moya saying, 'If you must take the coat off my back . . . ' It was just as well she marched out again as I got a fit of the giggles. We had been wondering how to get it from her as she was a holy show in it. Poor Moya actually thanked her for it later and was patronised for it.

I bought a book called *Bill the Minder,* a Heath Robinson children's book with wonderful colour illustrations of a kind that were all the thing among us students at the time. It had only just been published and I bought it as a special treat to myself, so I was fairly annoyed when I came home in the evening and it was not where I had left it on the dining-room table. I hadn't even opened it yet at this stage and I asked if anyone knew where it was. I was told that Ma had taken it (she was like a magpie with our property). This was a bit much, considering that she hadn't spoken to me for a month—the usual accusations of immoral conduct. I knocked on her bedroom door and she came out, dressed in her curious underwear. I asked her for my book and she said, 'Surely I have a right to look at any of your books!' I kept asking her and she worked herself into a tantrum and began trying to hit me but I was too strong for her, I was able to take her by the two arms and hold her at arm's

Tommy Dillon (seated on the right) after the conferring of his doctorate in 1912.

UCD chemistry class, 1912. Tommy Dillon is third from left, Gerry third from right. Minding her brother Joe took more of her time than she had expected so Gerry, to her regret, didn't finish her degree in chemistry but she did give a paper in the Royal Irish Academy in 1915, and contributed to an article on dyes in the Encyclopedia Britannica, *among many other things.*

length to prevent her from kicking me. Finally she threw the book at me and flung herself back into her room. Considering she was now in her fifties this was all quite extraordinary. I kept out of her way for the rest of the day and next morning went in to see Joe who was still ill in bed. I told him the story and while we were talking about it Ma came in and said, 'I suppose you've told him all about it'. Joe told Ma she shouldn't do such things and Ma said, 'Do you mean to say that I should apologise to my own children?' Joe said it would be the right thing to do. 'Well, all I can say is . . . I'm sorry.' For a considerable time, she avoided me, but that was the last physical violence on any of us. I was twenty-one.

The atmosphere in the house after the *Bill the Minder* episode was impossible. Looking back on it now I think that Ma was finding our society embarrassing so she took the opportunity to think up a scheme to get rid of us. In order to give Joe more room and comfort (she said) and the possibility of being properly looked after, she would give him the use of a house in Donnybrook. This offer extended to whichever of us girls would live with him and look after him. I was very happy to volunteer for this; in fact none of the other three were available and Joe and I were moved out of Fitzwilliam Street to Marlborough Road before Christmas of 1912.

No. 17 Marlborough Road was a nice redbrick house with four bedrooms and two sitting-rooms. When we moved in, it was re-wired and furnished sketchily for us with odds and ends bought at auctions. We already had two good oak beds and six dining-room chairs made by Anthony Marley. Ma suggested that these might be given to me when I got married and I did get them, but much later than that. One sitting-room had a little furniture, we had a bedroom each and a lot of shelves were put up in the big bedroom for Joe's books. In Fitzwilliam Street Joe had had a board laid out on the floor with switches and plugs on it which he used for wireless. This was brought to the Donnybrook house and wired up by some idiot of Ma's choosing so that it was never any good and blew all the electric fires when you plugged anything into it.

It was so pleasant to get away from the dreadful atmosphere of Fitzwilliam Street that Joe and I were prepared to put up with anything—'better a dinner of herbs with love than a stalled ox with hatred'—but the first few months in Marlborough Road were a bit spartan. Among other things we had no comfortable chairs, which was particularly hard on Joe and made him unnecessarily tired. One day Ma arrived at the door with a man carrying a lot of junk which he dumped in the hall. He disappeared out the door to reappear in a few minutes with more junk. She had just been at an auction of the house contents in No. 13 Marlborough Road (which she also owned) after the recent death of the Venerable Archdeacon Wills who had lived there. Ma could not resist an auction, we wanted furniture, so it was business and pleasure combined. She had bought a Nelson sideboard, a travelling writing desk in old

17 Marlborough Road in Donnybrook where Joe and Gerry set up house so that she could look after him as his tuberculosis was getting worse. Literary and political friends visited all the time and it was from here that Joe edited The Irish Review, *started the Hardwicke Street Theatre with Edward Martyn and Tomás MacDonagh and, with his brothers, Jack and George, played H. G. Wells' game of tactics, Little Wars.*

black leather inscribed 'Ven. Archdeacon Wills', two cut glass decanters without stoppers, an antique-style methylated spirit lamp for lighting cigars, a Sheffield plate bread basket, a worn floor mat, an old black leather armchair—not really uncomfortable. The last item was very welcome and the rest was added to the collection of useless objects we had been given when we left Fitzwilliam Street. They were quite at home with our set of entrée dishes which were silver hammered on to copper, quite impossible to clean, and a box of assorted rubbish. She said she would like to have bought the Archdeacon's wheelchair but was afraid that Joe would be annoyed. She looked around her with a smile and said, 'Now I think you have everything you want!'

Mary Bolger was brought in as a housekeeper; she was a rather mad spinster, somewhere between forty and forty-five, and she got madder, but she was devoted to Joe, kept his fire going and gave him neatly presented meals at the right times if I was not able to get in on time. Ma gave me £1 10s a week for our provisions, a very generous amount which allowed me to organise good, nutritious food for Joe. I had to find out what Joe, who was never really well from this time on, could eat. He didn't like milk puddings and he had seen a nasty fish shop when he was very small and been completely put off fish, but he liked lobster, whole and red on a plate without a salad or dressing, and he liked high-class cooking, game, sweetbreads, wood pigeon and the like. I had gone to classes in Leeson Street school where I learned how to gut chicken and haddock. I bought Soyer's cookbook and studying chemistry was useful for knowing how to substitute one food for another. I also found a cookbook for diabetics which helped (Joe didn't have diabetes but I thought this was the right area) and I made it a rule to use as little white flour as possible. I took a lot of trouble to make his food look good as well as taste good and, from eating very little, I gradually got him to eat a reasonable diet. When I was not there Mary could make brown bread and scrambled eggs but that was her entire cooking repertoire. Between us, we were trying to give him the care for his health and comfort which he had never had.

Ma used to gossip with Mary about me and I got plenty of side wipes from each of them as a result. Very occasionally I would find when I came home that Joe was looking upset and annoyed which always set back his health. It was caused each time by Ma who had dropped in for literally a few minutes. I did not ask him what she had said, he would not have told me, but I was pretty sure she had been complaining about how much it cost to keep him alive and saying that she could not afford it. I had heard this so often. In fact she had far too much money. Ma's generosity didn't last for more than a few months and, since we never lost the status of children from whom pocket money could be withheld as a punishment, as soon as we had a row, she took the £1 10s away from me again and gave it to Mary who hadn't a clue about food. I was still earning money as a demonstrator and by giving grinds, which gave me some protection, and it also meant I was able to extend this protection to Joe in some ways at least, and try to keep him on a decent diet.

Joe and I had always been very friendly and our interests had coincided in many ways. He would allow me to take care of him even when he was impatient with others and he told me that he used me as a person to talk to about everything that happened. I didn't at first quite realise how much this new life would interfere with my own work. Every time I started to work for my Finals, he got ill, and at lots of other times as well, so that I never did manage to sit those exams although Professor Ryan had promised to pass me if I sat for them at all. I was sorry afterwards that I didn't take him at his word. It was, however, a new era of independence for both of us. This independence was spiritual, political, philosophical, in some ways financial, and even more wonderful was the absence of criticism of every step we took. The atmosphere of Marlborough Road was generally friendly and as most of our friends were students and intellectuals they were not inclined to be critical of the discomfort. In spite of his constant bad health and long stretches of confinement to

Joe in the cloak his mother had made for him. Having travelled on the Continent he did not think it as odd as it seemed to others.

bed, Joe made many friends at this time, literary people whom he met through Tomás MacDonagh, young politicians and Nationalist workers, and scientific and medical people (including my classmates) from the university. Joe and Tommy Dillon got on really well and were good company for each other. They often went out together to meetings and made trips on Joe's motorbike and sidecar. Sometimes I had to put an end to their on-going arguments about the possibility of putting theoretical socialism or social equality into practice. Joe thought it should be tried, Tommy thought it would not work.

I could not afford to buy clothes for Joe and he was much criticised as an eccentric, partly because he wore a large dark blue cloak. As usual this was the result of one of Ma's whims. He was usually fairly well-dressed; at one stage Ma had taken a lot of trouble going round the wholesalers' with him to find the kind of fine grey tweed he liked and they found it in the Dublin Woollen Mills. When he needed a new suit he was allowed to get the same kind. However, she always had to go to extremes; he had an enormous frieze over-coat which went down to his heels but no waterproof or light coat and when he asked Ma for one, she put him off saying, 'You have one', so after a lot of family arguments, someone suggested he ask for a cloak. This delighted her and she got royal blue faced cloth and made him a circular, unlined cloak with a velvet collar. He had travelled in France and Italy and knew all sorts of foreigners so he did not think the cloak as odd as it seemed to others. Both he and Tomás had a liking for the flamboyant which Joe carried a bit further. He also liked colour, materials and fine work of all kinds, especially rings, not for

Tomás MacDonagh, barefoot, but otherwise formally dressed, on a beach. He was loved dearly and respected by all the Plunketts, he edited Joe's book of poems, The Circle and the Sword, *and got him involved in* The Irish Review. *It was mostly through Tomás that Joe got to know the other 1916 Rising leaders*

their value as jewels but for their beauty. He would have been very much at home in medieval Italy. By the time I had managed to get Ma to give him a light warm overcoat he had been so much annoyed by being forced to carry the heavy one that he at first refused to wear the light one and said he would stick to the cloak. When he got over that he used the cloak as an extra wrap. I understood how he felt about all this because until I was able to buy my own clothes, I had been continually embarrassed by being made to wear hideous shabby suits, and hats which sat on top of my big head.

Joe was now twenty-five. He was about five foot nine, but looked rather less as a rule, as he stooped in repose, and was very thin and muscular. He was dark-haired but his beard did not grow strongly, his skin was white and he had a good deal of colour in his lips and cheeks. His eyes were very large, his nose thin, high-bridged and delicately cut and his mouth was finely drawn and mobile. He was very active and loved motorbikes, rowing, and dancing. Some of the other young men and boys used to want to borrow his motorbike which was the kind you had to run along with until the belt started the engine. After one of these borrowings the belt caught suddenly and Joe was flung on the ground. He got sinovitis in both knees, which were also badly cut, and had to stay six weeks in bed. Dr Crofton took the opportunity to try the injection of a Turtlein—an anti-toxin from turtles. Joe's temperature went up to 104 degrees for eight or ten hours and we couldn't get Crofton as he had gone off to the theatre. Joe was flattened after this.

When he had to stay in bed (usually because his tuberculosis flared up) it was often for weeks at a time and he used to study anything and everything, philosophy, biography, mysticism, history and military history. He read enormous numbers of novels of all kinds, many of them complete rubbish, and he loved good detective stories. G. K. Chesterton's novels and the Father Brown stories were beginning to appear and we used to get the *Illustrated London News* because Chesterton had a weekly article in it. Joe frequently used Chesterton's and Belloc's political novels to illustrate the mistakes which people made in interpreting political news. He would also console himself with his fiddle, on which he played frivolously, refusing to learn it seriously. He used to sit up in bed playing for hours, popular tunes like 'Two lovely black eyes', 'Just because I happened to be there' and, after his trip to the USA, 'Ragtime cowboy Joe'. He continued to write poetry, serious or light, nonsense verse, ballads and triolets and he collected street ballads. I did not like all of his poems; the lyrical stuff which he wrote naturally and easily had little value to him and he was engaged in making several long philosophical poems in non-lyrical style, of which I only saw small sections. These were in a large red folder which he had with him up to the start of the Rising. I do not know what he did with it, he may have given it to someone to care for, but it has not appeared since. Several odd pieces which turned up were only duplicates of what we had already.

Tomás and Muriel MacDonagh moved to a house opposite the old St Enda's in Oakley Road, Ranelagh, after Donagh was born on St Cecilia's Day in December 1912, and between work and home Joe saw much less of him than previously. He missed him a lot so when he could get up out of bed but not go out, he used to get George, Theo McWeeney and Colm Ó Lochlainn (and anyone else he could capture) to play Little Wars with him. These younger ones enjoyed Joe's conversation and they took part in the plays which were always being got up. Little Wars was a game invented by H. G. Wells, who wrote a book about it explaining the rules. The whole floor of one of the rooms in Marlborough Road was a battlefield, covered with toy soldiers. There were rigid rules and it was all very exciting, with arguments lasting for hours, and they used to get so interested that they seemed to lose all sense of proportion and forget the real size of their armies. Joe learned a lot from it about tactics and strategy and it led him to look at historical battles and so on, all of which he used later when he made the plans for the Rising.

The students' National Literary Society used to meet in the Gaelic League hall in Parnell Square on Sunday nights for debates, one I remember being 'That the policy of Wolfe Tone is the true policy in Irish national affairs'. In 1910, when I first came across the society, Paddy McCartan was President and Tommy Black, Secretary. It was so full of life that it was put out of bounds for students of UCD by Dr Coffey. The members were all very young; they spent their time learning the revolutionary point of view in interminable discussions on fundamentals. Tommy Black was the only one who attempted to formulate an ideal Constitution for a free Ireland. We traced our evils, big and small, to England, and thought if we were politically free we would also be free of the political prostitutes who surrounded us. Whenever he was well enough I used to get Joe to come out with me to student gatherings and one of the publications he wrote poems for was the *National Student*. He came to a céilídhe in 25 Parnell Square which cost a half-crown in, started at eight-thirty and went on until six next morning when we went home in a cab. Joe got tired of dancing at about midnight and spent the rest of the night in intellectual flirtation with Kathleen Cruise O'Brien, afterwards Mrs Eimear O'Duffy.

I was very happy and very much at home in this company, and the kind of clothes I could afford to buy were fine for them, but the day after that céilídhe Moya told me she thought she really should complain to Ma about me, my clothes and my unsuitable carry-on. She used to repair vestments in St Francis Xavier Church, Gardiner Street, in company with a lot of sacristy Bessies and one of them said to her that I had been at the céilídhe and that indeed her greengrocer's daughter had been there too, meaning that I shouldn't be mixing in such low company! It took a lot of arguing to change Moya's mind. The company at the céilídhe that was supposed to be so unsuitable had included (besides the greengrocer's daughter) all the most distinguished figures in politics and the professions in this State for the next forty years, but Ma always referred to them as 'Gerry's low friends' and thought the National University was a rather disreputable institution.

On January 17th, 1913, the Home Rule Bill was passed in the British House of Commons for the second time and published in full for the first time and we got the details of it from the *Freeman's Journal*. There was a flood of congratulations to John Redmond and the Irish Party from all parts of the world and favourable resolutions passed by three-quarters of the public bodies of Ireland, and everyone tried to pretend we had got something worth having. The Bill proposed that a large number of services should remain permanently in English hands, including national health insurance, old age pensions, the police, the Post Office, the Board of Works, land annuities, road boards, factory and workshop acts, Customs and Excise, income tax and the army. There was a limited right to vary taxation but the vote for each service was to be settled in Westminster. All final appeals in law were to be dealt with by the Privy Council, an English-nominated Senate of forty would have the power to revise and delay legislation, forty-two Irish members were to remain at Westminster and proportional representation (PR) was accepted as a safeguard for the Unionist minority. This enormous and complicated Bill remained unpublished until it was almost completed and there was no time to examine the details before we were asked to approve of it. Most Nationalists swallowed it whole and met the criticism of others with a plain refusal to examine it. The Irish Party MPs were saying that they had Mr Redmond's assurance that the Bill would be interpreted in such a friendly way that the result would be much better than the appearance, and that it had been given a false front to deceive the Unionists. They said we should wait untill we saw the financial provisions. When we did, they only made it worse. When an English MP suggested that the 'dual control' would create friction, John Redmond declared that although the Irish leaders had been called liars and hypocrites for their protestations of loyalty, they meant them and were only waiting for the passing of this Act to become loyal Irish subjects of the British Empire. The younger Nationalists and all the Unionists took this statement with a grain of salt.

The state of Irish industry in 1913–14 was a good deal worse than people imagine. It was difficult for a Nationalist to make a living at any time, and sometimes it was impossible. A series of articles appeared in *The Irish Review* under various pen-names (in fact by Roger Casement) which gave a fair idea of the state to which we had been reduced. We were now promised that it would be worse. Hordes of English and Scots were imported to fill every decent job in the country. There were no public examinations for the civil service. (It had been tried one year but such a flood of nationalists topped the lists that it was stopped at once.) Since Ireland was, from the administration point of view, in the position of a 'Crown Colony', it was ruled by orders sent by the Cabinet in England rather than by proper legislation. English trade associations, such as the wool manufacturers, would appeal to their government to do something about, for instance, Irish tweed which seemed a menace to them, and an order in council would bring in some punitive measure against Irish tweed even though free trade was one of the principles of the Liberal Party. Every means was used to see that we only produced the raw material for England's trade.

Joe considered that the unfortunate position of the Irish Party in 1912–13 was due to their allowing themselves to become an integral part of the English Liberal Party, thereby losing their independence. He thought that this would lead in the end to their losing the leadership of the people, and he hoped that this would happen in such a way as to cause the least damage to the cause of freedom. This integration with the Liberals was not Redmond's fault; he had inherited it from Parnell, who had got it from Isaac Butt. Only expediency would make an English Liberal Party in power take any notice of the Irish need for justice. Work which had been begun under Parnell was continued under Redmond. Much good work was done on Land Acts, the National University replaced the inadequate Queen's Colleges and Royal University, and, of course, the creation of the National Museum, where Pa was Director, was a result of all this. It was well understood that the Liberal promise of Home Rule involved the Irish Party in a good deal of English and colonial business in parliament. Joe thought that taking part in the government of the Empire made us a sharer in its propagation of injustice. The Irish Party's contribution to the debates on imperial policy finally convinced us that their imperialism was real. Many of the Party had homes in London and they did

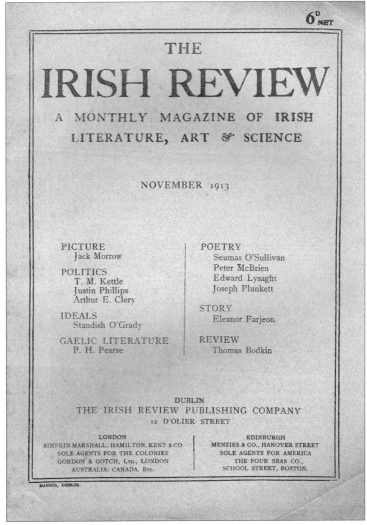

THE IRISH REVIEW

A MONTHLY MAGAZINE OF IRISH
LITERATURE, ART & SCIENCE

NOVEMBER 1913

PICTURE
  Jack Morrow

POLITICS
  T. M. Kettle
  Justin Phillips
  Arthur E. Clery

IDEALS
  Standish O'Grady

GAELIC LITERATURE
  P. H. Pearse

POETRY
  Seumas O'Sullivan
  Peter McBrien
  Edward Lysaght
  Joseph Plunkett

STORY
  Eleanor Farjeon

REVIEW
  Thomas Bodkin

DUBLIN
THE IRISH REVIEW PUBLISHING COMPANY
12 D'OLIER STREET

LONDON
SIMPKIN MARSHALL, HAMILTON, KENT & CO
SOLE AGENTS FOR THE COLONIES
GORDON & GOTCH, LTD., LONDON
AUSTRALIA, CANADA, ETC.

EDINBURGH
MENZIES & CO., HANOVER STREET
SOLE AGENTS FOR AMERICA
THE FOUR SEAS CO.,
SCHOOL STREET, BOSTON.

The Irish Review, *issue of November 1913. The* Review *was founded in 1911 to promote 'the application of Irish intelligence to Irish life'. By July 1913, when Joseph Plunkett became editor, the 'science' of the title had given way to history, economics and, most notably, politics. It foundered in 1914.*

not intend to come back to live in Ireland if and when the Home Rule Bill became law. Forty-two Irish members were to remain in Westminster and most of them wanted to stay. Redmond himself did not intend to stay at home, though he always spoke of the 'Old House in College Green' (where the Irish Parliament had been before 1800) as if we were going to get it back, though it was well known that after the Act of Union the British Government had ordered drastic changes to be made to the structure in order that it would be impossible to use it as a house of parliament ever again. When I first heard Redmond speak in public (he did not often do so), I thought him a very unimpressive speaker; his public statements and letters were incoherent and illogical and I thought it was surprising that his secretary had not put a better form on them before issuing them to the press.

All in all there was a lot of anger, frustration and disappointment after the publication of the Home Rule Bill, and a flurry of articles appeared in all sorts of newspapers and journals by people I knew and people I didn't know, but we were sure we had been sold a pup! When the last of the huge Home Rule meetings was held in O'Connell Street in 1913 we realised that the whole thing had gone stale.

Joe was still in love with Columba O'Carroll, although she had always made it clear she was not in love with him. She was his Egeria and 'The Vigil of Love' is part of one of the many poems he wrote for her. He had bought a little hand printing press from Tomás which he used to print Christmas cards, some of them designed by Mimi, and to experiment with printing nonsense rhymes. The printer, Mr Latchford, used to set up poems on the linotype for Joe and Joe printed them on the hand press on handmade paper. This was how the 25 copies of his book of poems, *Sonnets to Columba*, was printed. Most of these poems, including 'The Vigil of Love', were not printed elsewhere until the volume of poems we produced after his death.

> The wings of the imperishable Dove
> Unfold for flight, and we shall cease from sorrow;
> Song shall the beauty of dead Silence borrow
> When lips once mute now raise the chant above:
> Love to the loveless shall be given tomorrow,
> To-morrow for the lover shall be love.

From 'The Vigil of Love'

Joe was becoming more and more involved in literary projects in partnership with Tomás. In the summer of 1913 Tomás and David Houston asked Joe to take over *The Irish Review*. Pádraic Colum had been the editor for the previous year or two and he was now going to the USA to join his wife, Máire Maguire. She had beautiful red-gold hair like Tomás's wife, Muriel Gifford, and indeed Tomás had been engaged to Máire until it was decided that 'he wasn't good enough for her'. The *Review* had been losing money for some time and Houston had paid out more than he could afford. They did not want it to go to strange hands so if Joe could find about £200 to pay the debts he could have it with their blessing. Joe, who had been close to everything going on in the *Review* from the beginning, was very pleased at the offer and he felt it was an acceptance of his standing. At twenty-five he was regarded as one of the best of the younger poets, and several of his poems had been published in the *Review*, but the offer to own and edit it was something real. He was afraid that Ma, who was away having a holiday with Mimi and Moya in Shoreham, Kent, was in too much of a tear to buy anything for him but he sent her a telegram saying that he had been offered the *Review* for £200. A characteristic telegram arrived back from her saying 'Offer one hundred' so he wrote her a long letter explaining matters in detail. The idea of owning a magazine appealed to Ma and after a good deal of negotiation, she produced the money which enabled Joe to become the owner of *The Irish Review* on June 16th, 1913.

Our drawing-room in No. 17 Marlborough Road was turned into the office of the *Review* and the magazine became a very important part of our lives. Joe was in bed a lot of the time so Tomás used to bring people to the house who were interested in the *Review*. Tomás, of course, was part of the editing and the *Review* was already committed to articles and other material for the next couple of numbers. It was published by Ernest Manico, who owned a printing works in Temple Bar. He published anything and everything, including *Irish Society* and, I think, some trade papers but the *Review* was quite different from the others. The printer, Mr Latchford, was an artist at his profession and had perfect taste in layout, printing and centring poems on the page. To him each page was a separate picture. Joe and I both read all the books sent for review; we would have read very few of them otherwise. Joe had been very broadminded about literature until he read these books but now he developed a hatred of sloppy thinking and writing and became very critical of his own work. He had tried writing prose but found it very difficult and Tomás, who had been through this already, encouraged him to persevere.

Joe and Tomás were usually in complete agreement, expressed after heated argument and at great length, on literature and politics. They were deeply involved in the questions of taste which arise in publishing, styles of printing, layout of pages, bindings and so on. From the beginning the quality of the contributors to the *Review* was outstanding and included most of the best artists and intellectuals of the time. There was one art plate in every issue by such people as John B. Yeats and Jack B. Yeats, William Orpen, Beatrice Elvery, George Russell, Casimir Markievicz, Freda Perrott, Gabriel and Grace Gifford, Sarah Purser, Estella Solomons and Norman and Jack Morrow. Pádraig Pearse wrote in every issue (always in Irish) from beginning to end of the life of the journal. Tomás wrote poetry, articles and criticism and James Connolly wrote one article after the 1913 Lockout. James Stephens, whom I loved as a person and as a writer, was a regular contributor. James had just finished *The Charwoman's Daughter* which was serialised in the *Review* under the title *Mary— a Story*. He was now looking for a publisher for it under the title *Mary Makebelieve* but then found that there was an American book just published with that name—it was not in the same class at all. His next book was such a success that he and his wife decided to move to Paris. He was gentle and quiet and there was nothing in which he was not interested. James read his own work on English radio later and it was just as wonderful or more so.

Through editing the *Review* Joe began to find his feet in the literary world and made many friends whom he greatly valued, but as time went on poetry and literature always seemed to lead to politics, and in the writings of our friends the ideas of art and patriotism became so mingled that we could not imagine them as separate. The *Review* had included 'science' in the title from the outset and this had become an umbrella for history and economics. Inevitably these articles were political and became part of the expressions against poverty, deprivation, discrimination and the Home Rule Bill. Joe made this a more active policy and after a few months added the word 'politics' to the title.

Having always taken an intense interest in the *Review* and in the articles in it, Joe had come to the conclusion that some political articles in it, under pseudonyms such as *Shan Van Vocht*, were by Sir Roger Casement. Pa had known Casement since 1904 when he had come to see him with an introduction from Mr Redan, a friend in the English diplomatic service in Brazil. I remember Casement coming to lunch in Fitzwilliam Street, talking about his work in the Congo and in Peru, and we all followed his humanitarian career with interest which gave us ideas about international politics. Joe wrote to Casement saying that he hoped he would continue to write for the *Review*, but since Casement had made Pádraic Colum promise never to reveal who had written those articles, he at first thought that Pádraic had broken his word. He became very cordial when he found he was mistaken. He agreed to write further articles and did so. I met him a couple of times in Marlborough Road as he came in and out to see Joe but had no conversations with him—I was just the young sister—but Joe, who admired his intellect extremely, used to tell me about him afterwards. It was quite plain even to the casual eye that he lived in an intense preoccupation with whatever subject he was thinking about at the time and was quite oblivious of anything else. Among other things he had travelled in Connemara, leaving a fund of money to provide school meals in the Gaeltacht on condition that the children said Grace before every meal and sang a song in Irish after it.

Casement was a fine, sincere and very intelligent man, remarkably kind and charitable. He was a great asset to the *Review* on the political side, principally the articles, 'From Coffin Ship to Atlantic Greyhound', tracing the development of Atlantic liners from the emigrant ships, and 'Ireland, Germany and the Next War', which Joe published in the first issue he edited, July 1913. Joe re-printed these articles and Casement sent them to everyone he knew in all the European embassies. On the other hand, a dull nonentity of a man who produced some bad poetry and professed great interest in literature came again and again to Marlborough Road. We didn't know until after the Rising that he was a spy for Dublin Castle and this situation was new to us, although it became very familiar in the next few years.

Joe and Tomás used the opportunity of having the *Review* facilities to publish some books of poetry such as Tomás's *Lyrical Poems,* produced in the style that he and Joe thought right for poetry—on large pages, so that no lines would be turned and each poem placed on the page like a picture in a frame. They followed this with Pearse's *Suantraighe agus Goltraighe* and Joe's poems were to have been the next but events got in the way. In Joe's article 'Obscurity and Poetry' there is a great similarity to the character of Tomás's last book, *Literature in Ireland*, both in the matter, that is, in the aspects of the subject discussed, and in the curiously painstaking method of discussion. This was due, I believe, to the fact that they were dealing with what was, to them, an exact science for which they had no exact terms. Their spoken criticism also had the same characteristics—both of them as quick to construct as to destroy, to praise as to blame, not sparing in either, though Tomás was the more severe of the two. Later, when money was running out, Joe gave Manico a bill of sale on all unsold copies of the *Review* and on the books of poems in order to be able to carry on. Contributors to *The Irish Review*, while it lasted, included Joseph Campbell, Conal O'Riordan, James Cousins, Lord Dunsany, Darrell Figgis, Arthur Griffith, Mary Hayden, W. M. Letts, Susan Mitchell, Seumus O'Sullivan, M. A. Rathkyle, Frederick Ryan, Frank Sheehy-Skeffington, Peter MacBrien, Eleanor Farjeon, Francis Cruise O'Brien, Tom Kettle, Arthur Clery, Standish O'Grady, Edward Lysaght, Eoin MacNeill, Liam de Róiste, Col. Maurice Moore, Douglas Hyde and Alice Stopford Green along with Tomás, James Stephens, Pádraic Colum, Pádraig Pearse, Edward Martyn, David Houston and Sir Roger Casement. From this time on all Joe's interests began to lead, directly or indirectly, to the overpowering question of Ireland's freedom.

In August Joe went to Cloughaneely in Donegal on the motorbike to be with the O'Carrolls, particularly Columba of course, but came back depressed because Columba showed no sign of caring for him. He was on the point of thinking that it might be best to leave her alone and I did what I could to convince him it was useless to go on. The *Review* revived his spirits but he would have liked to do something more active, and the 1913 lockout and strike gave him that chance. I was in Dingle with Moya and our great friends, Con and Helen Curran, and then in Springfield with the Raffertys while Joe was away, and I got back to Marlborough Road a short while before he arrived home from Donegal; in that time the great lockout of 1913 started. William Martin Murphy, who owned the tram company, called a midnight meeting of tram-men in August and sacked 200 of them on the spot for belonging to the Transport Workers' Union. He then formed the Employers' Federation and they agreed to lock out all members of the Transport Workers' Union. From then till October Dublin was in an uproar with proscribed meetings, baton charges and prosecutions. The workers appeared to lose the fight but they actually won. I had been buying Labour weekly papers along with *Irish Freedom* in Tom Clarke's shop in Parnell Street for the previous year, and I was appalled at the old-fashioned fury in the ordinary daily papers and among business people at the mere idea of labour organisation. It was referred to as 'Larkinism—an invention of the devil' and the pretence was that it was only Larkin that they wished to destroy—in fact it was all trade unions.

By the time Joe got back from Donegal, the whole thing was in full swing and we followed the news carefully right the way through. Jim Larkin had done splendid work in Cork, Wexford and Belfast before he came to Dublin. One of the first things he did in Dublin was to put an end to the system of paying the dockers in certain pubs, by which the stevedores and publicans got a rake-off. There were plenty of abuses waiting to have an end put to them and hard cases were more a rule than an exception. There was the usual trouble in a badly-needed trade union. Only the men who already belonged to the union went on strike or were locked out, and they were usually the best paid and best treated. Living standards were appalling—well over 20,000 families in Dublin were living in one-room accommodation, and the poorly paid workers got from 2s 6d a week for the women in Jacob's to 17s for men on a 70-hour week. Even in those times this was rotten money. I was told by a doctor friend that when he visited a family living in one of the tenements, a Georgian terrace house, he found five families living in the one room, one family in each corner and one in the middle of the room.

The government was committed to an anti-labour policy in Ireland, however inconvenient they found its repercussions in England, and had brought in anti-union legislation the previous March. On account of their isolation and protection, the employers were altogether out of date. They tried to make labour organisation impossible and thought the government should make it illegal and they thought the military should be ordered out to protect them when they got into trouble. Larkin had been campaigning for better rates and conditions for the poorly paid workers, with some notable success in different places, and it was in reaction to this that William Martin Murphy sacked the tram-men on August 21st. A few days later, on the first day of the Horse Show, the tram drivers, in support of the sacked men, all left their trams where they were, pinned on their union badges and went on strike. Then the power-house men struck. A procession had to be abandoned because the police stopped it but there were several large meetings. More men were locked out by Murphy and other employers, more police were brought into the city. A monster meeting and procession was announced for Sunday 31st.

The Friday before the meeting, it was proscribed by the authorities as seditious, but Larkin said he would be there in spite of that. That Friday evening was the first baton charge by the police and many people were injured, and on Saturday there were more baton charges on Burgh Quay and Eden Quay. Two people were killed—James Nolan's skull was smashed in and

August 1913: crowds in O'Connell Street flee from the baton-charging police. Tomás MacDonagh described to the Plunketts, and to the official Inquiry, the noise of the police batons on people's heads.

John Byrne died several days later from the beating he received. The British Socialist Party wrote to the press protesting against the prosecution of Larkin and the others and the *Freeman* said that the crowd had been severely treated. In Brunswick Street there were plain-clothes men scattered through the crowd who took part in the baton charge and confused the crowd, who didn't know where to turn.

On Sunday 31st both the Dublin Metropolitan Police and the Royal Irish Constabulary took possession of all the side streets and both ends of O'Connell Street. A crowd gathered but was kept moving. Larkin, disguised in a suit belonging to Casimir Markievicz and a false beard, had been smuggled into the Imperial Hotel over Clery's. He suddenly appeared on the balcony, bowed to the crowd and said, 'Comrades and friends, the police have forbidden this meeting to take place in O'Connell Street today, but I am here to speak and will remain to speak till I am arrested.' He was arrested immediately and brought out by twenty police with drawn batons. Madame Markievicz and Tomás' sister-in-law, Sydney Gifford, drove up on an outside car and called for cheers for Larkin but hardly anyone had realised that it was Larkin on the balcony or heard what he said. Another of the Giffords, Nellie, had helped to smuggle Larkin into the hotel by posing as his niece and Tomás had gone to O'Connell Street, afraid that she would do something like this and get hurt. She was taken for questioning by the detectives but she gave a false name and was let go. That silly ass, Sir John Ross, Chief Commissioner of the police, was sitting on a white horse at the end of the street and personally gave the order for a baton charge. The police ran out from the side streets, caught people as they tried to run and batoned them. Anybody who moved was beaten down. Twenty people at a time were seen lying on the ground, old men and boys wounded and bleeding. Tomás was in a doorway in Prince's Street during all this and escaped injury by putting his bicycle in front of him. He was appalled at the savagery of the baton charge. Press photographs showed that the crowd was not dense and that the police kicked and batoned people lying on the ground. Five hundred were wounded and poured into the hospitals. The army was called out. The Lord Mayor demanded an inquiry.

There were more baton charges, more workers locked out and the Chamber of Com-

James Larkin in disguise and under arrest after fulfilling his promise to appear in O'Connell Street on Sunday August 31st, 1913.

merce passed a vote of thanks to William Martin Murphy, who turned on them and said that they were breeding Larkinism by their neglect of the workers. The men who had been batoned to death were given a public funeral. Jim Larkin and James Connolly were tried and jailed. Larkin was let out on bail and then released after about ten days; Connolly got three months but he went on hunger strike and was released in ten days. Afterwards the authorities discovered who Nellie Gifford was and her connection to Tomás and tried to use this to discredit Tomás when he gave evidence of the baton charge at the official Inquiry. He described to the Inquiry and to us the noise of the batons on people's heads.

Because of the depressing atmosphere of the family house in Fitzwilliam Street and the relaxed feeling in Marlborough Road, there was little temptation to visit home, but Joe and I had to attend on Sundays for family dinner. Our supplies would have been cut off, and Joe's health not only made it impossible for him to earn money but also caused considerable extra expense from time to time. When all the family were at home, ten people sat down to

Sunday dinner in Fitzwilliam Street. The seven of us ranged in age at this time from fifteen to twenty-six; Ma was fifty-six, Pa, sixty-two and Cousin Sarah was in her fifties. The traditional Sunday dinner was an enormous roast of beef with large dishes of vegetables followed by equally large apple pies with custard. We drank claret or Graves with this and sometimes brandy with the coffee and if we were in disgrace the whole ritual was gone through in perfect silence.

On our next Sunday visit after the beginning of the lockout Joe began to state his opinions. It seemed more than obvious to us that the workers had a just cause and the organisation of workers into unions was both desirable and inevitable. Joe wanted to discuss it with the rest of the family and get the right views supported. From his point of view justice was a whole. He knew that Ma underpaid the men she employed on repairs in the family house property, but we thought this was only natural meanness and anyway a great many other people did the same, but on this occasion we walked right into a hornets' nest. We had no idea that Ma had any views on labour and were surprised by the storm caused by our statements in support of Larkin. Joe was denounced in passionate and dramatic tones as having taken the side of the devil himself in the person of Larkin. Ma attacked him with fury, screamed and roared, flouncing about the place, in and out of the dining-room wanting to know (in a high dramatic tone) how her own family could actually tell her that the men were right. Her voice thrilled and shook, she said her heart was broken. 'Do you mean to tell me', she shouted, 'that they are right?' She had seen a procession of workmen carrying a banner demanding the right to work: 'I never heard of such a thing! They demand work! Well, the world is coming to an end!' she said. She always got an immoral excitement from fictitious vices and we found now that she was in the middle of a scandal whispering campaign against Jim Larkin—he was pretending he had a club foot but it was a cloven hoof in his surgical boot, he was the Anti-Christ. Poor Larkin was not club-footed, he was not even lame. To our horror Pa supported Ma. He was an awful coward when she was on the warpath. Pa was actually quite democratic—being in jail with working men later on was good for him. They were always very good to him.

It was no use telling Ma about the conditions under which men and women worked and which Larkin was trying to end. She would not listen, she said it was what they deserved. Moya used to bring food to people for the Vincent de Paul and those people's employers seemed not to mind having their employees supported by this kind of charitable subsidy. Ma couldn't see the point of this at all. Our meal was finished in silence and we left the house under a cloud of disapproval. Since we could not change our convictions and principles, and we could see that there could be no rational discussion on the question, we thought it better not to go home for the first two months of the lockout and we were able to make the excuse by telephone that Joe was not well, as of course he was not. Since Ma hardly ever came to see us this was easily accepted. Supply of food was maintained by Mary's weekly visits to Ma and she also brought her the household bills to be paid and the reports to her of our unsatisfactory conduct. Neither the atmosphere of disapproval at home nor our precarious financial position prevented Joe from continuing to take an intellectual and active part in the development of the strike.

Ma had now joined the army of people who underpaid from principle. She employed so few men on repairs, often only one handyman, that her personal interest in the labour situation did not explain the violence of her views. There had to be something else and it could not be a matter of principle, she did not know the meaning of the word. What we didn't know until years later was that she had bought a slum property in Upper Abbey Street and was keeping it a secret from us and everybody else, and of course Larkin was denouncing slum owners. She had found out how easy it was to buy property, and tenements in Abbey Street were her newest venture. I think she must have heard of people making fortunes out of tenements and the idea of making a fortune was always on her mind. She bought Abbey Street at an auction through a building society loan, borrowed the money from her solicitor and added it to her bill, but she did not pay the instalments when they came due. It was a four-storey redbrick house, let in single rooms, and a block of six flats down a lane beside the house. She thought redbrick houses were so well built, they needed no care. She was afraid of the tenants and avoided them. Her collectors cheated her, but the weekly rent collection came in in piles of silver shillings. She loved that because she liked the clink of coins and she pretended to herself that she lived on it and that the rest of the property did not pay. In September 1913 two tenements in Church Street collapsed, killing seven people and leaving many others injured and homeless, causing a lot of anger and a renewed campaign against landlords. Ma was well aware of all this, which is why she was so secretive about Abbey Street, and for years she referred to the income from it as 'ground rents of business houses'. During the 1913 strike Joe went down to Jim Larkin with a subscription which Larkin refused; in a speech the next day Larkin mentioned this, adding 'His people have rotten tenements'. Joe was terribly upset, particularly as he had always believed that the family property consisted solely of suburban houses and he thought it must be our grandfather who owned them. He never did know about Abbey Street.

After the lockout and strike started, a great many people, Pa among them, wrote to John Redmond, John Dillon and their own Irish Party MPs, telling them to come home and take charge of the situation, which was getting out of hand, but they stayed away from Dublin, acknowledging the letters but not answering them. Alderman Cotton, an Irish Party MP for Dublin, was a member of the Employers' Federation and Joe began by thinking that Cotton must be a source of embarrassment to the party who must see that their interests lay on the labour side. English Liberal policy was certainly not expressly anti-labour, but as time went on Joe began to think that the Irish Party considered that they could not take the labour side on account of Cotton. Cotton had not been a good candidate for South Dublin and was no asset to the Party. He was not popular and it did not seem to be worth prejudicing the whole Party position for a so-and-so like him. The Irish Party regarded anyone who opposed them as a crank or a sorehead. John D. Nugent and Stephen Hand brought a great deal of discredit to it; Nugent and his stooges even brought in a gang to a meeting to beat up the chairman who had disagreed with him. There is no doubt that the rank and file members were normally honest but they were chosen for their vote pulling, not their ability and most of them did not understand what had happened to Party morale. Their leader, John Redmond, did not like to be disturbed by the grievances of the people, which in any case he could do little to remedy, and he shut himself off like an oriental sultan. When problems arose Redmond usually advised waiting until we got Home Rule—live horse and you'll get grass!

My fiancé Tommy had always taken a good deal of interest in national politics. Tommy's father had followed his cousin John Dillon as an anti-Parnellite and there was a good deal of reverence in his family for John Dillon and his work in the Irish Party, but not enough criticism. The United Irish League was the official Irish Party organisation and Tom Kettle had founded the Young Ireland branch. Kettle was a lecturer in economics in UCD, where he and Tommy got to know each other. He had been a member of the Irish Party, representing a Tyrone constituency, but resigned when he got the university job. The Young Ireland branch was a thorn in the side of the Ancient Order of Hibernians as it contained all the younger intellectuals including Tommy, his friend Rory O'Connor and, the most noticeable because of his strong convictions and the extremity of his opinions, Frank Sheehy-Skeffington. After a time Tommy and Rory gave up attending the Young Ireland branch because the attitude of the party to it made it quite useless, but in spite of Tommy's advice Joe joined it in order to see for himself. After a couple of meetings he was convinced it was merely part of a party machine and he gave up on it also. The Young Ireland branch was eventually suppressed when an individual member criticised the Party.

It was plain that the lockout was going to last a long time and the situation got more disheartening every day. Tom Kettle was much affected, like so many of us, by the misery of the unskilled workers and called a meeting at the Mansion House where he proposed the formation of what he called a Peace Committee. The proposal was passed, Kettle was himself elected Chairman and he proposed Tommy as Secretary. As Joe had his motorbike with the sidecar, Tommy asked him to be his assistant and they were able to travel together to see people on the motorbike. Since the trams were involved in the strike, this was invaluable. Tommy also knew that Joe would be glad to get a chance to mix in something like this and in fact it was Joe's first time being engaged in

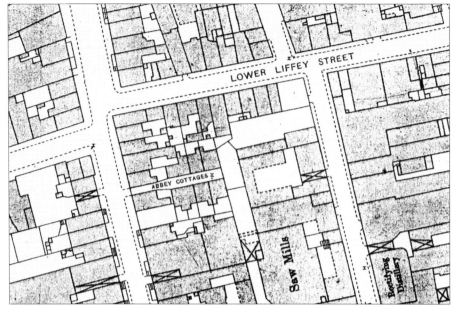

Map of Abbey Street showing Abbey Cottages and the tenement behind, both of which Countess Plunkett bought around 1912 but kept a secret from her family for years. When Joe Plunkett tried to join the workers in 1913, Larkin would not accept him as he said his family owned tenements. Joe never knew it was his mother who owned them.

public business. The Peace Committee sent letters of invitation to clergy of all creeds and public officials to join them. A fair number of people responded including the Lord Mayor, Lorcan Sherlock, the two Rabbis, Herzog and Gudansky, the Church of Ireland Dean of St Patrick's, the Capuchin monks, James Creed Meredith, Willie Yeats, Professor Oldham, Frank Sheehy-Skeffington and one employer, Edward Lee. Sheehy-Skeffington was the backbone of this committee, a very courageous man who was constantly in trouble.

The Committee held public meetings in the Mansion House but few besides the actual members went to them. They were theoretically neutral but it became obvious that their sympathies were with the workers. The secretaries (Tommy and Joe) called on the Catholic Archbishop, Dr Walsh, to ask him to join the committee. It was said that he had been vetoed for the cardinalate by the English Government and that this was what made him so reserved. Because of this reserve he was often misunderstood and he never explained his motives. He had not taken any action at this time; the Capuchin priests were helping the workers at Liberty Hall while a Rathmines curate was advising William Martin Murphy and neither side had been told to stop. Dr Walsh now told Tommy and Joe that he considered the workers were only demanding their rights, a living wage and the right to organise but he did not think he should join the Peace Committee or speak in public if it could be avoided because if he did, he would be asked to arbitrate, and he was concerned that the employers would not accept his decision, even if he made it plain that he was deciding purely on a theological basis. He was right. When the Trades Council openly appealed to him later he gave his decision in favour of the workers and the employers would not listen. Later he did make public statements on the side of the men.

The Peace Committee then invited both sides to agree to arbitration. The workers agreed and asked the Committee to find a basis for peace. The Employers' Federation, an extraordinary set of old humbugs with the exception of William Martin Murphy, seemed to think that they would be recognising the union if they allowed the workers' leaders to speak and were determined not to do so. They denounced the Peace Committee as pro-labour and spoke of 'interfering professors'. Edward Lee, who backed the unions and joined the Peace Committee, was the honourable exception. It was a complete deadlock. Having met the Dublin Trades Council, the Peace Committee finally met the MPs for Dublin known as the 'Dublin Six'. Tom Kettle had arranged this meeting at the Mansion House for himself and Tommy and Joe but he was having his own problems and did not appear, so that Joe and Tommy were left to face such of the MPs as turned up, most of whom were very annoyed with them. John Clancy, an old colleague of Parnell, did most of the talking. He abused them first for dragging the Party into it and then for not having brought them into it before. Then they walked out, all except the best of them, William Field, another survivor from Parnell's time, who remained behind for a talk on the situation. Tommy and Joe also went to see John Dillon but he would do nothing, it was a Party question.

The Peace Committee was not able to do very much but it would have been worse if it had not existed. Without it there would have been an impression that no 'respectable' person sympathised with the workers in their appalling hardship. Details of working conditions kept coming out, 2s 6d a week for so-called unemployables, 5s a week for men and women working in filthy cellars—an actual living wage was unthinkable. Rich men and women thanked God they had been the means of stopping the immorality of trade unionism. Before the Peace Committee ended Joe had a fine first experience of public and private conduct.

Jim Larkin went to England to get help and got a promise of £150,000, and the British ship *Hare* arrived in Dublin carrying food sent by the British Trades Union Congress, but it was not enough. In October, Mrs Dora Montefiore of London offered to bring the strikers' children to England and keep them until the trouble was over. The employers raised a howl of 'proselytising' and Dublin newspapers published Archbishop Walsh's letter urging Catholic mothers 'not to send away their little children to be cared for in a strange land, without security of any kind'. In fact, very few children went, but the Archbishop's letter was the excuse for real hysteria orchestrated by the Ancient Order of Hibernians and an angry mob was got up to police the railway stations and stop the children from going. Delia Larkin and her helpers were prevented from putting children on trains at Kingsbridge Station by the mob, and Frank Sheehy-Skeffington, who bravely fought them off, was badly beaten. The crowd also mobbed a man who was only bringing his own little girl to his relations in Hazelhatch in County Kildare. Sheehy-Skeffington fought a mob of hundreds that day and was cheered at a Peace Committee meeting that night.

Ma became involved in all this and got up a committee to save the workers' children from being proselytised. She bought Sandymount Castle, an empty boys' school, and put in a matron of some kind. Her committee was supposed to get the workers' children and house them there but as far as I could make out, not a single striking worker's child ever arrived there. There were fewer than twenty girls there including two pregnant sixteen-year-olds. After weeks of staying away from her after the dinner table row, Joe was ill again and I had to go to see her to arrange about something or other so I went at last, not caring about her and her tempers. She was quite mild and tried to tell me her troubles with this silly committee business, although she still kept on insinuating scandals. She told me that she had rung Archbishop Walsh to ask him if she should go on with it and he said 'I suppose you might as well', which she interpreted as meaning that he was on her side. When I ultimately managed to convey to her that the Archbishop was not on the employers' side she asked 'Why didn't he tell me?' There was, however, a sort of reconciliation with us based on avoiding discussion about the rights of the workers.

The employers succeeded in their plan to starve the workers back to work, and they gradually returned as desperate necessity forced them. By the end of January 1914 most of them were back, the last (in March) being the women workers in Jacob's biscuit factory. The workers appeared to lose the fight but a year later all the tram men belonged to the union, and the idea of trade unionism was established. By the time it was all over, Ma had had a sickener. Some of the girls in Sandymount Castle were very difficult to get rid of. Their relations, if they had any, had dumped them and did not want them back. There was a sum of £300 or £400 left over and she could get no direction from the Archbishop as to what to do with it. She appealed to me but I couldn't help. She left it in the bank and I suppose it's there yet. She also had Sandymount Castle still on her hands. She would not employ any man who was a member of a union, specially the Transport Union, for many years, in fact until long after the Treaty. When she fought with us about the lockout she said I was spending too much money, cancelled my housekeeping allowance and made Mary run bills and bring them in to her to be paid. This meant that I was not able to buy the pigeons and wild duck that Joe liked and I tried to explain this to Ma but she didn't care. She thought it didn't matter.

Larkin was sentenced to seven months in jail but actually served only about seventeen days, coming out in November, and after a couple of meetings here he went to England. There, he was constantly making speeches, which some-

Jacob's great factory in Bishop Street, where in 1916 185 men spent 'a very quiet week' munching biscuits and waiting for an enemy that never came, employed hundreds of young women and was a key site of the 1913 lock out.

times had little relation to the trouble at home. He was professing a good deal of internationalism and affiliation with the English Labour Party; he never seemed to realise that, as H. G. Wells said in his autobiography, the English Labour Party had decided to confine its internationalism to the British Empire. James Connolly did not make this mistake; Joe could support every word that Connolly said. On the other hand, it would be utterly ridiculous to minimise Larkin's work—in spite of his defects, he was a great man and did great work. There is no need to praise James Connolly. Joe admired and respected him above all for his honesty, for the way he listened to others and for his intellectual freedom. Sadly, when Tommy, who was keen on the labour movement, wanted to join it, Connolly said, 'We are not yet prepared to take people with education', although by this time he had educated himself to such a high point.

The Citizen Army was founded in November 1913, as a result of all, this to protect the workers on strike from the physical violence being offered them—one striking worker was even shot by a 'loyal' employee and the employers thought this was reasonable! There was another outburst of indignation from people like Ma. The men were out of work, badly clothed and undernourished. The only weapons they had to protect themselves against the employers' scabs, who were armed with revolvers, were short white staves, but the employers were terrified. This was the forerunner of revolution, of the Workers' Republic and worst of all, it was 'physical force'. Joe and I saw a little band of less than fifty men marching along College Green, holding their white staves. The most impressive thing about them was their cheerfulness. Ma said that 'physical force' was always wrong and had been condemned by the bishops, and that the Citizen Army was the last proof, she now gave up in despair of humanity. The terror caused by a few unarmed men marching in fours was incredible. It was a complete argument for even the shadow of military force.

7 War games 1913–1914

IN JUNE OF 1913 MA INVITED A CROWD OF US to a picnic in Larkfield, in Kimmage. None of us knew how or when she got possession of the place, but I had been there before. Kavanagh's, the Dame Street gunsmiths, rented a range in a field there which had butts for target practice and Joe and I, Phil and Willie Cosgrave went there to test revolvers. We discovered that revolvers cannot be aimed except as part of a movement and that Willie was a bad shot. On that occasion we took no interest in the other surroundings and did not know how extensive the buildings were. Larkfield was about twelve acres of land, with about four acres covered by the buildings, yards, paddocks, gardens and farm of Herron Connolly's old mill, which had been sold when the new mill was built. There was a manager's house with a garden and some cottages. The mill consisted of two big stone buildings, still full of machines, and a two-storey barn. There was a mill race, a tail race, a millpond, and a millwheel on the Poddle River. Ma told us she had bought it but she only paid the deposit, and ignored the demands from the Civil Service Building Society for the rest of the instalments. I don't think she had even seen it beforehand.

She got the grass cut and made into haycocks and then invited all of us, Kitty and Gracie McCormack and others, to a picnic tea in the Larkfield hayfield. I had a lovely afternoon lying in the sun watching the horses grazing. We had all been very lonely for green fields and this was a lovely and peaceful place. Then I got curious and began to explore. There were fields all round us with houses scattered among them and the remains of a brickworks on the other side of Dark Lane, now called Sundrive Road. I went into a kind of courtyard formed by the high three-storey stone-built mill, with its wheel and a boiler house, the very large two-storey barn and an assortment of smaller buildings. Backing on to the other side of this courtyard was the manager's house, a beautiful middle-size house with a garden full of roses and a hen yard. The house was let, but we never saw the tenant at that time.

On the rise above the mill was a romantic overgrown millpond surrounded by willows and high weeds. The Poddle flowed through the mill, turning the big wheel, while the head-race and tail-race enclosed a kind of island garden where vegetables grew. I could see a wooden windmill through the barred opening and a trout jumped further down in the sunny water. Spare millstones for grinding maize lay beside the door of the silent mill and all sorts of junk was lying around the yard. A faded sign along the front of the mill said 'Herron Connolly and Co.' and inside it was still full of milling machinery—

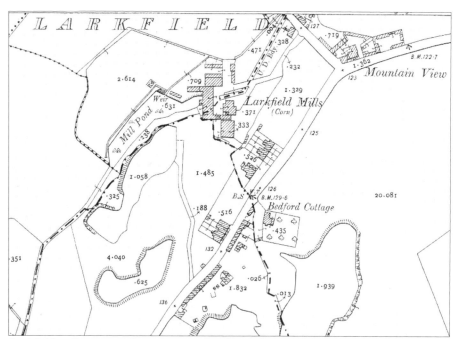

Larkfield in Kimmage, a few miles west of Dublin, which Countess Plunkett acquired in 1913. Besides the mill manager's house and two cottages, there was the mill itself, two barns and outbuildings where the 'Liverpool Lambs', refugees from British conscription, lived and prepared for the Rising.

long shafts with pulleys, milk rollers and great flour chutes the full height of the building, all as quiet as a scene from Sleeping Beauty. It was melancholy enough and I did not care to go in again. I went further along and opened the door of one of the small buildings before I realised that there were thumping noises coming from inside. A loom occupied most of the floor and a young man was weaving a wonderful blue poplin. He told me his name was Quinn and that he made poplin for a merchant. I was more careful opening the next door. It led to a bakery but the ovens were all drawn and I did not know it was being used until a floury man poked his head down the stairs to see what I wanted. The bakery was worked by the Quinns, brothers of the weaver. They made bread and set the sponge all night and then by day one of them drove the breadcart while the brother wove the poplin.

Now that she had Larkfield, Ma had to do something with it. She began by selling the big boiler and turning the boilerhouse into two four-roomed rather nasty cottages without an inch of garden or yard, but with bathrooms with baths, indoor lavatories, sinks and small ranges to heat the water. This made them palaces at once as workmen's houses at that time didn't have bathrooms. She let one of them for six shillings a week to James O'Neill, our gardener and coachman, who was very pleased to get one. He was a kind man who only got about a pound or a pound and five shillings a week. He cultivated the garden and the vegetable patch on the little island. Then Ma saw an advertisement in the newspaper offering Kerry cows for sale. She telegraphed the owner £80 and he replied with a telegram saying that he had put the cows on the train at Tralee and they would arrive at twelve noon that day. O'Neill the coachman and his son, Jimmy, went to meet the cows at Kingsbridge Station. Ma had sent what she thought was the price of two, but when the train came in, eleven little cows came out of the van! O'Neill didn't know what to do but Jimmy had an idea: he started to lead the first cow and the rest followed him like dogs all the way across the city and out to Kimmage.

It was on Joe's wenty-sixth birthday in November 1913 that he saw a little notice which appeared in certain papers, signed by Eoin MacNeill, calling a meeting to organise an Irish Volunteer force. Joe said to me 'Do you think I could be of any use? I'm afraid I won't be able to do very much.' The notice called for able-bodied men and he was certainly not that. I told him he ought to try anyway so he went to visit Professor MacNeill to ask if he might be of any use. We did not know him at this time, although he lived just across from us in Herbert Park, but he was very kind and encouraging to Joe and told him to come to the meeting. The response to the announcement was so great that the meeting, which was to have been held in the Rotunda Rooms on Parnell Square, was moved to the skating rink at the back of the Rooms which extended into the gardens. It was capable of holding several thousand people and there were two more overflow meetings in the hall and in the grounds. The police were there but had to be discreet because some G-men* using notebooks had been noticed, so they were forced to rely on their memories which were notoriously inaccurate. When Joe arrived at the meeting, to his great surprise, he was put on the platform and nominated to the Provisional Committee.

The group of people under MacNeill's chairmanship who organised the event included The O'Rahilly, Pádraig Pearse, Seán MacDiarmada, Eamon Ceannt, Bulmer Hobson, Piaras Beasley, W. J. Ryan, Colm Ó Lochlainn, Seumas O'Connor, Seán Fitzgibbon, J. A. Deakin and the poet Joseph Campbell. The speeches were not as reported in the newspapers next day, they were much more direct. The most important point made by MacNeill and Pearse was that the Volunteers were not being formed to fight the Ulster Volunteers, they were formed to fight all the enemies of the country, to defend its integrity and to demonstrate the right of the citizens to carry arms for the protection of the country. One speaker made a false note on this point and was corrected at once. The manifesto of about 1,000 words, which had been drawn up by the organisers and which Joe set up the next day to print in *The Irish Review,* was read out at the meeting and these extracts give a good idea of the whole thing:

> The object proposed for the Irish Volunteers is to secure and maintain the rights and liberties common to all the people of Ireland.

G-men were plain-clothes detectives of G Division of the Dublin Metropolitan Police, based in Dublin Castle and specialising in monitoring Nationalist activities.

Their duties will be defensive and protective, and they will not contemplate either aggression or domination.

Their ranks are open to all able-bodied Irishmen without distinction of creed, politics, or social grade. Means will be found whereby Irishmen unable to serve as ordinary Volunteers will be enabled to aid the Volunteer forces in various capacities.

There will also be work for women to do, and there are signs that the women of Ireland, true to their record, are especially enthusiastic for the success of the Irish Volunteers.

The Volunteers, once they have been enrolled, will form a prominent element in the National life under a National Government. . . .

In the name of National Unity, of National dignity, of National and individual Liberty, of manly citizenship, we appeal to our countrymen to recognise and accept without hesitation the opportunity that has been granted them to join the ranks of the Irish Volunteers, and to make the movement now begun not unworthy of the historic title which it has adopted.

It was voluntary, democratic, national and non-sectarian.

About 4,000 joined on that day, swelling to about 10,000 by Christmas. Joe came back full of enthusiasm and also full of wonder that he had been selected. Some of the organisers were members of the IRB and although Joe was not in the IRB at this time he was a friend of members of it and they were willing to accept him. The second meeting of the Provisional Committee was held in the Hardwicke Hall (which Ma had bought for a song in 1910) and then offices were rented in No. 206 Brunswick Street. Joe used to tell me when he got home what had happened at each meeting. After the meeting in the Hardwicke Hall, Ma chose to consider that Joe was the person who started the Volunteers. Years later she said to me, 'What do you think of that fellow Pearse that Joe got to help him start the Volunteers? I never thought much of him, he wasn't so important afterwards.' The Volunteers were an immediate success and companies were started in every parish, but it was noticed that official nationalists were inclined to hang back a little as if they were waiting for John Redmond to come to Dublin and make a speech to give them a proper start. MacNeill had been to see him and ask him for approval and got a grudging permission to go on, but it was unofficial.

It was taken for granted by most people that drilling on a British Army plan was the first essential. As the drill-sergeants were teaching them to march to English music-hall songs, Tomás MacDonagh wrote a marching song for the Volunteers and O'Brian-Butler offered to set it to music, but the tune he produced, while better than the words, did not fit them. They argued about it for a whole afternoon in our house and then abandoned it. Poor O'Brian-Butler was later drowned in the liner *Lusitania*, which was torpedoed off Kinsale in May 1915. The ex-British Army drill-sergeants nearly drilled the Volunteers out of existence; if the split had not taken them away there would have been no Volunteers left. Some of the boys who had been in the officers' training corps in English schools helped to teach also. Joe was one of the few who did

Eoin MacNeill (1867–1944) Professor of Irish at University College Dublin, a founder of the Gaelic League and Chief of Staff of the Irish Volunteeers— but he was not a member of the IRB and took no part in planning the Rising.

not agree with this heavy drilling policy and later others also discovered that voluntary discipline was the foundation of the kind of fighting we were likely to get here, but when they had difficulty getting halls for drilling, he asked Ma for the use of Sandymount Castle. She was quite pleased, at that time, to let the Volunteers have anything she could give them, and she willingly agreed to this, but I don't think she had any idea of what it was all about.

The Ulster Volunteers were being organised openly in the North as a protest against the Home Rule Bill. Although the aim of the Irish Volunteers was very different, they were allowed to organise, hold public meetings, drill men and have route marches because of the freedoms allowed to the Ulster Volunteers, but in December 1913 the King signed a government order banning the importation of arms to Ireland. Unionists here believed that there were now so many guns held by the Northern Unionists that it would be impossible to implement Home Rule. We could see some reason at the time why the Irish Volunteers were allowed so much rope, but from this on Joe lived for much of the time in expectation of proclamation and arrests. This prospect, though alarming at times, was not depressing. On the contrary, Joe was much exhilarated at finding that his philosophic speculation on the nature and necessity of spiritual and political freedom was leading to a practical conclusion.

I became familiar with the names of all the Volunteer committee, many of whom I never met. I did know Eoin MacNeill, Tom Kettle, Liam Gogan, The O'Rahilly, Roger Casement, Colonel Maurice Moore, Bulmer Hobson, Colm O Lochlainn, Seán MacDiarmada, Eamon Ceannt, Ted Sheehan, Liam Mellowes and, of course, Pearse and Tomás. Bulmer Hobson was the secretary to the Provisional Committee from the start. Joe published all the Volunteer manifestos in *The Irish Review* and as the *Review's* principal supporters had always been civil servants who could not now afford to be seen with it, the circulation went down. It had never been more than a thousand and the American order was ridiculously small. Tomás always said that the 'Four Seas Co.' who were the agents were just 'two men in an attic'.

When Cumann na mBan was started, I put my name down in one of the

Tommy Dillon (front), Rory O'Connor (right) and another.

offices taking names, but when I told Joe he said I was not to go on with it because he wanted me as a messenger. He could not use letters or telephone as it would not be safe and he was usually too ill to deliver the messages himself. It was from this time on that the secrecy which was so necessary was put into practice. Joe also wanted someone to talk to; it helped him to think, and thought was the principal and sometimes the only weapon we had, just as it was the only weapon Michael Collins had when he picked up the pieces later and put them together.

On January 21st the first afternoon drill was held in Larkfield. The 1st Battalion headquarters were in St Enda's, the 4th was in Larkfield. The 2nd and 3rd had to hire places to drill. On February 4th the first number of the *Irish Volunteer* was published. It contained articles by Roger Casement, Pearse, Tom Kettle, Liam Mellowes, Joe, and others. Joe also wrote unsigned articles fairly often. On January 30th, in the same week as the Lord Lieutenant, Lord Aberdeen, gave a lecture on tea-making saying that 'the water should be boiling but not too boiling', a sensation was caused in the Curragh. An arms store sentry was found gagged and bound, and arms were missing from the store.

On a night at the beginning of February, Joe told me that a Mr Nolan would be coming to see him and that I (not Mary) was to answer the door and bring him straight in without asking his business. He would be carrying a bag and I was to tell him to come right in with it. The man in question arrived on an outside car at our house in Marlborough Road. He had two old-fashioned Gladstone bags with him and he told the jarvey that he preferred to carry them himself as they contained valuable glass. He said his name was Nolan and asked for Joe. He came in, shut the door and put the bags down very carefully. 'Mr Nolan' was Liam Mellowes (this was the first time I had met him) and there was a half-a-hundredweight of gelignite in one bag and 4,000 rounds of .303 ammunition in the other. Someone had stolen the gelignite from the Arklow explosives factory and the ammunition had been bought from English soldiers in the Curragh. It was presumed by everyone that the arms from the Curragh store had been given to the Ulster Volunteers by the English officers, but Liam had managed to get some of it. From this time on it was always possible to buy arms and ammunition in small quantities from English soldiers. We kept the ammunition in the house until a few weeks later when Éamon de Valera, who lived round the corner in Morehampton Terrace, brought a message that Liam thought his journey (from the Curragh) had been traced. Joe was ill so de Valera and my brother Jack moved the ammunition to a safer place on the backs of bicycles. I helped to put the gelignite in a shed at the back of the house where Joe kept his motorbike. The gelignite was not strong enough to be of any use and was easy to get so it stayed there until after the Rising. Then we put it in a tin box and buried it in the garden of our house in Belgrave Road, where it stayed until we were forced to get rid of it because a man making a hen-run for me mistook the measurements I gave him and drove a post within an inch of it with a sledge-hammer!

In April 1914 the famous Larne gun-running took place. Ulster Volunteers took possession of both sides of Belfast Lough and landed something like 25,000 guns, from a tramp steamer from Hamburg. While the gun-running was in progress telephones were disconnected, armed men drew cordons across roads and held up traffic, and towns were isolated. From what we could make out at the time, the account of the number of guns was exaggerated. In the middle of May the Irish Party, having failed to destroy the Irish Volunteers by disapproving of them, moved in on them instead. John Redmond demanded that the Provisional Committee should give him control by adding 25 men, nominated by him, to the committee. With the official Party supporters already on the committee, this would give him a majority. As Joe described it to me, Redmond seemed to be as afraid of an Irish army as if he had been a member of the English government, and Joe was sure that if the Volunteers were handed over to Redmond he would destroy them, but equally Joe and

the Provisional Committee knew that if they did not come to some arrangement with Redmond the Volunteers would be destroyed in some other way.

Joe never did tell me in so many words that he had joined the IRB but I
came to know without being told. He was so often confined to bed or to the
house that I had to act as messenger and agent for him, and there was now a
change in the kind of people who came to the house. At first when I carried
messages, or when meetings were held in the house, it would be described as
'Volunteer business', but by degrees there was more mention of 'the organisation' which, as I quickly came to realise, was a controlling force in the Volunteers. From this time he used to say 'we have agreed' instead of telling me
different people's opinions, and of course it got much plainer as time went
on. Joe now told me that 'we' had agreed simply to accept Redmond's 25
nominees and if they proved completely intolerable, they could be rejected as
a whole. In the meantime, Joe said, they were to get a fair trial to prove
themselves sincere individually and collectively. At the June meeting of the
Volunteers Joe voted with the majority in favour of the nominees, because he
thought that if there were resistance to Redmond at this stage, nothing would
survive, but he was very worried and told me that they had agreed that if the
combined committee were a failure they would not continue to work with the
nominees. They thought they were bound in honour, however, to give it a fair
trial and as proof of this, training camps and other new schemes were held up
till the nominees should join them. Joe said he was determined to keep an
open mind and to give them every chance. Most Nationalists breathed a sigh
of relief. They thought the Irish Party had got control of the Volunteers in
order to use them for Ireland. Now that war was clearly imminent, the Irish
Party could have the proclamation against the importation of arms repealed
and the Volunteers would get guns to defend their liberty when the army was
out of the country.

Twenty-one of Redmond's nominees attended the first meeting of the combined committee in July. One of the priests told Joe he had not known he was
nominated and did not intend to come again. Most of them could fairly be
described as having no other value than a strong devotion to the Irish Party
and were unknown except as party hacks. John Redmond's brother, Major
Willie Redmond, was by far the best of them. Joe told me that from the
beginning it was quite plain that the nominees, except for Major Redmond,
were only obstructionist and were not interested in the Volunteers. They had
come, apparently, with the fixed idea that the Volunteers had been started by
the enemies of the Irish Party and that they must take it over, and Joe became
convinced they intended to destroy it. Michael Davitt was on the first list of
Redmondite nominees, and he told me that John Dillon sent for him and
told him he would be in the position of a puppet obeying the instructions of
the Party and that this would be the beginning of his political career. Michael
was indignant and refused.

The sub-committees for arms, uniforms, organisation and finance now had to be re-cast. Major Willie Redmond was made Chairman of the arms committee. He had just returned from a long tour of Australia—it was said that he had been sent there to keep him out of the Home Rule debates. Joe was a member of his committee and he said that there was no dirty work on it, that Willie Redmond was the only one of the nominees who treated the original committee members as honest men. Joe was also on the uniforms sub-Committee and, although most uniforms had been khaki, after the Party got control there was a rush of better-off men into the Volunteers and the appearance of a lot of very fancy uniforms with pink facings and so on. To put an end to this, the committee had to hurry up and get the grey/green tweed from Murroughs of Cork, which has been used ever since. One of the nominees, Cohane, proposed a British-style khaki uniform for a motorbike corps but the uniform committee was able to defeat this.

Radical Nationalists thought that John Redmond, leader of the Irish Parliamentary Party, spent too much time playing Westminster games. Cartoons such as this from Punch, *showing Redmond (centre), with (left) Colonial Secretary Bonar Law and Edward Carson, tended to confirm the impression. It was published in January 1916, after Redmond had successfully stifled a bill initially supported by Carson to impose conscription in Ireland.*

Although all this developed Joe's character and thinking, he found it terribly painful and he came back from meetings, sometimes after midnight, fed up and sometimes quite ill, often disgusted and saying that he did not see how he could attend another, but he always went again. He had a continual experience of frustration, disappointment and disillusion at the conduct, ethics and brains of Irish Party people who were supposed to be leaders. He told me after one meeting that John D. Nugent, a Redmond nominee, tried to provoke a row by accusing Pearse of embezzling the funds, a well-known way to annoy men into resigning from an organisation, and Pearse slapped the man's face. As he said afterwards to Joe, it was the only argument Nugent understood. Joe was delighted and said that he had wanted all the time to do it himself. The one priest who continued to attend the meetings drew a gun and threatened Pearse with it. Joe began to feel he knew more about political strategy, tactics, international politics and the conduct of business than the

Running the smuggled guns into Dublin after the Howth gun-running, Sunday 26 July 1914.

Party people and he had a better idea of how to treat the ordinary Irishman and the growing number of educated and intellectual young people whom the Irish Party either ignored or tried to suppress. The long discussions and arguments during this period were very useful to him, as he realised the value of his own gifts and began to see where he could be useful to Ireland.

During the summer Ma started up her hayfield teas at Larkfield again and at one of these I managed to shoot Jack in the shoulder with one of Ma's miniature .22 rifles. I didn't know that a .22 bullet would go through inch board until I aimed one of the rifles idly at a board and the bullet went straight through it, taking a piece out of Jack's shoulder as he was hiding behind a tree. Sometimes I had to try to get out of going on the picnics with the others because it was complicated by Ma's fantastic matchmaking. She used to ask men I was trying to avoid to come out with the family. They thought I had asked Ma to invite them but of course I hadn't. She thought she was entitled to offer us around as prospective wives, but that sort of thing had gone out. When I asked her not to invite a particular fellow-student of mine, as he would only think I had asked her to do so, she drew herself up in pride and said she would ask any friend she chose. He was not her friend and was very angry when I showed him my engagement ring. She was delighted she had embarrassed me.

The Marlborough Road house had been getting foggy from all the coal we used for cooking and heating. Joe did not want to go away for a holiday, although he had been feeling the need of a change, because he thought he should attend all the Volunteer Provisional Committee meetings, but he thought a month or two of summer in the country would be a good idea. So, with Ma's permission, he and I and Mary, the housekeeper, went to Kimmage to live in the vacant cottage in Larkfield. We brought a few bits of furniture but the place was not at all comfortable. The cottage had three bedrooms, a bathroom and WC but the rooms were dark and cold except for the kitchen, which was always full of flies. There was no garden, and it might as well have been down the town except that there was much more air out there. We were in Larkfield much longer than we expected because Joe had a haemorrhage and we had to stay until he was fit to move. I was doing some research in UCD under Professor Hugh Ryan on the synthesis of vanillin, and going into Earlsfort Terrace every day but, apart from attending Volunteer meetings, Joe was there in the cottage a lot of the time. His illness also meant that he needed a night nurse and luckily we had the use of a couple of rooms in an annexe to the house, a two-storey building across the yard. It was damp because the ridge tiles weren't mortared but it could be used at a pinch as somewhere for the nurse to sleep.

When the Ulster Volunteers had landed rifles in Larne no attempt was made to stop them. No guns were seized and no-one was charged. When I asked Joe about arms, he chuckled and said it had been taken care of. I was in Larkfield with him on Sunday, 26th July, the day of the Howth gun-running, and he was in a fever of excitement. He waited and waited all day for news to come and finally Theo McWeeney arrived. He had run all the way out of town to bring the news and it was altogether disastrous. He had been in O'Connell Street and had heard shots fired on Bachelors' Walk. He heard women wailing on the bridge and had seen dead men. He had also heard people saying that the Volunteers had been fired on and that all the rifles were captured by the English. Joe was bitterly disappointed and upset but too ill to leave the house to check the story. Some hours later Tomás arrived to console him with a true account and to tell him that the guns were safe.

The whole thing was organised by Roger Casement, Alice Stopford Green, Erskine Childers, his wife Molly Osgood, Mary Spring Rice and, at the Dublin end, Bulmer Hobson. Childers and Darrell Figgis bought arms and ammunition in Hamburg which were brought by German tug to the Belgian coast and put on the *Asgard*, a yacht given to Childers by his in-laws. The *Asgard* arrived in Howth with the 900 rifles (second-hand Mausers) and 29,000 rounds of ammunition, and was met by three companies of Volunteers under Hobson, Tomás and Sergeant Bodkin, who was one of the Volunteers' professional trainers. It was unloaded in less than half-an-hour and they began the march back to town.

Assistant Police Commissioner Harrell had called out sections of the police and the military to intercept the Volunteers. Afterwards he said that he felt fully justified, as he thought at the time that the military should have been called out to deal with the Ulster gun-running at Larne. When they met at Clontarf, Harrell said that the Volunteers must allow themselves to be arrested. Tomás refused and Harrell ordered the police to disarm them. To the surprise of both sides, most of the police refused and went back to the sea wall and leant on it (the sea used to come up to this wall at high tide). Harrell told Major Haig to order his soldiers, the Scottish Borderers, to disarm the Volunteers. Haig, instead, ordered them to charge with fixed bayonets. They did so, but the Volunteers stood firm and defended themselves with walking sticks and rifle butts (the Howth guns were not loaded). At the same time the doors of the two army ambulances which were behind the soldiers were opened and a machine gun projected from one of them but it was not fired. Some rifles were wrenched from Volunteers and three of them were slightly wounded. One of the soldiers was shot in the foot with a revolver by a Volunteer, acting against express orders. (Tomás told me that evening that he found he did not mind the sight of real blood at all, though talk of blood had always made him feel faint.)

Tomás and Darrell Figgis went with Harrell to a nearby front garden to argue the case. It was not illegal to own or carry a gun at that time but it was illegal to import arms. Dublin Castle had to prove that any individual gun had been imported illegally, which was impossible. Hobson (who knew that Harrell hadn't a chance in an argument with Tomás) had been drilling all but the front ranks of the Volunteers up and down the road as if they were restless horses. He gradually increased the distance until he brought them to the turn of the road and then round the turn and away. Harrell suddenly realised that the men and the guns were gone. He lost his temper and accused Tomás of cheating him. He said 'This is a disgraceful manoeuvre!' Tomás and Hobson sent the men away by back streets while Major Haig and his soldiers went by the straightest road to the Castle, through Abbey Street and along the quays. The Volunteers hid the rifles everywhere, in walls, in houses, in a field of standing corn belonging to the Christian Brothers in Marino, and then they went by roundabout ways home.

Word had spread fast and from the time they left Howth the Volunteers had been cheered all along the route and the crowds now followed the military into town. Rumour had spread that the soldiers had attacked and killed Volunteers and the crowd jeered and threw stones and banana peels at them. At Bachelors' Walk the Scottish Borderers turned on the crowd without warning, charged with fixed bayonets and fired, killing two men and a woman, James Brennan, Patrick Quinn and Mrs Duffy, and wounding more than 30 people. There were no Volunteers present for any of this. When Tomás came at last to Larkfield we heard the whole story and I heard it again that night from the Volunteer who had shot the soldier in the foot at Howth Road. The next day Joe and Tomás set out in a taxi driven by a Volunteer to collect the rifles from places where they had been hidden all over the city. They were followed by G-men and spies and also by people who were just nosing into other people's business. They came up to Larkfield with a carload of rifles, which they had to take away again and leave in our house in Fitzwilliam Street overnight because they could not get rid of a follower, but the next day they were taken away. On that day also the newspapers were full of interviews given by Darrell Figgis, describing him as the officer in charge of the Volunteers. He had taken part but was not an officer of the Volunteers. Figgis might have been able to make use of this claim to get onto the Committee and for this reason, and to answer wild rumours which were going about, Joe asked Tomás to write a true account of the gunrunning for publication. That account was published in *The Irish Review* in a supplement to the July/August edition.

There was a public funeral for the victims of the shooting on Bachelors' Walk, the first huge, political funeral of our generation, with crowds lining the route, Volunteers in formation behind the coffins, and a volley over the graves. Soldiers were confined to barracks. Songs and slogans appeared overnight. The Irish all over the world telegraphed their sympathy and indignation to John Redmond and the Irish Party, who passed a resolution calling for the arms proclamation to be revoked. The Government said it was under consideration. The Archbishop of Dublin opened a fund for the victims. Dr Louis Byrne, the Coroner, held an inquest. The Government held an inquiry and the verdict was 'unwise conduct' and that Assistant Commissioner Harrell had acted without proper authority. A week after the Howth gunrunning 600 rifles and 20,000 rounds of ammunition were landed safely at Kilcoole from the *Chotah*, a yacht belonging to Sir Thomas Myles, a Dublin surgeon. There was a fantastic immunity for 'seditious activity' on account of the Ulster Volunteers. The Government were pretending that there was civil war between two sections of the Irish and that they were only spectators, to intervene when it went too far, but the manifesto of the Irish Volunteers clearly stated that there was no question of their engaging in conflict with the Ulster Volunteers. War was now on the point of being declared in Europe, and Edward Carson offered the services of the Ulster Volunteers for home defence, but when asked if he would co-operate with the Irish Volunteers, he did not answer.

After the gunrunning very few of the nominees took the trouble to attend meetings and Joe said it made him sick. Many long hours of that summer were taken up in going over the rights and wrongs and internal difficulties of the Volunteer Committee. The conclusion reached in all discussions in our house was that Ireland's honour had to be redeemed. Ireland's spiritual and material needs required strong action, and 'England's difficulty was Ireland's opportunity'. There had been no armed protest against British rule since the Fenians and the approaching war with Germany could be the opportunity.

In August, England declared war on Germany. That made Mimi decide to come back from London, where she had been working as a seamstress in Harrod's and then as a dentist's receptionist. She wanted to try staying in Larkfield, where George was minding the laying of a new sewer down the avenue. Tommy and Rory O'Connor, recently home from Canada, started a small chemical factory, the Larkfield Chemical Company, with the intention of making aspirin and the like, but it was a very small affair. Jack was at school in Clongowes for a year and didn't like it, but he did join the Volunteers there as he said that he knew 'something was going to happen'. Fiona was in Fitzwilliam Street and Ma wanted to send her to France for safety. I pointed out that the war was in France and she said, 'Ah, but the French know how to manage these things'.

Rory O'Connor, possibly at Larkfield, where he and many others visited the Plunketts nearly every day. It was there that he and Tommy Dillon started the Larkfield Chemical Company.

In England war economies were carefully devised so as to preserve the institutions as far as possible. In Ireland the corresponding services were already on such a small scale that any economy wiped them out. A Retrenchment Committee sat in England and advised that in Ireland there should be no loans for public works, drainage, housing etc. Grants in the primary education sector were cut, by £10,000. All grants from central funds for the Poor Law and so on were heavily cut and the workhouse diet was margarine and potatoes. Destitute boys were no longer to be taken by Industrial Schools. The National Library, the National Gallery and the Museum were closed to the public and grants to the Royal Irish Academy and the Academy of Music were stopped. The Agricultural Colleges were already closed. There were no economies in the police or judiciary and real economies, such as the amalgamation of the workhouses, were quashed when proposed. The grant for Irish horse-breeding was stopped but the English one was increased. As part of all this, the teaching of science in secondary schools was stopped and this left Tommy without half of his income.

Redmond made a speech in the House of Commons the day war was declared, offering the Volunteers to defend the shores of Ireland from any invader other than England. The English took it as a declaration of loyalty to England. Many thought he was cleverly using the situation to further the cause of Home Rule. Plenty of Unionists thought the same and resented it. Joe told me that Pearse and Seán MacDiarmada suspected that it was in fact a plan to hand over the

Volunteers to the British War Office to be drafted into the army. They thought that this plan had been present from the time Redmond took control of the Volunteers. The IRB now had to wait until this became plain to break with Redmond. Joe thought it was treason to recruit for the British and Redmond was already recruiting for them. Droves of Irishmen joined up, including many of our friends and acquaintances. Lists of casualties full of Irish names appeared, and were used as an argument that more should go to join them. If we didn't, it meant that we were letting them down and showing we were not proud of them and that was represented as unthinkable.

Joe read every speech made at home and abroad and kept making pictures of the situation in his own mind. Some of these were surprising, such as the length of time the war would last, at least three years, instead of the three months prophesied by the Irish Party. He said to me that if real preparations were made to put the Home Rule Bill into effect at once, Nationalists, who still believed the Bill to be a real Home Rule Bill, would flood into the British Army. Every adult male would be slaughtered at the front line in such numbers that Ireland would be drained dry, leaving us quite hopeless when the war ended, but he said the governing classes in England were quite determined not to give an inch and so the question did not arise. It was bad enough as it was, 300,000 was the minimum number that went. Joe used to make me read national and international papers as well and give him a précis; it all mattered very much to him. In August, Redmond attended a Volunteer parade in Maryborough at which he said that he had several thousand rifles which he would shortly be able to distribute to them and that the Government was about to arm, equip and drill large numbers of Irish Volunteers for the defence of Ireland. In September thousands of these rifles arrived in Dublin and Joe saw one of them. They were Garibaldi rifles, completely useless; the barrels were crooked, no ammunition was supplied with them and none could be got to fit them. Some Volunteers bought them as no one except those who had actually seen them would believe that they were useless. The men were charged £1 each for them and it was said that they cost about five shillings each but Redmond must have lost a lot of money on them all the same.

I was wakened at five a.m. one fine September morning in Larkfield by the curious sound of 6,000 men talking quietly in the open air. They had gathered in the mill yard for the start of a route march and manoeuvres in the Dublin mountains. Tomás led one section and Pearse the other. They were a very mixed crowd, some in morning coats and striped trousers, some in uniform and some in rags. Training was carried out as best as could be done but it was not easy, as a great unwieldy mass of men with little or no time for training had enrolled. The field in Larkfield where Andy Clerkin grazed his horses was also used for drilling and the horses were used to train cavalry. It was a treat to see the Pope Flanagan fall off in his fancy uniform. The recruiters for the British Army had to be watched—Joe told me he was very surprised to learn that recruiters tried to join the Volunteers in the expectation of their being taken over by the War Office. The usual fee for every recruit handed over was 2s 6d but one man I knew got a fee of £1 for each one.

The Larkfield cottage became even more crowded when Eimar O'Duffy moved in. He had been told by his father, who was Dentist-in-Ordinary to the Lord Lieutenant, that he would have to join the British Army or leave the house. His father wanted Eimar to succeed him as a fashionable dentist but Eimar (who had a degree in dentistry) hated the whole thing. His father was afraid that he would be ruined if Eimar did not join up. Eimar had already had two plays performed in the Irish Literary Theatre and wanted to continue to write. His father got into a panic about the war and to prove his loyalty to the British Empire he used to throw up his front window and play 'Tipperary' on the gramophone each time he saw a squad of soldiers going from Portobello to the North Wall. When Eimar refused to join up, his father threw him out of the house and Eimar thought that he would have to sit on the front step and starve but he hadn't the guts to do it. Joe offered him a place so he came out to us. His father didn't approve of Joe; he said that all poets drank to excess and, prior to this, had invited Joe to lunch to test his table manners. Eimar was a bother to us and thought he could stay forever. He did not know how to live in any way except as in his father's big house, with three secretaries and five mechanics. Joe got him a job as a clerk in the Irish Volunteer office and then he did some organising and Joe thought he would leave, but he didn't. He didn't like the food and couldn't understand why we did not live better. Mary jeered him all the time, calling him 'Damn Lucky' or Lamb Ducky', and I could do nothing with her as Joe was too ill to be moved. I had to get a night nurse for Joe so I had to sleep in the annexe across the yard but still Eimar didn't go. So I sent him to Fitzwilliam Street and he didn't like that either. Fiona finally managed to move him out. She said he did not really exist, that she invented him and she had a bad mind. Eimar wrote a book later saying that Joe was mad and I was a pasty-faced ill-made girl, so perhaps I am biased!

Redmond offered to stand beside the Prime Minister, Asquith, at a recruiting meeting in the Mansion House in early September. The IRB and the Citizen Army intended to stop the meeting by taking over the Mansion House. Joe had his first long talk with James Connolly coming away from a planning meeting for this, and he came home very excited, saying that Connolly was the most intellectual and the greatest man he knew in every way. The military somehow got wind of the plan to stop the meeting and had occupied the whole street before they arrived, so that they couldn't get near it. Joe was terribly annoyed but decided to relieve his fury with a joke. He wrote on an envelope 'Herbert Henry Asquith' and gave it to George, who took it through shouting, 'Letter for Mr Asquith! Letter for Mr Asquith!' through all the sentries, down the street, up to the door of the Mansion House, 'Letter for Mr Asquith!' until at the Mansion House they opened the door and he handed it in. What it had in it was a quotation from G. K. Chesterton, 'Your beauty has not left me untouched' and it was signed 'Little Snowdrop'.

When I asked Joe what was going to happen now about Redmond, he told me that they were waiting for him to cross the line. On September 20th Redmond did cross the line. At a Volunteer review in Woodenbridge, he said that the Volunteers should join the British Army. Joe heard from one man who was there that Redmond shouted at the men to go at once, that they were a disgrace, but this was not reported in the newspapers. Joe said this was the final step. It would be impossible to go on acting with Redmond and they must let people know at once that they thought he was wrong. If they did not, men might distrust their judgement and join up. Joe had been ill at this time but IRB members of the Committee came to Larkfield to see him as soon as he was well enough and he agreed with their decisions.

A few days later the members of the original Volunteer Committee passed a manifesto which re-stated their position, signed by 21 of the original Committee members. It was not published in full in the newspapers, which were heavily censored at the time, so Joe put it in the September/November number of *The Irish Review*. Those who did not sign the manifesto and joined Redmond's section of the Volunteers included Maurice Moore, Tom and Larry Kettle, George Walsh and John Gore. Some of these realised afterwards they had made a mistake and soon got on terms with the original Committee again. A campaign of abuse followed with phrases like 'Pro-German Sinn Féiners alive, alive oh!' and so on. Joe told me that he had no idea of how many Volunteers agreed with them and that it would take some time to find out. At first he thought that they had all gone but in a matter of days they found that they were not alone. The split created two types of Nationalists forming companies and drilling; our group, the Irish Volunteers, secretly controlled by the IRB, and the far bigger National Volunteers, controlled by the Irish Party, which was regarded by the British Government as an excellent recruiting resource for the British Army. Because the Irish Volunteers almost went out of existence at the split, they were thought to be absolutely negligible by the authorities. This meant that in spite of the war and the Defence of the Realm Act (DORA) they were able to continue to organise and drill fairly openly. A completely new method of recruiting Volunteers was started on the IRB lines, with men bringing in those they trusted. Whenever this plan was not followed there was trouble.

About 10,000 men were found to remain in our group, and behind the scenes plans for an armed rising were taking shape. Arms became very important and guns began to come in more freely. Joe made me carry an automatic in a holster. He said if I carried it all the time I would not need it but if I didn't, I would not have it when it was wanted. I carried it nearly all the time in a holster under my jacket. I was afraid at first that it would be seen when I was going about my business. I was very little in the college because Joe was so ill, and I did not wear it there. Some of the boys carried guns but I did not know any girl who did. After a while I did not bother about it. The accidents usually happened to people who came out to Larkfield to practise shooting, not to people who carried guns all the time. Joe got a Mauser automatic, accurate up to 1,000 yards, and loved to take it apart and put all the little interlocking parts together again. Charlie Lawlor, who had a shop on Fownes Street where he sold sporting materials and sporting guns, used the shop to bring in a lot of guns for the Volunteers. (He was killed by Black-and-Tans on a tram in Dame Street in 1921.) Many guns were bought from British soldiers; the first prosecution of a soldier for stealing rifles to sell was in December 1914. Joe told me one day that an officer in Beggar's Bush barracks had given him his name and offered to get arms for him. After a good deal of thinking of ways to use this offer without being drawn into a trap, Joe did not keep the appointment with this man.

The Irish Volunteer Committee had also been left in possession of the offices in Kildare Street. The members of the Committee who had had experience of John D. Nugent's tactics thought it necessary to protect the office with barbed wire and Joe agreed with them, but there was no physical attack on them, the others were too busy. However, a horde of spies descended on Kildare Street—up to now they had not been quite sure who to spy on. A husband and wife team had been hanging round young Nationalists for several years; they had even founded some organisations like 'The Irish Self-Government Alliance' as a front and they belonged to every real and phoney organisation there was. Some were very phoney, making it obvious that the promoters were spies and *agents provocateurs*. We had been watching these two people for some time; they had been asking curious questions and would not be put off. The wife was the first sympathiser into Kildare Street where Joe came in and found her telling Tomás how right he was. He did not know whether Tomás knew she was a spy so he kicked his ankle a couple of times until Tomás said, 'What are you kicking me for?' Joe was mad and when she had gone away asked him what she had said. 'To tell you the truth,' said Tomás, 'I wasn't listening to what she was saying, I was watching the flea that was crawling up her blouse!' This couple continued their activities and I found the man in Larkfield one Sunday morning and he was most offensive when I asked him to go. In Black-and-Tan times he used his young children to gather information from their schoolmates about their fathers.

There were six full-time organisers for the Volunteers, Seán MacDiarmada, Liam Mellowes, Alfred Monaghan, Ginger O'Connell, Ernest Blythe and Herbert Moore Pim. Pim was a Belfast bank clerk, a Unionist who converted to Nationalism and Catholicism and left his wife and family to come to Dublin, where he was jailed for three months for a 'seditious speech'. He wrote a

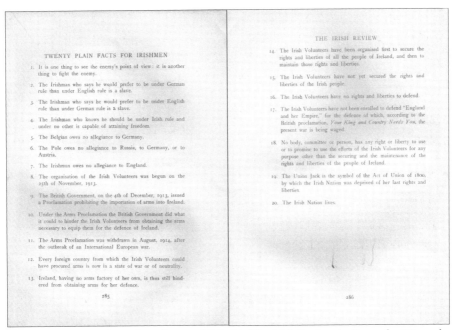

TWENTY PLAIN FACTS FOR IRISHMEN

1. It is one thing to see the enemy's point of view: it is another thing to fight the enemy.

2. The Irishman who says he would prefer to be under German rule than under English rule is a slave.

3. The Irishman who says he would prefer to be under English rule than under German rule is a slave.

4. The Irishman who knows he should be under Irish rule and under no other is capable of attaining freedom.

5. The Belgian owes no allegiance to Germany.

6. The Pole owes no allegiance to Russia, to Germany, or to Austria.

7. The Irishman owes no allegiance to England.

8. The organisation of the Irish Volunteers was begun on the 25th of November, 1913.

9. The British Government, on the 4th of December, 1913, issued a Proclamation prohibiting the importation of arms into Ireland.

10. Under the Arms Proclamation the British Government did what it could to hinder the Irish Volunteers from obtaining the arms necessary to equip them for the defence of Ireland.

11. The Arms Proclamation was withdrawn in August, 1914, after the outbreak of an International European war.

12. Every foreign country from which the Irish Volunteers could have procured arms is now in a state of war or of neutrality.

13. Ireland, having no arms factory of her own, is thus still hindered from obtaining arms for her defence.

285

THE IRISH REVIEW

14. The Irish Volunteers have been organised first to secure the rights and liberties of all the people of Ireland, and then to maintain those rights and liberties.

15. The Irish Volunteers have not yet secured the rights and liberties of the Irish people.

16. The Irish Volunteers have no rights and liberties to defend.

17. The Irish Volunteers have not been enrolled to defend "England and her Empire," for the defence of which, according to the British proclamation, *Your King and Country Needs You*, the present war is being waged.

18. No body, committee or person, has any right or liberty to use or to promise to use the efforts of the Irish Volunteers for any purpose other than the securing and the maintenance of the rights and liberties of the people of Ireland.

19. The Union Jack is the symbol of the Act of Union of 1800, by which the Irish Nation was deprived of her last rights and liberties.

20. The Irish Nation lives.

286

'Twenty Plain Facts for Irishmen' was published in The Irish Review *in September/November 1914, and copies were seized as a result. The magazine which, as Joe said 'was broke anyway', did not re-appear.*

ballad in jail, 'I tread the ground that felons tread', which was printed on Joe's handpress. When he got out of jail after his three months, Tomás brought him out to lunch in Larkfield, because he thought he was upset. He was upset—he said that he was disgraced forever, and he meant it literally, by having been in jail. Joe and Tomás tried to convince him that, on the contrary, he was now among the ranks of heroes, but he would have none of it. He went back to his wife and family, his job, his religion and his politics shortly afterwards. Another time, a young man in a great state of excitement came to Larkfield saying that the Little Flower, St Theresa, had told him to lead an army of ten thousand against Dublin Castle. Tommy had to bring him to his home in Mount Street where, he said, they all seemed a bit mad.

Censorship was now in full swing and even *Scissors and Paste*, which was entirely composed of cuttings from other papers, was stopped at once. *Nationality* survived for a while and the printers did their best, but the little penny papers such as *The Spark* were the only thing left. *The Spark* was printed by the printers after work and the owner was named as Marie Perolz. I think the Labour paper was protected by being printed in Belfast. When Joe published the manifesto of the Irish Volunteers and 'Twenty Plain Facts for Irishmen' in the September/November number of *The Irish Review* I told him that the censor would suppress the *Review*, but he said 'What harm? We're broke anyway' and in fact Manico gave him no more tick. They had had to give him the bill of

*Moya Plunkett was put off joining the Sisters of
Mercy and training as a nurse. She ended up
with the Sacred Heart nuns instead. She was, as
Gerry put it, 'always too biddable'. This
photograph was taken in 1906.*

sale anyway to get Tomás' *Lyrical Poems* published. The *Review* was not suppressed
under DORA but all the copies of it were seized because of 'Twenty Plain Facts'.
During that September Joe and I moved back to Marlborough Road. From now
on Joe's health got rather worse. Whenever he had a temperature, perhaps a third
of the time, he had to stay in bed.

My sister Moya decided that she could not go on living at home anymore
and made up her mind that she would have to go into a convent; she was just
at a dead end. She hoped to find a place where she would be of some use and
sensibly enough went to see the nuns in St Vincent's hospital to ask about
joining the Sisters of Mercy and training as a nurse. They said they would
accept her and she had everything arranged to go in when she made the unfortunate mistake of going to see a former friend of hers, Father Joey Wrafter,
in Gardiner Street Church to tell him of her decision. He had been her con-
fessor at some previous stage and he claimed that since she had not appointed
another one, he still was. He ordered her to give up the idea of going into St
Vincent's and to enter instead the order of the Sacred Heart, a teaching order,
in Roehampton in London. Her eyesight was still a big problem from the
time when she ran a stick into her eye and she had been reduced to such a
nervous state by Ma that she felt she could not study. I had been trying to get
her to do the UCD Matric and come to College but she would not try it and
had no heart to do it.

Moya was always too biddable and she did what Father Wrafter told her to do. She applied to the Sacred Heart nuns and was accepted. She had been left two houses on Elgin Road by Uncle Jack, who was her godfather, a share in the other houses which we all inherited from him (which Ma, his executor, never passed on to us) and she also stood to inherit a share, after Ma's life interest, in quite a number of other houses. Ma persuaded Moya to assign all of this to her but Moya told me that she never paid her for any of it. All she got in return was the price of her dowry into Roehampton, which was something like £200, far less than the value of the houses. Moya also needed about £150 for her nun's outfits and she couldn't get the money from Ma so she asked Grandpa Plunkett, who gave it to her. It cost every bit of the £150 and Ma complained because it meant she couldn't scrounge any of it from Moya. As a result of her problems Moya had very little secondary education and was slow at reading. In Roehampton they put her into some kind of training for teachers and when she was told to write an essay on Wordsworth she thought this was very stupid and said she did not like Wordsworth. They allowed her to choose for herself so she chose Blake, with whom she was really familiar, and wrote a good essay on him. Based on this they wanted her to go and do a degree and told her to study for the London Matric. This included a lot of subjects with which she was absolutely unfamiliar and after three months' study, which she told me was quite hopeless, she failed miserably, but she had to stay on to make the best of the whole thing.

Towards the end of 1914, just as *The Irish Review* was being forced, financially and politically, to end, Joe and Tomás started a theatre in the Hardwicke Hall. When Ma bought the hall in 1910 a builder offered her an extra £100 for it after the auction, but she was so delighted with the bargain and very pleased to find that someone else was after it that she wouldn't sell. She had no idea what to do with the hall. Little use of it was made in the first two years, then the Dun Emer Guild took over the rooms at the back when they had to move out of the house in Dundrum. We held a few dances in it and it was used for some charity variety shows, then Joe discovered that it had had a stage at one time and most of the timbers were still there, so everyone at home asked Ma to put it up again. Mimi, Joe, Kitty and Gracie McCormack and their friends had always loved acting and had been in various amateur plays—Sunday night in Dun Emer had always been the time for Charades. The eighteenth-century Hardwicke Street building had been a convent, a Methodist teacher training college and a Jesuit house and the hall, which had been a chapel, had a warren of rooms over it and a couple of big rooms at the back. Behind the building was a large yard and covered passage. There was a storage cellar and a lot of little rooms upstairs (probably the nuns' cells) which were used as dressing-rooms. The stage area was quite roomy and there was even a green room. The hall, which has now been demolished, held about 90 people and there was a sort of balcony high up at the back which had been the entrance to the 'priest's hole', a hiding place dating from the Poor Clare convent of Penal days.

Ma threw herself into the fun, she was always at her best when she was really busy. She had the stage put back up, very expensive velvet curtains made and got a lot of theatre seats. Strahan's were having an auction of things that were cluttering up their storage space, including carved and gilded large ornaments, serpents and a centrepiece which they had commissioned for the 1884 Exhibition. These made some kind of proscenium arch and made the stage real. The only bother was that the side wall was straight onto the street, a noisy slum, the place was very shabby and it had a bad entrance—up three steps and straight into the hall. The lighting and curtains often failed and there was a rather musty smell. Ma loved theatricals of any kind and helped with enthusiasm, although her tastes and ours were entirely different. Her idea of a really good play was Townley's eighteenth-century farce *High Life Below Stairs* and in this, most people at the time would have agreed with her; still, we were encouraged and helped and because she loved the excitement it was comparatively easy to get money from her for production costs.

For us the excitement was the influence of the Moscow Arts Theatre, which was beginning to make itself felt by a good number of people in Ireland, especially in our crowd. Tomás and Joe were very keen to put on Tchekov, Ibsen and other modern playwrights in Dublin and they frequently talked about the possibility of this. Tomás had said, 'We'll have to find a patron with money'. When he came to the house one day and told Joe he had found such a patron Joe didn't take him seriously at first but Tomás insisted. He told Joe that Edward Martyn was crazy about Ibsen and the Russian dramatists and brought him off to meet him. Joe knew who Edward was; he had read *The Heather Field* and thought it good, although he changed his mind about this later when he had more experience of production. Edward wrote an article for the *Review* with ideas for an international Irish theatre so similar to those Tomás and Joe had that they took him up with enthusiasm. A partnership was arranged between Edward Martyn, Tomás and Joe to run a company. Joe was to contribute the premises, the Hardwicke Hall, Edward was to pay the gas bill and the producer's salary and Tomás was to supervise production. The producer was Tomás's brother, John MacDonagh who, like Tomás, was an excellent actor; he had just come back to Ireland after years of singing and acting with touring companies in Europe and the USA. He acted well and had a good knowledge of production. They called the company 'The Irish Theatre' but it has been referred to constantly as 'Edward Martyn's Theatre'. The prospects were rosy. Tomás thought he could manage Edward Martyn and talk him into agreeing with him, and indeed he very often did.

Tomás had come across Edward Martyn after he parted brass rags with William Yeats over the Abbey Theatre 'peasant plays'. Martyn had remained friends with his cousin, George Moore, for some time after and they had discussed starting a theatre more representative of all aspects of life until George published his autobiographical *Ave atque Vale* (*Hail and Farewell*), causing

EDWARD MARTYN

"HAVING A WEEK OF IT" IN PARIS.

GRACE PLUNKETT

Grace Gifford's wicked cartoon of Edward Martyn (an 'old, fat, shy, bachelor') resisting temptation in Paris.

terrible offence to Edward in his description of him. Edward was tall, red-faced and bald, with a grey, fishy, googly eye, thick-lensed glasses and a rambling walk, an old, fat, shy bachelor. He said, 'I don't hate women, I think they're ridiculous—just look at them!'

George Moore's portrayal of him in *Hail and Farewell* made him frantic and he became obsessed with the idea of revenge by exposing Moore to the same kind of derision. He wrote a play about Moore called *The Dream Physician* in which he called him 'George Moon' and characterised him as a ridiculous person who wore a corset. This was the first play produced by the Irish Theatre and it opened on November 2nd 1914 , to an audience of about 100, not in the Hardwicke Hall, but in Madame Rock's little theatre in Upper O'Connell Street, where she had a dancing school, because the Hardwicke Hall was being re-wired and was not quite ready. The play was not a success but Edward was delighted with it and eager to go on.

He was much older than the others, inflexible and self-centred and thought that Tomás and Joe were negligible; he was the maestro and wanted to do his own plays first and did not see that even if they had been better plays, Tomás and Joe might like some variety. He had had plays staged by the Irish Literary Theatre but although they appear to be plays when read, the plots are too slight and Joe, Tomás and John said that they didn't like them, that they were almost impossible to produce successfully. As time went on, Edward got meaner and made more difficulties. I believe he lost some money in Russia and France during the war. He did pay for a frock for Una O'Connor (Agnes McGlade) when she played the lead in *The Cherry Orchard* and *Uncle Vanya* and although she was a really good, professional actress, the only payment she accepted was that dress. John MacDonagh played George Moon in *The Dream Physician* and Edward Martyn wanted him to put on the corset on stage but John refused and put it on a chair instead. After John was imprisoned in 1916, his sister, a nun, insisted on unpacking his trunk which was in the Oakley Road house. When she found the corset she was shocked and would not listen to any explanation whatever.

At that time theatre groups, intellectual and literary ones, were always slaughtered by the newspaper critics. The worst was Jacques of the *Evening Herald*. He had been a sports reporter and hated Russian and Scandinavian plays. His real name was J. A. Power and he became a good friend of mine when he was editing the *Connacht Tribune* thirty years later but he was not very steady in the head. Some people, however, were very encouraging, among whom must be mentioned Joe Holloway, who came to all the productions and kept a record of them in his notebooks. He spoke kindly every time but always left at ten thirty, it was his one rule. In his collection are also many of Grace Gifford's marvellous theatrical cartoons. I met Grace, who was Tomás's sister-in-law, in the MacDonaghs' flat in Baggot Street when Donagh was a small baby. Tomás disliked her very much, or perhaps it would be more accurate to say that he thought very little of her and did not trust her an inch. Joe thought the same at the time. I do not think that I have ever met anyone who put on more airs and graces—she patronised all other women, she thought anything serious was stuffy and dull and then presumed that we were all like that. She was a dreadful bore.

Sometimes there were only a dozen people in the audience at the Irish Theatre, but then the Abbey Theatre played to half-empty houses for years and their notices were just as bad. Anything native was fair game. Synge's *Playboy* was labelled indecent and obscene but Joe was delighted with it, it was just his brand of humour, and Tomás agreed with him but did not like the row. I didn't dare to go to it, the consequences from Ma, who only knew of it as a 'scandal', would have been intolerable. Even the *Playboy* did not fill the Abbey, it was O'Casey who did it first.

Over the next year and a bit there were probably ten Irish Theatre pro-grammes, each playing for a few nights including Tchekov's *The Bear, The Proposal, Swan Song, Uncle Vanya* and *The Cherry Orchard* and Ibsen's *Pillars of Society* and *An Enemy of the People*. Pearse got the hall for an Irish play and there were short plays by Eimear O'Duffy and Tomás MacDonagh. *The Dance of Osiris* was an experimental one-act play by Joe (under the name of 'Luke Killeen') to try out some Gordon Craig ideas on a small scale. My great friend, Kitty McCormack, was the dancer—I wasn't involved, I had enough other things to do at the time, but I did the hieroglyphs for the temple pillars in *The Dance of Osiris;* the pillars were made of hessian with hoops inside and quite effective. Regular members of the company were Kitty, her sister Gracie, the three elder Reddins, George and Mimi, Willie Pearse, Andrew Dillon, Joseph MacDonagh, Helena Moloney, Columba O'Carroll and, of course, Tomás and John MacDonagh, who could be very impressive, and Joe, who was a very good character actor. Martin Murphy, the stage carpenter of the Gaiety, came every time to help with stage settings and Bertie Smyllie (later Editor of *The Irish Times*) took part in one play. The complete record of their productions is in Joe Holloway's notebooks. Ernest Boyd knew all this when he wrote his book *Drama in Ireland*, which came out in 1916, but he told me he had left it out because his publisher would not publish the book if it contained Tomás's and Joe's names. I did not altogether believe him.

8 Guns and money 1915

AFTER CHRISTMAS JOE TOLD ME that he might be going to Germany on IRB business. This was his first really important task for the IRB and I assumed it was connected with arms and the talk of a rising. When the war started Roger Casement had decided to go to Berlin, because he knew of Redmond's pro-British decision and thought something drastic would have to be done. Joe told me at the time that Casement had no authorisation from anyone to go to Germany and had asked for none. He told me that the letters from Casement had been unsatisfactory and that the fears of the IRB Supreme Council about him seemed to be justified. Casement had told the German authorities what he thought was necessary for Ireland, including a huge invasion force, and they had been unable to agree to his suggestions. Since Joe was free to leave home, knew French and was a friend and admirer of Casement's, the IRB decided to send him and pay his expenses. He taught me the cipher which he would employ in any letters he wrote. It was a variation of the well-known diplomatic cipher which depended on a key word order. As a general plan, letters would be sent to our cousin, Aidan McCabe, and signed 'James Malcolm'. Aidan would pass them to me and I would bring them to Seán MacDiarmada or, failing him, to Pearse. I could ask de Valera or Batt O'Connor to bring messages but they did not know of Joe's journey.

Joe spread it about that he was going to Jersey for his health at Easter, and we heard afterwards that Dublin Castle opinion was that he had grown tired of the Volunteers and was making his health the excuse to leave them. He told Ma that he was going but she had not the slightest idea of what he was doing or the danger of it. All she cared about was that she would not have to pay his expenses. What he told her was that he was being sent on Volunteer business to the Continent and that he might have to go over the frontier into Germany. He said he would be passing through Florence and told her that she must say absolutely nothing about it to anyone. I asked him why on God's earth he had done such a thing. He said that he thought it would be worse if he didn't, that she would be rooting around trying to find out and that she had lost interest after she was told. On the other hand, I don't think he realised how stupid she was until he found out that she had written to Mrs Dunne in Florence telling her that Joe was going there. It never occurred to her that, being wartime, among other things, the letter might be opened by the Dublin Castle censor. When I asked her why she had done it she bridled

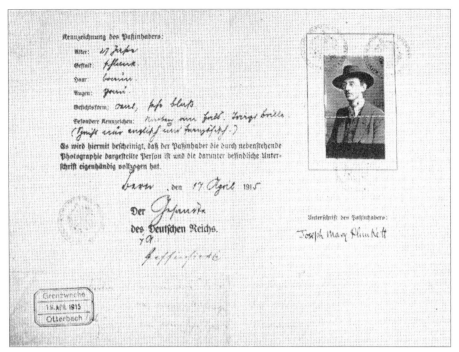

Joe Plunkett's German passport, April 1915. He spent three months in Berlin negotiating for arms, with Roger Casement's help, on behalf of the Irish Republican Brotherhood. He met the German Chancellor, several Ministers and Army officers, and the outcome was the shipload of arms, in the Aud, *which, arriving too early for the Rising, was pursued by the British and scuppered by the German captain.*

and said, 'Can I not write to my old friend about my son?' and she carried off her letter and posted it under my eyes.

My brother Jack has the original of Joe's diary of the journey and Joe told me about it when he came back. The first stage was by London and Paris to San Sebastian and thence to Barcelona, Genoa and Florence. He started on St Patrick's Day, 1915, by sailing to Liverpool. His original idea had been to go on by the Booth Line to Lisbon but when he got to Liverpool, he found that the Booth Line sailings to Spain had been cancelled, so he had to arrange to go through France to San Sebastian instead. On his way through London he got a passport and a visa for Spain from Ambrose Aliaga Kelly. His passport was checked everywhere, his luggage and person searched and all his letters read. In Paris he had twelve hours to spare so he went and found James Stephens and they talked for hours of people and ideas. He arrived in San Sebastian with a temperature and had to spend a week in bed before going on to Saragossa but, in spite of being ill, he was really enjoying himself. He was in Barcelona for Palm Sunday, got a visa for Italy from the Italian consul next day and left on a boat for Genoa on Tuesday, 30th March.

On Wednesday a shot was fired across the bows and the ship was boarded by officers from two French torpedo boats. In the middle of the next night they were stopped again by a French warship and examined and searched. He told me when he came home that half the passengers were German reservists going home, and one of them tried to pass by calling attention to another who was a much more important person and was nearly caught. One of them made friends with Joe over the incident and they travelled together for a day or two. By Easter Monday he was in Florence and ill again. He contacted the Dunne family, spent a few days with them and renewed other acquaintances in the city while waiting for word from Germany about the rest of the journey. From Charlie Dunne he learned how to spot the Italian version of G-men. He bought C. G. Leland's *Legends of Florence,* wrote a cipher poem in mock Latin in the front of it and afterwards sent it to me from Germany. He changed his name to James Malcolm as soon as he got word to go ahead to Germany.

He went to Lausanne via Milan and on to Berne where he contacted a German agent, the Argentinian consul, who was credited with acting for all sides. Then he met the German ambassador and had to wait for confirmation from him before travelling on to Germany. This took two weeks and in that time he grew a beard as a kind of disguise. He got a passport for Germany as 'Johann Peter' of San Francisco and a photograph taken for it, having destroyed every photograph of himself that he could find before he started on the journey. He wrote to Aidan McCabe, calling himself his 'cousin, James Malcolm', and he got a through train to Berlin. There were no sleepers and he says in the diary 'Train and train all day and night, Big towns and soldiers and soldiers and soldiers'; he was terribly tired when he reached Berlin. He went straight to the German Foreign Office and Count Von Wedel, whom he met there, rang up Roger Casement so Joe met him at once. Casement was not at all well and was worrying himself sick.

Casement's going to Berlin in the autumn of 1914 had caused a tremendous sensation and there was a good deal of publicity about his activities. Since he retired from the British diplomatic service he had been writing and speaking against the partition of Ireland and in October, 1914, he wrote an open letter from New York, published in the *Irish Independent*, against John Redmond's recruiting appeal. A second letter in stronger terms was censored out. The British Foreign Office wrote to him saying that he was liable for English service but he had resigned from the service. This was why, when he left for Berlin, he took pains to disguise himself and took Adler Christiansen with him as his servant, to carry his papers. They were not yet looking for him, however, and so he passed through to Berlin. It looked at times as if some kind of a trap was being laid for Casement and when Joe had a chance to make an estimate of Adler Christiansen afterwards he began to think that he was reporting on him to the British Government. Anyway, by this time there was a queer flavour of deceit and trouble. Every different variety of story has been told about Casement's going to Germany—he was not sent by Clan na

Gael, as John Devoy simply hated him, and he was not sent by the Dublin IRB either. He had realised that it must be done at once to be successful and Joe said that someone would have had to go so that it would be known that Ireland was not on England's side, that was what mattered, and we were very fortunate to have someone with such good standing as Casement. Joe met Christiansen with Casement in Berlin, as he was in continual attendance on Casement as a servant and messenger. Casement was paying for his training as a photographer in the Technische Hochschule. Joe said he had a curiously immobile face, not easy to decipher, and he did not allow Christiansen to be told his real name, although Casement was convinced he was reliable. The fact that it was discussed at all implies a doubt, but Casement said he had proofs of his fidelity.

A detailed plan was worked out between Joe, Casement and the Foreign Office officials over the next six weeks. Count Georg von Wedel arranged Joe's interviews. Count Nodolny, of the German General Staff, was the man with whom he had the most discussions, and among others involved were Captain Boehm and Richard Meyer, brother of Kuno Meyer. He told me that he had one long meeting with Von Bethmann-Hollweg, the Chancellor, which was perfectly satisfactory. The Germans had had doubts of Casement's credentials and distrusted his temperament. Joe told me when he came home that he and Von Bethmann-Hollweg came to terms at once on first principles without any difficulty. The groundwork for the agreement had been laid by Casement and now that the Germans found that the official IRB demands were reasonable, there was no difficulty and they agreed to them at once. Germany was to send a cargo of arms to Ireland at approximately Easter, 1916, on a date to be confirmed later. It was too early to make a final decision as a lot might happen to change it. A German offensive in the war was planned for the beginning of May, 1916, but in fact did not come off until October, 1916. If it fitted with the plans of the German Government, a skeleton force of officers and trained men were to come with the arms.

Joe, as the accredited IRB member, was delegated to draw up the written agreement with Germany, but he did discuss it with Casement. Casement was not a member of the IRB because of a scruple he had about oaths; having taken the oath of allegiance for the British diplomatic service, he did not think it right to take the IRB oath on top of that. He had a most unrealistic conviction that Germany should desire to give Ireland her freedom from the highest idealistic motives, and when he found later that they had no such motives his opinion of Germany dropped to the bottom. He said 'these people may free the seas but it will be by mistake'. Joe was a realist about international politics and knew what we required and exactly what effect revolt in Ireland would have on English strategy. He also knew that the German Foreign Office was quite ignorant of Irish affairs as, for instance, in the German hopes of civil war in Ulster, and since the deal Lord Carson and the Loyalists had made with them had fallen through, they were chary of putting any trust in Irishmen. Casement was convinced that the Volunteers could put up no fight without German leadership and was afraid that if Germany led the Irish to victory they would claim Ireland as part of the German Empire and we would have exchanged King Log for King Stork. Joe thought that Irish, rather than German, leadership would do better and that the German Army would make hopeless mistakes. He would have liked some trained officers and men but not an army, and he thought that a determined German offensive in France at the same time as an Irish rising would tear the English in two. Joe told me all this after he came home. Casement insisted on coming home at Easter, 1916, because he thought that the Volunteers were relying on German forces, but in fact they were only relying on the guns and these were sent to Ireland.

Joe told me that as 'Johann M. Peter' he had not allowed anyone under the rank of ambassador to know his real name and apparently no-one guessed his real identity. Berlin was swarming with spies, mostly Canadians pretending to be Americans. He finished writing the agreement on Wednesday 5th May and brought it with a covering letter to Count Nodolny in the Foreign Office, where it was signed by both sides.

Before Joe arrived in Germany, Casement had persuaded the German Government to allow him to start the Irish Brigade to fight for Ireland when the opportunity came. All the Irish soldiers the Germans had captured were in the Limburg prisoner-of-war camp near Frankfurt and the Irish Brigade was based there. In May, Joe and Casement went to the Limburg camp with a group of people including Captain Michael Kehoe, Quinlisk or 'Quin' (who later tried to betray Michael Collins to the British in 1919), and Joseph Dowling, members and organisers of the Irish Brigade. Joe had met them already and he told me that he had been quite hopeful, because of Casement's account, that a big enough number of Irish prisoners would join the Irish Brigade, but he soon changed his mind. Casement had not been in Ireland when the war started so he did not realise that, apart from the small number who joined the army because they thought Redmond had made a bargain about Home Rule, a small section who genuinely thought Germany wrong to invade Belgium, and the Unionists or Imperialists, the vast majority went because it was a job with a good allowance for the wife and family to live on. The number who joined the Irish Brigade therefore, was ridiculously small. The Germans had had great hopes of it at first and were bitterly disappointed. Joe told me that one of them told him that a real Irish Brigade would have been worth an army division to Germany. Bertie Smyllie, who was a prisoner in Limburg and had once acted in the Hardwicke Street theatre, recognised Joe when he addressed the Limburg prisoners about the brigade. Joe swore him to secrecy and Bertie told me about it later but gave me no details.

Most of Joe's time now was spent hanging around, waiting for things to happen, and he found it boring and frustrating. He offered the Germans a design for a plane; it was my brother Jack who told me about this. Joe's idea was for two narrow planes, mounted in parallel a short distance apart. Joe and Jack made a version of it and it behaved like a glider with very slow descent. The idea was to reverse the process and create lift. One of the German aeronautical men told Joe it would not work but they did try it out later and he was right, it didn't work! There was a lot of talking done with the group of people Joe was with and many discussions about the war. Joe began recording numbers of casualties from reports in the papers in his diary: '19th May, 174,000 . . . 20th May, 10,000 today . . . 21st May, 194,000, A large ship lost. Another large ship 4,800 prisoners, Friday 28th May 12,000 . . '

Joe says in the diary 'I made a talk-song (the Cuil Fhionn). Great heat.' Part of his diary entry for 24th May reads:

> If there is one thing about you more beautiful than another
> It is the back of your neck
> I am almost afraid to write of it
> It is so beautiful;
> Years ago—before you were grown up
> It was hidden by your hair.
> But I used to catch glimpses of it
> And go crazy;
> I used to walk behind you on purpose
> And feel like a criminal
> And I would think
> 'Some day she will put her hair up
> And everybody will be able to see'
> And I was horribly jealous
> And I swore.

He began writing the diary in not very good Irish from May 1st, giving new and sometimes more complicated names and ciphers to people and places. For example, Adler Christiansen became 'Iolar Mac Giolla Chríost', Quinlisk, Kehoe and Dowling became 'Trúir' and the Irish Brigade at Limburg became 'Fianna Fáil'. Among the many he met and talked with were Herr von Langwerth, Professor Schiemann, Dr Chatterton-Hill and Virendarath Chattopadhyaya. On Wednesday 16th June he was at Nodolny's office where he got his passport. On Thursday 17th he records '3 months today. At no 76 (the Foreign Office) in the morning. Waiting 1 hour. George Wedel, Richard Meyer and OR and attendant, secretary. (with Casement)' and this is where the diary ends. He left the diary in the Foreign Office in Berlin when he left for home. It was found there, almost miraculously, along with other documents and letters of his, by Gertrude Bannister, Casement's cousin, when she

*Sir Roger Casement was fifty in 1914 when, after a remarkable career as a
humanitarian in the British colonial service, he went to Germany to recruit Irish
prisoners of war and to buy arms for the Rising. He was hanged for treason in
August 1916.*

was going through documents after 1918. They were marked to be returned to
Joe's father with permission and this she did. Ma stuck them in the back of a
desk which she used but which actually belonged to Jack, and Jack found
them again when he recovered his desk.

Joe had to wait until he got instructions from the Military Council in
Dublin to go home again, so he and Casement went out to the Grunewald to
stay and he was there the best part of a month. I believe that before leaving
Germany he told Casement that he must stay there and Casement agreed to
it, for the time being at any rate. It was impossible for him to find any place
to be safe except in Germany. Casement was tubercular, very lonely and both
his mind and body were in a miserable condition. Joe admired and trusted
him but he thought that he was too restless, nervous and inclined to worry
himself sick to stay in Berlin until the war was over, as he would now have to

Pádraig Pearse's cottage in Rosmuc, County Galway, where Gerry, Jack and Fiona spent a happy holiday in 1915. The roof leaked, because, it was said, Pearse had been cheated by a thatcher with beautiful Irish. The photograph shows Father Aloysius OFM Cap. and some friends. He ministered to Pearse and MacDonagh before their executions but they were shot without a priest being present. Father Aloysius protested and was allowed to attend James Connolly at his execution.

do. It seemed incredible that he had reached Berlin safely in the first place; it was too much to hope that he would be able to leave it and find some other safe place to stay.

While Joe was away I saw a newspaper report that a tall man with a black beard was with Casement in the Limburg camp and had made a speech to the Irish prisoners urging them to join Casement's brigade. At this time I had heard nothing from Joe but took it for granted that he reached Germany because I had heard nothing. I was afraid that this man must be Joe and that he would in some way be identified if he took part in Casement's public activities. He had told me before he left that he intended to come home, that he would not stay in Germany. If he was identified he would be caught, if jailed, he would surely die. The *Legends of Florence* arrived in May and I was supposed to take it to Seán MacDiarmada but he had just been arrested for a statement which, incidentally, he did not make. When I heard about his

arrest, I went over to Eoin MacNeill's house to see if he had any news. MacNeill told me that all Seán's papers had been got out of the way before the detectives had arrived to search his room. He told me that he knew Joe was in Germany and what he was doing there and apparently he had no objection to it. I then brought the message to Pearse in St Enda's and he took me into his study to look at it and see if it was the message he was waiting for. His sister Maggie kept hopping in and out of the room, madly trying to find out what was going on, but Pearse stopped speaking while she was in the room. She left the door wide open each time and each time he got up and closed it before speaking again. He was a most impressive person. I would have done whatever he told me to do because of his authority, not, as in Seán MacDiarmada's case, because I loved him.

When Joe was on his way back John MacDonagh met him in London on a tram and said with his usual stutter, 'I don't believe you were in Jersey at all,

Plunkett, I think you were in Germany', at the top of his voice, for a joke. Joe nearly jumped out of his skin.

Joe had told me before he left that Pearse said I could have his cottage in Rosmuc for a holiday, so in June, while Joe was still in Germany, I made arrangements with Pearse and left for Rosmuc with Fiona and Jack. On the way to the Broadstone station Fiona collided with a donkey cart and the back wheel of her bike was buckled but she still managed to cycle over our bit of country. When we got to the station a porter meanly made such difficulty about getting my bike out of the cloakroom that I lost the train and had to wait for the next one, so Jack and Fiona had to wait for me in Galway. I had never seen Galway before but George and Jack knew it well, having cycled across Ireland several times with their friends. They used to stop at farms along the way but were never allowed to pay for the hospitality; they paid what they could with music and songs. Frank and Gertie Connolly were friends of ours and their parents were the teachers in Gortmore, in the neck of the Rosmuc peninsula. Mrs Connolly sent a sidecar to meet us at Maam Cross to take our bundles of luggage. She also had a huge fire in the hearth at the cottage and some pots and pans and a pot oven. I had not thought of these, I presumed they would be there. I was told to bring bedclothes but no other information. We were very tired and hungry and the sandwiches we had brought with us were soon gone. We were twenty-four hours without a meal and there wasn't even bread to be got and when we did find some, it was very poor. We forgot to cover the fire so it went out but after a day or two we were better organised. Jack soon got very good with the fire and I got into a routine of making two cakes of bread, brown and white, every second day which were better than any I have made since. Local girls brought us milk and chickens and we got eggs and cocoa from O'Malley's shop and they also gave us baskets of rock bream. I made stews of chicken and rice and once a week a man brought meat. We had plenty. There is a little lake in front of the house and Jack brought it up in buckets. Willie Pearse had tried to teach Pearse to swim on this lake by tying a rope around him and keeping him afloat while he gave him advice from the shore but they laughed so much that they didn't make much progress.

A friend of mine from Dublin, Nancy O'Halloran, joined us in the cottage for a while and Frank Connolly spent a lot of time with us. We walked with him up the hill and found the little lake in the pocket of the hill with the trout rising. In the stream coming from the lake was an eel with a trout in its mouth. Frank took the trout from the eel and the eel bit him. Another time we cycled down to the point and the little pool of a harbour where we bought báinín in Conroy's shop which I made into jackets for us. Lena Rafferty came down from Dublin when Nancy O'Halloran left and we tried to get to Aran in a boat. It had a cargo of straw which was too light so it did not rise well to the waves. The main sheet broke and before the men could mend it with a crios we had drifted in too close to the cliffs. If we had touched the bottom then we would not have risen again so we turned home again to Kilciarán. At one point I could see porpoises dancing on the top of a wave higher than the mast. As we turned home we were passed by a bigger boat and one of the men leaned over the side to laugh at us and shouted, 'Were ye seeeck?' Lena said afterwards that she was wondering what she would say to our mother if we were all drowned, forgetting that she would have been drowned too. The weather was fine until the last week and then the rain came in on Jack who was sleeping in the loft. He found a waterproof coat and spread it over the bed. We had been told that Pearse had been cheated by the thatcher, who had not put proper straw under the thatch, but Pearse did not care because the thatcher had such beautiful Irish and talked all the time to cover the bad work. We got a postcard from Pearse saying not to mind the demand for rates as he did not intend to pay it. He knew that the card would be read and indeed the O'Malleys in the shop told us all about it.

Joe came home to Larkfield in the middle of July. When he arrived he asked about the two reports he had sent and when he found that a letter which Christiansen had undertaken to send had not arrived he had to sit down and think whether this would matter and decided that it would not. In that letter he had asked for confirmation of his order to Casement to stay where he was and this had not come, so being somewhat worried as to whether he had been right in insisting on Casement remaining in Germany, he went straight to the Military Council and came back greatly relieved to find that he had been correct. Joe was very busy running around; even when he came back he kept up the pretence of having been away for his health and indeed he seemed to be in much better health than he had been for a long time. He was still wearing a slight moustache, a little imperial, because he intended to go to the USA, but his beard was hardly noticeable. It would not have disguised him, but it meant that the description of him as 'a black bearded man' would not fit. People who knew him already seemed to presume that he had not shaved that morning. He was in very good form, having drunk a lot of Bulgarian milk in Germany which he found very good for his tuberculosis.

A few years ago I received this letter from my very old friend and solicitor, Arthur Cox:

> Dear Gerry,
> I was very interested in Joe's diary. It reminded me of a little bit of history. Sometime late in 1915 I was in Aidan McCabe's flat. Joe came in. We were sitting by the fire. After a while, he took out a gold hunter watch which he wore. He opened it. He took out a small red wafer which was hidden in the back. He threw it into the fire. Saying 'There goes the seal of the German Foreign Office'.

The old Fenian, O'Donovan Rossa, died on the 30th of June and his body was brought home from the United States. The Volunteers were stewards and

Ten thousand people attended the funeral of the Fenian, Jeremiah O'Donovan Rossa, organised as a show of Nationalist sentiment by Tomás MacDonagh. Count Plunkett can be seen on the left, a few rows from the grave. Pearse is at the graveside making his famous speech.

marshals at the funeral which was on August 1st. Huge crowds followed the coffin to Glasnevin and I was standing on Parnell Square watching it pass. Those who got in to the graveyard heard Pearse's famous speech, including Pa who was standing very close to him, with its famous ending: 'They have left us our Fenian dead, and while Ireland holds these graves, Ireland unfree shall never be at peace.' Joe was still trying to keep a low profile, as he was leaving shortly for the USA on Military Council business, but he put on his Volunteer uniform and went to the funeral in the same carriage as Ted Sheehan but didn't go to the graveside. Jack was also there as a messenger on Joe's staff, using Joe's motorbike, but he told me he had very little to do, Tomás MacDonagh organised the whole thing and Jack described it as 'perfect organisation with a completely successful scheme to prevent arrests.' After the funeral the atmosphere became fairly tense. The ties between the Irish Party and Dublin Castle tightened and John Redmond was being consulted constantly by the Castle. At that time Redmond still thought it would be bad for his prestige if the Volunteers were suppressed and Dublin Castle was being fairly careful about arrests, but of course this made each one seem more important.

I had arranged with Joe that I would move the household from Marlborough Road to Larkfield while he was in Germany. By the time he came back we were installed, and it was so much pleasanter to live there than in Fitzwilliam Street that the rest of the family, apart from Moya who was in the convent at Roehampton, drifted out for the summer. We had asked Ma to let us live in what had been the mill manager's house when the tenants left during the winter of 1914. The house backed on to the courtyard and it was so damp that the drawing-room could not be used. It was wet halfway up the wall until I managed to drain the water from under it by making an open drain—the water ran out for three weeks. At the time this was fine for us as we did not need a drawing-room. It was otherwise a lovely house with a charming small garden, five bedrooms and three sitting-rooms. The big square hall had a gallery to two bedrooms and there was a back stairs to the other bedrooms; a good kitchen and scullery led to a two-storey extension.

Ma stayed out in Larkfield with us, going in to Fitzwilliam Street every day to collect her letters, until Sarah Ferrall announced that she was going back home to Minneapolis. She said her sister, Julie, was ill and wanted her, but Joe thought that seeing the Howth rifles stacked in the hall of Fitzwilliam Street after the gunrunning had terrified Sarah and she had wanted to go home ever since. In August Ma said that she would go back with Sarah for a holiday and suggested that she would like to see all her relations in Minneapolis again—in the event she never went near them. Ma and Sarah started making the worst souvenirs I have ever seen—little purple poplin bags decorated with orange crochet in a sort of Irish design, they said it was real American taste. Ma also took with her all the lace made by the two Limerick girls in No. 27 Marlborough Road six years before, to sell. Since she knew nothing about selling anything in New York, she had to bring it all back with her again. She got a tailor to make her a Cumann na mBan uniform although she was not a member of it, and I tried telling her that she had no right to wear it but she only got indignant—of course she had the right, if necessary she would join, but she never did. Mimi told me afterwards that Ma wore the uniform a lot in the States; she was at her fattest then, or nearly, and must have looked a holy show! It must have been about then that she started to regard herself as the Queen of Ireland, a position she then never gave up. Before she left for the USA she concocted a lecture on the life of Oliver Plunkett and told me that she was going to use this lecture to collect funds for the expenses of his beatification. She had signature forms prepared for a petition to the Vatican for the beatification, but she must have omitted to look for the necessary permission because she was later told to stop as it was not correct to do so in Canon Law. In New York she stayed all the time in a hostel kept by nuns and she did collect about $2,000, but the money created a lot of trouble as no-one was willing to accept it in Ireland and the matter was not settled until after her death.

She came to Larkfield for a few days before she left and took on a cook and a housemaid who got pregnant and left, so the cook got another maid who

The hollow walking stick that Joe Plunkett used for carrying documents, including the agreement with the German government. On the way to the USA he had a bad moment when the customs man took the stick and looked at it but he gave it back without further examination. Joe's brother Jack had bored out the centre of the stick and then replaced the ferrule.

tried to blackmail me later. We also still had Mary there. Ma gave strict instructions that all three staff were to stay until she came back. In September, as she and Sarah Ferrall set sail for the States, Ma said to me that she thought it was time that she lived her own life. When I told Mimi this, she burst out laughing. After they had gone, the dreadful cook in Fitzwilliam Street—a thief and a drinker—left. That meant Pa had no place to go but Larkfield, where he was welcome. He went to his work in the Museum every day and he loved the walk back from the tram at Harold's Cross to Larkfield. The house in Fitzwilliam Street was not really shut up, there was just no one in it. Mimi, who had acted as housekeeper there, announced her decision to stay out of the place and then the others felt justified in doing the same. Only Pa continued to call there for books and letters, and a cloud of dust settled down on the whole house.

In September, Joe was sent to New York by the Military Council to inform Clan na Gael, in particular John Devoy and Joe McGarrity, of the German agreement and to give the duplicate to McGarrity. He did not go in the same boat as Ma. Before he left Jack spent hours copying documents, including the agreement, into code with details of everything for Clan na Gael. The code was a simple one with an agreed relation between certain letters and certain figures. Joe brought the documents in a cane, expertly hollowed out by Jack so as to keep its balance. He did not let it out of his sight, but he had a bad moment when a customs man took it and looked at it; he gave it back to Joe without examining it any further. Joe was not happy with his meeting with John Devoy and he told me that Devoy was now very old and had forgotten what it was like to live in Ireland. Joe said that none of the people he came across in New York seemed to realise that a careless word spoken in America could jail a man in Ireland. Not only were there many British spies there but the American Government agencies were prepared to work on behalf of the British Government. Joe was worried about the way that Devoy confided in Judge Cohalan who, he said, was using Irish affairs to play his American politics and because of this Joe did not give Devoy the copy of the agreement. Joe McGarrity, whom Joe trusted far more, lived in Philadelphia and was away from home when Joe arrived in New York so he waited about ten days for him to get home then went to Philadelphia for a day to give McGarrity the copy.

While he was waiting in New York he got to know some of the young American writers and literary figures including Joyce Kilmer, who told him how dissatisfied he was with his own work. Kilmer gave him an inscribed copy of his *Trees and Other Poems* which had been published the previous year. After the 1916 Rising Kilmer wrote a poem, 'Easter Week', dedicated to Joe's memory. Joe also saw Pádraic Colum, who wrote that he was 'impressed by the decision and command he had attained to'. Joe had been drinking Bulgarian sour milk when he was in Berlin but he could not get it in New York so he drank beer instead, quarts of it, and found it agreed with him very well! He came home in mid-October and plunged straight into work. He was ill again by the end of the month and I remember this because he was upstairs in bed during the big flood.

That was on Halloweve, October 31st , when there was a storm of rain and the water began to pour off the field behind the mill in a flood because the layer of brick clay under the land couldn't absorb it. Then the Poddle overflowed higher up, where cows had trodden down the banks, and it made a lake ten feet deep behind the hen-run walls while the yard filled with water. Rory O'Connor and Tommy were with us for lunch, as they usually were, and Rory tried to get home to Monkstown in the afternoon but arrived back at Larkfield having found the flood at Merrion impassable. I was worried about my hens, who lived on broken bread from the bakery, and Tommy and Rory helped me, all of us up to our necks in water, to rescue them and bring them in to the house. Jack never forgave me for bringing them in. We walked in and out with bags of squawking hens, put them in one of the rooms and shut the door on them. The ducks were already in the house and Pa sat by the extinguished fire minding them on his lap and reading a book with my cat, Augusta, beside him. Tommy threw out the ducks and said 'you can swim', but the poor things were caught in the wire netting and drowned. Suddenly a flood came in the back door and out the front carrying shoes and sods of turf with it—a melancholy sight. The ovens were put out and things were floating round the kitchen. We used to get hot brown buttermilk rolls for supper from the bakery every night, and we had just got them that night when the flood put the fire out. There was a loud noise and the wall behind the henhouse collapsed from the weight of ten feet of water behind it. We had broken holes in the garden wall and the water ran out through them. The two maids and the cook stood screaming on the stairs, although the hens were the only ones in any danger and they were busy making an awful mess of the room they were in. Next morning the whole place was covered with frozen pools.

Some of the people who helped us to make dams and trenches to direct the flood were the first of the refugees from conscription, christened 'the Liverpool Lambs' by George. Up to the time the Lambs arrived in Larkfield it was a rather desolate place. The bakery worked quietly at night. Some days Volunteers drilled in the barn. Tommy and Rory O'Connor were still trying to get the tar still for their chemical factory erected. The double-sided, three-storey mill was nearly empty. Suddenly one morning about 40 young men descended on us. Many of them were members of the IRB, or their fathers were, and they had come over to avoid conscription and join the Volunteers. The first serious attempt at conscription had just begun in England. George was put in charge of them and they set up living quarters in the barn. When they got an agricultural boiler and tried to boil a stew in it, George came in to the house to ask me, 'How long does it take to boil potatoes?' I told him three quarters of an hour and he said, 'Well, they should be boiled now, it's three hours since they started.' The poor things knew nothing. Some of them found digs at once and their people sent them money, others had to stay on in Larkfield and they got better at looking after themselves quite quickly. George said they were a handful and that they grumbled all the time, especially at having to sleep on mattresses on the floor. George stopped the grumbling by giving up his bedroom in the house and bringing his mattress out to the barn to sleep there. They posted regular sentries, but one night the sentry fell asleep and someone had got into the mill and up to the first floor when the sentry woke up with a yell and the man fell down the steep stairs. Some of them found work and went away, and Tommy's chemical company used to give others a day's work now and then.

When Ma was leaving for America she told Mimi to look after all the house property, which was about 60 houses and a good number of ground rents, but after she had gone Mimi said she had no intention of doing it. She always said it was worth nothing and instead she decided to keep the books for the Larkfield Chemical Company. Then the bills started coming in. I went to the grocer and the butcher when they sent enormous bills, but each of them said they would give us no more credit. Demands began to come in for ground rents, fees, rates, mortgage interest and repairs. I wrote a letter to all of them saying that Countess Plunkett had been ill and had gone to the USA for a holiday, but they all insisted on being paid. I had to do something about all this since Mimi wouldn't, and I knew a bit about it, so I got the rent books and sent rent demands to a good number of tenants. The rents were all due quarterly and at various dates but everyone wrote back to say they had paid already, some had even paid in advance, and had receipts or cheques to prove it. I had to apologise and explain myself and I began to see what was going on. Ma had collected all possible rents, some of them six months in advance, but she did not enter any of them in the rent books. She had paid no household bills, no grocer or butcher, no rates, no ground rents, no interest on the two mortgages on Uncle Jack's property, no annuity to Aunt Marie. She was always careless but this was all a bit much.

Then there was a flood of civil bills, threatening prosecution, and I went with whatever money I had collected to the man who sent the first one. He was an old friend of the family and I had been to scores of parties in his house. His sons and daughters were our friends and one of the boys was a particular friend. He bluffed Ma one day into lending him £50 by telling her he was going to shoot himself—I afterwards heard of him doing this to several different people. I paid him and his partner most of what was due to them and he followed me to the door stammering some excuse that he had been given orders he had to take. I did not know then that Dublin Castle thought that Ma was financing the Volunteers, which was not true, and that orders had been sent out through the Freemasons to bankrupt her. (I was told this later by a friendly solicitor who had not taken these orders.) Rumours that the family was bankrupt encouraged more creditors to press for payment. Up to now my Pa had handed me his salary cheque every month for the housekeeping as we had a large household, Pa, Mimi, Joe, myself, George, Jack, three staff, very often Tommy and Rory, and frequent extras to feed and maintain. Aunt Marie wrote Pa a bitter letter saying that she had not been paid her annuity for three years, and drawing down her jam and her white cow which Ma had absconded with when Uncle Jack died. Of course Ma rarely allowed Pa, who was joint owner of the property, any hand in the running of things, so he had had nothing to do with Aunt Marie's money or the lack of it. Ma had always tried to get out of paying the annuity and said that Aunt Marie didn't need it anyway, that she had enough and she had told Pa it was paid when it wasn't. Pa sent Aunt Marie all the money he had with his usual polite letter saying he had not known. She wrote back kindly saying that if she had known that he was unaware of it she would not have written such a letter. I remember all this stuff, but I also found both Marie's letters and Pa's draft reply when I was burning papers after Ma died.

There was now no money and a large household, including the three staff Ma had said we could not discharge, and no provision for it. We would have been much worse off for food if we had not had some real assets. James O'Neill had made a vegetable garden where the main Poddle stream and the tail race formed an island, and kept us well supplied from this. We had milk from the Kerry cows, the two remaining of the eleven Ma had bought by telegram a couple of years before to keep the grass down. One of them was not much bigger than a St Bernard dog and gave twice as much milk as the other. We also had a churn so we churned the cream for butter. We gave buttermilk to

Quinn's bakery in the mill and they gave us the brown rolls, fresh at eleven o'clock at night, and bread in return, and on Saturdays Jack and I used to buy three rabbits in South William Street for the pie on Sunday. We had constant callers of all kinds and people came in as easily by the back door as the front. We were never quite sure how many we would have for lunch and much of the food was cheap and bad, but there was always coffee and buns to make up. Pa never complained; instead he remarked, surveying our friends, that they were very fine young people and wanted to know why we did not know them long ago. The amount of laughter in the house must have seemed unusual. No one had the heart to tell him that we would not have dared to bring our friends into the house in this way when Ma was at home.

Ma was also overdrawn in the bank, but a few cheques came, and I found that if I lodged money I could draw against it. Mimi was good at signing Ma's name, she had often had to do it before. Rents started coming in again and the bank accepted them, which helped to pay expenses, but there was no credit anywhere. I could not get Ma to understand the urgency of the situation. It took close on six weeks to get a letter to her in New York, as the smaller boats were being used for this route, and the same time for one to come back. I told her creditors, who were pressing me, that I was writing to her about the question, whatever it was, and I did this at once in each case, but it would have taken about three months to get an answer from Ma if she had written one, which she did only once. That letter concerned the worst problem, a civil bill from North's for £28. Ma wrote that the last two items were wrong and I sent it back to North's saying that Ma was in the USA. I got back another civil bill so I paid all but the two items and North's were very pleased and accepted. In that letter she also wrote about another of the civil bills saying the contractor had done this work four or five years previously. I offered him half the money and he took it. Otherwise she did not write home at all, not even to Pa. Often we did not know her address but she said afterwards that she thought we did.

After the war began the old easygoing business methods had gone in a hurry, the cost of repairs to house property had seriously increased and there was a financial panic. Houses were idle because everyone who could had given them up, stored their furniture and moved into hotels and lodgings. There were a lot of Ma's houses un-let. In one empty house a painter and handyman, who was inefficient, old and sickly and a Methodist preacher in his spare time, had been doing some kind of repairs and decoration for nearly a year. I think there were 20 houses idle. I managed to get some of them let. Dockrell's, hardware merchants and house agents, were owed £120 by Ma for supplies of paint and general hardware for maintaining the houses. There had been a habit of giving two years' credit to property owners and Ma had had the same arrangement with Dockrell's, but with the start of the war, this had come to an end. Dockrell's allowed me to pay cash when I could and they let

Michael Collins' first job on his return from London in 1915 was managing the Plunkett family rents.

our houses until Ma's debt to them was paid. I found a couple of painters but I had to explain to them first that if my Ma caught me employing a trade union member I would be in trouble. Luckily they were not members. We used to decorate the two sitting-rooms in good taste, with the folding doors open to show them, and leave the hall door open for people to come in. Between myself and these two men we let 20 houses one after the other and I gave them a bonus. Ma never thanked me for any of this.

There were two mortgages on the Elgin Road houses, taken out to pay off Uncle Jack's debts when he died in 1904, and the worst problem was the interest on these. I got along fairly well until the bank managers in Merrion Row stopped a cheque, part of all the trouble-making for our family going on at the time. One of the solicitors, Sir John Lynch, insisted on making me the receiver for the Elgin Road houses, which made my life hell for years. Lynch thought that he was getting his hands on the whole of Ma's property and was quite disconcerted when I laughed at him. He tried to interfere with other family property, pretending he did not understand, and once I caught him trying to act for three sides of a question at the same time. The Pembroke Estate solicitor was a very decent old bloke who told me what to do and how to manage those leases, as there was a forfeiture clause on some of them and the ground rent had not been paid for two years. Ma's own solicitor was Sydney Matthews, who had bought Master Denning's share in Hoey and Denning, and he certainly didn't have her best interests at heart.

In the Larkfield mill, Quinns, the bakers, couldn't pay their debt to Pauls', their flour suppliers. Pauls' solicitor, Frank Scallan, announced an auction of contents to pay the debt and I went to see him. The auction would have been disastrous! By this time Larkfield was effectively an armed camp with 300 Liverpool and Glasgow men, the Liverpool Lambs living in the mill, the barn being used for .303 practice with the precious Howth rifles, and all sorts of things not meant to be seen by outsiders. I couldn't tell Scallan that but I did argue that there was nothing there of sufficient value to auction. Scallan said stiffly, 'Paul's must have their money', so I was going to have to think again. As I was going down the stairs, Arthur Cox, who was apprenticed there, leaned over the rails of the upper floor and whispered, 'They're out for your blood!' He had heard that Dublin Castle were organising the clampdown on our finances and trying to bankrupt us. The eldest Quinn brother told me that they had no flour to bake with and they had come to the end of everything. They had paid no rent to Ma for months so he gave me formal possession of the bakery. The weaver took his lovely poplin away and they got rid of the van somewhere else. When some men arrived to make an inventory for the auction I told them I had had vacant possession for some time and that if there was anything worth auctioning, it should go to pay the rent to Ma. They went away then but the auction was eventually held there after the Rising in 1916. The only thing of value in the place was the big dough mixer which they couldn't get down the stairs from the top floor as it was so heavy. I heard later that someone did manage it and Ma sold it off but I don't know how it was done. Some of the Quinns finished up weaving for Gerald Elliot and remembered me long after.

I was now minding the house property, looking after Joe, giving grinds and doing laboratory demonstration work and having a paper on dyes read in the Royal Irish Academy. By November I found myself constantly running about Dublin seeing solicitors and business people and then rushing home to write letters. It was just two years since the Volunteers had been started, tension was fairly high and it was now a question of how long this could go on. It was impossible to prophesy. We were compelled into one course or another about many things in a way we would not have expected and it affected the way I had to do business. I could not carry on any longer by myself, Mimi refused to help, Fiona was hopelessly incompetent, Jack was now working on wireless on Joe's staff and Moya was in her English convent. I realised that I couldn't carry on any longer without someone experienced to help with the clerical part of the work and I told Joe I would have to have a clerk for half the week and asked him to get me a Volunteer to avoid having a spy planted on us. I could not bring any other into an armed camp.

A few days later Joe told me that two men would come that day to see me and that one was all right and the other doubtful and that I was to pick the right one. It was apparently a test of my judgment. That afternoon a very tired young man—I can still see him—arrived from London and asked for me. The other one didn't turn up and I never heard why. This man was slim and of medium height and I thought not remarkable until I looked at his eyes. He was completely honest and direct and it was quite obvious that he was the right man. He was twenty-five, I was just about to be twenty-four, but looked a few years younger. This was Michael Collins (we knew him as Mick) and no one ever had a better clerk. He had been a boy clerk in the post office in London, followed by work in a bank and then in a stockbroker's as a stock exchange clerk. He lived there with his sister Hannah, who was also a post office clerk, and he told me that she was the one of his family for whom he had the most respect. I quickly realised that he was far too good for the work I had for him to do but he did not despise it. He was shrewd, serious and downright, very quick and clear. I paid him £1 a week and he took pot luck with the family. For about three months he did a couple of hours' work every day making new rent books, answering letters and filing papers. He had never before done this kind of work, which was all related to the family house property, but thanks to his help the property was gradually being put in order and it was wonderful to see.

A few days later I told Joe that Mick was much too good for the job and Joe, who had never met him before either, told me that he was very glad Mick lived up to the account which had come with him from Art O'Brien and Diarmuid O'Leary in London, where Mick had been an important member of the London IRB for several years. Mick came to Ireland at this time in order to avoid having to register for national service, the first step to conscription. When leaving London he had asked his employers for leave to see a very sick relative, a Miss Kathleen Ní Houlihan. Joe put Mick on his staff after only a few days; they got on very well together and Mick sometimes acted as Joe's bodyguard, becoming deeply attached to him. Various people have noted that Mick Collins used to read G. K. Chesterton's novels. It was Joe who introduced him to them, particularly *The Man who was Thursday*, which was of course a spy story within a spy story in which nothing is as it seems. Apart from the witty, flibberty-gibbet style which appealed to Joe, he used the tale to encourage people to open their eyes, examine their surroundings alive or dead, and judge for themselves. When he was young he also liked the fantastic side of the story but as time went on there was no longer any need for fantasy; the reality was fantastic enough. Joe always used books to illustrate his arguments and in Mick's case he used *The Man who was Thursday* to broaden his views of the use of the IRB and conspiracy in general. This accounts for Mick's reported affection for this book. For his part, Mick was a good actor and could be the silly countryman with a Cork accent and so pass unnoticed through police cordons. He had no experience of culture and had never read any fiction so Joe spent a lot of time talking to him, in particular to encourage him to have standards with which to judge people. Mick had left home when he was very young and his education had been almost altogether commercial. Apart from his knowledge of Irish history, he had read too little and he told me after a week or two that he was only beginning to be able to follow the conversation at lunch or tea.

He was an active man with a humorous and pleasant manner. In our house he was quiet and did not talk much in the beginning. When he was thinking, which was most of the time, the corners of his eyes and his mouth would lift with a kind of quirk which gave him a good-humoured look even when he was annoyed. He was unsophisticated, except financially, but he was really intelligent and his business judgment was excellent. His social manner was not so good and often offended people who did not understand his sincerity. They thought him materialistic, but he was only a realist. When we heard people say he was rough afterwards we could not believe it, because he was invariably pleasant in our house. By December we were on such friendly terms that we invited him to spend Christmas with us, but he thought he should stay with his comrades in the house in Mountjoy Street where he lodged.

Earlier that December (the 2nd to be exact) I was sitting and reading in Larkfield along with Pa, Mimi, George, Fiona and Jack when Joe came in in high good humour and said, 'I am going to marry Grace Gifford'. It was a bombshell for all of us—we didn't know they took that much interest in each other nor did we know that he had given up the idea of Columba O'Carroll, although Columba had come out to Larkfield to tell him that it must come to a complete end. Mimi was shocked and almost said so but I managed to stop her in time. It would have been no use. Grace had no interest in what we were interested in. Her first link with Joe had to do with her desire to become a Catholic and she said that was what they talked about all the time. He was helping her with the preparation and was concerned that after she was baptised, she would probably be thrown out of home. Part of his reason for marrying her was to protect her in such an event. She seemed to have no realisation of how ill Joe was—she said later that 'he might have had bronchitis' whereas the tuberculosis he had had all his life was by now confining him to bed almost constantly. From the time that he came back from the USA, the gland in the centre of his right cheek began to get troublesome and he had to stay in bed a good deal before and after Christmas.

NEW LOVE

The day I knew you loved me we had lain
Deep in Coill Doraca down by Gleann na Scath
Unknown to each till suddenly I saw
You in the shadow, knew oppressive pain
Stopping my heart, and there you did remain
In dreadful beauty fair without a flaw,
Blinding the eyes that yet could not withdraw
Till wild between us drove the wind and rain.
Breathless we reached the brugh before the west
Burst in full fury—then with lightning stroke
The tempest in my heart roared up and broke
Its barriers, and I swore I would not rest
Till that mad heart was worthy of your breast
Or dead for you—and then this love awoke.

Joseph Plunkett

9 Preparing for the Rising, January–April 1916

JOE WAS NOW A MEMBER OF THE IRB MILITARY COUNCIL, and I knew what he meant when he said, 'It has been decided' or, 'The others think', when he was giving me messages or instructions. Immediately after Christmas 1915 the Military Council sent Mimi to New York with despatches for Clan na Gael; Joe did not tell me what Mimi's message was—it concerned the date of the Rising and the arms from Germany—until he had to send her a second time, in March, then I heard a lot about it.

One day in January Joe went out and stayed out until long after I had gone to bed, and left again at cockcrow the next morning. He had been ill in bed so I was worried about him and when he was out late again I tackled him and protested, 'You can't go on like this, you're killing yourself'. He smiled at me and said, 'I suppose you'll have to know, we have been kidnapping James Connolly!' I was horrified and said, 'I'd as soon kidnap a tiger!' until he ex-plained that this was Connolly's joke. Joe said, 'It's all right, he's coming in with us, it's wonderful! We couldn't have him leading the Citizen Army out, it would have been fatal.' He went back to bed feeling glorious. Before Christ-mas, Joe had told me that the Military Council were told that Connolly had said he was fed up waiting for the Volunteers to start something and that if they did not, he was going to bring the Citizen Army out in a rising himself. The Citizen Army numbered about 200 at this time and as they were almost completely unarmed, this would have been a massacre, a disaster. There would have been no hope of any result except a release for Connolly's 'savage indignation'. In addition, Joe was afraid that if Connolly did this, it would completely destroy any chance of bringing off a Volunteer rising at Easter.

I asked him why they did not tell Connolly of their plans and he said that they had made several appointments with him but he always put them off at the last minute and said he was busy. He said he thought that Connolly did not believe they were serious or had any plan of action because of the long delay in acting, and had made up his mind that the Volunteers were going to let the war slip by without a rising. He said that the Military Council had got tired of sending messages to Connolly to meet them and that when the mat-ter became urgent some of them, in a rented car driven by an IRB man, had waited for him outside Liberty Hall. There were two unarmed guards with two members of the Military Council, not to intimidate Connolly, which would have been impossible, but to protect their own leaders in case anything went wrong. The two leaders must have been MacDiarmada (Connolly had always been friendly with him) and Ceannt because I know the other four were not there. When Connolly came out of Liberty Hall one of them told him that he must come with them; he was unwilling, saying it was no use, but they insisted. He said, 'Are you kidnapping me?' and that was how it came to be called 'the kidnapping of Connolly'. They told him at once that they had a rising planned for Easter and he said he wanted to know the plans so they went in the taxi to an empty house in Dolphin's Barn where Joe and the remaining members of the Military Council (I'm not sure if Tom Clarke was there) were waiting to meet him. Joe told me that the house was at the disposal of a friend in some way. There was a little furniture in it and they all went into an upstairs back room where there was a table and some chairs. After some very plain speaking, Connolly agreed to a detailed discussion of the whole matter.

First of all he wrote a letter to his wife to say he was all right and would be home in a day or two, and then a discussion began which as far as I could make out lasted for two days and two nights without rest. They told Connolly that they had detailed military plans for a rising (which Joe had ready by this time) and had arranged for possible help from Germany. They discussed the plans in detail and Connolly agreed with Joe about seizing the centre of the city and all that went with it. They then discussed the social programme for a new Irish State, and convinced Connolly that they had no interest in founding a State without civil and religious liberty and equal rights and opportunities for all citizens. Pearse might have trusted the people to do right as soon as they were free, but he thought justice as essential as Connolly did. Connolly had become convinced that men must be free if they were to be just. This conviction dated particularly from the end of the 1913 strike. He said then that Internationalism was a trap, a straitjacket, and he told Joe he would have to write all he had written over again because of his conviction that freedom came first. Connolly wanted his country as well as social justice and they wanted social justice as well as their country.

Connolly always walked up and down while talking and thinking and he walked and talked now until everyone else was worn out. Joe went into another room and lay down on a bare iron bedstead for an hour or two and when he woke up, the others were still talking and Connolly still walking. Some kind of meals were brought in for Connolly but the guards were forgotten until their relief arrived. Connolly had been very angry at first but by the end of it he had come to complete agreement with them and said afterwards, 'I have been beaten at my own game'. Finally, after Connolly had provisionally approved of Joe's plans for the Rising, he was persuaded with difficulty to go home. He went to the house of Madame Markievicz in Leinster Road, Rathmines, and when he arrived there it was obvious that he was very tired. He told someone that he must have walked 40 miles that day and of course it was thought that he must have been 40 miles away. By the time he got to Madame's house,

James Connolly, 1868–1916, militant anti-capitalist and organiser of the Citizen Army. The IRB were afraid that, in his impatience for action, he would bring out his army in a rising, so they insisted that he meet them. After two day's discussion he came in with them and joined the Military Council.

there was a good deal of anxiety about him so the Citizen Army people were greatly relieved to see him. Mrs Connolly had gone unexpectedly to Belfast and the letter from Connolly, telling her he would be back in a couple of days, was forwarded to her unopened. She got it on Saturday morning but did not mention its contents to anyone, so even Connolly's daughter, Nora, did not know of it and neither did the people at Liberty Hall. That was how it was thought Connolly was missing and the Citizen Army was not certain whether it was the Volunteers or the Castle who had taken him. Joe and the others all thought that Mrs Connolly had got the letter and they were not thinking about the effect of his absence on other people. When it was all over they were surprised to learn that a Citizen Army search party was on the point of setting out and that there had been mention of Connolly's disappearance in the newspapers. Afterwards Joe was very tired, but he was so happy about the agreement with Connolly, it did him no harm. I was told all these things at the time.

From this time Connolly was a member of the Military Council and commander in Dublin for the Rising. Joe was director of military operations and from here on checked all the plans with Connolly, who made some alterations. Sadly, I never met Connolly but his daughter, Nora, told me before she died that Joe and Connolly became very close. Connolly had not previously been friendly with Tomás, I think he had misunderstood his manner and thought him frivolous, but now he changed his mind completely about him. I was told later that Pearse presented one of his books to Connolly with an inscription dated January 21st, 1916. That was the date of the end of this meeting which had begun at midday on Wednesday 19th January, 1916 and when he lent this book to Cathal O'Shannon Connolly told him to be careful of it as he attached great importance to it.

Joe threw himself into the military plans for the Rising. He was confined to bed a good deal until Easter but whether in bed or out of it, most of his time was spent on the plans. From the days of playing Little Wars in Marlborough Road he had developed his own ideas about tactics and strategy, and his bed was now always covered with maps, procured for him from the Ordnance Survey by Captain Robert Monteith, and British military handbooks. It was illegal to have any of these things. He studied them more to measure the mentality of the enemy than for use by the Volunteers. The author of one of those textbooks on tactics that Joe used was one of Ma's tenants in No. 31 Marlborough Road, Captain Kinsman. His headquarters as military intelligence officer was in Beggar's Bush Barracks at the time, and was he mad when the Rising came off! He had known nothing of it.

Joe was sure that Dublin Castle's expectations were that if and when the Volunteers acted, they would take to the hills in small numbers without proper plans; he thought Dublin Castle's idea of an Irish rebellion was 'ten bloody fools in a field surrounded by machine guns' and he was determined that this time would be entirely different. The most important thing would be for the plans to be unexpected: if Dublin Castle was prepared for hill fighting, the Volunteers should do the exact opposite. It may seem simple now but at the time, even the more sophisticated people thought the idea of doing the unexpected was fantastic. Joe had been very much struck in 1911 by Peter the Painter holding out against a regiment of soldiers and police in a house in Sydney Street in London. He could see from that how one well-armed man could defend even an ordinary house, and he proposed to use this to the full. He thought it would be ridiculous to throw away the advantage of even semi-fortified positions on buildings which would be difficult to dominate without large-scale artillery, and he knew the British military forces were not prepared for this.

He told me he had come to the conclusion that there was only one way the British Army would approach the city when they brought in additional forces. They would have to land in Kingstown and march in by the coast road through Ballsbridge, Northumberland Road, Lower Mount Street and Nassau Street to College Green. When I argued that this was limiting their chance too much, he said they would have to do that because it was according to the rules laid down in the British Army handbooks. He thought he might be presuming too much on the rigidity of the Army training but, as it turned out, the Army was indeed bound by its own textbooks. 'We need not keep their rules,' said Joe, 'but they have to.' One of the reasons for the planned occupation of big buildings such as the General Post Office was that they were not dominated by surrounding buildings. The other was that General Friend, the General in command in Dublin up to the date of the Rising, was known to have said at a Council meeting in the Castle that he was completely opposed to the shelling of the city under any circumstances. He thought it

The Citizen Army, seen here mustered outside the soon-to-be-destroyed Liberty Hall, numbered about 200 men. It was orignally founded as a defensive and enforcing arm of the ITGWU during the 1913 lock-out.

would be a confession of failure to do so. Unfortunately, he was on leave in England at Easter and was superseded by General Maxwell. Otherwise the thing might have lasted longer.

It was the general policy of the Military Council to keep information and plans of all kinds unwritten and memorised in a series of water-tight compartments, each delegated to the charge of one man. Without these regulations it would have been impossible to keep out spies. Seán MacDiarmada, who was not long out of jail (six months' hard labour, splitting wood), had a good deal of information about Dublin Castle spies. The plans for the Rising were also kept inside a very small circle whose opinions were very well known. Helpers and associates were observed, no risks were taken, men were sometimes cut off for a chance word and those who it was obvious would not carry on to the end were dropped very early. Inside this circle the facts were well-known and it seemed impossible that Dublin Castle did not know them also, but they did not. It turned out that they had no spy who had any actual knowledge of the plans.

Joe's health was so bad that the others used to come to Larkfield for meetings. Larkfield as an armed camp became more organised; no strangers were allowed near the buildings and an English soldier in uniform who came in was chased down the avenue with knives. A platoon of British soldiers marched up to the gate one night. They did nothing, but I heard curlews all night and I believe it was them signalling each other. I found an offensive person poking around about the millstream one Sunday morning and identified him as our local

Joe working on his wireless apparatus. His idea was to get the news of the Rising transmitted to America and the world as quickly as possible, thereby side-stepping British censorship.

spy. Another time I found a well-known Sergeant-Major and his crony stand-ing in the yard. I told him it was private property and he said, 'I hope I have not injured your little bit of grass by standing on it', but he went. Seán MacDiarmada said he was one of the special recruiting sergeants who got an extra fee for each recruit. Guns of all kinds were quite common, but it must be remembered that they were in no way illegal at this time (it was only illegal to import them) and there was constant practice at the targets in the big barn with the Howth .303 rifles and revolvers. Men and boys sometimes damaged themselves with guns and would come in to have wounds dressed. We kept up a good pretence that all this was commonplace and talked in loud and cheerful tones with much laughter whenever strangers were present. Small arms were smuggled in, revolvers and small automatics were common enough and it was always possible to buy arms and ammunition from English sol-diers. Tommy showed Mick Collins how to make bombs out of big gun-barrel caps cut like pineapples. Gun-barrel fittings were hard to get so the Liverpool men made some bombs out of tin cans and Tommy was able to get a certain amount of stuff to fill them, but they were not good. Buckshot was cast in moulds and a few pikes were made by fixing twelve-inch knives on six-foot poles. These were not a very practical proposition but when the King's Own Scottish Borderers met them on the Quays they ran away! Very few of all these were kept in the house.

In January of 1916 Mick Collins went back to London for a week to settle his business affairs and to tell his stockbroker employers that he would not be returning. He told me afterwards that they asked him what he was going to do and he told them that he was going to 'join up'. To them that meant he was going to enlist in the British Army and to his horror they presented him with a month's pay and congratulated him. They were so nice to him that he was really upset and could not laugh at it; he did not want to deceive them. After he came back his money was running short and he had to find a better job than his work with us—by that time I did not need his help so much anyway. He got a job with Craig Gardner, a big city firm of accountants. He came out to see Joe nearly every day and carried letters for him to the other members of the Military Council. He was very good to Joe and looked after him well when he was his bodyguard for the last few weeks before the Rising. He did everything he could for his comrades before and after the Rising and at all times. He also acted as Seán MacDiarmada's bodyguard on occasions, which was very important on account of Seán's lameness (a result of childhood polio).

Joe gathered a staff to work with him consisting of Jack and George, Mick Collins, Tommy as his chemical expert and Rory O'Connor in charge of engineering, with Con Keating and Fergus Kelly working on radio, all members of the IRB. Joe was a wireless expert; he had followed the Marconi experiment from the beginning, read everything he could get and made sets which worked. He was the only one on the Military Council who knew about radio and it was now that his model wireless station became a serious proposition. He had had sets working from 1907 but only up to a range of two miles, only in Morse and not portable. He had been working on wireless with Jack from 1915—'an awful lot of work with no result', Jack said. Con Keating trained in Atlantic College in O'Connell Street and had been radio officer on ships for several years. He was a small lively Kerryman, about twenty-five years old, but his black hair and big brown eyes made him look younger. He had travelled around the world and used to describe Africa, and other places he had been, to us. Fergus Kelly, an engineering student in UCD and a friend of George's, was Con's assistant. The four of them set up a transmitter in Joe's bedroom, but it was not powerful enough and they were afraid to call attention to it by erecting an aerial outside the house. It has been taken for granted by many people that the purpose of the wireless was to get in touch with the German arms ship and direct it, but it had no radio—very few ships had—and no one supposed it would. Joe thought that publicity was most important, so the real purpose of the wireless was to get the news of the Rising transmitted to the world, especially to America.

The result of all this work by Joe was that the house was full of people from morning till night and often on to midnight. We had dinner in the evening and did not often have more than one extra for this meal, but there might be four or five extra for lunch and tea. Tommy and Rory were always there, and usually Con Keating, Mick Collins and Fergus Kelly. Seán Neeson used to come for weekends when he came to Dublin from Belfast for concerts. George brought people like Colm Ó Lochlainn and so on. All this strained the housekeeping money to the limit: with the war prices were rising daily and we were hard put to it to keep up appearances. It was stew three times a week and rabbit pie on Sundays.

Early in March, Joe told me that a letter had come from Casement to the Military Council in Dublin in which he said that the Germans were going to let them down and make a mess of the whole thing. He wanted to land from a submarine in Howth or Bray to meet the Military Council secretly to completely re-cast the

Mimi Plunkett went twice to the US in 1916, carrrying information on the forthcoming Rising and returning with money and responses.

plans for the Rising and change the date. Joe said that Casement thought he was to be the military leader in command of the Rising and that every one of these things would be a disaster—it was far too late to re-cast plans, Casement was no leader and he could not be concealed at all. He would be arrested at once, action would be taken against the Volunteers and all the initiative would be taken from them. Joe said that the early landing of arms would have the same effect and in any case there was no need to have them beforehand; there were enough arms to start the Rising and with commandeered trains and lorries it would be comparatively easy to distribute the consignment once it was landed. If I am to judge from Joe's expressed views, the Military Council had never from the start made their plans dependent on a German invasion, and Casement's obsession about it never seemed reasonable to them. They thought it would be absolutely fatal if the arms were landed before Sunday or more than a few hours before then, as landing a large quantity of arms would have been notice to the English that armed action was intended and they would have taken immediate action. Casement's obsession about an invasion may well have been the reason that the German Government did not regard the date of landing as terribly important, or he may even have told them that he thought it would be better to be early than late. Perhaps they were just doing their best.

On March 17th, St Patrick's Day, the Irish Volunteers took possession of College Green and held a review. MacNeill took the salute from a lorry near the

Grattan statue. All the companies who had uniforms were there and some who had not. The men with hats pulled down over their eyes were those who would have lost their jobs if they were seen. I heard that evening that there were 5,000 present. The police reported 4,500. The police did not try to interfere, but the usual carload of English officers tried to force their way through and lost their tempers when they were stopped. This review was ordered at very short notice, so that sections on their way to it could not be cut off and disarmed. A tram driver tried to force his way through but was stopped by an armed cycle scout who pulled him off the tram. On Sunday March 19th, the Tullamore Volunteers were attacked by a crowd, mostly people coming from a football match, and the next night the Volunteer Hall there was attacked by a crowd carrying Union Jacks. Some of the Cumann na mBan were in the hall and the men got them out, but not before they were attacked and kicked and one of the girls was hurt. The police did not interfere until a Volunteer made the mistake of firing a shot over the heads of the crowd, whereupon the police, headed by the County Inspector, rushed in and tried to search the Volunteers for arms. After the County Inspector was hit with a hurley and a constable was wounded by an automatic, four Volunteers were arrested and the remainder nearly killed by the crowd. The captain of the Volunteers pretended he was badly hurt and got away to Dublin and stayed in Larkfield mill. Joe said that the captain had not acted wisely, he might have started more than he knew.

It was about six weeks before the Rising when Mimi arrived home from New York the first time. The message she delivered to John Devoy was that the date of the Rising had been settled as Easter Sunday, which was the first time that this had been stated. John Devoy thus knew the date of the Rising from February and there was no alteration from Ireland of this date or of the date for the landing of arms. The message asked for instructions to be forwarded to Germany that the arms were not to arrive here before Holy Saturday and confirmed the request for a skeleton staff of German officers and a submarine to be sent to Dublin Bay, arrangements which Joe had provisionally made with the German General Staff. Mimi delivered the despatches to John Devoy but he did not seem to take the instructions seriously. He thought that the decision ought to rest with Clan na Gael and telephoned Judge Cohalan while Mimi was present and told him a good deal of what was in the despatches, far too much, Mimi thought. This greatly surprised her because she knew that Judge Cohalan was not in the inner circle of Clan na Gael. Devoy did not tell Judge Cohalan the proposed date of the Rising.

Devoy sent Mimi back with a message arguing that arms could be smuggled in beforehand; it was obvious that if this was his advice, he had not sent the correct message to Germany but had either altered it or not sent it at all. In fact he had sent his own version to the Germans, that the arms should be sent between Holy Thursday and Easter Sunday. I was there when Mimi told all this to Joe when she came back. She brought £2,000 from Clan na Gael back to Ireland in a chamois bag tied around her thigh. I think the money must have been in bearer bonds or something, not in gold, because she said, although it was uncomfortable, it was not too heavy. She came home at the end of March, the crossing each way taking between five and six weeks. Devoy had also asked that he be allowed to tell all the details of the scheme, including the actual date of the Rising, to Judge Cohalan. This message was another bother as Judge Cohalan was a member of Clan na Gael but had been unsuccessful in his attempt to be elected to its Council. This request by Devoy should have been referred to the Council and by them to Dublin. Devoy's attitude explains why it has been said that the date of the gunrunning was changed at the last minute. It would have been better if word had always been sent direct to Germany instead of through Devoy, but it was thought essential to keep on terms with Clan na Gael. They did provide some money but the larger amount always came from the Volunteers themselves. Clan na Gael were always cautious about guns and when they were asked to send guns here at the beginning of the war they decided not to. There was definite feeling in Ireland that Clan na Gael considered that it was the senior body and that it was they who should make the decisions. In spite of the fact that individual members of Clan na Gael had expressed a perfectly correct understanding of the situation here the Yankee superiority complex had spread to others of the Irish and they thought they were the only people competent to direct the campaign in Ireland. McGarrity knew better, Devoy did not and Cohalan's commitment was to American politics. Joe told me a lot of this.

With the authority of the Military Council, Joe sent Mimi straight back to New York with a reply for Devoy, but he was at his wits' end to devise a message in words strong enough to convince Devoy that the date of the arms landing was absolutely vital. Joe told me that the man by whom some messages were being brought to the USA was Tommy O'Connor, a steward on a liner, and that he had sent word that his route was being changed and he could not be sure that he would arrive on time, so Joe was sending Mimi back to New York with a duplicate of his message. O'Connor actually did arrive before Mimi. The message for John Devoy was thus brought to him by O'Connor and by Mimi in identical terms in cipher, saying that arms must not be landed before the night of Easter Sunday 23rd: '*this is vital, smuggling impossible, let us know if submarine will come, to Dublin Bay.*' John Devoy did send this second message and it arrived in Berlin on April 6th before the arms ship left, but the previous message he had sent said 'between Holy Thursday and Easter Sunday' and the German Government chose to take this as correct. Mimi also brought to New York an absolute refusal to allow Judge Cohalan to be told the date of the Rising.

One evening in March, Tommy and I were coming home from town when a troop of RIC with rifles passed us. When we walked up to Larkfield from the Harold's Cross tram, we found that the house and ground, which was a rough triangle, was surrounded by soldiers and police with rifles. When we got in to the house we found that Con Keating, Fergus Kelly, Rory O'Connor, Mick Collins and Jack were putting up the shutters and backing them with furniture, preparing to defend the house to the last. Con was delighted with the prospect! George was out in the mill with the Liverpool Lambs, some of them acting as sentries and outposts on the hedges and the two avenues, and the rest, armed to the teeth, preparing to defend the mill. Joe was expecting an immediate attack and planning the defences, although what he really needed was a plan to silence the servant girls who were having hysterics on the stairs. My father sat reading by the fire and smiling quietly at the boys. It could have been the expected move against the Volunteers and if so, it would have been a fight to the death. Of all present no one seemed to know this but myself. Yes, they did of course, but they would have been dead and I would have had to clean up after it was all over. I was wondering what kind of mess the place would be in after the fight when suddenly George came in to say that they had gone. Everyone had been prepared to fight to the last and nothing at all happened. The RIC and soldiers just went away but they left an outer ring of guards for a while. Joe told me he thought that this must be a demonstration, retaliation for manoeuvres and the taking of a gun from a policeman by a Volunteer company, acting against orders, around Dublin Castle some nights previously. Just after this a Wexford motor was caught in College Green with a load of guns and ammunition and the men in it, Kenny and Doyle, were arrested and given a three-month sentence. The Larkfield siege happened the day the telegram arrived from Ma.

The telegram was from London, addressed to Mimi and telling her to go there at once. As Mimi had left for New York for the second time the day before and it appeared that there was something seriously the matter, I went over the same night. Although there was a Zeppelin bomb scare, the blackout was not very serious. Ma was in the guesthouse of the Roehampton Convent where Moya was a novice. Ma told me that she had arrived back in Liverpool from New York a week before and that on her journey back she had an inside cabin and got bilge gas poisoning because the bilges had not been pumped out in New York as they should have been. She had gone straight to Moya's convent where, as far as I could see, neither of them were welcome, as the convent had had enough trouble already with police investigating a German nun as a spy; because of the war, anybody Irish was also regarded as a problem. Ma looked a bit yellow but had not been really ill and she was furious that I had come instead of Mimi and furious that Mimi had gone back to the USA—in fact, she was furious. She kept on saying to me, 'He must get his answer, the man is entitled to his answer. Why does he not get his answer?' It took a long time to get a coherent account from her. She took it for granted that I knew what she was talking about and was being obstructive. Then a doubt came into her so-called mind and she told me the story.

Mimi had visited Ma the first time she went to New York but of course hadn't told her the purpose of her visit. Important information was always kept from her as her conduct was incalculable and she had a fatal habit of making friends with spies. Ma said that after Mimi had gone back to Dublin, Judge Cohalan sent for her. She had met him previously but did not know him well and he staged an act to induce her to return to Ireland, walking up and down his study in what she described as a terrible state. He told her he wanted her to follow Mimi to Dublin and that she was to insist on Mimi's telling him or sending him the answer to his question and that he must have it at once. He did not tell her what the question was. He said, 'I must know, I have a right to know'. He seemed to her to refer to a particular piece of information that had been withheld from him. She took it for granted that Mimi was in the wrong and Judge Cohalan right and was intrigued at what this question could be that was so important. I could see all this on her face when she told me about it. She said that she had asked Cohalan why he had wanted her to go home as she had not planned to go for some time longer. What a pity she did come! Judge Cohalan then added that he was worried about Mimi's safety as she was carrying a large sum of money and might be attacked. Ma did not believe this until he told her that Mimi had brought £2,000 back to Ireland with her and Ma was of course interested at once. She wanted to know why Mimi had the money and although she had not the slightest notion of what all the fuss was about, she agreed to go home and to insist on Mimi's giving him his answer. She always sided with the stranger against her family. I told her now that Mimi had gone back with the answer—a plain refusal to tell Judge Cohalan what it was not his business to know. I had to say it several times before I got it into her head and then she said that perhaps she had made a mistake, that the man had been most insistent. She also said that Cohalan had told her to tell 'them' (she did not know who, but she obviously thought it was Joe and others) that Casement and the arms were to arrive on Good Friday. This in itself would be disastrous but it was also appalling to hear it from someone who had no business to know it and so long before the Rising.

The last big public meeting before the Rising was held in the Mansion House on March 30th. I was there with Fiona, Rory O'Connor and Tommy in the gallery. The place was full. Two G-men were recognised and put out. The meeting was held to protest against the deportation of Ernest Blythe and Liam Mellowes, who were Volunteer organisers. The Deputy Lord Mayor, Alderman Corrigan, presided. Eoin MacNeill spoke, then Pearse gave a wonderful speech and held the hall full of people completely silent. The time seemed to flash by. Bulmer Hobson spoke openly against fighting. He advised the Volunteers that they would never be able to fight England now or at any other time. It must have taken great courage to say this. I knew that he had already persuaded Ginger O'Connell that no military action could be taken with success without about ten years' military training. There was silence when Hobson ceased speaking, then a growl arose and a scene seemed to be imminent. The Volunteers began to stir and to shuffle their feet. I heard a slight scuffle but could see nothing. I heard afterwards that a Volunteer in the audience pulled out his gun to shoot Hobson. A fracas ensued and the men beside him stopped him in time. When Hobson sat down, Father O'Flanagan sprang up, and his fighting speech put Hobson's out of people's minds. The meeting ended on a very high note but it was quiet and restrained enough.

To his sisters' astonishment Joe Plunkett became engaged to Grace Gifford in December 1915. The engagement was announced in the newspapers in February 1916.

One of the detectives who had been put out was waiting outside. He tried to arrest a young lad saying he had broken a motor lamp, which was not true. The detective said he was shot at, the Volunteers said they had only beaten him. Someone said a shot did go off. According to the authorities later, 'The meeting was followed by very disorderly conduct in the streets through which traffic was held up and two policemen fired at.' Regret for this was expressed by various speakers at a meeting held outside Liberty Hall next evening and at meetings against the deportations held every evening in the following week. The regret was expressed in order to make sure that incidents such as this and the arrests in Tullamore would not be made an excuse for Dublin Castle action. The Castle officials thought that the speeches were a climbdown. The newspaper account of the meeting said that Alderman Tom Kelly, Eoin MacNeill, Frank Sheehy-Skeffington, Father Costello and Peter Macken spoke, but this was not so. The Castle admitted afterwards that they did not know what went on at the meeting and the press reports as to demonstrations in the streets are also incorrect.

Joe and Grace had publicly announced their engagement in February, to great opposition from Grace's mother. Now Joe was trying to make it impossible for her mother, who was a Protestant, to get hold of her again, because of her bigotry, which was savage. Grace's father, a solicitor, was Catholic but her mother would not allow him a priest on his deathbed. On April 7th Grace was baptised in University Chuch, St Stephen's Green, with Fiona as her godmother. She was received into the Catholic Church and at the same time thrown out of home by her mother.

To Grace

On the Morning of her Christening
April 7th 1916

The powerful words that from my head
Alive and throbbing leap and sing,
Shall bind the dragon's jaws apart
Or bring you back a vanished spring;
They shall unseal and seal again
The fount of wisdom's awful flow,
So this one guerdon they shall gain
That your wild beauty still they show.
The joy of Spring leaps from your eyes,
The strength of dragons in your hair,
In your young soul we still surprise
The secret wisdom flowing there;
But never word shall speak or sing
Inadequate music where above
Your burning heart now spreads its wing
In the wild beauty of your Love.

—

Joseph Plunkett

In the spring of 1916 Dublin Castle offered Pa the directorship of the National Gallery as well as the National Museum, with the proviso that he and his family would stay out of politics. He thought this was funny and turned the offer down, but in doing so he lost the one thing he wanted most in his life; the National Gallery had been his life's dream. When he was imprisoned after the Rising he lost the Museum as well. On March 31st we read in the papers that Asquith, the British Prime Minister, had been visiting the Pope, Benedict XV. Casement had warned Eoin MacNeill nearly two years before this that England was using her influence in the Vatican against Ireland and Joe had been given confirmation of this in Germany. A danger was that the Pope would be asked to instruct the Irish bishops to condemn as unjustifiable any political action in Ireland which was taken without the authorisation of the Irish Party. Joe now swore Pa into the IRB and Pa said to me that he was very pleased that his son was now his superior officer. At the beginning of April Joe sent him to Rome as he had a right, as a Papal Count, to an audience with the Pope. He was sent officially on behalf of the Military Council but it was Joe who gave him his orders. He also got Pa to memorise a letter to Casement which he was to send from Switzerland on his way to Rome. Pa travelled night and day without stop in case of obstacles, as restrictions were increasing because of the war, and in Berne he went to the agent at the Argentine Consulate. He did not like the way in which the man agreed to send a letter to Berlin and he was right, as this letter never arrived, so he left a duplicate letter to be sent to Casement in the German Consulate. That letter was delivered to Casement through the Foreign Office. The letter was signed 'A friend of James Malcolm' and had Joe's authenticating word 'Aisling', so Casement thought Joe was in Berne and had sent him this letter. It got to Casement on April 6th before the German arms ship, the *Aud,* left. Later, Joe told me it was a duplicate of the one Mimi brought to Devoy in the USA. Various garbled versions of this letter have been published but I do not know where they were obtained. As to the date proposed for the landing of the arms, Pa was told to say 'no earlier than Sunday'. He memorised the messages and carried no papers.

Pa then went on to Rome and saw the Pope at once. The Pope told him that Asquith had told him some months before that the Irish now had Home Rule and that the Irish question was settled. Asquith did not tell him that Home Rule was hung up by a suspending Bill and a government guarantee that it would not be put into operation without an amending Bill, substantially meeting the views of the Unionist minority. Pa was able to tell this to the Pope and that there had been no elections in Ireland for six years, that the Home Rule Act was not in operation as had been represented to him and might never be put into operation. He gave the Pope a proper account of the position in Ireland and told him that the Volunteers intended insurrection, and that the prospects were desperate and asked him for the blessing which all Catholics are entitled to when they are setting out on an enterprise which they believe to be right. They spoke French and Pa told me that the Pope sent them his blessing while the tears of sympathy poured down his face and he said '*Les pauvres hommes, les pauvres hommes*'. After visiting the Irish College, Pa came home as quickly as he could, arriving back in Ireland on Holy Thursday, but he was so worried by what the bishops might do that he went straight down the country to visit various of them, I think five. He warned them that if there was trouble in the immediate future they should not take any action and asked them to refrain from condemning what they did not understand. He was so tired by this time that he was never quite sure whom he had seen, but he told me that he thought none of the bishops he interviewed condemned the Rising

The tubercular abscess on Joe's cheek was becoming so acute that he could only do a certain amount, and it had to be opened. He went in to Mrs Quinn's nursing home on Mountjoy Square the day after I left to meet Ma in Roehampton, and he was operated on almost at once by Charlie MacAuley, who took the utmost care of him. I had known and respected Charlie as a student for his character and brilliance, and he was my first choice as a surgeon of those Dr Michael O'Hea suggested. Joe was obviously so fragile that the greatest care had to be taken and Charlie told me afterwards that he thought Joe had only two weeks to live but I was quite unable to take this in at the time. Joe stood the operation well but made himself tired working on maps and plans. Mick Collins, who was acting as his guard, went with him and looked after him for the time he was there. Joe told me that I was not to go to see him unless he sent for me, which he did a few times, to bring him some books and maps. He slept in the nursing home every night but after the first week came to Larkfield several times for a few hours, in fact quite often during the day. All the other leaders remained away from their homes most of the time during those last weeks. They were being very closely watched by the police and at any time now Dublin Castle might start wholesale arrests and raids. The Castle plan, as revealed later, was to arrest all the leaders at their own homes, but they seemed to be unaware that they were not at their homes. Until General Stafford's letter to General Friend arrived at the last minute warning him about the Rising, they did not know that an insurrection was planned for Easter. Even then they did not believe it, as Stafford made light of it and said 'the Navy would take care of it'.

Sometime before Pa started for Rome, Joe had told me that a friend of the organisation, who had a clerical job in Dublin Castle, had been using his position for some time to give information and warnings to the IRB. Joe was delighted at the idea of having a spy in the Castle and told me that the man had got some information from a file he had seen, which was not in his charge, about the Castle plans against the Volunteers. I asked Joe if he had any indication of its contents but he said Mr X did not want to give it piecemeal but wanted to wait until he had the whole. Mr X had been trying to make opportunities to look at this file, to which he had access in the course of his work, and to memorise it. He had to be careful not to be seen reading it so he left days between each reading. It was April when he felt that he was being suspected so he gave what he had to his IRB contact in normal handwritten script and it was then put into code to protect it en route before being given to Joe. Joe deciphered it and brought it to the Military Council. When I started writing this Mr X was still alive and did not want his name published until he retired, but I can give it now as Eugene Smith, later Donagh MacDonagh's father-in-law.

In early April I came home to find that a meeting of the Military Council had been held in Larkfield. Joe was gone to hospital when I came back so I got no account from him of the meeting except indirectly. Rory and George told me that the meeting lasted an hour and a half or so and that when it was breaking up they heard a good deal of laughter. Joe had come home from the nursing home for it and the meeting was in his bedroom with (unusually) Tom Clarke as well as all the other members present. It seems to have been good-humoured and rather noisy. The publication of the document from Dublin Castle was authorised by the whole Military Council at this meeting. They decided that it must be published to disconcert the Castle and let the Irish people know that there was a plan to attack the Volunteers. When the meeting was over Joe saw Colm Ó Lochlainn, who had been sent for and was waiting during the meeting to be called, and asked him to print the document which he gave him. Colm seems to have got the impression that the document was an invention, partly because it was in Joe's handwriting and partly because he had heard the laughter and talk coming from the meeting in Joe's bedroom. He had not known about the man in the Castle and he was not told about him now.

The document was to be printed in Larkfield and Colm helped at the start, but said he was too busy to stay and soon left, so it was done by Rory and George. Colm's account of the matter in *The Book Lover* is sheer nonsense and quite impossible to correct except by re-casting the whole. George and Rory printed a number of copies on the little hand press Joe had bought from Tomás four years before. They were not used to typesetting and got very bored with it so they sang all the time, mostly Herbert Moore Pim's 'I Tread the Ground that Felons Tread' to every tune from 'The Croppy Boy' to 'God Save the King'. When they were half-way through, one of them knocked the type over with his elbow and it had to be done over again. They told me that there were only a few pounds of type and they ran out of capitals and punctuation marks almost at once. They asked Joe what they were to do about it. There was no way of getting more type so he told them to go ahead without them. This was afterwards supposed to be some kind of cute dodge to create the illusion of a de-coded cipher. Rory and George came to an obvious error: the Archbishop of Dublin's house was given as Ara Coeli, which was the name of the Primate's house in Armagh. Rory and George sent Jack over to the nursing home to ask Joe what to do and Joe thought about how the error might have crept in for a moment or two and then said, 'Correct it, of course'.

The document (without any capitals or punctuation of any sort) was sent to all the newspapers but none of them even mentioned it, and Dublin Castle denied a few days later that they had censored it out of the newspapers. When it became plain that the newspapers would not publish it, Rory brought it to Paddy Little, the owner and editor of *New Ireland*, a weekly moderate paper, with whom he had always been friendly. Paddy Little agreed to send out the document with a covering letter in which he said that an attack on the Volunteers would provoke armed resistance. Copies of the document and Paddy

The gates of Dublin Castle, the seat of the colonial administration. One of the first casualties of the Rising was the unarmed guard (the only one) shot here by a detachment of the Citizens' Army. Despite its real vulnerability, it was not in the plans to take the Castle and this initial success was not followed up.

Little's letter were brought to all the newspapers as well as to MPs and many prominent people, but in fact it was not reproduced in any paper except *New Ireland*. When Paddy was told by someone that the document was bogus he was afraid that he had been dishonestly used and that he had caused things to happen, and I had to assure him that the document was in fact genuine. He told me afterwards that he was satisfied of this. Frank Sheehy-Skeffington, just returned from a lecture tour of the USA where he had done some IRB work, went to Alderman Tom Kelly to ask him to bring the letter and the document before the next meeting of Dublin Corporation. Tom Kelly did not know anything about the business except what Sheehy-Skeffington told him. At the Corporation meeting on April 19th, the Wednesday of Holy Week, he read out the letter and the document. He said he did not want to do anything that would lead to irritation but if it was the hope of the authorities to drive the Volunteers into premature insurrection they should be guided by moderation, patience and fortitude. After this reading of the document into the Dublin Corporation records, the papers could ignore the thing no longer and it received a good deal of publicity.

The document was compiled from the measures that were to be taken on receiving an order from the Chief Secretary's office. There was a list of all the organisations whose members were to be arrested, arrangements for confining citizens to their houses, for pickets and mounted patrols, and the occupation and isolation of premises, a list of which included our house at Larkfield and MacNeill's house, O'Rahilly's house, St Enda's, the Mansion House, the Volunteer HQ in Dawson Street and the Archbishop's house. The only things added to Eugene Smith's document were some introductory lines and a couple of reference numbers. The *Freeman* was indignant—if this was true, coercion was going to start again. The Irish Party and the Dublin Castle officials called the document bogus and this is the origin of that label. The *Evening Mail* editorial said they had the word of the military authorities that there was not a word of truth in it. Joe knew that Dublin Castle would take action very shortly and he hoped that publication would do two things: make the Castle hesitate to do the things they were accused of planning, and make the public realise what was planned whether there was a Rising or not. Joe was quite capable of inventing it if necessary but there was no need to do so, in fact the closer it was to the truth of the Castle plans, the better the effect would be. Joe questioned me very closely when I saw him again about the effect of the document on public opinion. I was able to tell him there was a good deal of public indignation and it was said that if it were true, that the Castle had no justification.

Although all these things in the document were very ordinary military measures, they were thought by the public to be very shocking. There would be an attack on the Volunteers who, up to this time, had done nothing to provoke it. Only political and recruiting considerations had prevented these measures from being put into action long before. Though some Castle officials had been in favour of suppressing both the Ulster and the Irish Volunteers and the Citizen Army from the start, directions came from the English Cabinet and had to be obeyed. Some military men would have liked to treat us as savages; the permanent officials would have preferred quiet arrests and imprisonment for the leaders and the disarming of the men. As we found out afterwards, all of them agreed that the Volunteer Headquarters should be raided and arms taken from all kinds of Volunteers.

10 'The last time I saw Joe'
April 21st–May 3rd 1916

THE RISING WAS PLANNED FOR EASTER SUNDAY and the orders and announcements of the insurrection were to be given to the assembled Volunteers at the parades on that day. We always thought there was a possibility that the parade would in fact be prevented by mass arrests of the leaders or similar action by Dublin Castle, which up to this had not happened. Castle plans would have to be very well concealed if our people were not to get some wind of them and take counteracting measures but it was always possible.

GOOD FRIDAY APRIL 21ST

On Good Friday morning, all the wireless equipment was taken away from Larkfield. Joe and his radio staff had decided to send Con Keating to capture the wireless station in Cahirsiveen, as that transmitter was the most powerful in the country and they knew that their own transmitter was not powerful enough to transmit the news of the Rising to the rest of the world. Joe thought this was essential because we knew from experience that Nationalist versions would be suppressed. That afternoon Con put his head in the dining-room door at Larkfield and said goodbye. I asked Joe when Con would be back and he said, 'He may not come back'. Con was charming and the best of company and we all loved him.

Joe slept every night in the nursing home in Mountjoy Square until that Friday evening when Mick Collins, who was acting as his guard, brought him and his luggage to the Metropole Hotel on O'Connell Street where he stayed until Easter Monday.

HOLY SATURDAY APRIL 22ND

On Holy Saturday, Joe came out to Larkfield in the morning to see Tomás but I didn't see either of them as I was out. None of the leaders had been home for more than a few minutes in the last week. That morning there was a short paragraph in the newspapers about two men being arrested at Banna Strand in County Kerry the day before. It gave no description of them but said that three men had landed in a rubber dinghy, apparently from a submarine, and that one of them had got away and was being searched for. In the evening papers there was a report of a tall bearded man being arrested in Kerry with no word of who he was but a horrible suspicion that it was Casement, in spite

216

of all the orders to stay where he was in Berlin. This seemed disastrous, as we had been certain that the arms were not to come until Easter Sunday and that Casement was not to come at all. At the same time, there was a report of a car plunging into the river or the sea at Ballykissane pier and at least three of the occupants being drowned. Then the news came to Larkfield that Eoin MacNeill, commander-in chief of the Volunteers, had issued an order countermanding the parade on Easter Sunday, which he had signed in Seumas O'Kelly's house in Rathgar on Friday night. Too many things were happening at once and we were missing a lot of information. The boat captured on Banna Strand was not necessarily our boat full of arms; if it was, why was it three days too early? That would be a dreadful mistake. There were rumours and counter-rumours. Personally, my first thought was that the Rising was now impossible and must be postponed perhaps for a week, perhaps for longer.

After all this I was dumbfounded when, at twelve noon, Tommy got his mobilisation orders for Sunday from Mick Collins. I asked Mick if it was going ahead and he nodded. I had to know now what was going to happen. Tommy and I were to be married that Easter Sunday and it was to have been a double wedding with Joe and Grace. We went to visit Joe in the Metropole Hotel at about eight thirty that evening, partly to find out what Tommy's duties would be if something did happen. Joe was seeing people at the hotel and we just got him for an hour in between. Joe wrote out Tommy's commission and gave it to him and said that Tommy could go to the Imperial Hotel over Clery's and wait for news. If and when the chemical factories were captured, Tommy was to take them over and make munitions of war. Rory O'Connor's orders were the same in respect of engineering. Joe told us that the Military Council was waiting for information and he did not know yet what was going to happen. It was fairly certain that there would be no Rising on the Sunday and whether it would take place on Monday or a week later would depend on the nature of the information. We could only wait and see. We agreed to stay in the Imperial Hotel until further orders.

We then had a long talk. Joe told us that he did not know yet what was going to happen. He said that MacNeill's countermanding order had caused complete confusion. He gave me a rough account of how it happened. First of all, Joe said that Bulmer Hobson had told Eoin MacNeill that the parade on Sunday was to be a Rising, that MacNeill accused Pearse of deceiving him and that Pearse had told him that it had been inevitable and reminded him that he had told him long ago to go ahead with his plans. Joe said that MacNeill agreed to join the Military Council after he had been told the plans for the Rising, which included the landing of arms. Hobson was then arrested by the Military Council as they knew that he was utterly opposed to such a rising as this though Joe thought that Hobson's own plans were not very practical. Then Joe told me of how O'Rahilly had come back from a three-day tour of the country and had heard of Hobson's arrest and how he had gone to St

Enda's and abused Pearse for it. He said that he and Tomás MacDonagh had been trying to get hold of O'Rahilly to tell him about the Rising from the Tuesday of Holy Week. Tomás had gone to his house twice and had been told he was ill in bed and could see nobody. O'Rahilly was completely sincere and reliable but rather indiscreet and that was why he had not been told before. Joe and Tomás now got hold of him and told him what had happened. O'Rahilly was absolutely in favour of a rising, it had been his object for years. When he realised that Hobson was against the Rising he got very upset. He told Joe and Tomás that he had been sent by Hobson to places round the country with documents for delivery to various commandants. O'Rahilly had not examined any of the documents he had delivered.

Joe next said that Casement was the man arrested in Kerry. He knew that the arms were gone. He said he had no hope now of MacNeill's co-operation. It would be impossible to find out the position throughout the country for at least a week, perhaps ten days. There might be no Rising after all but until they heard what the Castle was going to do, there would be no final decision.

There was a button missing from Joe's shirt and I had a needle and thread behind the reveres of my jacket so I sewed it on while he went on talking. He said they were waiting for news from their friend in the Castle of what happened at a meeting that was being held that evening. If the officials came to no decision that evening, neither would the Military Council. He said delay was entirely in Volunteer favour. If the Castle took no action for the whole week it might be possible to get in touch with the rest of the country. If the Castle decided to arrest the leaders at once and to attack, the Rising would go on no matter how few took part in it. If not, it was certainly off for the moment. There was still time for the leaders to escape but if they did so, leaving the rank and file to bear the punishment, or if they were arrested without a fight, Joe said that Ireland might never fight again and so they had decided not to go on the run.

Joe said that he thought that if there was no Rising now and if no opportunity arose later in the war that we would get nothing, not even the Home Rule Bill, without fighting for it. He said the Irish would be conscripted if they did not fight now (and he was right). He said that a Rising now could not be a success; the Castle knew from Casement's landing that action was intended, the *Aud* was gone with the guns and there was little hope of capturing any from the enemy on their guard. In spite of all this he was satisfied that it was right to go on if they were forced to do so by a Castle decision to disarm, attack and arrest.

On the other side, if the news got to Germany quickly the Germans might think it worthwhile to attack in strength and so enable the Volunteers to hold out longer than would otherwise be possible. They might even send more help. If a sufficient number of Volunteers came out in spite of MacNeill's order as soon as they realised that a rising had begun, they might hold out for a possible month even without German help. As England could not spare many soldiers for Ireland, and those already here were reported to be not much use, he had already come to the opinion that soldiers would have to be brought from England rather than from all over Ireland and this proved to be accurate. He said that it would be a victory if they held out against England even for a short time, it would be a first step on the road to freedom. I asked Joe what he thought would be the utmost that could be got from a rising. He said that if they held out for a month (and he had no real hope of it) he thought that it might result in something like the repeal of the Act of Union, with alterations of course! He said that everything had been done to give the Volunteers belligerent status. They were uniformed and officered. They would declare a republic with a president and council and a provisional civil government. He did not expect the English to respect this for a moment but he said it would become known in the end and would have its effect.

He had arranged a long time ago to get married at the same time as Tommy and me on Easter Sunday, but now he said that it would not be fair to Grace as she did not know the smallest thing about the political situation and had no idea whatever of such things. He had postponed their wedding because of all the disasters and the re-organisation of the Rising, but if the Castle did not act, he would get married at once, even if he could not avoid being arrested later. If he were arrested before a rising, he would try to arrange to get married in jail. Unless there was an actual rising, he thought only the executive would be interned, probably deported, and Grace could be with him and they would go home in the end. He was afraid that if he did not marry her, her mother

The pier at Ballykissane, where the expedition to capture the radio station at Cahirsiveen came to a tragic end.

Tommy Dillon and Gerry Plunkett were married on Easter Sunday 1916. It was to have been a joint wedding with Joe Plunkett and Grace Gifford but that wedding was postponed becausse of the Rising.

would try every means to get her to give up her religion. He said that he did not by any means want to die.

We were about an hour and a half with him and Colm Ó Lochlainn was due to come in at nine o'clock to report on the expedition to Cahirsiveen. He was in the first car, Con Keating being in the second. Joe told me that Colm had been left out of everything since he had failed to do a job he had been directed to do with others; he trusted that Colm would rise to this occasion. When we left about ten o'clock Colm was arriving.

Much later we learned what had happened. Con and the others were met at the Killarney train with two cars to take them to Cahirsiveen. Con, Dan Sheehan and Alf Monaghan were in the second car. By the time the two cars got to Killorglin in Kerry it was dark night. Their driver lost sight of the tail light of the first car, missed his turn and drove off the pier at Ballykissane. The driver survived but Con, Dan Sheehan and Alf Monaghan died. Con could swim ten miles but he was trapped under the car hood. He had been in charge of this expedition and the men in the other car did not know what the orders were, so they returned home to report. Joe's fears were confirmed now that Con Keating was dead.

EASTER SUNDAY APRIL 23RD

Ma knew that I was getting married and had told me that I could have a house to live in. There were plenty vacant, so I moved Tommy's mother, Mrs Dillon, from Edenvale Road to 13 Belgrave Road, made curtains for the new house and took some unwanted pieces of furniture there, all as if I did not know that the whole thing might come to an end in a few days. As the Rising came nearer I did not see how we could have any kind of ordinary wedding celebrations and felt inclined to cut them all out, but Ma was home now and although she did not give me any money for clothes, she insisted on having a wedding breakfast to which she asked a couple of annoying relations. In fact she made a row about the fact that I bought a hat and a few pounds' worth of clothes because I was too busy looking after her property to make them myself. I paid for everything else out of money I had earned.

I got a terrific send-off from the Liverpool Lambs at Larkfield, and Ma and I went to the church in a taxi. Tommy and I got married on Easter Sunday in Rathmines Church but until we got to the church I did not know that the Lenten regulations at that time extended to the end of Easter Week. No weddings were allowed in the body of the church before Low Sunday, and the priest, Father O'Loughlin, was very rude to us about it, so we were married in the sacristy. George and Jack were there in Volunteer uniform and Rory O'Connor (not in uniform) was best man. Fiona was bridesmaid. Two G-men pushed their way into the sacristy but George, Jack and Rory took great pleasure in putting them out. Joe was unable to come; there were too many meetings going on and, like all the other leaders, he was keeping out of sight lest there be any last minute arrests. Pa was not there either as he was still down the country visiting the bishops, telling them about his meeting with the Pope. We did not know yet whether the Rising was to be on Sunday or Monday.

Afterwards my mother and mother-in-law shared a car back to the house and discussed why I had got married on that particular day. Ma persuaded Mrs Dillon that I must be pregnant and succeeded in convincing her of this, but she did apologise to me a year later when my first child was born. The real reasons for marrying Tommy just then were that the Rising would put an end to my world, nothing would be the same again and I was not going back to that hellhole of family life. We had the breakfast in No. 13 Belgrave Road and afterwards Tommy and I put our bicycles on top of a cab and went to the Imperial Hotel, which was over Clery's opposite the General Post Office. A telephone message came from Ma during the morning to say that a report of MacNeill's countermanding order was in the *Sunday Independent*. Rory came in that afternoon and confirmed that, adding that it was not settled what was actually going to happen but that as far as he knew the Rising was off for that day but to look out from twelve o'clock the next day. I knew then that Dublin Castle must have decided to act and so from now on we were sitting in the window, watching.

The Imperial Hotel, where Gerry and her husband Tommy Dillon spent the first night of their honeymoon, was across O'Connell Street from the GPO and the front rooms afforded a grandstand view of the early scenes of the Rising. Both buildings were destroyed by British shells.

EASTER MONDAY APRIL 24TH

From about ten o'clock on Easter Monday Tommy and I kept looking out the windows of our sitting-room in the hotel and from noon, on this beautiful day, we were sitting and watching through the open second-storey windows. It was breathless. At ten past twelve a company of about 100 uniformed Volunteers wheeled round from Abbey Street, marched up O'Connell Street and halted in front of the GPO. They wheeled left and entered by the main door, which is now closed up. I was looking out for Joe and saw that Mick was with him. Joe was in his new uniform and looking all right. I did not see Jack and George at all and of course we couldn't hear much from where we were. As the troops entered the GPO, we recognised Pearse, Connolly, MacDiarmada and Willie Pearse. Just as the last were going in there was a small bang and a commotion and then someone was carried off on a stretcher; we could not see who it was. When Rory came later he told us it was Liam Clarke. He had slipped as he went in the door and the bomb which he had in his hand had exploded on the lovely, new, bright blue tessellated pavement of the doorway. Then he dropped and was immediately carried away on a stretcher.

There was a fairly large crowd in the street, a holiday crowd, walking about with their families and friends and a constant stream of racegoers on their way to Fairyhouse in their cars. None of them seemed to notice anything out of the way. They were used to seeing Volunteers parading in uniform and manoeuvring in the streets. We watched the Volunteers stopping milkcarts and food carts and bringing the food into the GPO and some supplies were brought in from the Metropole Hotel. All of a sudden the Post Office staff, mostly girls, began to run out of the doors, clutching their hats and coats over their arms, their mouths open, frightened for their lives. Then the Volunteers appeared at all the windows facing onto O'Connell Street and broke out the glass with the butts of their rifles. The men on the street tried to keep the crowd away from the flying glass. A Volunteer came out of the GPO and ripped off the thick pads of recruiting posters which had been defacing the pillars for over a year and that was a pleasure. Then the tricolour was hoisted up the flagstaff on the south front corner of the building and there was quite a cheer from the crowd. From this time on the crowd behaved in a manner which I found quite unexpected. They got so excited that they cared nothing for danger. This had nothing to do with being sympathetic; the sympathisers seemed quite cool and fearless and willing to help. The crowd did not seem to care whether they were cut by the glass or not. The police had vanished and the crowd knew this and knew that they could now do as they chose. There were too few Volunteers to control them and anyway the crowd were not afraid of them. George stood on the front steps of the GPO with an automatic, trying to keep them at a safe distance, but they knew he would not shoot them. He pulled out a long knife and they ran away but they were soon back again.

Most of the crowd were indifferent to what was going on, they were enjoying the drama as spectators. There were, however, a fair number of women who were violently hostile—these were the Separation Allowance women whose men were in the British Army, and we found out afterwards that they thought the sole purpose of the Rising was to put an end to their weekly money and their pensions. These women began picking up pieces of the glass which the Volunteers had broken out of the Post Office windows and threw them in at the windows. Every time they were driven off, they returned like Furies. Some knelt down in the street to curse the Volunteers and I remember one kneeling with her scapular in her outstretched hands, screaming curses at them. George came out again waving his knife at them, which produced some effect. I saw a man driving up and getting out of a car and Tommy said it was Major John MacBride. He was not in uniform and gave the impression of being casual. He had told Joe during a long personal conversation with him that he had thought he would only bring discredit on the Volunteers if he joined before the fighting started, but he had got a promise that as soon as there was any fighting, he would be told at once. Tommy went down to the front door of the hotel to scout for news. He found that the manager, very indignant because of all the glass being broken, had telephoned William Martin Murphy who owned the hotel. William Martin Murphy told him not to worry because, he said, the military would have a big gun in the Dublin mountains in half-an-hour and one shell on the GPO would end the whole thing. There was all sorts of excitement and clamour about the destruction of property going on and the customers were giving out about the police for not stopping it.

Something was happening at the top of the street behind the Parnell statue—some cavalry men appeared near the Rotunda Hospital but they were gone again in a moment. The Volunteers started to make a barricade in Prince's Street with motor cars commandeered from people going to Fairyhouse races. We could hear the racegoers, who seemed to be all English officers, shouting and threatening the men. They seemed to think that this was a piece of impertinence which would be well punished. When Rory came over he told us stories about some of the owners, army officers saying they would complain to the military authorities. The crowd in the street were getting rather excited and started running about when a lot of men in black suddenly appeared out of Marlborough Street and in a moment we realised that they were priests, about forty or fifty of them, who must have been at some meeting in the Pro-Cathedral or the presbytery. They urged and pushed people off the street into Earl Street, Marlborough Street and Abbey Street, but some of them would not go. A tall man in black near the Father Mathew statue would not move, but the street was practically empty inside a minute. The Volunteers aimed their rifles at the street from each window, there was a pause and then a company of cavalry charged down the street. Rory told us afterwards that the Volunteers had orders to hold their fire until the cavalry was level, but the first shots were fired when the vanguard was opposite the tramway office and two thirds of the company turned and galloped back up the street. The rest swept past and when they came level, the bullets started to whistle past us and we had to duck. As the charge went on down the street I could see one man and horse on the ground, one hanging on to his horse's neck and a wounded man on a horse supported on each side by his comrades. They were gone in a moment, it was quite senseless. A horse dropped dead and the rider ran off down the street with the rest of the cavalry towards the quays. The tall man in black at the foot of the Father Mathew statue stood for what seemed quite a few minutes and then dropped dead.

I think it was then that Pearse came out of the GPO with Joe and some others, I could not see who they were. Pearse read the Proclamation of the Republic from a printed sheet, first on the steps and then he moved to the middle of the street, a few yards down from Prince's Street, and read it again. There was absolute silence for a minute, then he gave the remaining copies to some newsboys to distribute and Tommy went out and got one.

Rory came over to fill us in on what was happening. Very few Volunteers had come out in Dublin. Tomás was in Jacob's factory, the Four Courts was held, as were the South Dublin Union, the Corner House at Phibsborough, Davey's at Portobello, Boland's Mills and the Northumberland Road area,

The wrecked tram which served as a barricade on the corner of Earl Street. Gerry, watching from the Imperial Hotel, saw Joe put a bomb in the tram and shoot at it with his Mauser; the bomb exploded and smashed the chassis. That was the last time she saw Joe.

and the Citizen Army was in Stephen's Green. There were a lot of other places, some of which would be very hard to hold without support. The timing had been good and all the occupation had been done inside twenty minutes. There was no intention to capture Dublin Castle because it was overlooked by high buildings, but there had been some hope of capturing arms in the Ship Street cavalry barracks. The worst news was the failure to take the telephone exchange (the company who were to take it simply did not turn out), as it left the enemy in control of communications. Fergus Kelly took over the Atlantic College's little radio station in O'Connell Street and sent the news out over and over again, '*Irish Republic declared in Dublin, Pearse first President*'. It was in Morse and only carried halfway across the Atlantic, but it was picked up by a tramp steamer which brought the news to the United States. His heroic efforts were some compensation for the loss of Con Keating. There was absolutely no news from the country and we heard nothing of what happened in Galway or Enniscorthy or even Ashbourne until long afterwards.

We watched out of the window again when Rory had gone and Joe and George and other Volunteers came out into the street. One of the Volunteers got into a tram which had been abandoned at the Pillar, and tried to get up enough speed to ram it into another one in the Earl Street opening to wreck it. This was to make a barricade, because Earl Street is just opposite the GPO, but he did not succeed. Then he threw a bomb at the Earl Street tram but it did not explode. Joe put another bomb in the tram and shot at it with his Mauser from about thirty yards—he was a beautiful shot. The shot exploded the bomb and smashed the chassis. The tram settled down on the bogies and now could not be moved, which served the purpose intended. That was the last time I saw Joe.

When the bomb exploded in the tram it broke the windows of Noblett's shop and a boy discovered that he could stretch in his hand and get the sweets and then the crowd helped him. An hour later there was not a window left in the street. Some of the incidents were very funny: the dummies from the dress shops were taken dancing down the street, an old lady wore a top hat and a large checked ulster, a man sat down on the kerb to read a pile of books, but he did not seem to care for them as he threw them in the gutter and went back for more, another man fired several revolver shots in the air but no-one noticed them. George came out of the GPO with some white staves and called for some volunteer police and the men who took them did their best but it was quite useless. The sound of breaking glass in Abbey Street drew most of the crowd away.

It was about six o'clock when Rory came across again from the GPO where he had been talking with Joe. I had asked Rory to ask Joe to let me help in the Post Office, but he brought back the answer that I was not to do so. He said that it was already crowded and they had more than enough help for cooking and nursing for the number of men there. He said we were to go now and try to get back to Belgrave Road. Joe had said I was to go to Larkfield with Tommy and Rory to help them to try to get the tar-still working in case of it being needed, and that if by any impossible, wild chance things went better than they could, we should make some explosives there. Tommy had made a list of the chemical factories but he gave up when Rory told him that the situation was as bad as we feared. I was so used to doing what Joe ordered that I tried to take his order seriously in spite of Rory's news. He had no news of the condition of our way back and it was of course possible that we would be stopped and turned back, that the road would be held by British soldiers, even if they were in small parties. Rory thought he could get home to his father's house in Monkstown by going through Ringsend. If both parties succeeded in getting home he would meet us in Larkfield the next day, if we could get there.

It was getting dark and then suddenly the street lights flickered and lit up. It was great carbon arcs in those days. We got our bicycles and with a small bag strapped on to one of them, we cycled without any opposition across O'Connell Bridge, along D'Olier Street, Brunswick Street, Westland Row, the Green, Harcourt Street, up through Belgrave Square to 13 Belgrave Road. We met nothing on the way, very few people, no soldiers, no police. We saw that the Rising was a complete surprise to the English. Every hour's delay was a disaster to Dublin Castle rule. Joe must have been right when he said that there were no big guns in Dublin barracks. The bulk of our luggage was left in the hotel and was, of course, burnt with the rest.

EASTER TUESDAY APRIL 25TH

On Tuesday morning we got out to Larkfield on bicycles without meeting any soldiers. Rory was there and he had already been in to the GPO, having walked in by Sandymount strand. He said that there was absolute quiet downtown and the Volunteers could only wait for the coming fight. Joe was all right but very tired. Fiona joined us in Larkfield while Rory was there. Tommy and Rory discussed whether it would be any use for them to go down to the GPO and Rory said he agreed with Joe, that it would not improve the position if more men went in there. He did not think anything could be done to help, so he proposed to carry messages in and out but would not remain. He also brought us messages, mostly bad news. The Glasgow firm which had supplied the tar-still was trying to fix it around that time but it would not work. The Larkfield Chemical Company, Tommy, Rory and two sleeping partners called Supple, of the glove shop in Grafton Street, claimed, and afterwards obtained, compensation from the Glasgow firm in respect of this. It was hopeless trying to get it going, and anyway it would have been no use, but it was not a question of explosives but inaction that was dreadful. Rory felt as useless as we did, so we filled the drawers of a desk, which Rory had given us as a wedding present, with cotton waste and sent it in to Belgrave Road on a donkey cart.

Fiona went back to Fitzwilliam Street, where she had been with Ma and Pa, and Dr Kathleen Dillon, my sister-in-law, who was called to the College of Surgeons to look after a wounded girl. Mimi was caught in New York for the Rising and stayed there for six months with the Cohalans, and Moya was still in her convent in England. Pa had arrived back from the country and he came over to Belgrave Road to give me a little bag of sovereigns as a wedding present. He had gone down to the GPO to ask that he be taken on as a Volunteer but Joe told him that there were more than enough there and to go home; Pa was then sixty-five. He had a long conversation with James Connolly there and Connolly told him, as he had told Joe, that if he lived, he would like to re-write everything he had written in the light of what he now thought, that freedom came first, but he smiled then and said he did not think he would have the time. He talked affectionately and enthusiastically of his comrades.

The MacDonaghs were now living down the road in Oakley Road and we went down there, as we often did from then on, to see if Muriel had any more news than we had, but she didn't. Martial law was declared.

From Wednesday morning, Rathmines, like all the outlying areas, was completely cut off and there was no question of getting out of it, but I was able to get a basket of food. The machine guns rattled all day and night. The two Florence Dillons, Tommy's sister-in-law and her daughter, arrived to take refuge in 13 Belgrave Road after a sniper killed the curate from the tower on

Haddington Road Church near their house. Rory managed to get in to the GPO and bring back news again. The complications of the Rising could not be guessed at; we would have to wait and see what happened and pretend to ourselves that, by some miracle, another boatload of arms might come or the troop transports might be torpedoed on their way from England. A proclamation was posted imposing curfew from six o'clock, but Tommy and I went down all the same to see Muriel and exchange news. Hanna Sheehy-Skeffington, who also lived on Belgrave Road, was there. She told us that Frank was missing since Monday and that she could get no news of him. She was sure he had been arrested, but since he was a known pacifist she hoped he was safe.

The battle of Mount Street Bridge had begun. This was the part of Joe's plan that worked far beyond his expectations. Seventeen men in houses at the bridge held up a column of British troops on their way from Kingstown, and inflicted the greatest number of casualties of the entire Rising.

Winifred Carney, Connolly's personal secretary in the GPO, said afterwards that Connolly had a very high opinion of Joe. Miss Carney saw Joe's appearance, his bangle and rings, as unsoldierly, but Connolly smiled and said that Joe could please himself, as he could teach them all in military science, and that he was 'clear-minded and a man of his word'. Joe was physically very frail but I was told that as the week went on, as British reinforcements arrived and the shelling grew worse, he put all his energy into keeping up spirits in the GPO. He walked up and down the line of men at the front windows, shouting encouragement, and at one point announced, 'It is the first time that a capital has been burned since Moscow!'

EASTER THURSDAY APRIL 27TH

On Thursday morning early we woke to the boom of the big guns. Machine guns rattled night and day without stopping. Rory was fired at trying to get to the GPO, and had to turn back. Our house began to fill with more refugees, friends and relations who thought Rathmines was safe. We ran down to see Muriel but none of us had any news.

EASTER FRIDAY APRIL 28TH

On Friday morning the whole of Rathmines, including our road, was covered with huge sheets of burnt paper. This was from the *Freeman* newspaper office in Prince's Street, but we did not know this at the time. We had made some of the cotton waste from Larkfield into gun-cotton in the bathroom during the week and when we heard the house was going to be searched, I stuffed a cushion with it and put it in a cushion cover. When we saw the searches start, we buried our guns in the garden. The soldiers searched all the houses and were advised by one of our neighbours to search ours again. They came back a third time with a police list. The soldiers were weedy lads, dressed in wretched uniforms; one of them thought they were in Norway. We all sat in the drawing-room (I sat on the cushion full of gun-cotton) trying to keep a refugee child occupied, guarded by a poor, dirty, almost ragged boy soldier with fixed bayonet. My mother-in-law was raging with me, I had brought trouble on them.

Pa was arrested at 26 Fitzwilliam Street that day.

When we got down to Muriel's, Hanna told us that she had been searching Dublin for Frank. She had heard that he was in Portobello Barracks. She and her sisters, Mrs Tom Kettle and Mrs Culhane, went there to inquire. They were arrested for some hours in spite of their pointing out that Tom Kettle was in the British Army as was their brother, Captain Sheehy. They were refused information. She said she would appeal to Father O'Loughlin, the Rathmines curate, again. He had told her he knew nothing of her husband, but this seems to have been untrue. After dark, the fires in the city filled the sky with an orange light which slowly changed to a terrible glow of red and then died away.

EASTER SATURDAY APRIL 29TH

When Hanna Sheehy-Skeffington saw Father O'Loughlin again, he told her, brutally, that she might as well make up her mind to it that her husband was dead and buried. That was on the Saturday of Easter Week, but on the previous night, after she had left Muriel MacDonagh's, Captain Bowen Colthurst and another officer had led a raiding party on her house. They fired a volley through the windows, burst open the door and held Hanna, her small son and the maid under arrest while they searched the house and removed all her textbooks. She was a teacher of languages with high university degrees. Colthurst, later judged insane, had already killed her husband. Frank had been trying to get a volunteer police force together to stop looting. On Wednesday, April 26th, Bowen Colthurst ordered a firing party of seven soldiers to shoot two men, Dixon and McIntyre, and Frank Sheehy-Skeffington in the yard of Portobello Barracks. None of them were involved in the Rising. Of course, we didn't hear any of this until two weeks later when the Inquiry into the business began. I last met Frank at Shrovetide, 1916, in the Abbey Theatre. He had just returned from the USA and we asked him what he thought of the way things were going in Ireland and he said he knew what was going to happen. He was more than sympathetic, he was one of the revolutionaries.

On Saturday, during the day, we heard news of the surrender but no details. Fiona arrived in a cab at midday with Rice, the solicitor, who brought her to me when Ma was arrested when they were on their way across town. Ma had been trying to get to Dublin Castle to get news of Pa and my brothers. She had a little attaché case filled with Woodbine cigarettes to give to the soldiers, and this got her through cordon after cordon until she got close enough to be arrested. She told me later that she was really trying to find someone in authority to establish that she had no connection with the Rising. I went to Fitzwilliam Street; the door was banging open and a man across the street had wanted to close it but his wife, who was terrified, wouldn't let him. Nothing was gone from the house.

SUNDAY APRIL 30TH

Kathleen Dillon came to us the next day, so we had a full house. There was no food to be got, no bread even. We had a half stone of flour, some carrots, a tin or two of milk. We walked down Rathmines through a rejoicing crowd, who were shouting to one other that the rebels would all be shot. In the crowd there were also young men with caps pulled well down—the ones that got away. We heard details of the surrender, that the leaders expected to be shot but had tried to negotiate for the rank and file. Someone who had escaped told me how, after the surrender, the Volunteers in the GPO had been made to lie down in the Rotunda Gardens all night on the wet grass under searchlights and about the furious British officers who had bullied them and screamed at them in the traditional manner of British officers to natives everywhere. I have heard since that it was much worse than anything I was told at the time. Joe seemed to be dying. Winifred Carney covered him with her coat. I found it hard to believe those who told me then that he was dying. I had nursed him for so long that I felt he could survive almost anything and I thought that if I could have got him back, I could have nursed him to health. We lost heart when we heard all these things.

Rory O'Connor got his father to write a letter to some high Castle official asking him to use his influence to keep Jack and George from being executed, but before he could deliver it he was hit in the ankle by a stray bullet at the corner of Grafton Street and was brought to Mercer's Hospital. The nurses kept saying he was a Sinn Féiner and should be shot because he had a holy medal in his pocket that Fiona had given him. Dr Maunsel heard this and moved him to a nursing home in Leeson Street and it was three weeks before his brother, Norbert, found him.

MONDAY MAY 1ST

On Monday the courts martial began and we heard rumours that the leaders were all to be shot at once but hoped that it was not going to be as complete as that.

TUESDAY MAY 2ND

Muriel MacDonagh was brought a message by a private soldier that Tomás was to be shot. He told her that if she rang the barracks she could see Tomás but he omitted to give her a pass and when she tried to get down to

A page from Joe Plunkett's court martial. He was executed on the day after Patrick Pearse and Tomás MacDonagh. The continued series of executions had a more inflammatory effect on public opinion than the Rising itself.

Kilmainham Jail to see him, she was stopped each time at the cordons. She tried to get a message to the Castle to ask if she could see him and Dr Hennessey, who lived on Oakley Road, helped her to find a phone but the owners of the only phone on the road refused to let her use it. She never got to see Tomás.

WEDNESDAY MAY 3RD

On Wednesday we heard first that Pearse had been shot. That night Muriel ran down after curfew to us in Belgrave Road at about eleven o'clock with her brother, Liebert, who had turned up from the British Navy and was staying with her, and while we were talking at the gate my mother-in-law was standing on the top step at the hall door shouting over and over again, 'Don't let her into the house!' Poor Muriel! There was nothing we could do.

Muriel then told me that Tomás had been shot that morning and Joe was to be shot next morning. That was that.

THE DARK WAY

Rougher than Death the road I choose
Yet shall my feet not walk astray,
Though dark, my way I shall not lose
For this way is the darkest way . . .

Now I have chosen in the dark
The desolate way to walk alone
Yet strive to keep alive one spark
Of your known grace and grace unknown.

And when I leave you lest my love
Should seal your spirit's ark with clay,
Spread your bright wings, O shining dove—
But my way is the darkest way.

—

Joseph Plunkett

11 After the Rising May–December 1916

Almost at once after Joe's execution a kind lawyer, J. J. McDonald, brought me news of Pa and Ma, that they were still alive. In the atmosphere of the time, when almost anything might have happened, this was a relief, though to tell the truth I could not feel very much. A lot of people were annoyed at the mean and savage way we had been treated and did what they could for us. Then on Thursday we read a story in the *Independent* about a Grafton Street jeweller named Stokes who had opened his shop so that Grace could buy a wedding ring. Grace herself arrived in Belgrave Road later to tell us of how she and Joe had been married at midnight. She had managed the most incredible things, the permission, the ring, getting into the prison. She told us there were six soldiers with fixed bayonets in the little chapel with them, and there were soldiers with them again when she saw him later that night in his cell for just ten minutes. She had not believed that Joe would be shot; the officer in charge told her several times that he thought Joe would not be shot, that he was dying. I did not know until long afterwards that that

After the Rising hundreds of Volunteer prisoners were marched off to jail in Britain.

officer was Niall O'Morchoe; he and Joe had played together as children in Kilternan. If Joe had shown any signs of life after the rifle shots O'Morchoe, as officer in charge, would have had to finish him off with a revolver. He refused to give the order to fire and was dishonourably discharged and ruined as a result.

Some said Joe's wedding had lost some sympathy for the Rising. It was said, of course, that Grace must have been pregnant; the curate who got permission for the marriage must have thought so. Grace said that she told him she must get married and that he asked her, 'Must you?' and she said, 'Yes'. The story which went round was that she was going to have a baby but that Joe was not the father. I was told on good authority that this story was put about by Dublin Castle. Another one was that Grace had had a baby three months before and that we were all at the christening dressed in green. I was also supposed to have had a baby and two old asses who kept a newspaper shop on Kimmage Road came to our house and solemnly asked me if this was true.

Mrs Gifford came down to the MacDonagh house in Oakley Road, and brought Muriel and Grace and the two children, Donagh and Barbara, to the Gifford family home in Palmerston Road, but she could not resist making insulting remarks about Tomás as selfish for abandoning his wife and family, so Muriel took her children and went straight back to Oakley Road. Fiona went down to her and stayed to help with the housekeeping.

On Friday, 5th May, a lorry full of soldiers, with an officer in charge, went to Larkfield and took away anything of any value down to bedclothes and clothing. They turned the office files onto the floor, mostly looking for photographs of Joe to sell to the newspapers. O'Neill, the gardener, saved my christening mug by putting it under his hat and Cook saved my linen by saying it was hers. The housemaid's father tried to blackmail me, saying he had seen something white (the gun-cotton), but I developed a poker face and gave the girl her fare home. As soon as I could I spent several hours a day clearing up after the soldiers but they had made such a mess that I had to leave a big barrel of the papers as they were. My mother-in-law was raging with me for bringing trouble on the household. She said, 'The leaders must be a mean crew, a rotten lot, to bring all that trouble on the people. They must have expected to get something for themselves out of it. It was ambition made them do it'. It was no use saying anything to her. Kathleen, my sister-in-law, told me not to mind her. She was on our side but she had to go back to her work in the hospital in Mullingar.

Professor Hugh Ryan had been asked if Tommy could have been making bombs and he said that he could. Dr Denis Coffey, President of UCD, held up Tommy's and Johnny Nolan's salaries (£12 10s a month) for two months until he had made them say that they had nothing to do with the Rising (which was not true). Florence Dillon was not on our side and although she

George and Jack Plunkett (second and third from left, aged twenty-two and eighteen respectively) in Volunteer uniforms at Richmond Barracks after their arrest. George and Jack were both sentenced to death, commuted to life and were in English jails until June, 1917.

and young Florence were in the house for at least a fortnight and knew that Tommy had no money, she never offered to pay a penny. Now Pa's wedding present, the little bag of sovereigns, came in handy.

When the newspapers came out on Saturday the 6th we saw that George and Jack had also been sentenced to death and the sentence commuted to ten years. Jack told me afterwards that he had been told first of the death sentence and that the officer had then paused for a whole minute before telling him it had been commuted. Jack and George were brought to Mountjoy Jail for a few days, and then brought in a cattle boat to Holyhead. They spent six months in Portland Prison before being moved to Parkhurst, on the Isle of Wight.

I got some South African medal ribbon because it was green, white and orange and made it into a bow which I wore everywhere. A big policeman in Dame Street stopped me and said the tricolour would get me into trouble. I said, 'I have one brother shot and two brothers sentenced to death and my father and mother in jail'. He said 'You're Plunkett, you can wear it.' He was seven foot tall. When I went riding with Alice Doyle, she begged me to take off the tricolour brooch. She said Tommy was such a nice man she was sure he wouldn't like it. As she didn't know Tommy I asked her, 'What makes you think he's a nice man?' Alice said, 'Because he married you.' I took that as a compliment.

A letter from Ma to Fiona arrived:

6a Married Quarters
C/o Sgt Maj Lewis
Richmond Barracks
7th May 1916
Dear Fiona
I've just been told that I am to leave here today—I will try to let you know where I go to.

I believe you can send me clothes and food but I'm not sure about the regulations in the next place, but Pappy could receive clothes and food and cigs to give away and a few better ones to smoke while he is here as Mc N is with him I think, so he might like to divide—I'd like my little cheque book later on and take out any papers that are in it such as lodgments dockets—and keep them safe for me. If Lena is not afraid of being in sympathy you might go to her if she will have you—Trust in God obstinately.

These things come but to try us and keep us steadfast in the ways of virtue, steadfastness and good works.
Tell Ger to look after Grace and give her my love
Your loving Mother

Fiona and I had searched the town and the jails for Pa and Ma before this and hadn't been able to find them. The day after Ma's letter arrived, we went to Richmond Barracks and asked for Pa but we were told he wasn't there. A few days later we got word that Ma was in Mountjoy Jail and we brought food and clothes there for her, but we were not allowed see her.

About Sunday, 7th May, Father McCann SJ came to Tommy to see what could be done for the dependants of the executed and the prisoners. Tommy sent him on to Kit Ryan with the advice that as many neutral and Irish Party names as possible should be got as supporters to prevent the funds being confiscated and so the National Aid Association was started. The money poured in at the rate of £1,000 a month but every penny was needed. It was hard to hold fundraising concerts and so on because all functions were prohibited under martial law.

One night after curfew two English army officers arrived and brought me a letter from Pa from Richmond Barracks. They told me they would call at eight-thirty next morning to bring me to him. In the letter he asked me for food, soap and a towel:

F Block Richmond Barracks
Goldenbridge
12 May 1916
My Dear Gerry
Could you send me at once a change of linen (set of woollens, socks, shirt, collars, cuffs), brush and comb, toothbrush, sponge, towel and soap. Also a tin of condensed milk and 1lb butter, which I need and £1 in small silver.

Visitors can come here between 11am and 10c,
[parts missing here]
    I am praying for you all always; we are in God's hands.
    With all my love to each —
    Your Loving Father
    Keep up your hearts. I am very well, D.G. I have heard the worst but God is good
[part missing]
    God Bless.
    Also some notepaper, pen and ink and . . . penny stamps

Next morning Fiona and I brought these things to Richmond Barracks and were kept waiting a long time in the office of the Provost Marshal, Colonel Foster, while we were inspected by Major Dudley Heathcote,* the intelligence officer. Father Augustine, one of the Capuchin priests who had seen Joe just before he went out to be shot, was on the next bench. He gave Joe's love to us and told us how he had died. He had been with him until the last minute and praised him in every way. Father Augustine had a bit of Joe's hair for Ma and he gave me Joe's spectacles, which he took off at the last minute saying he would not need them. He also gave me Joe's keys of Larkfield. Father Augustine's kindness was a wonderful relief from the complete panic we had been enduring from others. All this time Major Heathcote kept scolding a young officer who had released Desmond FitzGerald without orders.

We were taken upstairs to a guardroom where Pa was alone, sitting on the bed. I hardly recognised him. He had been arrested more than a fortnight before and was extremely dirty and miserable and more pleased to see the

Richmond Barracks, where four members of the Plunkett family—the Count and Countess, George and Jack —were imprisoned after the Rising, and a fifth, Joe, was court-martialled.

This is not the Dudley Heathcote who 'married' Columba O'Carroll; he was probably a cousin.

soap and towel than the food. His beard had practically all fallen off and although he was only sixty-five, he looked eighty-five, a poor, tired old man. I hugged and kissed him and cried, but Fiona could not move—old stoic habits. He told us all that had happened.

After his arrest in Fitzwilliam Street on the Friday of Easter Week he and other prisoners were marched through town, taking more prisoners on the way including a poor old tramp on the quays. At Richmond Barracks they were all pushed into an already full cell, making about thirty of them crammed into this cell meant for two—a black hole—for the whole night. The sanitation can only be imagined—as slop buckets were left unemptied before long the floor was awash. The older and feebler took turns to sit on the seat and the younger men made a pile of their coats for Pa, as the oldest and weakest, to lie on. He said that by far the kindest man there was the old tramp who had been picked up for no reason. The next day Pa and 35 others were put in a room meant for eight. They had bully beef, black tea and dog biscuits and Pa broke his last tooth. He told me he was got at by an officer who used to make him and old James Sweetman run with buckets across the parade ground. As all the courts martial were held in Richmond Barracks, Pa had known all about them and some of the men, held in the same room with him, tried helping when Pa himself was put in line for a court martial three times and sent back three times. He found out afterwards that a number of powerful old friends and very influential people had been doing their utmost to save him. He also had a great many friends outside Ireland, where he was better known as an art critic, trying to help.

I had not known before this that Pa was in Richmond Barracks the day of Joe's drumhead court martial and had seen, from the guardroom window on the first storey, Joe standing in the pouring rain in the barrack square; Joe saw him and they stayed looking at one another for a long twenty minutes till Joe was moved on. Pa knew by then that Joe would soon be shot and he was weeping as he told me this. Even after the executions it was not thought right to weep openly, but Pa did, and it was one of the reasons I loved him.

On the night of May 3rd Pa and Ma were brought to Kilmainham Jail and put in a cell there. At four o'clock in the morning Pa heard the shots of the firing party and knew it was Joe's execution, but Ma slept. They never saw Joe, were never told why they were there and the next day they were brought back to their separate cells in Richmond Barracks. They were probably brought to Kilmainham to see Joe and his marriage to Grace must have stopped it, but other leaders saw more than one of their relatives before their execution.

I kept bringing food and clothes to Pa in Richmond Barracks until he told me he was now getting a really good dinner every day straight from the officers' mess. No explanation was given until the tremendous cook-sergeant of the Highland regiment arrived in Pa's cell in his full Black Watch dress uniform, saluted, and said he hoped that the dinners were satisfactory. Pa, very surprised, said the food was excellent and the cook said 'Mr Dewar said *Remember!*' He saluted again and left. Pa was mystified and it took some time to discover that it was Mr Dewar of Dewar's Whisky who was responsible. He was a Jacobite who had refused a title from the British Government and when he came to Kingstown on Sir Thomas Lipton's yacht he asked to meet 'the person who had helped translate the Jacobite officer's diary'. My father had collaborated with Father Edmund Hogan in deciphering and publishing Charles O'Kelly's diary, *The Jacobite War in Ireland,* and so met Dewar on Tommy Lipton's yacht and made friends with him. Mr Dewar had instructed his friends in the Black Watch to do what they could for my father in jail. *Remember!* is the Jacobite slogan, the last word King Charles the First spoke on the scaffold.

Ma wrote to me from jail:

1019 Countess Plunkett
HM Prison Service
Mountjoy - Prison
16.5-16

Dear Gerry

We can receive one visit each day and even three people can come together, so I hope you will come see me tomorrow, before one, if possible, & if not, later. I want you to do something for me so bring pencil & paper to write so as not to forget. I told Grace to come on Friday—Bring a few eggs and flowers if there are any in the garden—my steel knitting needles are in the basket in the dining room and some more coarse cotton—some hairpins and a penny looking glass—

Love to all
Your Mammy
(Josephine) JM Plunkett
Some MS paper would be a boon and a green book on dining room table "Ancient Civilization "

I saw Ma and brought things to her at Mountjoy Jail the day after her letter arrived. She had discovered that she could have dinners sent in from the local shop. While I was waiting in the hall, a number of dinners were delivered and I saw the doorman lifting off the lids to allow them to get cold. When I asked him what he thought he was doing, he said, 'If they wanted hot dinners they should have stayed out of Mountjoy.' Ma told me that some looters had been caught with jewellery and Ma had identified some jewels brought to her as her mother's diamonds.

After the Rising odd things happened.

My cousin Mary White told me that she could not know me now, as it would be bad for her brother, Dudley's, career. As Pa had helped them so much after their father died, this was funny.

Captain Kinsman, our Marlborough Road tenant and the author of one of the handbooks on tactics that Joe used for the Rising, left the house in a rage

Count Plunkett's study in Fitzwilliam Street, wrecked by looting British soldiers. In 1918 the family lawyer called to offer the Count £2,000 compensation on condition he attended the Trinity College Convention. Mimi laughed and said 'I'm sure he'd want more than that.'

a week after the Rising; perhaps he was dismissed. He tore all the light fittings out of the wall and left without notice. No manners! I made him pay up for £40 worth of repairs and rent for a quarter.

I got a request from Eimar O'Duffy to tell his mother he was safe and well. He was in Monaghan where he had gone with the countermanding order. His sister was very rude to me but his mother thanked me.

I went to Edward Martyn, who had got very old and shyer than ever, and asked him if he wanted to carry on with the Hardwicke Street Theatre. He said he did and agreed to pay John MacDonagh's salary, the gas and electric bill and a very small rent, but he did not pay them. He sacked John and brought in an English ex-officer as producer and spoke rudely to the company about it. They were an unpaid company and had never cared for him, most of them were Joe and Tomás's personal friends, so nearly all of them walked out. Later Ma had some kind of annoyance with Edward and took the Hardwicke Hall back from him.

We heard that Sarah Ferrall, the American cousin who had lived with us for seven years and who had become quite fond of the family, had died as a result of the shock of learning about the Rising and Joe's death.

At some point we heard that Liam Mellowes, Robert Monteith and six others had reached the USA safely and Darrell Figgis came up to Dublin from Achill and gave me a Mauser, a lovely gun, to keep for him. It was much too good for him so I gave it to Mick Collins when he came home from internment at Christmas. Mick gave Figgis a revolver in exchange.

Seán MacDiarmada had a room on the floor above the printing works in Temple Bar and when I went to see if Joe had left anything in the *Irish Review* office, Manico told me that he had helped the English soldiers to search Seán's room and after they had left, Manico noticed that Seán's pocket book was on the mantelpiece and ran down the street after them to give it to them. In 1914 Joe had given Manico a bill of sale on all unsold copies of the *Irish Review* and Joe's own poems, in order to keep the *Review* going. Immediately after the Rising Manico sold them all for half-a-crown apiece. A week later they were selling for thirty shillings.

The Rising put an end to Pa's job in the Museum. The Royal Dublin Society also dropped him and many organisations took his name off their lists. On the other hand, the Protestant Primate, Dr Crozier, wrote him a letter of sympathy—they had been students together.

It was obvious as early as the 7th of May that General Maxwell was carrying out orders from the military and that executions in Dublin did not tally with government opinion. The executions were an unavoidable piece of stupidity for them and the ruin of the Irish Party. Ordinary Irish people began to recover from the fright they had been given, and their opinion seemed to be that while the shooting of Pearse was inevitable, it was going too far to shoot Seán Mac Diarmada, who was a cripple, Connolly, who was wounded and Joe, who was dying. John Redmond asked for clemency, but only for the rank and file; even Carson said that nothing should be done in a hurry, but the English and Irish Tory papers howled for blood and more blood. Even when thousands had been interned, one hundred and thirty-four sentenced to penal servitude and hard labour, fifteen executed (Casement was the sixteenth), the so-called leaders of public opinion wanted martial law continued. It was said that the Rising was an orgy of murder, that the Volunteers had been brutal to their prisoners and that they had fired on the Red Cross. The prisoners concerned, soldiers mostly, wrote to the newspapers denying that they had been treated badly and saying that they had been treated with great kindness, but the politicians took the charges as proved. It was plain that the Irish Party was glad that the Rising was a failure but they were disconcerted by the reprisals being carried out with so little regard for the appearance of justice. In fact these immediate reprisals were only one factor in the change in public opinion. Others were the revelations at the Inquiry into the murder of Frank Sheehy-Skeffington, the trial and hanging of Roger Casement and the wholesale deportation and internment of thousands of men who had previously little connection with the Volunteers.

There were calls for clemency and it was a matter, they said, for statesmen not soldiers. In fact, there was no right way of dealing with it. It was known that General Maxwell had taken control of the telegraph and telephone companies and given orders that only military messages should be received or sent, so no protests could be made to London. When Sir William De Courcy

Wheeler became aware that General Maxwell intended to execute large numbers of Volunteers, at least one hundred and twenty, and a great pit had been dug to hold the bodies, he protested to Maxwell but to no effect. He was not permitted to telephone or telegraph, but he managed to get the commander of a gunboat to carry him to Holyhead 'on official business' and went straight to the Prime Minister, Asquith, to protest. On that same day, May 8th, Ceannt, Colbert, Heuston and Mallin were shot. The shooting of Thomas Kent in Cork on May 9th was announced to be 'for murder'.

These were all drumhead courts martial; no defence was allowed nor lawyers admitted until Eoin MacNeill was tried. The only evidence given to the court was the formal identification of the accused by the Castle intelligence officers. The two leaders left to be 'dealt with' at this stage were James Connolly and Seán MacDiarmada. Public opinion credited William Martin Murphy with hounding Connolly to execution as a labour leader. At the House of Commons debate on May 11th John Dillon suggested that Prime Minister Asquith was being kept in the dark by the military. He asked about Frank Sheehy-Skeffington and said,

> 'I do not come here to raise one word in defence of murder. If there be a case of cold-blooded murder, by all means try the man openly, before a court martial if you like but let the public know what the evidence is and prove that he is a murderer and then do what you like with him. But it is not murderers who are being executed, it is insurgents who have fought a clean fight, a brave fight, however misguided and it would be a damn good thing for you if your soldiers were able to put out as good a fight as these men did in Dublin—3,000 men against 20,000.'

(Actually it had been less than 1,000 against 30,000.) Asquith refused at first to give an undertaking that there would be no more executions without a Commons debate, but the next day he agreed to this. It is difficult not to think that the delay was deliberate and designed to allow the military men to complete their work.

James Connolly and Seán MacDiarmada were executed on May 12th and the day after their executions Prime Minister Asquith came to Dublin. He had an interview with General Maxwell, inspected the barracks and spoke to the prisoners, shook hands with some of them and said they had put up a clean fight. This was reported in a newspaper and I was told it by some of the prisoners when they were released, but it was denied at once officially.

On May 12th we began to get the details of Frank Sheehy-Skeffington's murder from the papers. On Easter Tuesday he had been arrested at Portobello Bridge while distributing leaflets calling on the public to prevent looting, and these were the only documents found on Frank of any importance. Questioned by Captain Bowen Colthurst, Frank stated that he was in favour of passive resistance and opposed to militarism. Bowen Colthurst was going to raid Alderman J. J. Kelly's house in Harrington Street and took Frank with him as a hostage. He ordered Frank's hands to be tied behind him and told him to say his prayers and they went in a lorry with soldiers along Rathmines Road where Bowen Colthurst shot a boy named Coade and another man who were going about their business and had nothing to do with the Rising. They went along 'firing so as to keep people indoors' leaving Frank with a guard at the canal bridge, with orders to shoot him if the military party was fired on. They threw a bomb into J. J. Kelly's shop and arrested Kelly and Dixon and MacIntyre, the Unionist editors of two nondescript weekly journals who had no connection with the Volunteers. The next day Bowen Colthurst went into the guardroom and ordered Dixon, MacIntyre and Sheehy-Skeffington out into the yard where the firing party, seven soldiers, shot them. Frank was seen to move and Colthurst ordered another volley. The murdered men were buried in sheets in the barracks yard and exhumed for the Inquiry. In Colthurst's report he said nothing of taking Frank as a hostage and called the three shot men leaders of the rebels and desperate men. He raved about all sorts of rumours.

It was Coade's father who told Hanna Sheehy-Skeffington that he had seen the body of a man with a beard beside his son's body in the barracks. George Bernard Shaw wrote to Hanna about her husband and the scandal could not be ignored. Captain Bowen Colthurst was a member of a Cork ascendancy family, an officer of sixteen years' standing who had been sent back from France during the war as 'unreliable in action'. He was hag-ridden with ascendancy and colonial traditions, but the only officer who attempted to stop his course of action was Sir Francis Vane, who was appalled and had tried to get his superior officers to act. Their response was to promote Bowen Colthurst to the command of Portobello Barracks. Colthurst was placed under open arrest on May 6th, court martialled and committed to Broadmoor as insane. I saw him the day after the court martial staggering down Wicklow Street with a bottle of whiskey sticking out of his pocket. I was already familiar with his appearance, a big fair-haired horse-faced man; a pattern of our Norman masters. Sir Francis Vane was retired as over-age.

We read the proceedings of the Commission of Inquiry into the Rising when they were published day by day in the papers, beginning on 18th May. Dublin Castle officials had found themselves in a position of very real difficulty and had to give their version of what happened at this full dress Commission. Many of them thought that they were being made responsible for the mistakes of their political superiors as every measure proposed by them had been turned down by Chief Secretary Augustine Birrell with the British Cabinet, either for political reasons or because it would stop recruiting. Birrell thought it would be a good thing if the War Office could send more soldiers to be trained in Ireland because even if they were not much use as soldiers, he thought they could be marched up and down to overawe the civilian popula-

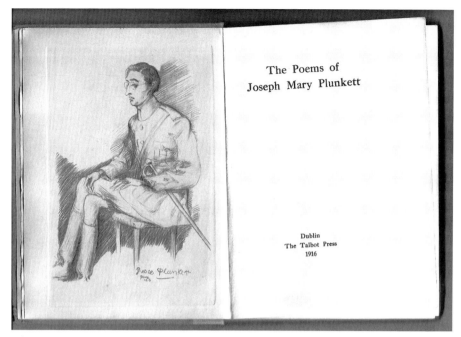

The warrior aesthete: a collection of Joe Plunkett's poetry was published by the Talbot Press, September 1916, with an introduction by Gerry Plunkett Dillon, dated June 1916, one month after his execution, and a memory drawing by Grace Gifford Plunkett. The book was reprinted three times.

tion. He said, 'The people are not law-abiding but they yield to firm control if it is impartial and just.' This had never been tried! Birrell thought a rebellion would not start at that time of day, that sort of thing usually started earlier than half-past twelve; a rebellion should start just after breakfast. He thought the date of the outbreak very well timed and said that they had no spies on the Volunteer Executive but he seemed to think it was not good form of the Germans to encourage rebellion in Ireland. The Lord Lieutenant, Lord Wimborne, had heard the Volunteers derided from the time he had first come to Dublin, but he had come to the conclusion that they were dangerous, although he had great difficulty in getting police reports. Dublin Castle relied on their chief intelligence officer, Major Ivor Price, to tell them if the situation was serious. He was a promoted policeman who was not clever and hated the Volunteers. We used to hear about his intelligence reports from our contacts in Dublin Castle and they were not true. He was the principal witness at the drumhead courts martial after the Rising. This was usually just identification, but after Seán MacDiarmada's trial, Seán told a friend that Major Price had told a fearsome pack of lies. The police reported what was said at meetings and reviews, sometimes accurately but often wildly, and Tomás MacDonagh once said that he found he could say anything he liked at a meeting because the police never believed him to be serious.

The English Admiralty had had information from their spies that a cargo

IRISH REBELLION, MAY 1916.

JOSEPH PLUNKETT (son of Count Plunkett),
Commandant-General Irish Republican Army,
Executed May 4th, 1916.
Who was married a few hours before his execution.

A commemoration postcard issued in 1916. The photograph was taken when Joe was about twenty. Before he went to Germany to arrange for the arms shipment he destroyed as many photographs of himself as he could find, so that the British could not use them to recognise him. This photograph brings out the aesthete in him. According to Roddy Connolly, James Connolly's son, he turned out for the Rising 'gorgeously apparelled'.

of arms was on its way to Ireland from Germany to start a Rising. Casement was arrested on Good Friday and on Saturday Dublin Castle knew who he was. On Easter Sunday morning a large amount of gelignite was stolen from the De Selby quarries and brought to Liberty Hall. The incident helped Under Secretary Nathan to make up his mind and he told Lord Wimborne that he proposed to raid Liberty Hall, Larkfield, and Father Mathew Park that night. There was a delay in this because it was thought that these places were arsenals which would be defended if attacked and that big guns, which would have to be brought up from the Curragh, would be needed. If they had only known how little we had! By Easter Monday Nathan thought all danger was over with Casement's arrest, and at twelve noon Lord Wimborne sat down to write a letter to this effect to Birrell and the Prime Minister. He had to re-open the envelope to say that instead the worst had happened—the police had just telephoned to say that the Rising had started.

At the Commission, Sir Matthew Nathan said:

> 'Concealed as much as possible in or on the top of these buildings they [the Volunteers] were able to inflict severe losses on the troops moving against them, and were only finally dislodged when an area was surrounded and the buildings in it destroyed, as in the attack of a hostile town . . . the planning and conduct of the insurrection showed greater organising power and more military skill than had been attributed to the Volunteers, and they also appear from all reports to have acted with greater courage. These things and the high character of some of the idealists who took part in the insurrection no doubt account for some of the sympathy, which the beaten Volunteers have undoubtedly excited among a large—probably the larger part of the people of Dublin—and in many places in the country. There are also the deeper grounds of a passionate national feeling for Ireland and of a long hatred of England.'

The Commission finished on June 7th.

After a few weeks in jail, my parents, although neither tried nor sentenced, were offered deportation to England because the authorities were windy and began to hedge. The alternative was continued imprisonment for both of them. Pa would have preferred to stay with the other prisoners, but Ma was raising Cain in Mountjoy and Pa accepted deportation for her sake. They were given a choice of two or three towns from which Pa chose Oxford because he wanted to read in the Bodleian Library. During June Requiem Masses were held for the executed men in Dublin churches, and there was a chanted Requiem Mass for Joe in Whitefriar Street Church when Ma and Pa were allowed out for three days before being deported. There were immense crowds at all of the Masses and they stayed outside singing patriotic songs and hymns and 'Hail Glorious St Patrick' when they couldn't remember any more. When the crowds got so large that the streets were filled, the military occupied the streets and we were forced to stop the Masses. Soldiers were often hissed at and booed and on the whole they were kept off the streets. The RIC were on duty instead, armed with revolvers in Dublin, but with carbines and rifles through the country. Martial law was still in force and continued most of the time off and on until the Truce in 1921.

Pa and Ma left for Oxford and Fiona went with them. Ma had told me that I was to refer everything to her solicitor, but I found that he was working directly against her interests and trying to get her to sign a power of attorney. He was also trying to get evidence that she had been financing the Rising, which was quite ridiculous. I was sending them £2 10s each week to live on, but very little money was coming in rents as a lot of tenants expected that my parents' property would be confiscated and they held their rent over, telling me that if they paid, they might have to pay it all over again to the government. I pointed out that my parents had not been tried or executed and that property, even of the executed, had not been confiscated, so they started to pay again. On the other hand, I got a lot of kindness from plain bloody Freemasons like Martley and Barlee, the Westland Row solicitors to the Pembroke estate, and Donaldson, the builders' providers of Capel Street, who (he told me) refused to withdraw me from the discount list in spite of orders from the Freemasons' Lodge.

Because everyone was at me to keep Grace in the public eye and in the Plunkett home, I pressed her to go to stay in Larkfield when she was thrown out of home again and I got one of our maids to stay with her. I thought Grace had many good points, and I got on better with her than the rest of the family, but while she was staying in Larkfield she took every advantage of the position; she was destructive and a messer and I thought her silly and dangerous. It cost a good deal more to keep her in Larkfield than to keep Fiona and my parents in Oxford. She invited all her friends to stay there. I asked Marie Perolz to stay with her when she came back and Perolz said that she could not see how Grace had kept out of trouble all her life.

I went out to Larkfield to see Grace and was told that she was upstairs in bed. When I went into her bedroom I saw a large white chamberpot full of blood and foetus. She said nothing and I said nothing.

An ex-fiancé of Grace's named Moore sent her a postcard, congratulating her on the birth of a son, and she wrote back telling him it was not true and asking him to call on her. They made it up then but quarrelled again and she went to Henry B. O'Hanlon asking him to take an action against Moore. He very kindly sent for me and told me about it and he managed to keep her from doing anything. Various spies made up to her, they must have thought she knew a lot, and this included one of those curious people whose job it was to report on trends of opinion in the young intellectuals, Land Commissioner William Bailey. He asked Grace to tea with him and, although Marie Perolz asked her not to go, she went. She said that she did not see why not, he was a very nice man but he was wasting his time, she knew nothing of use to him. She also went to tea with Major Dudley Heathcote, now Provost Marshal of Dublin.

A tall, handsome, oldish man called on me in Belgrave Road. This turned out to be our family remittance man, my celebrated uncle, Frank Cranny, who had got my address from our family solicitor. I did not recognise him, I had not seen him since I was very young, but I soon saw that he had eyes exactly the same as my mother's. They had the same look that seemed to see through you and make you think you had to tell them everything, but by now I knew that look meant nothing at all. He had been sent to Australia at the age of seventeen, out of control, having seduced the housemaid and pinched £1,700 from his father, for whom he had been acting as a building clerk-of-

Grace Gifford Plunkett's cartoon of Countess Plunkett. Joe had hoped that his family would look after Grace as they both expected that she would be thrown out of home for becoming a Catholic. Grace did not realise that her mother-in-law, the Countess, who held the purse strings, did not even give her own children what was rightfully theirs. Grace took an action against the Plunketts in the 1930s and they settled out of court for £700.

works. He said that his mother, Maria Cranny, and eldest brother, Jack, had stolen the money and blamed him for it. In Australia he had taken up land and bred horses and married the beautiful daughter of a North-of-Ireland parson. He led her an awful life and I found out from letters that the children were very unhappy. The eldest boy, John, could not go to school because he had to attend his father with a horse and trap outside every hotel and bar in Melbourne. Ma had agreed to give him ten shillings a week and for years I had posted a letter every week for her containing a ten shilling postal order, and I knew that it was conditional on his living out of Ireland. When he appeared after Easter Week, 1916, he had not got his ten shillings for several weeks and said he had sent several telegrams about it. They may have been sent to Fitzwilliam Street or the censor may have stopped them. I told him I had no money and asked him why he had come, didn't he know my parents were in jail? He then said that that was why he had come, to look after his dear sister and do everything for her. I told him that I did not think that there was anything he could do. He suggested that he had influential friends and when I said nothing, he turned ugly and said he supposed that I had been told lies about him by Ma. On the contrary I said she never mentioned his name. He was upset, but he went and I did not see him again until the next year.

Roger Casement's trial for treason began in London on June 26th and, on the 29th, he was sentenced to be hanged. Casement called himself 'the leprechaun of Irish politics', and said 'Ireland should not sell her soul for any mess of Empire'. My father and Joe admired him very much and we always heard him spoken of with respect and liking. I never had more than a few words with him but his great height, his characteristic walk, emaciation and nervous manner made him impossible to miss. When he exerted himself to please, he was irresistible. These scandalous stories about him were made up out of the whole cloth for use on people who had never seen the man. He had an excellent standing among diplomatists and was very well known and admired in many places in the world. He was hanged on Thursday 3rd August, 1916.

Ma told me later that shortly after they went to Oxford she had written to the Home Office offering to tell them everything she knew about Roger Casement (which was nothing) if they would let her two sons out of jail. She hated Casement and when he came to dinner in Fitzwilliam Street, she froze him out. Fiona, who was with them all the time in Oxford, told me that Ma had gone up to London at least twice on business, with her 'very important' air. There was no result, of course. I should think it would be more likely that she offered the information on condition she and my father were allowed home. She was paid for her trouble by the Home Office (which gave her ideas) and I understood then why she hadn't demanded that I send more money from Dublin. In Lavery's painting of Casement's trial there is a woman in the picture identified simply as 'a countess'.

Joe had asked me, as his literary executor, to make a selection of his poems for publishing, and Mr Lyons of the Educational Book Company got Manico to print them. I wrote an introduction and Grace did a memory drawing for the frontispiece. The first section of the volume, *Occulta*, was to have been Joe's next book and he had arranged the order of it himself, making an unbroken sequence of thought. In the second part I gathered some late verse and any early poems he would have considered worthy of republication, including some from *The Circle and the Sword* (1911), but I did not include anything he thought second-rate, and many of his poems had been destroyed. In his recent writing he had outgrown all false standards, and gone to simplicity, which is so hard to achieve. The poems in this book have an appearance of ease, but they were written after very hard labour and it is this that makes them flow.

To him, expressed thought was more important than versifying. Although Joe employed the symbolism of the mystics, he applied the term 'mystic' to only a very small part of his own work. He showed me two or three poems that he called mystic, but I have not been able to find them again and must presume them destroyed. This volume of his collected poems ran to four printings.

When the National Aid Fund was started very shortly after the Rising the Lord Mayor and other sympathetic moderates were put on the list of organisers as a precaution against confiscation by the authorities, but Miss McMahon of Cumann na mBan went to Mrs Kathleen Clarke, who had been very ill after a miscarriage, and told her that the fund was in the wrong hands. Mrs Clarke was always stubborn and refused to listen to reason, and she started another fund called the Volunteer Aid Fund. John Archdeacon Murphy came over from Clan na Gael in America with some funds for the widows of the executed men and refused to part with a penny until the dispute was ended, so agreement was reached between all of us and it meant that Grace and Mrs Clarke and all the other widows had from £500 down to £100 given to each of them to last the next year. Mrs Wyse Power (Jenny O'Toole) got Grace to agree to put the money in their joint names in the bank and to take out so much each quarter.

The family solicitor had told me to let Larkfield, so I had moved Grace to Fitzwilliam Street and when she left there the place was an awful mess. She took things and sold them or gave them away. Money or possessions meant nothing to her except to play with for a little while and then give away to the first person who asked. Mimi was particularly annoyed at having some of her clothes, including a paisley evening cloak, taken by Grace to dress dolls and make cushions. On the other hand, she seemed to think that the eldest son of a family got all his parents' money, even while they were still alive. Grace finally left Fitzwilliam Street at eleven-thirty one night and went to stay with Mrs O'Doherty down the road. Grace told her that I had thrown her out with no money and nowhere to go. In fact, she had her income from the National Aid. She then did the same thing to Mrs O'Doherty and to Katie Wilson, her own sister. Mrs O'Doherty told everyone at first that I had thrown Grace out but she took it all back afterwards. I started getting Fitzwilliam Street cleaned for whenever my parents returned. Ma wrote to Grace from Oxford offering her a home but Grace refused, and when Ma came back from Oxford and found that I had let Grace leave Fitzwilliam Street, she got on her high horse and said I had no right to get between her and Joe's widow.

Mimi came home at the end of October from the USA, by which time I was expecting my first child. I had moved Muriel MacDonagh and her children from Oakley Road to No. 50 Marlborough Road and Mimi moved in with them. I bought Mimi a few bits of furniture and bedding for her room but when Ma came home she confiscated the lot and even when Mimi married in 1918 she did not get them all back.

Larkfield got into an odd position; Dublin Corporation wanted some land which the military had in Portobello and the military offered them instead some land which they said they controlled as allotments—part of the war effort. Dublin Corporation accepted it and then found it was Larkfield! There was no notice of this served on us and in fact the military had not commandeered the land. The first I heard of it was one day when Tommy and I went to Larkfield on bicycles on the canal bank. As we went along the canal we heard military trumpeters practising under every canal bridge from Leeson Street to Rialto, and the slow melancholy sound reverberated along the water from one bridge to another. We arrived at Larkfield to find men breaking the sod in the fields. Tommy went to the Corporation to protest but got no satisfaction. Even when he went to Willie Cosgrave after his release from jail, Willie said it was against Dublin Corporation policy to interfere. Of course we didn't know then, and I didn't know for another thirty years, that it had been repossessed by the Civil Service Building Society and that Ma had only paid the deposit in 1913 and nothing further. The Corporation took it over and later built on it.

About November, I had to go over to Oxford to see Ma about the power of attorney the solicitor was proposing. When they first arrived there Ma and Pa had gone to a guesthouse but they were not welcome; they were spied on all the time and then asked to leave. They managed to rent a tiny four-storey house with one room on each floor and orange-box furniture where the landlord was quite kind to them. Ma took to making furniture (it wasn't very good

Pat Plunkett as an old man (1915). A year after this photograph was taken, his son and daughter-in-law, the Count and Countess, were in exile, another son had been killed in the Dardanelles, two of his grandsons were in prison and another had been executed. Pat Plunkett died in 1918.

but it kept her out of mischief) and they got a few sticks of it as well. Pa used to light the fires and keep them alight with twists of newspaper and lumps of sugar, and Fiona did the shopping. Pa was as nice as ever but Fiona was miserable. Pa wanted to read in the Bodleian Library. He had known McCann, who was Master of one of the colleges, as a young man, but when he wrote to him asking him to sign his library ticket McCann refused and said that he did not think Pa was a suitable person to get a ticket. He probably could have got somebody else to sign but he did not bother further. Eleanor Hull, translator of the *Táin,* and her daughter were living in Oxford with her father, also the head of a college, and she came to see my parents and invited them to her home but my father would not ask again to have his ticket signed. Mrs Victor Rickard, a cousin of the Gwynns, was also living in Oxford and she was kind to them.

When the men came back from internment at Christmas we kept one or two of them until they got fixed up and so did lots of others. Many of them called and told me their stories of the Rising, including Jim Grace and another man who gave me an account of their fight in the battle of Mount Street Bridge. The rank and file who had gone to Frongoch were organised there by Mick Collins and his helpers to start the fight all over again, and as soon as Mick arrived back, he took charge and reorganised National Aid at once. He started a club in South William Street with Marie Perolz in charge to keep the released men together and there was regular weekly pay for Volunteers who had not got their jobs back. He also started to get guns at once, mostly from soldiers; conscript soldiers were willing to sell their guns for £2 to £4 apiece. I was told of this by a Volunteer and, appalled at being given such information, I told Mick, who sacked the man who had told me. It was at this time that I gave Mick Darrell Figgis' Mauser, which had been left in my keeping, and I told him not to give it back to him.

I found out later that Mick gave Ma £600 which she said she had lost as a result of the Rising. By rights Mimi and I, who had lost all our clothes and many other possessions, Mimi some rings and brooches as well, should have been given some of this, but she did not let us know she had got it. I had spent all I had on feeding and clothing her and Pa; however, I did not think we should have been given money from the National Aid. Ma had plenty of property and the money should have been kept for the men out of work. I told Mick he should not have done it, but he only smiled at me.

12 Laying foundations 1917–1919

THE WHOLE COUNTRY BEGAN TO LOOK UP. Even before Mick Collins had been released at Christmas, Cathal Brugha and a small number of other Volunteers had begun gathering arms, ammunition and explosives. Cathal Brugha was the managing director of a firm of church candle manufacturers, a small fair man, not clever but kind, hard-working, brave as a lion, stubborn, narrow-minded and very much in earnest about the Irish language. During Easter Week he was in the South Dublin Union and he kept back a whole company of English soldiers by himself. He was so badly wounded that the others put him to bed in a ward and no one thought he could recover. He was not executed because he could not even have sat in a chair to be shot, as James Connolly was. A year afterwards he was barely able to walk. He was chief of staff in 1918, with Mick Collins as his right hand, and had the appearance of a man who would come to an early and violent death.

Mick had kept the men together in the internment camp and after they came home did not let them disperse until he had arranged to contact them. In their Dublin club-room they started to buy arms and make explosives in the months before the penal servitude men were released. The guerilla war which Mick prepared for was different from what could have been done before the Rising and included a good deal of street fighting. There was strong opposition to action by the Volunteers of any kind and if the individual commands had not taken it on their own responsibility, much less would have been done. Along with a secret organisation and arming for the renewal of fighting, a public campaign was necessary to lay the democratic foundation of the new State, which we were all determined would result, and the election of separatists who would not attend the British Parliament was essential to that end. All these things were necessary, but they seemed to some to be antagonistic and although the division was by no means clear-cut, the foundations were now laid for the Civil War.

After the death of James J. Kelly, the Irish Party MP for North Roscommon, Father Michael O'Flanagan, the curate in Crossna, got Pa nominated as an Independent candidate and as soon as he was invited to stand my parents came home from Oxford without waiting for permission to do so. Their release from parole followed almost at once but the campaign, organised by Father O'Flanagan, was already well started, and my parents already back in Dublin when the Home Office notified them that they could return. This was a very short time before polling and they moved into Fitzwilliam Street with Fiona and Mimi, who was most reluctant to leave Marlborough Road.

Count Plunkett and Larry Ginnell MP on the station at Roscommon,
1917. Count Plunkett stood for election as an Independent MP in the
by-election for Roscommon North on February 3rd and Larry Ginnell
was his agent. The snow was so heavy, it was thought Count Plunkett
could not win, but the people cleared the roads and he was elected with
a majority of well over a thousand.

From the time they came back, Grace started ringing up Pa saying she must
have £50 or she would kill herself. Even Pa got tired of this after giving her the
money the first few times. Pa now went down to Roscommon as soon as he
could and joined the campaign.

Nearly all the prominent people were in jail, but everyone who could
manage it had gone to help with the canvassing and clerical work—Larry
Ginnell MP, who acted as Pa's election agent, Tommy, Mimi, Arthur Griffith,
Mick Collins, Mick Staines, Kevin O Sheil, Tomás MacDonagh's brother John,
O'Leary Curtis, Big John O'Mahoney, Rory O'Connor, Dan MacCarthy,
Darrell Figgis and a score of names I have forgotten. I had been told by my
doctor not to go, as my baby was due in April and I was having a difficult
pregnancy, but they all told me about it when they came home. The organis-

ers were hampered by having only three weeks in which to canvass votes, procure speakers for meetings and impersonation officers for the day of the election, and arrange transport to bring Pa, as the candidate, around the constituency, but everyone worked night and day with the greatest willingness. Pa made a favourable impression of good feeling, culture and proper democracy and he would go into a pub and take a drink and converse politely with everyone. Joe's death was still a heavy grief to him and, in spite of his efforts not to show it, it got him down sometimes. Ma, who joined him there, was not a success. She condescended too much and her political gossip was idiotic.

No-one had the smallest idea of the chances of victory, except perhaps Father O'Flanagan, who would not have considered anything else. It was too much to hope for; there were two other candidates, an Independent, Jasper Tully, and an Irish Party man, Thomas Devine, and the Irish Party took victory for granted. The election was exciting and dramatic: three days before the poll it snowed in Roscommon and nowhere else in Ireland. It was a wild snowstorm which covered the constituency with deep drifts and seemed as if it would keep the country people from the polling station. This favoured the Irish Party candidate, as the towns were thought to be on his side, but Father O'Flanagan organised the whole constituency and the country people went out with shovels and cleared lanes through the snow, piling it six feet high on the roadsides. This allowed the campaigners' cars to pass as well and wherever they went there were scenes of enthusiasm so, in spite of the arctic conditions, the usual meetings and speechmaking went on and people could get to the polling station in Boyle.

The Volunteers were at the polling station on the Saturday of the election, the 3rd of February, and after the booths closed they joined the local RIC in keeping guard over the ballot boxes from Saturday evening until Monday morning when the count began. Tommy had to leave Roscommon before the result was announced, because Cathal Brugha had sent for him to go to Limerick to advise on explosives. The counting began at ten o'clock in the morning and the result was announced that afternoon at two o'clock. Pa polled 3,022 votes and was elected with a majority of about 1,200. We had thought he might scrape in but the big majority was incredible. There was great rejoicing. The people in sympathy were experiencing a sensation new to people of that time, a sensation of success—a new kind of victory for them and for Ireland. The actual amount of support for a revolutionary policy was surprising and it became apparent that the work had to go on and that it was being pushed from below. The Irish Party followers were stunned, they described the Roscommon result as ruinous and took it very badly.

Pa addressed his followers outside the racecourse in Boyle, where the votes had been counted, and after thanking the returning officer and his staff, he said:

Electioneering in Longford: Count and Countess Plunkett in the car and Larry Ginnell on the ground. The Countess had no real sympathy with Nationalist politics and offered information on her family to the authorities. Her devotion to her husband, however, kept her on the fringes of Republicanism until she died in 1944.

'My place henceforth will be beside you in your own country, for it is in Ireland with the people of Ireland that the battle of Irish liberty will be fought. I recognise no Parliament in existence as having a right over the people of Ireland, just as I deny the right of England to one inch of the soil of Ireland.'

The Irish Times set down what the Roscommon election meant:

'Here is a constituency where three-fourths of the electorate are peasant proprietors. ... They were never getting better prices for their produce and they were never better off. The Post Office Savings Bank deposits and the local banks are eloquent proofs of this. Yet 3,022 of these men recorded their votes for the candidate who was recommended to them because he was the father of one of the leaders executed after Easter Week. '

Larry Ginnell MP had been campaigning for Pa and he came back to Dublin with him now. I was in Fitzwilliam Street to meet them. There had been no mention of policy up to this time, only resistance to England and support for the man with three sons in the Rising. Pa now told Larry that he had definitely made up his mind that he was not going to take his seat in Westminster and he asked Larry if he would come in with him. Larry was now an old, not too healthy man, whose principal source of income was what he received as an active MP at Westminster, and this income made him very independent to do as he thought right. He had been a member of the Irish Party when it was well supplied with money, but the Party published no balance sheet. Larry told me that this was the reason he left the Party in 1905,

256

but they denied it and said he was a crank. He went on to be elected as an Independent for North Westmeath with a large majority. Abstentionism would mean giving up an MP's pay and Larry said to Pa, 'Give me twenty minutes to think it out', but it was only five minutes when he came back and said he was coming in with him. Larry had the loyal support of his wife, one of the King family of Mullingar, who worked as a journalist to support both of them.

On March 17th Pa made the formal announcement that he would not go to Westminster and was starting a new organisation, the Liberty Clubs, to be based on the Proclamation of the Republic. He was not a member of Sinn Féin but a separatist, supported by a combination of separatists and almost all advanced Nationalist opinion. He wrote after his return,

> 'I am returned to Dublin pledged by the electors of North Roscommon to recognise no foreign authority, to maintain the rights of Ireland to independence and to initiate Ireland's work of taking control of her own affairs.'

This caused Arthur Griffith of Sinn Féin to write several savage letters to him accusing him of making political capital of his dead son; he did not seem to realise that Pa was a member of the IRB from before the Rising. Pa answered him with his habitual courtesy. He was well aware of Griffith's policy for Ireland of a House of Lords and House of Commons under an English king and had no intention of working under this banner. The name 'Sinn Féiners' was originally given to the Volunteers as a term of abuse, a description of a futile and ridiculous movement and as President of Sinn Féin, Griffith was in a very curious position because the Rising had been labelled 'the Sinn Féin Rebellion' by the British Government and others although there was very little connection with it.

Griffith, who had been employed by the IRB as editor of a succession of newspapers issued before the Rising, most of which were suppressed, was a splendid editor, a great journalist with a fine historical sense and complete control of his sources of information, and Joe and I had admired him because of his policies of self-reliance, protection for industry and abstention from Westminster and for his pamphlet, *The Resurrection of Hungary*. Most official Nationalists anathematised Griffith, attacking him for his best ideas, which were in fact to become essential points in the next few years. Griffith was a Volunteer from the beginning. He was at the Howth gunrunning and carried his gun back to Dublin but he did not attend drill as he disliked that kind of thing. He was very athletic, a fine swimmer and rescued children from drowning in the canals. He was no leader and not treated as one by the British, but deported and interned in Reading, returning at Christmas 1916. He now took the position that the Rising was a failure and proposed that Sinn Féin should take over. He never really gave up the idea of King, Lords and Commons and he told Tommy that he had taken part with The O'Rahilly in an offer of kingship of Ireland to Rupert of Bavaria, or the Duke of Anhalt, or to a de-

The Mansion House Convention April 19th 1917. Despite its dramatic increase in support, there was no umbrella group to represent Nationalism, so Count Plunkett started the 'Liberty Clubs' and called a Convention of all political organisations to discuss the future.

scendant of Brian Boru. He told Joe that the King of England would be the only possible king but Joe thought this was somewhat old-fashioned, that a new movement should not attach itself to an obsolete monarchy.

The Liberty Clubs were started and Pa announced a meeting at the Mansion House on April 19th which Rory O'Connor and Tommy organised. They sent out circulars to all public bodies, asking them to send delegates, but a great many put them in their wastepaper baskets as nearly all these bodies had Irish Party majorities. Every person with any kind of public position was invited and in the end there were 1200 men and women present in the Mansion House. Arthur Griffith was invited but did not intend to go until Tommy persuaded him. He sat at the back of the hall and at one stage was going to leave but the people, led by Father O'Flanagan and Father Ferris, absolutely refused to let him go and Father O'Flanagan managed to persuade him to meet them in another room. After some argument Griffith agreed that a committee should be formed to promote independence for Ireland, abstention from the English parliament and an appeal to the International Peace Conference at the end of the war. To form the committee, Griffith chose Stephen O'Mara and Seán Milroy and Father O'Flanagan chose Tommy, who was made secretary of the committee, and Cathal Brugha. When Griffith announced the names at the full meeting he added that there should be a Labour representative also and named William O'Brien. This had not been agreed so Father O'Flanagan, who had not previously known William O'Brien and thought it was a majority-gaining trick, jumped up and said there must be a woman and named Ma. We told him this was a mistake and that she was not suitable.

Just before this Rory had caught Ma putting her foot in it, saying that Griffith had always been in favour of going to Westminster, whereas in fact he had invented Abstention, so Rory insisted on her keeping out of interviews. By June, she had been persuaded to give up her place to Dr Kathleen Lynn.

The Longford election came on almost immediately afterwards on 9TH May and everyone went to help, including Larry Ginnell and my parents, who went in their car. Our candidate, Joe McGuinness, was a prisoner still in Lewes, a sentenced man. The slogan was 'Put him in to get him out'. This was a much nearer thing and the majority was only 37. The first result was the other way, but one of our agents had noticed an Irish Party agent straightening a bundle of votes and insisted on a recount. The crowd had been preparing to beat up the Volunteer supporters but now changed their minds. This made three MPs for the new departure. When the Longford Election Committee came to the Mansion House Committee and told them they must find a way to unify, they spoke to the already converted.

We were keeping up our acquaintance with everyone in the movement, and also with Helen and Con Curran, while all this political stuff was going on, but life in our house was very unpleasant. The maid was clean but useless and then she said that her father, an ex-British soldier, would not let her work in our house. Tommy's mother, Mrs Dillon, said she was right. She hated the whole thing and blamed me for all her discomforts, which were in fact due to the war. She thought I managed badly but refused to take any part in it. Tommy had £150 a year, Kathleen gave her mother £6 a month and prices were rising every day. It was impossible for the four of us and a maid to live on this, but Mrs Dillon refused to live without a maid. When I didn't get one she went out and got one after another, each worse than the last. Mrs Dillon bought butter with Kathleen's money for herself and Tommy's brother, Andrew, to eat while Tommy and I ate margarine at the same table. I didn't mind her, but Andrew was now twenty-five, had never done any work and was treated as a child by his mother. He had a pass degree in Arts and did a course in book-keeping and then blamed me for his not having a job in the English Diplomatic Service which he had never applied for, nor anything else either. He should have been in a bank.

Moya was born on the 12th of April and Lena Rafferty was her godmother. Lena and Mr Rafferty kindly came and collected me from the Coombe Hospital in their car and brought me home to No.13 Belgrave Road. I brought Moya upstairs to change her and when I came down, I found the Raffertys sitting in silence while Mrs Dillon sat glowering in a corner. Helen Curran was also very kind, she gave me a pram for Moya and a cot. I pawned my watch to get clothes for her. Ma paid for the hospital and gave me some dreadful old-fashioned long baby dresses. I brought Moya round to Palmerston Road to show her to her great-grandfather, Pat Plunkett; she was his first great-grandchild. 'Look at me,' he said to me, 'I can't even lift my hand to my mouth! I never allowed anyone to do anything for me and look at me now!' He had to have helpers now and he was very annoyed. He made no allowance for being one hundred years old!

While I was still in hospital and not very well, Fiona came to tell me that Jack and George were being treated very badly in jail, and given so little food that it was thought they could not live. They were allowed to get letters once a month and we all joined in writing them. In June, a meeting in Beresford Place was announced, to protest against the treatment of the prisoners in English jails, in particular against the raping of the younger prisoners, which I knew afterwards, from Jack's nightmares, did happen. The meeting was proscribed by Dublin Castle but people gathered all the same. A lorry drove up with Pa, who was to speak at it, and others on it. Pa stood up to speak and Superintendent Mills attempted to get into the lorry to arrest him. A man in the crowd hit Mills on the back of the head with a hurling stick and he fell dead on the ground. Pa was grabbed and hustled off by other police and as he was dragged away he saw Mills lying on the ground and said, 'Oh, the poor man, I hope he's not hurt.' He was brought to Store Street station and Mimi went there to find out about him, but the police threw her down the stone steps onto her back. Tommy was late for the meeting and on his way down Abbey Street to it he met the G-man, Johnny Bruton, who gave him a swipe across the jaw with his baton. Ma went to her solicitor, Sydney Matthews, and offered to tell all she knew and sell the Republic to get Pa out of jail, and Matthews complied by bringing her to a Dublin Castle agent. When she told me about this, I asked her why she did it, and she said she was afraid Pa would be accused of the murder of Mills, which was quite ridiculous, there was no question of this; everyone had seen what happened and Pa was released afterwards.

George and Jack were released less than a fortnight after this meeting and were home a couple of days after that. They had been sent first to Portland Jail, which was well known to be severe, and I never liked to ask very much about this time. After a lot of agitation all the prisoners were moved to Lewes Jail and for a time there was some relief. I think what started the next row was a new governor who started to put a severe discipline into force; anyway, they took the jail apart and made a wreck of the whole place, walls and all—it took years to repair it—at the end of which they were all dragged off in chains to different jails. Jack and George were sent to Parkhurst and treated with great brutality. Their food ration was half a pot of porridge and bread each day and they said it was worse than nothing. They shared jails with, among others, Bob Brennan, Thomas Ashe, Willie Cosgrave and Éamon de Valera. As soon as they came home they went down to Clare to help get de Valera elected, and Willie Cosgrave a month later in Kilkenny, both as abstentionists.

A house had been rented in Skerries, County Dublin, as a holiday place for the families of the executed men and in August that year Muriel MacDonagh,

George (front right) and Jack (front left) Plunkett and friends after their return from jail, June 1917. Michael Collins arranged for all the returning prisoners to be photographed before they went home. From Jack's account of their release: '. . . dressed in Martin Henry clothing, we were brought in charabancs to Euston Station where there was a crowd of London Irish to see us off. Art Ó Briain shook hands with us. Seoirse (George) was with me in all the prisons; a week in Parkhurst and the rest of the time in Lewes.'

Tomás's widow, went there with the children. Muriel thought that she could swim to St Patrick's Island but it was too far. When some of the party saw she was in trouble and tried to get help, they were refused a boat. Rory O'Connor found her the next day, her hair spread out on the wet sand. She had died of heart failure. Grace wanted to have the children but John MacDonagh got them and handed them over to his sister, the nun (Muriel had become a Catholic), who had no way of managing it. Grace, who was deeply affected by Muriel's death, changed a lot and she was always very good to the children, giving them everything she could.

The British Government set up a packed 'Assembly' (although there were honest men in it), known as the Trinity College Convention, chaired by Horace Plunkett, and the Mansion House Committee issued a statement against it. Pa was offered a large bribe if he would attend it. Matthews, Ma's solicitor, came to Mimi and told her that if Pa attended the Trinity College Convention, he would get £2,000 compensation for losses and damage done in 1916 by looting soldiers. Mimi laughed at him and said, 'I'm sure he'd want a bigger price than that.' A sub-committee was appointed by the Mansion House Committee to secure unity of action between all organisations with the same objects, and Cathal Brugha spoke very frankly to them, pointing out that the country was looking to them for guidance, for instructions as to which organisation they should join, and that they must come to an agreement on the subject. They got agreement on June 7th to summon a Convention not later than the following October to replace existing organisations with a body composed of the Mansion House Committee, the Liberty League and Sinn Féin, but Griffith said that Sinn Féin could not give up its name. This meeting was held in Cathal Brugha's house and it was with his help that unity was achieved and this phase of Irish history ended. There were six delegates added to the executive after the general release of prisoners in mid-June including Madame Markievicz, Éamon de Valera, Piaras Béaslai and Austin Stack. Up to then, Mick Collins represented the Volunteers. They drew up a constitution to present to the October conference and, to appease Griffith, Countess Markievicz drafted a resolution that, after Ireland got her freedom, she might adopt any form of government she chose.

It was at the end of September that Tom Ashe died from pneumonia after forcible feeding in Mountjoy Jail. Dr Lynn was with him at the end in the Mater Hospital. At this time very little was known about hunger strikes and both sides were terrified of the effects. In Belgrave Road we put out a Celtic cross in tricolour, made in the Liberty Hall workroom, with hatchments (black flags) for Tom Ashe. A respectable lady from Palmerston Road spat on the ground when she saw them.

In October about 1,700 delegates at the Sinn Féin Ard Fheis in the Mansion House voted in the constitution and, after Pa and Griffith had stood aside, voted Éamon de Valera as president. The Sinn Féin executive which then came into existence acted as Dáil Eireann until the 1918 election. Tommy was made a member of this new executive and was proposed as secretary but did not accept the position as he had to get back to work so Darrell Figgis and Austin Stack were made joint honorary secretaries. As well as Pa and Tommy, and Grace, the executive included Arthur Griffith, Father O'Flanagan, Willie Cosgrave, Larry Ginnell, Cathal Brugha, Mick Collins, Seán T. O'Kelly, Madame Markievicz, Dr Kathleen Lynn, Mrs Tom Clarke, Harry Boland, Ernest Blythe, J. J. Walsh, Seán MacEntee, Eoin MacNeill, and Joe McGuinness, Though Pa and Griffith were both willing to work in the new organisation, they remained suspicious of one another.

By 1918 it was getting quite impossible to live on what we had. Meat was 3s 6d a pound, milk, 1s a pint, bread, 1s a loaf and now everything was adulterated except potatoes and oatmeal. Eggs were 9d each in summer. We had a duck which laid an egg a day the whole year. The maid had killed the hens with boiling food and they were too dear to replace. I gave the baby, Moya, a piece of bread when she was a year old and it nearly killed her. They were allowing bakers to use white pine sawdust to knead the bread. Barley and beans were in it and sometimes half a loaf would be full of ashes and dirt. Finally, they allowed, or forced, Allenbury's to adulterate the infant food, and there was nothing left but porridge and potatoes, and an egg for the baby when I could get it as a favour. We were surrounded with people whose incomes had gone up with the extra profits on war bonuses. A list appeared in the papers of things that a pregnant woman should have to eat and I found it funny because I had none of them and I was pregnant again.

By this time England had conscription and it was imminent in Ireland. It was accepted, even by the Irish Party, that it would be an appalling disaster for Ireland but the Party's protests proved to be purely formal. John Dillon was the only leader of the Irish Party who did anything: he joined the National Anti-Conscription Committee. The Government now made it clear that they were not going to exempt clerical students and this brought the Catholic Church in on our side at last. In just a few days, £150,000 was subscribed by the public and in April there was a one-day strike against conscription. As anti-conscription meetings were against the law, the Catholic Church authorised the holding of meetings in the churches and Tommy spoke from the steps of the altar in Rathmines Church. He was introduced from the pulpit by Canon Fricker, who luckily mumbled so much that no-one could hear that he was talking about the fact that Tommy and John Dillon were related. The whole thing was in itself a revolution and an utter challenge to the Government.

In May it was announced that there would be a general election in September (later changed to December) and the whole Sinn Féin organisation set out to sweep the entire country with Dan MacCarthy as the director of elections and making a good job of it. The Sinn Féin executive had been warned at Christmas that it was probable they would all be arrested and then Mrs Dillon wanted to know what was going on and I told her about it as I thought it would be less of a shock to her if they came to arrest Tommy in the house. Tommy's sister, Kathleen, thought I should not have done it but I could not agree. Anyway, Mrs Dillon got a stroke a short time later and Kathleen came up from Mullingar Hospital, where she worked, and nursed her. She also got a night nurse in, so finances were worse than ever and Andrew more ill-mannered. After three months of this Kathleen had to go back to her job or be fired so she moved her mother to a home.

The arrest of the Sinn Féin executive was near the end of this fantastic conscription crisis—Tommy was at a meeting of the Executive at which they were told that information had come from Dublin Castle that they were all going to be arrested that night. Some of them went on the run, but Tommy decided not to and came home to Belgrave Road to tell me about it. Kathleen Lynn, who was also on the executive, had come in to see me when there was a ring at the door and I went to answer it. The hall filled up with large men in plain clothes and Dr Lynn said, 'Excuse me', and walked out between them

MAGNIFICAT

GERALDINE PLUNKETT

ILLUSTRATED BY
JACK MORROW

THE CANDLE PRESS
158 RATHGAR ROAD
DUBLIN . . . . . MCMXVII

In 1917 Geraldine Plunkett published (with The Candle Press) a small volume of eight poems under the title Magnificat. *Jack Morrow, the Belfast artist and cartoonist, recently released from prison, drew the frontispiece.*

While you are in Kilkenny town
I see your grace in every tree,
Your hair is as the beeches brown,
The birches have your bravery.

Your strength in mountain oaks I find,
Eagles in this have built their nest,
With supple sally twigs you bind
My willing heart unto your breast.

Cyprus and cedar spreading wide,
Under your peace my heart will sleep,
O rowan tree that grows beside
My pool of love, your roots drink deep!

Geraldine Plunkett

and went on the run in her Sunday best. (Madame Markievicz disguised herself as a scout master.) Tommy handed me all the papers out of his pockets and then the men took him away. Tommy had made it look as though the papers were business affairs I had to see to but in fact they were notes about manufacturers of explosives and so on. Pa was also lifted and jailed in Birmingham. The next day the newspapers were full of scare headings about a Sinn Féin German plot (this was afterwards completely discredited) and the tone they took was such that it seemed quite possible that the whole Executive would be shot.

Tommy was lifted on May 17th, his mother died less than a week later and my second daughter, Blanaid, was born three days after that, on 26th May, in the Coombe Hospital. While I was still in the Coombe, the Governor of Gloucester Prison where Tommy had been jailed wrote to me, and Ma, finding the letter in the house in Belgrave Road, opened it. The letter, which was about regulations, said that the only money Tommy was allowed was £1 (20s) in change and that it could be sent to the Governor. Ma, without asking me, sent it off to him and came straight to the hospital to get it back from me. I told her I had nothing but actually I had 33s, the price of eleven days in the Coombe Hospital at 3s a day. Anastasia, the wife of Padraic Óg Ó Connaire, was in the next bed and was very kind to me. Unfortunately, when I went into the Coombe, I had to leave Moya with Ma and Ma said that Moya had defied her and that she had had to break her spirit. Moya was only thirteen months old and whatever it was that Ma did to her had a lasting effect.

There were constant threats of conscription and, in an attempt to put it over in a popular manner, three speakers were given a large fee to hold a series of meetings, mostly in Dublin. From the first the crowd took part in the proceedings and enjoyed themselves so much that the speakers tried to hold succeeding ones hidden round the corner or in odd places, with the crowd pursuing them and roaring with laughter. The highlight was the meeting at the James's Street fountain at which Pádraic Ó Conaire offered to speak in Irish and made a lovely anti-English speech. The crowd's reaction showed that they knew a good deal of Irish and one of the official speakers sat smiling on the lorry until he suddenly realised what he had let himself in for and tried to stop Pádraic but the crowd would not let him. Andrew Dillon was at this meeting, sitting under the lorry; he could see nothing but he heard it all.

In the middle of June the weather was blazing hot and then the 'flu hit us. It was the first real epidemic of flu for about fifteen years and was accompanied by a very large amount of pneumonia. Fiona had stayed with me. She minded me and the two babies and Andrew until she got it herself. Then she went home to 26 Fitzwilliam Street and had a bad dose of it. Kathleen Dillon came in to see us and found us all flat. She got the nurse who had nursed her mother to come and stay, which she very kindly did. I remember trying to

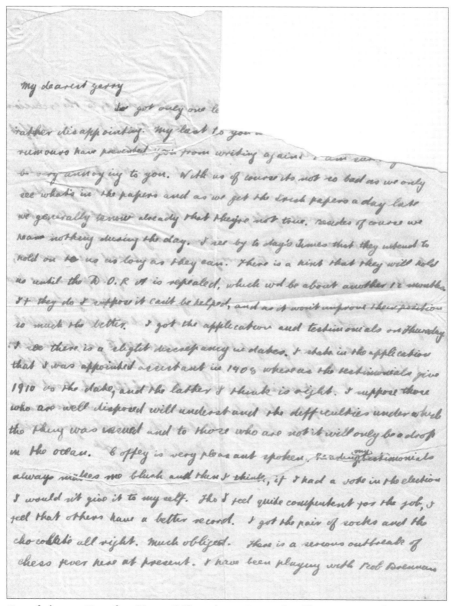

Part of a letter to Gerry from Tommy Dillon who was interned in Gloucester Prison from May 1918 to January 1919.

nurse poor Bláth, who was a month old and had got it badly with a temperature of 104 degrees. I would wake up to find myself waking her up by singing her to sleep in a loud voice. Andrew had got himself a job working in the Dun Emer Guild and was contributing 10s a week to his keep. He now took himself off to live in digs, taking with him all the family portraits and books. That meant that Fiona and I and the children were left in a rather large house, so I let it furnished and we went to live in Fitzwilliam Street.

Blánaid (in the chair) and Moya Dillon, 1918. This was one of a number of photos taken to send to Tommy Dillon in Gloucester Jail. A week after he was jailed in May his mother died and a few days later Blanaid was born; he did not see her until she was nine months old.

Ma, George and Jack were also in Fitzwilliam Street, and Ernie O'Malley stayed there when he was in Dublin, but he was frequently away organising the Volunteers, now known as the Irish Republican Army (IRA). Ernie was like the young Cuchulainn; he was thin and hawk-faced and had red hair. He was very pleasant company and very kind. He continued to be like this until he went to the USA and got married when he seemed to change his nature completely. It was either George or Jack who used to take Bláth and her cradle and run all the way up the stairs with her at night to our bedroom at the top of the house and all the way down again in the morning. Jack used to say he was the only one who could make her laugh and even Ma, whom I still made sure to keep away from little Moya, liked Bláth.

Uncle Frank Cranny was back in Dublin and going from one solicitor to another trying to get them to take an action against Ma to get the 10s allowance without his going away, but they all refused until that summer, P. W. Joyce, who had often been a guest in our house at dances, agreed to take the action to court. I was told at the time that the Castle had guaranteed the costs and indeed this was obvious, as Frank had no means whatsoever and no case and no consideration had been given for the 10s a week Ma had already paid him for over ten years. Further proof was the way the newspapers handled it. The *Herald* had a large heading, right across the top of the page: COUNTESS ACCUSED OF UNDUE INFLUENCE OVER DOCTOR and no mention of the fact that the doctor in question, who left her a life interest in his property, was her own brother. I went to the court with Ma. Her solicitor, Sydney Matthews, wanted her to give in but I backed her in refusing. Judge Dodds had been a personal friend of Uncle Jack Cranny and he got more and more annoyed as the case went on. Frank made a holy show of himself in the witness box, saying that Uncle Jack had owned half Dublin and that he and his mother had plotted against him. Patrick Cranny's will was proved in solemn form by Master Denning and the verdict was against Frank. Ma's counsel, Murnaghan, compared him to Uncle Danny in *The Drone*.

Frank did not go away but managed to hang around Dublin supported by his unfortunate family. He was looked after by an old friend from his youth, McGlade, the frame maker, who used to come to Ma and get a few pounds from her to furnish a room for Frank, as he would not be taken in any digs. He would live in it until he got a bad fit and then smash and sell the few poor sticks of furniture, go on a booze and end up in the gutter. After he got out of jail or hospital, poor McGlade would come and get a few pounds to set him up again.

Mimi got married to Diarmuid O'Leary on August 12th. She and Min Ryan (Mary Mulcahy) were secretaries of Cumann na mBan after 1916 and he had come over from London where he was in shipping and in the London IRB. Here in Dublin he had been working for Larry Nugent at the Pasteur Dairy, but he lost his job on the day of their wedding. Ma prided herself on giving her nothing for her wedding because, as she said, Mimi was marrying a poor man so she wouldn't be doing any entertaining. I told Ma she was making little of herself and so she gave Mimi some necessary furniture, but Mimi was bitter about it. As a sister, Mimi had found fault with everything but when she got out of that nasty house in Fitzwilliam Street, she became a gentle and friendly person.

On September 21st Pat Plunkett died, aged 101. His son, Gerald, who had joined the British Army, had been killed in the Dardanelles during the war, his grandson, Joe, had been executed in 1916 and at the time of his death, his son, my father, was in jail in Birmingham.

After a few months of living in Fitzwilliam Street, which was miserable with Pa away in jail and Mimi gone, I moved out with my babies to the top flat in No. 10 Belgrave Road, which was being rented by Bob and Una Brennan from my mother. I could afford to do this because the Anti-Conscription Committee used their funds to support the dependants of the men arrested for their anti-conscription activities. Alderman Tom Kelly was in charge and Mrs Eamon Ceannt went around looking after the families. They gave me a few pounds a month and some extra at Christmas and paid some very pressing debts such as Paddy Gleeson's. The butcher told me not to worry. Bob Brennan had been the second director of elections for Sinn Féin and he was now arrested and sent to join Tommy in Gloucester Prison. In UCD, Dr Coffey proposed to sack Tommy, but the Chemistry Department, led by Joe Algar, said they would go on strike if he did. They offered to do Tommy's work so that I got his £12 10s a month. At intervals the government would hold up all the letters from jail for a month and upset everybody. At first I sent parcels but after a while Tommy told me not to send anything but a kind of biscuit made of oatmeal and golden syrup because Desmond FitzGerald liked them. Desmond found it very hard to live on the jail food; his mother had brought up her family in London on cake because she did not think bread was good enough for them.

The war ended in November with Germany defeated. The men in jail thought that this was the end of all our hopes but we, outside, did not feel quite like that. Public opinion was much more informed and support for us had been growing. Armistice night in Dublin was a very ignorant demonstration by the English and that night I went over to Kathleen Lynn's newly started hospital, St Ultan's, which was just an old empty house on Charlemont Street, and I bathed the first baby that came into it. Dr Lynn had taken over the baby after its mother died of 'flu in the workhouse hospital. In the kitchen Madame Markievicz was scrubbing the dirty flagged floor, Mrs Dryhurst, Robert Lynn's mother-in-law, was cleaning the old gas stove and Maud Gonne was cleaning the oil lamps which were the only lights. Dr Lynn was an angel to Una Brennan and myself and kept us going. She lived next door to us in No. 9 Belgrave Road and she had two cats who fought on the wall between the back gardens of the two houses one day and fell off on to my duck and killed her!

We all voted in the general election on December 14th with Sinn Féin contesting nearly every seat in the country. This election changed the whole position of the country and the position of everyone in it..

As the general election results came out, we put out tricolour flags for every Republican victory. Soon we were leaving them out all the time except for the four Northern constituencies which MacNeill had unfortunately agreed to. Sinn Féin won 73 seats, 47 of those elected were in jail, the Unionists won 26 and the Irish Parliamentary Party 6. Sinn Féin had swept the board. There was an entirely new situation, with no pretence at loyalty.

In Gloucester Prison at Christmas they managed a kind of dinner with green, white and orange jellies, while Una Brennan and I and the two lots of children had a most miserable small party. I tried to make pancakes from tinned eggs. They were awful but we giggled a lot! I visited 26 Fitzwilliam Street, where Ma stayed in bed while poor Fiona burned the pudding in the kitchen four storeys below her. There was one old carbon bulb hanging from the dining-room ceiling. It was horrid and I was very glad to go

On December 31st Pa, who had kept his seat in Roscommon, was released from jail because of illness and came home. If it had not been for this illness, he would not have been at the opening of the First Dáil.

I was at the first meeting of Dáil Eireann on January 21st 1919 in the Mansion House. We had no idea what the meeting would be like, we'd never even set out to go to anything like it before. I got someone to mind the children, Rory O'Connor collected me and Fiona from Belgrave Road and we went into town on the No. 12 tram. As far as I remember it was a fine dry day and Dawson Street was packed with people. There were over 2,000 people in the Round Room of the Mansion House and we didn't throw any spies out, we just didn't let them in. I sat on the right hand side and saw Pa, looking very distinguished, lead in the newly elected members. Pa sat on his own and announced the meeting and called on the members to elect Cathal Brugha to the chair. It was completely impressive but it wasn't half as tense as people tried to make out; the great thing was how orderly and dignified the proceedings were. There seemed to be a period of peace almost. On other occasions when we were having meetings we would expect the doors to burst open and police to file in, but nobody expected anything like that today. We knew we had a right to be there and that was what was important. About half of those who had been elected were in jail or on the run and they were answered for in Irish 'Fé ghlas ag Gallaibh' (locked up by the foreigner). When Father O'Flanagan read prayers there was cheering, but there was nothing excessive in the way of noise, no-one there was in any mind to shout or anything like that. If you were there, you were one of the lads and that meant you supported everything that went on. We felt we had really made it that day; if they let us away with holding the meeting we were right. The papers commented on the number of priests and women there but of course there were a great many; the men were either on the run or in jail. It has been said that Mick Collins was not there, but he was (I saw him) and at his very best. It was he who answered in Irish for the absent TDs.

The women who were there, many of us with husbands and brothers in jail, looked terrible. Clothes were poor then anyway, and we didn't wear our best clothes, we wore our only clothes. The priests looked like country curates. People seemed to think it was full of drama but the only drama was holding it in the first place. What we were used to was hearing that Ireland couldn't run her own affairs, couldn't do this and that and the other, and now we were all amazed at the way things happened. Pa was made Minister for Foreign Affairs, there were speeches and resolutions and motions and nominations, we'd never seen such things before. The audience was enthusiastic but not hysterical. With an election just over and God knows what just coming, we were hardly in the mood for that. Everyone was well-behaved and left patiently and qui-

The opening of the First Dáil January 21st 1919; Count Plunkett is standing in the centre giving the opening address in which he called on the meeting to elect Cathal Brugha as acting president. Gerry Plunkett Dillon is somewhere on the right hand side. She always maintained that she saw Michael Collins there, as did two others who knew him, Máire Comerford and Dr Eileen McCarville, but this is contradicted by official reports.

etly when it was all over at five o'clock, and there was no particular celebration afterwards for the new Dáil members. Rory and Fiona and I left with the others and I went home to mind my babies.

While Tommy was in Gloucester Jail, the professor of chemistry in UCG, Dr Senier, died. He and Tommy were friends and Dr Senier had always told Tommy that he should get the job when he retired but he died before retirement. Liam Ó Briain came and told me that there would be support for Tommy if he applied and that Father Hynes had said Tommy was the man for the job at Senier's funeral. I got the regulations and forms and sent the application to Gloucester to Tommy who wrote it and sent it back. I collected the letters of reference; some were already there but most of them had to be new. Tom Nolan and a man named Reilly had been working on munitions for the English and wanted to come home and when they applied for the job, Joe Algar was annoyed as he thought Tommy should be given a walkover so he also applied. When Joe Algar asked Dr Coffey, President of UCD, for a letter of recommendation he refused, saying that if he gave it to one he would have to give it to all of them, but Joe told me it was because Coffey did not want to give a reference to Tommy. I refused to accept this, as I thought that if Tommy had not a reference from the head of the place he worked, it could be said that there was something specific against him. I called on Dr Coffey and he put me off but I had known him a long time and was more obstinate than he was and called on him three more times (once the porter tried to stop me, I think on Coffey's orders). Each time, although he knew I had two babies at home to mind, he talked for an hour about everything he was ignorant of (such as that no child could learn to read under the age of seven—I didn't contradict him!) and on the last occasion he suddenly stopped and said 'What do you want?' and dashed off the letter of reference. I told Joe Algar so that he could get a reference for himself, but he was so offended by Coffey that he refused to ask him again. With all the rumours of release I had thought that Tommy would be released in time to call on all the members of the Governing Body and Senate, but time ran short and I called on all the Dublin members of the Senate that I could and that I knew, like Sir Joseph McGrath, Michael Cox, Father Corcoran and Douglas Hyde. They were all very kind.

One evening at the end of January there was a paragraph in the *Evening Herald* late column saying that the 'flu epidemic had hit Gloucester Jail and that twenty-eight men had been removed to a nursing home, giving its address. Tommy and Desmond FitzGerald's names were given. I got the night boat from the North Wall and arrived in Gloucester after eighteen hours' journey. I found the nursing home, in which all the staff had 'flu as well as the patients. They were all very ill and Peadar O'Keefe was pale green and I did not think he would live, but the sight of someone from home helped him. I was the first to arrive; Katy O'Keefe and Mabel FitzGerald came next day. There was a big ward with about twenty men in it and a small ward with about eight, both closely packed. Tommy, Pierce McCann, Desmond FitzGerald, Ginger O'Connell and others were in the small ward. The doctor, an Irishman named James Bell, had divided them in his wisdom with great care between the rooms. He had refused to be responsible unless the men were taken out of the jail and put in hospital, although he knew that they would cease to be prisoners if they were taken out and would have to be re-arrested. Tom Hunter was in the county infirmary and I went to see him at once after seeing the others. He had pneumonia and had been the first to be taken out of the jail and put into hospital. His doctor in the county infirmary was a South African and he and Tom made great friends and kept up their friendship. I only saw Tom Hunter twice, as the infirmary was then isolated because of a case of cerebral spinal meningitis in it. The men in the nursing home had high temperatures and were light-headed and very excited and insisted on telling me that they would not go back to jail.

I found the maid in the kitchen passing out with the 'flu and I cooked whatever I could find and they ate it and praised it as 'heavenly'. A box of eggs arrived from home, about ten dozen, mostly broken; the box was left in the hall of the nursing home overnight and it all ran down the stairs but I made omelettes of what was left. The box was addressed to 'The Prisoners, Gloucester Jail'—no wonder it got hard treatment! At first their food had been very badly cooked but after some months in the jail, a lot of prisoners from Usk in Monmouth, including Bob Loughran, were transferred to Gloucester after Dick Coleman died in Usk of pneumonia, and Bob, who was a cook, was allowed a gas stove and made their rations eatable at last. When the prisoners' clothes wore out they were given what were called 'Mallaby-Deelys' after the manufacturer, who made a fortune out of them as civvies for the conscription army. These just fell to pieces and they went back to their worn-out clothes. I mended lots of them when I was in Gloucester; some of their trousers had not a single button. Some of the men managed to keep clean and neat but Tommy and Griffith had no idea of washing clothes or keeping rooms and their clothes were awful. Tommy had learnt chess from Griffith and Irish from Pierce McCann. A day nurse was got for the men, May Biggs, a baker's daughter from Belfast, and Johnny MacEntee, who was engaged to Nancy Power and writing to Maggie Brown, made up to her. I posted letters to all three girls at the same time!

Katy O'Keefe and Mabel FitzGerald had come straight to the nursing home when they arrived but Johnny MacEntee's parents had not known the address and went to the jail. The governor would not give them the address until they promised to visit Johnny for one hour with supervision, as if he were still in jail. This started a fine row, with everyone telling the MacEntees that they should not have promised this, and when the governor put his nose into the large ward, they all shouted at him and he ran away. He had told the MacEntees that Johnny was still a prisoner, which was not true, and he told me that I should advise Tommy to go quietly back to jail when he was well enough and said he could be looked after very well there. I said I would not and he threatened me with vague penalties. Next day the Home Office doctor, another Irishman, Dr Ahern, came to see me and argued for an hour or more about how much wiser it would be for me to advise Tommy to go back to jail. He said he would come back again but he did not.

Pierce McCann had got very excited and kept popping his head and shoulders out the window, although he was warned not to, trying to see how they could escape if necessary. We had to get a couple of warders from the jail to help with Pierce as he was over six feet tall, very strong and with the high temperature very violent, and he nearly killed one of them. He got pneumonia and was put in another room and his family arrived with his fiancée, Jo Ahern. I wrote to Mick Collins telling him that the men were determined not to be re-arrested and asking him to deal with it and I enclosed the letter in a sealed letter to Father Michael Curran of the Archbishop's House. I had no right to do this and Father Curran ticked me off for it but I had no other way. Mick sent Seán Nunan over but by the time he arrived, it was too late, Pierce

McCann had died on March 6th. I and others thought there should be a national funeral but his parents refused to permit this. Jo Ahern told me that this was because they were afraid they would have to pay for it. Seán Nunan settled that and told them it would all be paid for, so they agreed. Mrs McCann asked me to get a photographer in the town to take a photograph of Pierce laid out. She said she wanted it to hang beside the photographs of her other son and daughter, as they were also dead.

Pierce McCann's death brought the whole thing to an end and a few days later the men started to go home, but some of them were still too ill to travel and were going to have to stay behind. Griffith and the rest of the men from the jail arrived at the hall door of the nursing home where I had been helping all day and I opened it. He knew who I was and he said they had been released but had refused to go home until they knew that the sick men were being properly treated, so the long procession of men tramped up the stairs and in and out of the rooms and kissed every man goodbye. The same thing happened when our lot were going—all of them kissed the two men we had to leave behind. Some of our lot refused to go until they got more respectable clothes and they did get some things. We had two carriages full on the train to the boat, a very tight squash. Tom Hunter had managed to get a bottle of whiskey, but they did not get out of hand. When we got to the Holyhead boat, I was stopped because my ticket was for the North Wall, but the Dublin G-man at the gangway said I was to be let through. The boat was full of soldiers going on leave and we had a good deal of trouble finding places for our sick men to lie down. I sat at a table in the saloon, my head falling onto the table with a bang whenever I went to sleep.

13 Terror in Galway 1919–1920

W HEN WE GOT HOME FROM GLOUCESTER IN MARCH Tommy was just in
time to go down to University College Galway for the Governing Body
meeting. He had no clothes and very little money, so he wore an enormous
frieze overcoat which had been made for me but was just right for him; in the
fashion of the time my overcoat was like a man's. He got the job but in a
hoofling manner so that it was only by one vote. I heard a complete account of
the voting from others; members of the Governing Body had approached the
bishop and asked him not to attend the meeting to keep the voting even or
nearly so, in the hope that the National University of Ireland Senate might
not approve Tommy, and they hedged and fixed votes in other ways. It was
my first encounter with academic intrigue and I found the whole thing hard
to believe. The Senate, on the other hand, were largely made up of old friends
of Tommy and myself and they gave him the job by a good majority, to the
surprise of the other lot. Tommy went to tell Ma he had got the job and came
back with a queer grin, carrying a present of butter and eggs. I sent them to
Mimi, who was starving. Tommy's job in University College, Dublin ended
in July, the new one did not start until October and he would get no money
until January because he had high-mindedly refused to take any more money
from UCD.

In April Pa, Griffith and de Valera represented the Dáil at the post-war
peace talks and tried to get Ireland's case considered. They were not accepted
there, of course, and the Irish Party made no claim for a place at the conference and allowed statements by British ministers to go unchallenged. Pa de-
plored this and their attitude to the Rising.

I went to Galway to look for a house. Ma said she would guarantee me in
the bank if we had to buy one but she demanded the house in Belgrave Road
back when I wanted to let it. She said that she had only lent it to me for my
personal use. I should have asked Pa to help me, as it was his house, but his
health had broken down from when he was in prison in Birmingham before
Christmas. After looking at a few places we found the only house available,
which was on College Road, and cost £1,000. I was brought to Louis O'Dea,
the chairman of the town council, who brought me to the National Bank. We
bought the house from another Tom Dillon, the jeweller, who auctioned the
furniture in the house and Ma, who came down with me to settle me in,
enjoyed herself at the auction, bidding for nothing I wanted, and everything
I didn't want, with my money, which I had not got.

Tommy Dillon was thirty-five when he was appointed Professor of Chemistry in University College Galway after his release from jail in 1919. From very basic conditions he built a highly respected faculty and his pupils included the first two women professors of chemistry in Ireland.

Uncle Frank died. In the end his kidneys went back on him, he could drink no more and he died in misery. Ma followed him alone to his grave. I told her she should have let me know and I would have come up from Galway to be with her. She was very unhappy about him.

In Galway it was a hot dry summer and the road through the town was not paved or macadammed, it was just limestone dust which became a sea of mud in winter and was mended by throwing limestone chips on it. The horse trams were just gone and the tracks were being taken up and that summer there was a continual cloud of dust and I got an awful sore throat. We were, of course, made acquainted with all sorts of people and asked to parties of all kinds; the standard was not too high for us and Chris and Michael O'Malley were really kind. It was a quiet time politically and it was possible to hold the Sinn Féin courts, started by the Dáil, in the house. Tommy took part in everything that went on and he had lectures to prepare and so on. University College Galway was in a very bad financial position. Its grant had not been increased from the time it had been a Queen's College, with the staff paid partly from fees, and during the First World War and later there were few students and the staff was very badly paid. Part of the old Queen's College staff were still in possession; these were English Government appointments, in some cases quite unfit for their work, no qualification having been required, others were merely out of date. There was hardly any equipment in the chemistry department, the laboratory was not up to much, the quarters were cramped and there were no research students. The first-year chemical laboratory was a room in the abandoned Model School and the lab for the rest was a room in the main college building. There was a provision in the National University Act that the county councils could strike a halfpenny rate in support of the College and if they did this they could elect a member to the Governing Body of the College. A group of Nationalist Republicans organised the county councils and managed to get a majority on the Governing Body of the College. From this on, ordinary Irish people were appointed to the professorships. Some of the old staff, like the president, Alexander Anderson, had been brilliant as were some of the new.

I found quite a lot of snobbery in Galway, high highs to low lows, but it was quite phoney as, except for the English Colonel of the Connaught Rangers, no one in the town had that kind of position or money to justify it. Galway was a garrison town and the English Army were socially, politically and economically the top and were accepted as such by far too many people. When I bought a white duck in the market and carried it home under my arm, some of the ladies were seriously annoyed with me and decided that they did not like me. In any case I talked politics with men, which was regarded as most unsuitable for a young woman. I found their position ridiculous and had no interest in their card parties. We met a lot of people on our own side and it took me a long time to sort them out. Louis O'Dea, Tom Walsh and George Nicholls were the most prominent politically and I heard of many others but did not meet them till later.

The most unpleasant experience I had at this time was a visit to the RIC barracks in Eglinton Street to get a sugar ration card. Sugar had been practically the only thing rationed during the war, though there was a lot of unofficial rationing by traders, and my sugar ration card was with the grocer in Rathmines who had applied for it for me as a customer. In Galway I found a different regulation and could get no sugar, so I went to the barracks and explained the matter to Sergeant Fox and several others. They were very rude and nasty and took the opportunity to pretend they had a lot of power. I had never lived in a town with RIC except on holidays and I thought their behaviour absurd—Bolsheviks, how are you! I told some Galway people my experience and they found it hard to believe, Sergeant Fox was always polite to them, but Mickey Allen knew about him.

I had thought that now at last I could join Cumann na mBan, but there was nothing to join. It had broken up because Mrs O'Dea and some other

The Model School, Galway, where the Dillons lived for a time with rats in the bedrooms and sandbags at the doors. The children, however, loved the classrooms where they could put on plays and make speeches. The school later became the home of the University College Galway Chemistry Department.

ladies had refused to belong to the same branch as their maids and after a few months both branches had disintegrated. The only thing left was a student branch in the College and that was not doing very well. The Volunteers were a different thing altogether. The Volunteers in the town had been through a bad time, first at the time of the Redmondite split in the Volunteers, when they were beaten up by soldiers with their belts, and then after the Rising. Liam Mellowes, who had delivered the gelignite and ammunition to us in Marlborough Road in 1914, had commanded the men who turned out in Galway for the Rising. In July, 1915, he had been served with an order under the Aliens' Restriction Act excluding him from all four military areas of Ireland. Liam did not obey the order and was arrested and given three months in jail. When he was released he was served with another order and did not obey it and was forcibly removed to England. There he had to live in a restricted area, under the eye of the police, but managed to escape in time to take up the Galway command in 1916.

Under these conditions the campaign was not a fair test of his ability. He was joined by about 2,000 Galway Volunteers, first at Athenry, then at Moyode Castle. A gunboat in Galway Bay sent a shell in their general direction and it landed in a field near the racecourse, twenty miles wide of the mark. They were not attacked except by a Home Guard and police contingent from Galway city, which in turn was ambushed by a Volunteer outpost at Carnmore Cross. One RIC man named Whelan was killed but this was the only casualty. When the week was over, Liam dispersed his men and escaped to the USA. The police did not know who had taken part in it so they arrested all those who were away from home during the week. The English Government tried to get Liam arrested in America after the USA joined the Allies in the war. He tried to get back to Ireland, but the boat he was to go on was attacked. When de Valera arrived in the States he sent Liam back to Ireland as a messenger and told him to return as soon as he could, but he stayed in Ireland. During the Rising many of the male population of the town had signed up as special constables against the Volunteers. One of them told me that they had been persuaded to do so by being told that the Rising was an attack on John Redmond and the Irish Party. After the Rising, the *Galway Express* was bought by Sinn Féiners when it came up for sale and it was then the only Sinn Féin newspaper in the country. In University College there was a Volunteer command and when practically everyone else was on the run the students were able to put up a show. A lot of people were much too afraid of losing their jobs.

One day, about 150 men on horses, carrying tricolours and each with a small bag of oats tied to his saddlebow, came clathering past our house into the town. They were tenant farmers on the Alcorn estate near Headford who had descended on the Alcorn house, got the old man and tied a rope to him and dumped him in and out of the lake until he agreed to sell the land to the tenants. They then helped themselves to his oats and rode into the town in triumph. Alcorn kept his word. When the officers and officials in the County Club saw this tenant cavalry apparently take possession of the Square they were furious. They went to Hildebrand, the RIC District Inspector, who was playing billiards and told him he must get his men out at once and that he must ask for military help. DI Hildebrand delayed and delayed and when he finally went out the horsemen had gone home.

My third daughter, Eilís, was born on March 7th, 1920 in Galway. I had such a bad time with the births of each of my children that I was advised not to have any more as it would probably kill me. I had read and heard about the Marie Stopes Clinics so I went to my doctor and asked him for some kind of contraception. He told me that he couldn't do anything for me as it was against the laws of the Church. I was raging but I couldn't see what else I could do.

This year was remarkable for the takeover of the civil government from the British. There were only a certain number of ways that this could be done but there was a general direction from the Dáil that it was to be done. The Republican Courts, set up under the Minister for Justice, Austin Stack, were arbitration courts and, as there was no compulsion to attend them, were not illegal. Some police work was done but it was not well managed and a lot of land settlement work came in, some of it not well done either, but it did keep the land question from interfering with the main question of political freedom for a time. The civil disobedience campaign was quite successful and local government was almost at a standstill. Books were not sent for audit, or were removed by the IRA. There was an almost complete breakdown of civil government in the West. The daily resignations of Justices of the Peace, the empty law courts and the full Sinn Fein courts, the missing minute books and account books all made the government think of Galway as a hotbed of rebellion, which was very far from being the case.

Lloyd George announced his intention of dealing with the Irish as murderers. Shortly afterwards supplementary English recruits to the RIC, called Black-and-Tans for their unmatched uniforms, and a bit later the Auxiliary Cadets or Auxies, also nominally under RIC command, started arriving. During the summer they came into Galway in increasing numbers, and more and more soldiers also arrived. The Auxiliaries took over Lenaboy Castle, the property of the O'Hara family, with its extensive grounds, and the RIC were brought in from all the villages and small towns to the bigger ones. There were now 20,000 soldiers and police to the 14,000 citizens of Galway. The members of the old RIC were sharply divided into those who wanted to get out of it as quickly as they could, and those who had always hated rebels and were going to get their opportunity at last. The first section had already resigned in large numbers, with or without pensions, and this left the Castle with no means of identifying suspects and without the reports on which they depended so much, so resignations were stopped and those who tried to get out, on the plea of ill health or the like, were beaten up to teach them to know better. This left us with a lot of friends in the police barracks and they gave us all the information they could.

The Black-and-Tans usually lived in the barracks with the RIC. Promotion among both sections was rapid; every constable could hope to be a district inspector and every sergeant a chief inspector, provided he showed his loyalty to England and his willingness to kill, maim and torture. After a while the worst of the two lots were indistinguishable, except that the old RIC knew who we were as a rule and took a good deal of pleasure in being insolent. The Auxies were supposed to be officers and gentlemen and as such were welcomed by the friends of the old garrison, but they were not accepted by high society and thought themselves insulted by the discrimination, with amusing results. The Auxies who were married, or supposed to be married, lived in lodgings in the town and some of them had their children with them; twenty-six sets of divorce papers were served on them in one day. They seemed to us to be a set of lunatics and by the time they left, their lives were as silly and fantastic as any film scenario. Their colonel brought his wife with him and a great point was made of his being a Catholic, but this only made it more amusing when he got engaged to the sister of a Black-and-Tan and the poor man could not get a divorce because he was a Catholic. They said that the brassy-haired six-footer that was married to another of them belonged to a good family who had offered her any money if she would leave him. They spent their money on drink and lived on loot—pigs, hens and ducks stolen from country people. They drank anything, a mixture of Bovril, whiskey, gin and rum. They stole everything down to the old ladies' red petticoats and sent them to their friends in England as souvenirs. We heard from people in England of the wonderful things their friends were getting and did not realise that they were stolen. Nine extra trainloads of parcels of poultry were sent from the Galway post office at Christmas. They fought amongst themselves, sometimes with guns, and some were even dismissed for conduct unbecoming to an officer and a gentleman.

During their visits to Galway, the official murder gang were stationed in the Retreat in Rockbarton, which had been commandeered from the Kennedys. The cadets and Black-and-Tans settled down happily with their lady friends, bought new clothes with their pound a day and waited for the fun to start. It was known that when it did start, they would be allowed to loot freely and that they had been told this when they were engaged. This was all they were interested in and, except for the official murder gang, they did the looting and the old RIC did the killing. These military authorities, meaning that curious mixture of old RIC, Black-and-Tans, Auxiliaries and regular army, did not always work well together. The police had orders through their weekly gazette, *The Weekly Summary*, to 'make Ireland an appropriate hell for those whose trade is agitation and whose method is murder'. Some regiments took these orders and some did not.

Tommy and I met DI Hildebrand on the Weir Bridge in Galway in August. Hildebrand was a kindly man who had lived a long time in Galway and took the decent official view that maladministration and injustice were the cause of all the trouble in Ireland. He stopped us and said that we were in for trouble, that a man had been sent to Galway and told to make as much trouble as would lead to the sack of the town but that so far he had been able to stop him, and as long as he, Hildebrand, was in control, he would not allow this trouble to happen. He said he expected to be transferred if he refused to co-operate and that when we heard he was gone, we were to look out for squalls. He did not know why so many troops had been sent into Galway and was very worried by it. He also said that Irishmen only wanted justice and if they got it they never made any trouble, which struck us as the point of view of a decent policeman. Captain Harrison was the man who came to make trouble.

My brother George had been in Waterford giving a course in tactics and manoeuvres with the Volunteers there and one day, when about twenty of them were out for practice, they saw several lorries of Black-and-Tans on the road. George thought this would be good experience for the Volunteers so he allowed them to attack. The lorries fled, the IRA followed them across fields and attacked again and repeated it. The Tans reported being attacked by at least 300 and made a whole battle of it. George was now on the run and staying with us and after he had been with us a few days a Franciscan priest,

Father Fidelis, arrived at the house one afternoon in a great hurry saying he had been told to tell me to get George away as he was going to be arrested. An RIC man had gone over from the Eglinton Street barracks to the Franciscan church, the Abbey, which was just across the road, saying he was going to confession and had sent Father Fidelis to give me the warning. George was not in but came in a few minutes afterwards and I ran him out and as he went down the road he passed a company of soldiers. They surrounded the house but went away peaceably after searching for George. Fergus Kelly came in afterwards, found George for me and took him off to Mayo for a week out of the way. They had a fine time in Killala helping to make poitín and brought back a bottle of it to me as a present.

Seán Mulvoy: he was shot dead by a Black-and-Tan in a fight on Galway railway station.

While they were away we were told that Hildebrand had been moved to somewhere in the North.

On September 8th, a few days after Hildebrand left, we were in Louis O'Dea's house to meet a priest from Ironton, Ohio, who wanted to tell everyone about the great work he was doing for Ireland. The evening papers used to come in on the train from Dublin, arriving at 11.30 p.m. Tommy went out to get one and we heard the train and then several loud shots and a lot of shouting and noise. When Tommy came back he told us what had happened. A Black-and-Tan lorry driver named Krumm had spent the evening drinking. In one pub he boasted about his aim and insisted on setting up a row of bottles as targets to show his skill. Tom Hynes, the IRA intelligence officer, heard of this and sent his brother Michael to warn any Volunteers that an armed man seemed to be preparing to create trouble. The Volunteers were in the habit of going to the station every night to meet the train, watch the troop movement, collect despatches and meet Volunteers from other districts, and this night they were also going to collect arms from the Longford area. Krumm and a companion went on to the platform by the gate on the arrivals side. The Volunteers warned the men arriving with the Longford guns and the train stopped for a moment outside the station while they went out by the signal box with the guns. The train came into the station and as the

Séamus Quirke was taken from his lodgings and shot through the stomach eleven times. He crawled on his hands and knees from the lamp-post on the quay where he was shot, to the door of his house. He died at dawn.

passengers started to go out the gate Krumm drew his gun and made as if to shoot into the crowd. Seán Turke jumped on his back, pulled him to the ground and tried to get his gun from him. Seán Mulvoy went to help him and Krumm managed to fire all the rounds in his gun in the struggle, killing Mulvoy and wounding another man. Another Volunteer shot Krumm just as Tom Fahy and Michael Hynes came to help and they took the gun away. Krumm's companion was still with him but he seems to have taken no part in the business. Tommy and the others carried Mulvoy to his lodgings but he was dead on arrival.

A quarter of an hour after we got home from Louis O'Dea's, we heard several armoured cars go tearing down the road from Renmore and we knew the trouble Hildebrand had warned us about had started. We got the children, Moya, Bláth and Eilís, and the maid and ourselves into our friends', the Griffiths, house and they found room for us all. We had told them that we thought we might be a mark and they had very kindly said that they would always take us in. I opened the window in the dark and sat down on the floor beside it. It was a wonderful still warm night and I could hear every sound in the town from where we were on the shore of Lough Atalia. The lorries full of armed men tore down the road from Renmore and the shooting began. The first shots sounded like a machine gun followed by a dreadful screaming. This was when Sergeant Fox shot young Séamus Quirke. Quirke was taken from his lodgings in the new dock and shot through the stomach eleven times. He crawled on his hands and knees from the lamppost on the quay where he was shot, to the door of his house. This screaming was the background to all the horrors of the next five hours until the poor boy died at dawn. Father Griffin was sent for and stayed with him till he died. It was thought that the police mistakenly believed Seamus Quirke had shot Krumm.

The finish of their rampage was a volley of shots when the troops put Johnny Broderick and Cummins up against the big gate at the railway station and shot them. Cummins was wounded in the leg and fell, but Broderick's head was only grazed and he cleverly fell also, pretending to be dead. Seeing him covered with blood the police left him. The next thing was the sound of Johnny's mother, Mrs Broderick, screaming when they shut her in her house on Prospect Hill and set it on fire with petrol. The neighbours ran to put it out but were shot at and had to wait until the RIC went away again. A party of RIC led by Sergeant Fox ranged the town looking for Volunteers, who had nearly all got away at the sound of the first shots. They searched for Tom Fahy, who was gone, and Paddy McAvinue, who got up on the roof of his mother-in-law's house where he could hear Sergeant Fox howling for his blood in the street. One after another the lorries went back to the barracks, leaving the RIC alone in the streets quite mad with blood. It was a planned outbreak of terror. While the RIC and Tans were doing all this, the Auxies were enjoying themselves working down a list of houses which were to be looted, Moylette's, Kennedy's, Séamus Murphy's and so on. They took silver and valuables of all kinds and if they did not like anything they left it in the next house. The *Galway Express* office was completely wrecked.

The next day some of the type of the *Galway Express* was got together and a leaflet was printed giving the main facts of the previous night's orgy of murder and wreckage. It formally accused the police, that is to say the RIC, of the murders and advised the people to 'keep cool'. The next morning we went down the town to see what had happened. We met Louis O'Dea. As inquests were prohibited in Ireland by military order, he proposed, as chairman of the town council, to hold a public inquiry into Mulvoy's and Quirke's deaths. When he tried to do so he was met by a company of soldiers with DI Cruise who occupied the office and ordered him to stop. It was made quite plain to Louis that he would also be murdered and he had to go on the run. Cruise, who came here from Cork, was Hildebrand's replacement and was accepted as a gentleman in Galway. He slept in Eglinton Street barracks with steel shutters round his bed. He used to lead all the raids and seemed to us to be possessed of a devil. I often saw him, his head muffled in a waterproof, in the Crossley tenders which tore along the road full of screaming police.

In September the Dáil was declared a 'dangerous association' and its meetings were prohibited. Three days later our house, among many others, was raided and searched. Over the next few days 23 newspapers were suppressed, 14,000 houses raided, 476 attacks were made on peaceful meetings, 260 men, women and children were wounded by bayonet thrusts, rifle butts or fire, 959 arrests for alleged political offences were made, 20 leaders were deported and 332 attacks were made on civilians by police and military, with 8 civilians killed and no-one charged for it. There was one death in prison, 227 courts martial, Fermoy was sacked, martial law was declared and fairs and markets were suppressed in Tipperary, Cork, Kerry, Limerick, Clare, Galway and Mayo. In Galway, the terror rose higher and higher and a farcical military inquiry

The funeral of Séamus Quirke and Seán Mulvoy. Requiem Mass was celebrated for them with the Bishop presiding and the Last Post was sounded. No public funerals, apart from Father Griffin's, were allowed after this.

into the murder of Séamus Quirke was held and adjourned. Requiem Mass was celebrated for Quirke and Mulvoy with the bishop presiding and the Last Post was sounded. No public funerals were allowed after this.

Tommy and I could not see what we were to do. We had seen how easily our College Road house could be surrounded when the soldiers had come for George. Each day we went home during the day, and at night put the children and maid in the Griffiths' and stayed in Mickey Allen's in Shantalla ourselves. After a few days we decided to shut up the house and go to the Stella Maris hostel in Salthill. We did not know then that, although we were on the Dublin Metropolitan Police list in Dublin, we had not yet been put on the Galway RIC list. We were too recent newcomers and the disorganisation of the police, due mainly to the number of resigned and dismissed, had caused confusion and they had lost track of us. Then we thought of going to Barna. We moved some of the furniture to a house belonging to Willie Hickey and managed to get the rest of it into one of the college cellars with the help of Tom Hynes, the porter in the Physiology Departmen and a couple of other porters All the porters, except O'Hare in Physics, were in the IRB. The house was left empty and when the Tans came to burn it afterwards, Ronan Healy, the son of the chemical lab porter (a boy at the time), was standing near and he told them that we had gone away long before and sold the house.

The authorities wished us to know what was happening in different parts of the country so that we would be terrified, but they didn't want the news to get abroad and were in a dilemma as to whether news should be published or not. It was extraordinary which reports they allowed and still more extraordinary which they suppressed. *The Connacht Tribune* was allowed to say that the police broke out, that they killed Seamus Quirke, but later the paper was threatened with reprisals if other information was given out. Reports of burnings and shootings all over Ireland began to reach the English papers as the hard work of the propaganda department of Dáil Eireann began to have effect. A steady stream of English journalists was sent all over Ireland; many of them were in Galway and attended Republican courts. They were told the history of recent years in Ireland and saw the condition of the country and the *Irish Bulletin* was sent to them every week. For the first time they knew something about us and the reports given to them by their own government were recognised to be untrue. The *Manchester Guardian* published an article by Ivor Brown saying that the police were being permitted to run amok. The *New Statesman* pointed out that Sir Henry Wilson was trying to explode rebellion in the manner of Castlereagh. They said that the military and police were acting on direct orders from Downing Street over the heads of Dublin Castle. The idea was to provoke us into disorganised and senseless action and so work us out of our hard-won position as rulers of our own country, through our own elected representatives, but this did not allow for the speed of modern communications. The news was carried to the furthest corners of the earth and men of goodwill, including decent Englishmen, helped us to put an end to it.

Press men from all over the world, journalists from England and the USA were sent on to us in Galway by Bob Brennan and Desmond FitzGerald. Childers and Collins were in charge of a lot of this work in Dublin. We gave the press men hospitality and food. They were a mixed lot. We thought we had made little impression on Ivor Brown but when he went back to the *Manchester Guardian* he wrote splendid leaders. Gary Mostyn of the USA was one of us who afterwards fought alongside the IRA in an ambush. The worst was Charlie Shaw, who wrote anti-Irish novels under the name of Shaw Desmond. He arrived and asked us to get some prominent Sinn Féiners together as he had a message for them from England, so we got Liam O Briain and Michael and Chris O'Malley and Tomás O Máille and others to an evening party. Shaw began to talk to them in a patronising tone as people who had never been abroad, whereas most of those present had lived in London for years or studied in Germany and elsewhere. He began to get worried and then he came out with his message, 'The great heart of English Labour is sound!' and everyone burst out laughing.

The next thing, on September 20th, was the sack of the town of Balbriggan, 54 houses and a factory burned and the whole place shot up by police and military, and it was plain that another Cromwellian plan was starting. As far as I could see, it would be with torture and floggings, but when I said this

The Bal (Ballinasloe House) with Mr and Mrs Grehan at the left of the door. Mrs Grehan was a Republican and sent messages to Gerry for the local IRA unit from Michael Collins.

many people thought that it was not possible in that day and age. Certain Galway houses had practically daily raids—Joe Grehan's, Donnelly's, Fegan's in Barna. Paddy McAvinue's and Harry Shield's were commandeered. Four girls had their hair cut off, which was more of a tragedy then than it would be now. Tuam had a horrible night of raids and shootings. A young man named Harry Burke was made crawl on his hands and knees up and down the Square in his nightshirt and when his knees were cut to pieces, a Black-and-Tan took him by the heels and made him finish it on his hands. The Archbishop said that the destruction of life and property took on the hideous colours of hell. There were lorries going about all night in Galway firing rifles. Louis O'Dea's office was bombed, Pat Moylette's shop looted. The Bal (Ballinasloe House) in Salthill, owned by Joe Grehan, was looted while the Tans beat a shop boy, played the melodeon and spat on the crucifix. The old malt house was searched for Michael Walsh, the Republican outfitters was looted, George Nicholls,

Charlie Costelloe and Reynolds, foreman porter at the railway station, were arrested and University College was raided.

Through October men were stripped and beaten, one an ex-RIC man. Humiliation and indignity were recognised as the objects of whippings, so men were usually stripped in front of crowds of women before being beaten with buckled belts or with specially made scourges. There were terrors by the Black-and-Tans, the Auxies and the RIC in Barna and Moycullen, in Ardrahan and Labane, in Athenry and Gort, in Clifden and Oranmore. Town halls were shot up, parochial halls burnt down by soldiers, houses and haggards burnt. Houses were looted and daubed with filth and parlours used as lavatories, men were shot up. There were raids on shops—Keane's, Powell's, O'Dea's, Fegan's, Moylette's raided and looted nearly every night—and Donnelly's was set on fire three times in one night but each time the local Volunteers put out the fires. J. J. Ward was ordered to provide drivers for looters' cars and refused, so he had to drive Black-and-Tans about all night with a gun pressed to his back as they looted his friends' houses. The printers of the *Galway Express* were court-martialled. *The Connacht Tribune's* leader was headed 'The Darkest Hour'.

Advertisements had appeared in all the Irish newspapers offering rewards and protection to anyone who wrote to the authorities giving information about persons engaged in illegal activities. The Galway Volunteers in the GPO were instructed to take possession of all letters of this kind and among those stopped in the GPO were three from Joyce, the schoolmaster of Barna boys' school, giving the names of the men of the East Connemara Brigade, some of them also teachers, and their meeting place and saying that they were actively working against the British Government. Tom Hynes, of the Galway city company, sent word to Dublin, the matter was investigated and an order for Joyce's execution was sent to Galway and carried out a week later. Father Tom Burke attended Joyce but the authorities believed that it was Father Griffin. Joyce's body was buried and has never been found. About half an hour after the men had taken Joyce away, Joyce's son went for the police and the Black-and-Tans were sent for. It was presumed, of course, that the police would take action at once and all concerned were on their guard. They thought it best to stay at their usual work as far as possible, but the police had very precise information about the east Connemara brigade and it is likely that all Joyce's information had already got to them in spite of those letters being stopped. They acted apparently on the presumption that Joyce was being held as a hostage. They rushed out along the road next day in lorries and tenders and whenever they saw a few men together or even singly they stopped and beat them up.

We thought that we would be still further lost if we moved again, so we rented a house in Spiddal for a month. The day we moved to Spiddal was also the day our furniture was being brought to be stored in Hickeys' house in Barna, and it was the day after the execution of Joyce, but we did not know that when we started out. We went to Barna on an outside car and waited there for the furniture to arrive. Suddenly we heard shots and then a lorry full of armed RIC and Tans passed quickly. When the Duggans arrived with the float there was a bullet hole in one of their caps. They said that as they met Tom MacDonagh, the teacher in Cappagh, on his bicycle, the Tan lorry over-took them. They caught MacDonagh and a very big man lifted him above his head and dashed him to the ground, breaking his leg, and then smashed the bicycle the same way. MacDonagh had been taken to hospital. We put the furniture in Hickeys' house and drove on towards Spiddal. It was now getting dark. At Furbough, Miceál O Droighneáin came out of the dark and walked beside the car, talking to Tommy. He told him about Joyce having been shot the night before and told him to look out. We heard a lorry coming from Spiddal and Miceál dived backwards through the fuchsia hedge and away but some of the RIC men had seen him and were after him. We could hear shout-ing but no shots. They had screamed as they passed and one man had a waterproof wrapped round his head and when it blew away from his face we could see it was DI Cruise.

When we reached Spiddal we found Eamon Breathnach with a great cut over his eye and the whole place in an uproar. The lorries had gone out by Moycullen and over the hill to Spiddal, stripping and horsewhipping the young men in Killanin. One man had the whip, which seemed to be a spe-cially made type of large dog whip. They arrived in Spiddal, without warning, by the bog road and caught Eamon Breathnach in the Co-op where he worked. They beat him on the head with their rifle butts and fired shots off beside his ears and all the time they shouted that Joyce must be brought back by next day or they would come back and burn the village and kill everyone in it. We did not believe the threats, as a large number of the inhabitants of Spiddal were ex-RIC and soldiers. All this was on Saturday. On Sunday morning Fa-ther MacElhinney told us in his sermon, first in Irish, then in English for strangers, how Cruise had ordered him to denounce the 'kidnapping' of Joyce and said he would not take orders as to what he was to say in his own church. From that time there were almost daily raids by soldiers and police. Immedi-ately after these incidents Dr O'Dea, Bishop of Galway, asked Tommy if Joyce had been executed with the proper authority as, if not, he would have to denounce it as murder. Tommy told him that he knew it had been authorised by the Dáil but that he would obtain formal assurance if it was necessary and he did so within a few days. Dublin Castle had expected denunciation by the Bishop and waited for it, but Dr O'Dea said nothing. He got a threatening letter denouncing him for favouring the IRA and saying he would be shot. The priests of Galway diocese were now marked for murder. The town of Loughrea was shot up and burnings of houses and farms continued. Hugh Martin of the *Daily News* wrote an article about the terror called 'The Knout in Ireland'.

The three children, myself and the maid were alone most of the time. Every couple of days Tommy would come for an hour or two. One day we were warned of a raid and I put the maid and the three children away at the top of the long garden and waited at the back of the house. It was a raid by soldiers and police on Josie Lydon's next door. A soldier with a rifle was sentry at the back door and I could hear revolver shots and shouting, so I asked the sentry what was going on in there. He said it was the officer-in-charge's idea of fun and then his face got red and he said in his cockney soldier's accent that he was from Tipperary, that they thought he was English because of his accent, but he had been on leave in his own county and had seen what 'they' had done to it. If he could only get a chance at them, they'd see what he would do. There was a noise at the door, he sprang to attention with a sign to me not to speak, and I pretended to be walking past the side of the house. That night our Spiddal house was searched by soldiers, who said that they had been advised to do so by the owners of a pub in the village, and my rings were stolen.

A couple of nights later we were warned that our house would be bombed that night and Michael Dillon, the gardener at Killanin's, and his wife took us in. The three children and the maid were stuffed into a single bed. I sat in a chair in the kitchen with Mrs Dillon most of the night and Tommy went to sleep in a goatcave with Mairtin Thornton and a couple more. The Thorntons used to stay in their own house until they heard the lorry at the end of the bohereen and then go, but now the Crossley tenders, which were quite silent, had arrived and the boys were nearly caught. They went out the back door as the Tans and RIC came in the front, and Mairtin spent hours lying in a pond under an overhanging stone with his nose above water. It was a marvellous autumn, warm and dry, more like summer and lasted into December, so that the men were able to sleep out in the fields. The day after the raid warning to us, Canon MacElhinney came into Michael Dillon's lodge to get his breakfast (I don't know why, I believe it was out of penuriousness). While he was eating he told us that he had just been in the Spiddal Irish College down the road as he had been told that it had been broken into by Tans. He said they had forced a latch, broken a pane of glass and torn a map of Ireland in two. That was all. He then went into Galway on a side car. I followed him on a bicycle, arriving an hour or so after him, and by the time I caught up with the story there were not two bricks left on top of each other and all invented by the poor Canon.

I went into Galway and arranged to go back to the Stella Maris, as I could not see that we would be any worse off in the town and Tommy was more exposed when travelling in and out to Spiddal. The day after we went back there, Michael Walsh was murdered. He had given assistance to the Volunteers and the use of his farm in the country as a prison for prisoners of the Republican Courts, of which former prisoners had told the police. Masked

An Teach Beag Bán, the Dillons' house near the Eglinton Hotel, Salthill. 'We lived in the small house on the right, from which we could see a lot of the Black & Tans. I stood at the window for hours on the night that Father Michael Griffin was shot and saw the outside car which carried the informer etc and the truck which carried his body to the bog at Barna. It was a very wild night.'

men entered his shop and told him that they would kill him in half an hour. This was heard by the people who were cleared out of the shop but no-one went to get help. Maybe they did not know where to go. The men got nervous and did not wait the full time. After about twenty minutes, they took him away. They walked him down to the quay between two rows of people lining the road, shot him on the quay at the fish market and threw his body into the Corrib. Jim Fleming, a cousin of Seán Turke's, was in the crowd and armed, so he told me, but I was not surprised when he also told me that he did not see what he could have done.

There was an order issued at once prohibiting anyone following Michael Walsh's funeral except the immediate relatives. In spite of that the people came along both sides of the street, creeping along trying to keep up with the hearse. I walked along the footpath wheeling my bicycle. As the hearse came to Eyre Square there was a sudden setback and confusion. The four mounted soldiers of the 17th Lancers who had been riding beside the hearse turned round and, on an order shouted at them by an officer in uniform, charged the crowd. Unless horses are trained to do so, they will not actually charge people and do their best to avoid them, so no one was injured. We all got quickly out of the way. I got into McCullaghs' doorway with the bicycle across in front of me and one of the McCullaghs came down and brought me into the room over the shop where they were all looking out the window at the scene in the street. Captain Harrison, who was the liaison officer between the RIC and the Auxies, was dancing about in front of the people waving a revolver and screaming with rage. He pointed the revolver at all the windows filled with people in turn. This was kept up for at least ten minutes. He had kept the people from following the hearse to the cemetery but even the most pro-British Army people of Galway despised the exhibition. From this time on the women made the rule that they would always be the ones to open the door to a knock, and Loyalists drew a sharp line between military and police.

We got a small house or two-storey cottage on the beach in Salthill. It had four small rooms and a kitchen in it, but there were beds for fourteen people, feather beds and full of fleas. It belonged to a Mrs Murphy who had a key with which she constantly came in the back door as soon as I went out and abused my unfortunate maid. She had a jar of rotten dripping on the top shelf and was furious when I threw it out. We now heard that police had been looking for Tommy in 13 Belgrave Road, which meant that we were lost officially for the time being and Tommy was able to stay a good deal with us in the house. In the college the men would always warn him of danger. On November 11th, Armistice Day, I had gone up the town, forgetting what day it was, and as I got near the Four Corners I saw an old man staggering down the street with his face laid open in a long diagonal. The Black-and-Tans had waited for the people coming in to the market—it was a Saturday—to make them observe a two minutes' silence, an institution of which the country people had never heard, and when they did not do so, they lashed them across the faces with ash plants. I heard afterwards that the old man I had seen had died soon after and that his son killed the Tan who had struck his father. In University College a 'Kitchener Scholar' named Dryden told the military that two of the students had been larking about in the drawing school of the engineering building during the two minutes' silence. A company of soldiers arrived at the college the next day and ordered all the students into the quadrangle. Everyone expected at least some of them to be shot, but they were only made to stand to attention while a band played 'God Save the King'. Some of the students took Dryden for a walk up the railway line to Clifden and left him there to punish him.

As we were riding round by the jail the next day, November 12th, a Tan lorry came speeding round the corner and drove us into the camber which was a very exaggerated one. I fell, and Tommy fell on top of me, tearing the ligaments of both my knees. The driver was normal, he stopped and offered to bring me home. Naturally I refused and got as far as the College. So I was hobbling about on two sticks with both legs bandaged and sleeping downstairs on a chair bed because I could not climb the stairs.

Father Michael Griffin was twenty-six years old when he was killed. He had been three years in Galway as a curate in Rahoon, a very big parish. He knew little or no Irish when he came to Galway and during those three years he learned enough to converse fluently with native speakers and to preach an excellent sermon. There was no house where he was not welcome. He was invited into thieves' houses, houses with tight shut doors, houses where the people were ashamed to let their poverty be seen. He gave money away as though it was burning a hole in his pocket and he never had a penny for himself. He was very wise for so young a priest; his advice was sound and moderate, and I never saw him lose his temper or get really annoyed. He spent himself in the service of others as if he knew he only had a short time. He was big and fair and his face was rather reminiscent of the Leonardo composite head of Christ. He acted on the Republican Court, which always had a priest on it, and he knew all the Volunteers. Father O'Meehan, the most important of the clergy in the IRA confidence, was sent a death notice so he went on the run. This left the parish short-handed and Father Griffin had to do most of the parish sick calls. He had a motorbike and I used to have an image of him lying on the road with a bullet wound in the temple. It was a persistent image so I told him about it and he took it seriously enough to give up the motorbike and instead asked people to send sidecars to fetch him This was the only precaution he took as he did not think he was very important.

It was on November 14th that he was shot, a wild night of storm and rain. Dr Michael O'Malley and Chris and some friends were playing cards in the Kennedys' house in Salthill. There was a loud knock at the hall door and three smallish men, not in uniform, came in waving revolvers and shouting for 'the Professor'. There was no Professor there; it was only next day that it was remembered that Professor Tomás O Máille was always called so by the townspeople. He had been sleeping in Kennedys; on the run because of the activities of his brother, Pádraig, who had a camp of Volunteers and refugees in Connemara. It was only by chance that he was not there that night. After searching the house the three men allowed the O'Malleys and the O'Byrnes to leave while they stayed talking to the Kennedys and to each other, calling each other by the names of Barker and Smith and Ward. The Kennedys were terrified that they would start shooting, as they were still waving their guns and the babies were in their cots overhead, but they got a bit quieter after a time. They said that this was quite a nice raid, that they had a terrible job to do that night later on; they were quite upset about it. We lived opposite Kennedys and the O'Malleys called in as they passed us and told us what had happened. They then went on home, they were not the mark for that night. As I have said, no one realised until the next day that Tomás O Máille was the mark and although there had been no special notice taken of us recently, Tommy had to go elsewhere for the night. Liam Ó Briain was staying in the Stella Maris so Tommy warned him to go out also. Tommy, Liam and Tomás Ó Máille all spent the night in Lavelles' house in University Road, unknown to one another. Mrs Lavelle didn't tell any one of them about the others.

After Tommy had gone, I stood at the window in the dark and after a long time, it was after ten o'clock, the three men came down from Kennedys. No one else had passed. It was a terrible night; the wind was lifting puddles off

Father Griffin's funeral in Loughrea. He was murdered because the Black and Tans thought he had attended Joyce, the schoolmaster informer, at his killing by the IRA. They were wrong—it was Father Tom Burke. Father Griffin feared he was going to his death when he was called out as if for a sick call.

the road in sheets and splashing it down again a few yards on. The men knocked on Finans' door as if they wanted to get in for a drink but no one answered and they went on. Some time afterwards, about an hour, a lorry came by at a terrible belt. I stepped back behind the curtains, as a face at a window might get a bullet. A short time later an outside car went by with the three men on it. The lorry had the body of Father Griffin and the three men, Barker, Smith and Ward, were his murderers. The cook in Lenaboy Castle told me later that the Tans in the lorry had refused to go any further with the body unless these three men came with them. I did not know about Father Griffin at the time but it was plain that something hideous was going on. When he was missing the next day we knew what to expect. He and I had talked some time before about his position if he were called out, and he had said that if it were a sick call, he would have to go, even it was to Black-and-Tan headquarters. It was a Galway RIC man who had knocked at the door and asked Father Griffin to come out. All this and more was heard at the time and put together by Tom Hynes.

It was infuriating to have to stay at home. I had crutches now and could get about better but not go out. Tommy brought me all the news. On 20th November the *Connacht Tribune* asked 'Where is Father Griffin?' It was the Barna men, who loved Father Griffin most, who found the body in a shallow grave in the bog. They washed it and wrapped it in a sheet and brought it into town in an ass and cart. They brought his clothes in separately. The little ass and cart was left, forgotten until evening, in the street.

Everyone on all sides went to the funeral, the military pretending that the IRA had killed him. We would have liked to bury him in Galway, but he had been on loan to Galway diocese from Loughrea and the bishop there claimed him and buried him in his, the bishop's, own grave. It never occurred to us at the time that the police were making the mistake of thinking that Father Griffin had attended Joyce, when it had been Father Tom Burke. Father Griffin had been named in Joyce's letter to the police as a man who should be shot but so had several others. We heard a lot of this at the time and I put it together in sequence but a few details came out over the years. Tom Hynes actually traced the route of the lorry.

Individual units of the IRA, now terribly isolated and practically unarmed, managed to show that they still existed by ambushes and attacks on barracks, burning abandoned police and military barracks and attacking occupied ones. Hardly a day passed without something. They continued to hold arbitration courts, although they were declared to be illegal, and to make government by the Castle impossible by taking possession of the account books of public bodies. Railway workers refused to carry arms or armed soldiers.

Liam Ó Briain was arrested and put with 143 men in the town hall which was serving as jail. These men were very badly fed, so the shop assistants of Galway each gave one shilling a week out of their wages and this paid for a hamper of food. The money was collected in each place of business and given to Bid McHugh who bought and prepared the food, and when the money was not enough, she made it up herself. She also sent in a special dinner every day to Liam. Bid and I went to see Liam in the town hall, which was all barbed wire and soldiers, but the soldiers were kind and one named Willie was always running messages for them. The place was very smelly and dirty, there was an awful lot of noise and Liam looked very tired, there must have been no peace in the place. Later the same Sherwood Foresters saved his life when the Tans wanted to kill him while he was attempting to escape.

The weather was now much colder, there was frost and the men could not sleep out any longer. Tommy went to Dublin for the Christmas holidays where he was apparently fairly safe. The day of the Christmas Fair, the Tans got the ex-British soldiers of Galway to go through the crowd at the fair and mark the IRA men who had come to sell their cattle. I was outside our house when I saw a Crossley tender full of prisoners coming with the Tans howling like devils. They brought them out to Barna and threw them in the river and when they crawled out they were taken in their dripping clothes and put in the doghouse huts in the barracks at the Earl's Island old distillery behind University College, where the 17th Lancers were quartered. It was here that Michael Moran of Tuam was shot dead, just behind the college handball alley. The semi-circular huts were full of prisoners, one of whom told me that when a soldier wanted to give them blankets in the cold weather an officer stopped him, saying that he never heard of swine wanting blankets. At Christmas the people thought that at least they could go to midnight Mass, but they were held up and searched and shots were fired; women panicked and ran screaming down the street.

14 Endings 1921–1948

IN JANUARY 1921 ABOUT FIFTEEN TANS AND AUXIES going to the market in Headford were ambushed by Volunteers at Kilroe. They had rifles, revolvers and shotguns but very little ammunition and some of the shotguns only had birdshot; the Tans and Auxies had a machine gun among other things. The ambush would have been much more successful if Baby Duggan had not been so excitable. He didn't wait for the Black-and-Tan lorries to get level and that was really why the Tans got the chance to take cover. He was called 'Baby' because he was the youngest member of Liam Mellowes' command in 1916. Baby Duggan fired early and the Tans and Auxies managed to take cover and the shooting, which could be heard in Claregalway and Cornundulla, went on for about twenty minutes. The ambushers, in a poor position, were forced to break off the engagement when the Lewis gun on the lorry got into action.

Five Tans were wounded but Charlie Quinn was the only Irish casualty. His right hand was pierced by a rifle bullet which ran through the knuckles, almost severing the index finger, and Dr Michael O'Malley took him into his nursing home, St Bride's, a few doors from our house, where Barham, one of the five Black-and-Tans wounded at Kilroe, was already being treated. When that became unsafe Charlie's brother, Martin, and Pat Carr came in and took him away. In the reprisals Brian Molloy's, Newells' and Mulryans' were all burnt as well as Kynes' of Kiltrogue, where Maud Shields stored her furniture when her house in Galway was commandeered.

Black-and-Tans maximise their menace by lining a road prior to a funeral.

Months afterwards, individual Black-and-Tans and Auxiliaries took an action for damages under the Malicious Injuries Act. They claimed that eleven cadets were attacked by at least sixty men at Kilroe. Eight of them claimed compensation and evidence was given that five were wounded, one of them with a rifle and the rest with pellets of one kind or another. The rest claimed that they suffered from shock, had acquired a stammer or found it unpleasant to travel in a car. One gave his evidence with gestures and was unable to speak. They were all ex-British soldiers who had seen service in Flanders and had a medical history of the same kind as they produced now. One got £6,800, another got £1,750, and the rest from £100 to £350. If this was to be collected from the Galway rates by the Tans there was going to be a very serious position and another excuse for violence. On the other hand, the only people who took it on themselves to protest were a number of pro-Britishers who formed a ratepayers' association. What we got out of it was the publication of the court proceedings which contained details of the raids, burnings and killings. Barham, the Tan who was wounded at Kilroe, had been in St Bride's nursing home ever since. He had got a charge of birdshot and the doctors had been picking it out of his skin all the time. Barham's sister appeared in Galway and was at first a great social success among loyalists. She was supposed to be a widow but I found afterwards that she was supporting her husband in Canada all the time. She set up a beauty parlour and one long-legged daughter in socks and short frocks arrived and then another.

Sir John French of Ypres, Lord Lieutenant of Ireland, was a nasty old man who talked a lot with little or no authority and the principal duty of his personal guard was to escort his ladyfriends. It was in an attempt to kill him that Martin Savage was killed at Ashtown level crossing. Lord French's sister, Mrs Despard, thought that she should try to keep her brother from being damned by doing all she could to counteract his actions and the actions of those for whom he was taking responsibility. Her only choice was counter-propaganda, so when she arrived in Galway she went around collecting information against the Black-and-Tans and brought it back to England to use against Lloyd George. We told her all we could but she seemed rather hysterical. The Lenten pastorals were published in the *Connacht Tribune* of February 12th. The archbishop, Dr Gilmartin, enjoined the clergy to persuade all their charge to cut their connection with associations, the members of which might be called on to obey orders which might contravene the Commandments, but he did not tell the RIC that they were wrong to belong to the police. We could only surmise that he still thought that the English government was the right one for Ireland, in spite of the 1918 election and the establishment of the Dáil. He called for a return to constitutional methods, by us not by them, and said that he would not support socialism, that is, popular government. Our bishop, Dr O'Dea, only asked us to pray for a just peace. There were more courts martial and the reports of these were often printed; this was good for us as it showed us that

St Bride's nursing home, Salthill, Galway, where the IRA intelligence officer, Tom Hynes, and a wounded Tan, Barlow, who was so nervous he had to have a guard around the clock, were patients at the same time.

there were plenty of people on our side. The untried prisoners were removed in batches from the town hall and other camps to Ballykinlar. Those who were sentenced were in the jails. All possible jails and camps were packed to bursting. Various social events were reported and the Galway Blazers continued to hunt the fox.

Shortly after the Kilroe ambush Mrs Grehan of the 'Bal' sent for me, and when I got there she introduced me to a tall man with fairish hair whom she called Joe Byrne. I think his name was really Tom Byrne. He asked me if I would accept him as a messenger from headquarters in Dublin, but in spite of Mrs Grehan's introduction I did not accept him without a good look at him. When I told him I would, he took off his shoe and sock, with an apology, and produced a note which he had in his sock from Mick Collins telling me to tell the commandants of the IRA Connemara brigades that he wanted their reports. Tom Byrne asked me about the IRA situation in the town; he said headquarters was worried about it and wanted to know if any activity was possible. I told him I did not see that much could be done in the actual town and he said that it looked bad for nothing to be done. After a day or two in the town he could see for himself that it was like living in a barracks, but even so he urged that something should be done. I do not know for certain why he did not go to Tom Hynes, the intelligence officer, with the message but from what Liam Mellowes told me later it must have been because of Séamus Murphy's adverse report on the Galway city brigade in 1919. Gerald Bartly later confirmed this to me. Byrne went on to say that he wanted a report from Miceál Ó Droighneáin, the schoolteacher who was commandant of the East Connemara brigade, and in fact would have liked to meet him. I had a job to convince him that Miceál could not venture into the town to meet him--he would have been caught at once. The place was riddled with spies who knew him personally and the way into the town was a bottleneck between the sea and the lake. He gave me a letter for Miceál and I went to Tom Hynes who said that since it was a military job, he would have to swear me into the IRB before I could carry the messages back and forth. I swore that I was prepared to obey his orders as an officer.

Dr Michael O'Malley was the person with a car in the IRB and he drove me to Furbough to Miceál Ó Droighneáin, with the message. He was on the run down by the shore, with the permission of the parish priest to take a holiday from the school for this purpose, so Michael O'Malley drove me out to Spiddal instead to deliver the message to his wife. She promised to give it to him although she was very nervous about handling it as she thought it was orders to take action—and of course it was. Miceál was to pass on the message to the Western brigade. Tom Byrne wanted to stay a few days in Galway, so I asked Marjorie Neville who was living in the old Mill House belonging to Miss Somerville of Somerville and Ross (now the CYMS) if she would put him up and pretend he was her boy-friend. She lived and had her studio on the middle floor and Miss Somerville was in the top but we never saw her. Marjorie was the domestic economy teacher in the technical school and an artist but she had to give up when she became too arthritic. Marjorie brought Tom Byrne round as if he was her boyfriend and allowed him to use her sitting-room to meet people. She did it all very well and saw him off affectionately at the train when he left.

Tom Hynes got a despatch from him at Marjorie's for John Geoghegan of the East Connemara brigade and gave it to him the same day, and late that night John Geoghegan was taken out of his house in Moycullen and shot by Tans. While he was putting on his clothes to go out to be shot, he managed to hide the despatch and his brother got it and dealt with it. The Tans put a notice on his body after he was shot, 'Yours faithfully, Michael Collins'. Twenty-four civilians were reported as shot during the same week, some of them children. It was quite a long time before Tom Hynes' report came back. By this time he was in the St Bride's nursing home with appendicitis so that when I went looking for him to get him to send it up to Dublin, I could not find him at first. It was not a very safe thing to do, to go up to the door of St Bride's and ask for Mr Hynes, as Barham, the Tan, was still a patient there and was so nervous he had to have a guard all the time. Tom Hynes sent me to Joe Togher who sent me to the men on the mailvan of the train, who delivered it in Dublin. A few weeks later Marjorie Neville's flat was raided; presumably someone had talked carelessly about Byrne and she said then that she should have been told more. Miss Somerville, who was an extreme loyalist, had her rooms searched also.

Tommy organised the raid on the courthouse for county council books in February. He contacted two students at the college, Jack D'Arcy and Michael Dwyer, who, with Kilfeather and Martin Brennan, arranged with Seamus Carter who was a clerk in the courthouse, that the essential county council books should be in a certain place on a certain date. Carter carefully went out of the building a few minutes before they arrived and they walked into the courthouse under the eyes of the sentry on guard at the town hall opposite, took the books and put them into a motor car which Bill Garvey had just driven up. Garvey ran the books out to the sandy bridge on the crossroad between the Tuam and Oranmore roads and the Castlegar men took them over there. As always, the effect on the police was out of all proportion to the job.

The White Cross organisation was started by James Douglas, a Quaker Dublin businessman who had been promised some money by his co-religionists in the USA, and he took the opportunity to get a relief organisation going to help the dependants of Volunteers. The Central Committee in Dublin had as members the chief rabbi, bishops of all denominations, public men of all kinds etc. I was asked by James Douglas to start a committee in Galway so I asked a lot of public men and clerics to join it. It finally consisted of the bishop, Dr O'Dea, the three parish priests of the town parishes and a Labour member of the town council, Tom Rea, a laboratory porter in UCG. The old Redmondite members of the town council, Martin Mór MacDonagh and others, refused on the grounds that they would only be playing into the hands of their political enemies, Sinn Féin. Martin at first agreed and then went back on it, getting me into a fine row with one priest, Father Davis, who thought I was a liar. The Central Committee wanted a committee in each parish and I had to explain to them that there were only two people who could be on such a committee in a Connemara parish, the parish priest and the teacher, and that both of them might be on the run themselves, so they allowed us to run it from Galway town. Maureen O'Kelly acted as secretary and was followed from house to house by the police who threatened the people she visited. Pope Benedict XV (whom Pa had seen before the Rising and again at the beatification of Oliver Plunkett) gave £5,000 to the White Cross fund.

Two English women arrived in Galway as police searchers, and it got more difficult for the women to carry despatches. Bid McHugh and myself were searched three times in one week. Both of us were carrying documents at the time but we managed to slip them about inside our clothes and they were not found. Bid was carrying dispatches from the North West brigade and I was carrying accounts of the savagery that was being done in the Eglinton Street barracks. Small bundles of papers giving accounts of the ill-treatment of prisoners in the town hall, in the 17th Lancers' camp, and the Eglinton Street barracks had been put in our letterbox. One of the young men who had been beaten in the barracks had put in accounts of his and others' beatings. I made copies of all of them and sent them to Erskine Childers, who was editing *The Irish Bulletin*, and they filled three editions. I gave another set to Albinia Broderick, Lord Middleton's sister, who was doing what she could to make up for her brother's sins. Another lot was sent by just giving it to the man in the train post office van, as nearly all the staff of the railway and such services were acting as messengers for Mick Collins.

In March two young men, Paddy Moran and Tom Whelan, who was from Clifden, were hanged in Mountjoy Jail. Tom Whelan's mother was allowed to see him before he was hanged and he sang for her in the condemned cell her favourite song, 'The Shawl of Galway Grey'. They were accused of having taken part in the Bloody Sunday killings of fourteen police spies in Dublin the previous November, the sequel to which had been a machine-gunning of the football crowd in Croke Park by Black-and-Tans, with twelve casualties. There was no evidence against the two boys and these hangings had a very big effect on Galway town. I walked down the town the day they were hanged and everyone was crying, big tears running down their faces, even loyalists and ex-British soldiers; public opinion had definitely turned. The archbishop, Dr Gilmartin, appealed for mercy for them, and spoke of the doubtful evidence, but it was useless. The police were sure that even if the men had not been in the place at the time, they were Volunteers and that was enough. Lloyd George said he was anxious to explore all avenues for a peaceful settlement with Ireland, though questions were asked in the House of Commons about the murders of the Lord Mayor and ex-Lord Mayor of Limerick, George Clancy and Michael O'Callaghan, and the hanging of the boys. These questions were asked by Commander Kenworthy MP and Joseph King MP. The burnings, shootings and beatings continued.

On St Patrick's Day in Clifden, Volunteers lay in wait for a Tan patrol, which usually passed at a certain hour. Two ordinary RIC, harmless people, passed before the patrol and were shot by the Volunteers before they realised that they were the wrong men. The news was telephoned to Eglinton Street barracks and a fleet of lorries dashed out the fifty miles to Clifden. I saw them loading the petrol barrels and the Tans running out of the barracks with their bottles of whiskey and their rifles. They went to Dr Michael O'Malley and insisted on his going with them to treat the police, one of whom had not died. When he arrived at Clifden he found that the police were systematically burning M. J. Lydon's houses and property, nine different places in which he had an interest of some kind. M. J. Lydon was Michael O'Malley's brother-in-law. He was an old man and he had to get out of the window of his house in his nightshirt and run for his life. He got pneumonia and did not live very long after. Mrs Lydon was the head of the Clifden Cumann na mBan. While Michael O'Malley was trying to save the life of the wounded policeman, the Tans came into the house where they were, and tried to turn them out of it so that it could be burnt, but Michael lost his temper with them then. John J.

MacDonnell of MacDonnell's Hotel was shot dead; the parish priest, Monsignor MacAlpine, tried to save his people but was ordered off the streets. Men, women and children rushed to him for safety and, carrying whatever they could snatch up, crowded into the workhouse, three hundred of them. The Tans rushed up and down firing their guns and carrying the petrol to burn the place while a cruiser in the bay lit up the scene with a searchlight. About £70,000 worth of damage was done. When they had gone a notice was found painted on a wall, 'Clifden will remember and so will the RIC'. Colonel Hackett, who was then the owner of the Railway Hotel, gave an interview to an English newspaper saying he had seen the whole thing. The usual lies were given out by the official agency, that shots had been fired from those houses which were burned. Monsignor MacAlpine said that this was a lie. Dr Gilmartin said it was plain that government agents had murdered, but he still kept on appealing for a truce. Westport was burned. The Galway Blazers continued to hunt the fox.

At the end of March Louis D'Arcy was killed. He was going to Dublin to find out what had happened to the guns for which he had already sent money to Dublin. He went to the railway station of Attymon accompanied by a man named Lally, and they were seen and arrested by an RIC man. Lally heard D'Arcy screaming with the torture all night from the next room. D'Arcy was being brought into Galway the next day and on the road near Merlin Park, just outside the town, he was tied with a rope and dragged behind the lorry until a Tan kindly put a bullet in him. D'Arcy used to come in to Galway about once a fortnight, usually on a Wednesday, and would walk out along the Clifden railway to meet Geoghegan from Moycullen. No-one knew till long afterwards that a Tan used to watch the line for them, concealed in a big bushy lime tree which still stands just on the far side of the wall of the lawn of Dangan House. He had been let pass through the grounds by the tenant who came back years afterwards, when we were living there, to get his gun which had been left in the tree.

On Easter Monday, March 28th I was arrested and put in jail. This was my own fault for being caught in a most stupid manner by two district inspectors with the account of the beatings in Eglinton Street barracks. I'd gone out to buy some bread and found when I came back that there had been a bad police raid on our house. No-one was in but the maid and our three children, Moya, aged four, Blánaid, nearly three and Eilís, who was just over a year. The maid, Peggy, had opened the door and the police rushed into the house waving their guns and shouting that they were going to shoot me. They threw all the books in Irish onto the fire. They turned the place upside down and they took the soiled underclothes and sanitary towels and they draped them round as decorations. They made Moya, the eldest of my little girls, show them the way to the garden, where they said I was hiding. They searched it and then told her they were going to shoot me. I was so angry when I saw the mess they had made of the house that when they came back again, I abused them for their conduct and it took them aback so much that they were quite quiet this time. They put me on the back of the lorry and I was able to wave goodbye to the children, and they drove the lorry through the town to make a show of me but I did not care at all. When we got to the jail, the police went with me into the offices to hand me over to the governor and recovered their spirits enough to be insulting, saying, 'I'm surprised at a lady like you telling lies about the police,' and stuff like that.

It was beautifully quiet in the jail but it was the usual mess and very dirty. I was wakened in the middle of the night being bitten by such vermin as I have never seen before or since for size and variety, which were only got rid of by several disinfectant baths. Eight Galway county councillors had been arrested a few months before; Alice Cashell, the vice-chairman, was court-martialled and sentenced to six months for having documents and Dr Ada English of the mental hospital got nine months. They were great people and both in the so-called hospital of the jail; Dr English had got some kind of food poisoning and Miss Cashell was nursing her, the usual prison arrangement. My friend Bid McHugh sent in a dinner each day for me until, after three days, I was put in the hospital and spent my time cooking for Dr English, Alice Cashell and myself, which I really enjoyed. I cooked the prison rations which they had requested to be sent in raw, but there was not enough food for any length of time and it was quite mad. A lump of meat, four black potatoes, a piece of dirty bread and margarine, milk, but no vegetables. I cooked at the open fire in the hospital room in a frying pan and a smuggled saucepan and made bread puddings in a cake tin. The only other woman political prisoner was Miss Anita MacMahon from Westport, who did not mix with the rest of us except for an occasional hour of Bridge. Except for certain times when the prison spy was expected, the doors were not locked and there were little or no regulations. The prison doctor, Dr Kincaid, was a loyalist and a savage. He used to inspect the hospital very early in the morning but never came back except once, when he reported the hospital as dirty for three crumbs on a floor and the medical inspector arrived from Dublin. He just chatted to Dr English for an hour about mental illnesses and went away laughing.

The ordinary jailees, mostly tinkers, were nice and kind. They were practically starving—their diet dated from a hundred years back—and in order to make a separate jail for the politicals they were put in the laundry building where the cells were six feet by four, and where they slept and worked. The head wardress used to leave their cell doors open at night, as she said that they might die if she did not. One woman had her child with her, another, a very tough lady, had a beautiful voice and sang loudly in the chapel on Sundays. They did the washing and hung it on the railing which divided the recreation ground and the handknitted socks came out a mass of ravelled thread. The priest came to see us every day and brought the news. As the chapel was in the

Galway Jail where Gerry was imprisoned for a month in 1921 for possession of accounts of police beatings. Her children were aged four, three and one at the time. A question was asked about her in the House of Commons:

'MR J. JONES asked the Chief Secretary whether he was aware that Mrs Dillon, wife of Professor Dillon of Galway University, has been arrested; that she is a delicate lady with three children, the youngest being only three months of age; that the documents alleged to have been found upon her related only to the relief of distress caused by arson and robbery on the part of Crown Forces; and whether directions will be given for this lady's immediate release.

MR HENRY (Chief Secretary) replied that Mrs Geraldine Dillon, wife of Professor Dillon of Galway University has been arrested on a charge of having in her possession documents prepared for the purpose of spreading false reports against the Crown Forces. These reports are being sent to General Headquarters for examination and at present it is not considered advisable to release Mrs Dillon. Her youngest child is six months old and in the charge of a nurse.' [The youngest, later the novelist Eilís Dillon, was actually just over one year old at the time.]

women's prison, the men used to parade for mass in the courtyard of the women's prison and we were able to wave to them, if we were careful. Charlie Costello always managed to have a rosebud in his buttonhole. The visiting justice refused at first to allow my little daughter, Moya, to see me but afterwards she was allowed to come and I saw her at the gate. A question was asked in the House of Commons about me and I was just let out one morning.

Near the end of April a patrol of fourteen police on bicycles stopped near a supposedly empty house at Kilmilkin and noticed that it was inhabited, that smoke rose from the chimneys and doors opened and shut. This was Muintir Eoin, Padraic O Maille TD's house and farm, where he had a camp for men on the run. The numbers in it had been growing and the police, who had been informed about it, were afraid that a mass attack could be directed from it. Padraic Mór used to stride over the hills in his frieze overcoat carrying rifles and ammunition and it was his people who attacked the escort at Screeb.

We estimated that there were about thirty men there. The police had to take refuge from rifle fire behind a turf stack and a wall and one of them was shot dead. They could see men leaving the house and making for the hills which were about 1400 feet above the road. They said that they only saw seven men leave the house, but they believed there were at least sixty in it. The battle lasted from five a.m. to four p.m. and in the middle of it a motor belonging to T. F. Joyce of Leenane drove up and the police jumped on it and told the driver to 'Go like hell', which he did. An RIC man named Ruttledge was wounded as he was getting into the car. They got a message to Galway and within an hour and a half seven lorries arrived, including one of the new armoured cars with Rolls engine and machine guns. DI Cruise was in charge. Within a short time the house had been taken, as the men had all left for the hills and there were only women left, Mrs Eamon Ó Máille and her children and Padraic's sister, Janie. We heard that they kept up the defence while the men got away. A troop train was sent to Clifden, thousands of soldiers and police were out, aeroplanes searched the hills but not a man or a gun was taken.

All fairs and markets were now prohibited in the County Galway and since this is the way the people sell their produce there was nearly a standstill in supply in the town. No eggs, potatoes, vegetable or poultry were allowed to be brought into Galway for sale. Carts were turned back and men beaten. Men were flogged in Loughrea for enforcing the Sinn Féin boycott of goods against loyalist bigotry in Belfast. There were raids and arrests everywhere. Prisoners were deported to Ballykinlar in batches. Cardinal Logue, who was a timid old Redmondite, said in a statement that if the people of Ireland abandoned crime, they could obtain anything that was necessary for the country. This sort of thing hurt, but as no reasonable person thought it was a crime to fight for their country we could disregard it. It was not good publicity, however. The cardinal made it still worse by sending messages to Rome, but the pope in reply did not denounce the IRA. In fact we had no alternative to fighting, there was no possibility of living in our own country under any terms so far offered to us. Many bishops took the republican view and spoke freely in spite of the danger.

In May, a Kitchener scholar at UCG who was friendly with the Tans had a row with some of them in a pub in Salthill about a box of matches. That night he was taken out and shot through the lungs, beaten, thrown in the tide and riddled with revolver bullets. He managed to keep from drowning and Dr Michael O'Malley was fetched to tie up his wounds which took hours, there were so many. While Dr O'Malley was trying to save his life, the house was raided, apparently in order to pretend that the man had been shot by 'Shinners'. Another man, Johnny Greene, who lived in the same digs, was treated in much the same way and another digs a few doors down was then raided. Johnny Greene was a long time recovering and was awarded big compensation.

On the same day there were a few shots fired in Spiddal to keep the police from buying turf in the Spiddal turf market. This was the last barracks for many miles around and the police took the opportunity to exaggerate the whole thing into an ambush and a battle. They said that between thirty and sixty men were engaged and the usual lorries rushed to the scene. Eight houses, the old schoolhouse in Moycullen, and Miceál Ó Droighneáin's tiny house in Furbough, were burned and bombed. A bomb was thrown in his door but luckily his wife and children were not in at the time. Whenever he thought he could safely teach for a few days, the boys were set to watch the roads. At the first sign of a lorry he'd be away off down to the seashore. They searched the seashore, too, but they never caught him. Father Davis helpfully shut the school whenever there was the slightest 'scare' of an epidemic of measles or mumps, which simplified matters. On this day, the people knew the Tans were coming and got all the furniture and stuff out and hidden in the fields in time. The police were very glad of an excuse to harry Spiddal and its neighbourhood. In Belclare, around the same time, a family of children, the eldest a young girl of sixteen or so whose father and mother were dead, had the house set on fire over their heads. When the eldest girl was trying to get the youngest out of its cot the Tans kicked her back into the flames, but she was saved.

We had moved several times in Galway from College Road to Salthill, to Spiddal, to Barna and various friends' houses, and we had now been in a house in Montpelier Terrace for a couple of months. It had a very narrow staircase, so narrow that we could get none of our furniture up the stairs and had to camp. The garden was full of rats because the people next door used to feed their hens by throwing out a lot of food for them last thing at night. Tommy rarely slept at home; he went to the houses of different friends, to Lavelles, Allens or others. He spent the holidays in Dublin where there was a procession of men on the run going from the house of one sympathiser to another or in digs. Anyway on this night, 20th May, he was tired and decided to risk one night at home, but the dog kept barking and we could not get to sleep. Then we heard a noise and looking out saw five men at the hall door. One had his coat turned inside out as a disguise but we were able to identify him as Captain Harrison, who had made the scene at Michael Walsh's funeral. We had made plans for such a thing as this long before but nothing ever turns out exactly as you think it will. There had been so many killings that I did not see why we should just plain open the door and let men in to kill us, so first of all I said I would not open the door but would talk out the window. Then, if they got in, I planned to throw everything on top of them down the narrow staircase and perhaps block it with mattresses. Tommy thought he had a chance of getting away while I was talking to them, so he lit out in his pyjamas with his jacket over them and his trousers round his neck and off out the back.

I asked them who they were and they said they were IRA and told me to come and let them in. It was a three-storey house and I went and talked to them out the top window. I kept up the talk as long as I could, but in the end I told them I did not believe them. I should, of course, have told them some story that the children had scarlatina or typhoid but I was not smart enough. After a lot more, I said that I did not believe that they were IRA and they started trying to break in the door. This hall door sometimes stuck and could not be opened even with a key, and sometimes opened by itself, unexpectedly. We should have put a bolt on it but had omitted to do so. This time it stuck but every moment I expected it to give. I remembered the noise they found useful in Belfast and I started to shout. At first I shouted 'Help!' and I began to see what a fool I was to call for help inside a barracks so I shouted 'Murder!' instead and found that I was able to shout louder and louder. The men looked up and down the road and tried the door again, crashing against it while I screeched. Suddenly Captain Harrison spoke to them and they went away. I thought they had gone to get more men or something to batter the door in, but I was afraid to leave my post to go downstairs to try to barricade the door. One of the children woke up and wanted to know what the noise was, and when I came back to the window from settling her, I saw three Black-and-Tans coming towards the house. They asked me what was going on and I said that some men had been trying to get in to the house and that they said they were the IRA but I didn't believe them. They told me that they were the guard at St Bride's nursing home, only a few doors from us. They said that they would see that nothing more happened. Obviously they had not known that the raid was intended or they would have kept away. There was no good-will between one section of these people and another. I heard afterwards that they intended to kill me as well as my husband, but that did not occur to me at the time.

In the meantime, Tommy had got out over the garden wall and through some lanes at the back, losing his trousers on the way. He came to the back of a house where he was known, but could hear men talking at the front. He thought of climbing up the waste pipe but it was just as well he didn't, as two students who lived in the house had seen him and thought his pyjamas were tennis flannels, which only a Tan would wear at that time in Galway. They were preparing to bat him over the head when he got to the top. The Tans, who really were in front of the house looking for him, went away, so he didn't try the climb. He got to St Mary's Diocesan College, found a window open and found a door with the name of Father Sexton, a patriotic young priest. He got him a bed for the night and fetched his clothes the next day. The bishop had to be told about it and he said it was all very well for once but not to do it again. The woman who found the trousers on her back wall would not give them back to me. The same old RIC man, who had sent me a warning the previous summer that my brother George was going to be arrested, sent me a police whistle to make a noise if the Tans came back again. Up to this time it was thought that if there was an officer in charge or a lorry it was more or less safe to open the door to a raiding party and perhaps safer to do so as to avoid causing anger. From this time, so the old RIC man said, we were not to open the door. Previously, official raids meant searches but not murder; now all pretence was being laid aside.

There were complaints that children were not being sent to school and there were long discussions about it in the press, but no-one said that the schoolmasters were all on the run or that the roads were not safe for the children to travel. In Mayo it was worse, as there seems to have been a particularly bad sadist in the Tans there, who hated crippled boys. However, all this time, serious plans were being discussed for the amalgamation of the various institutions, for a children's home, apart from the workhouse, for a county home for old people, for improvements to the mental hospital and so on, a great many of which were put into operation a few years afterwards. The holding of meetings of public bodies became very difficult; not only was it dangerous to say anything at them but also public men of any kind were now a mark for killing. There was also very little money to administer any institution and in many cases, the workhouses or infirmaries had been commandeered by the police or the military. The courts martial went on all the time—for being found near an ambush, for guns being found in your house, for having documents relating to the Volunteers, to arbitration courts, to the Dáil. When men came to give evidence for the defence at a court martial in Renmore, they were stripped and flogged in Mainguard Street. The lawyers were on the run, except for some loyal attorneys and a drunken barrister who used to ride around with the Tans on the lorries to the raids and burnings, so if the prisoners did not say anything for themselves they were not defended. It was best for them to say nothing, unless they were loyalists who had been arrested by mistake. Some attempts were made to accuse Tans of looting, but they were acquitted, and newspapers which had printed reports of their behaviour had to print corrections. When houses were burnt the papers had to announce that it was done by civilians. There were rumours of negotiations with Lloyd George, but no serious offer had been made at this stage.

The general election was held in the middle of all this and since anyone of any importance was in jail or on the run, it was very difficult to hold a convention to select candidates and to collect the money for the deposits. It was decided that candidates must be properly selected at a convention so Tommy, Micky Allen, and Father Donnelly, the candidates for Galway City, went to meet the delegates from the rest of the county. They managed to meet in Athenry, in Brodericks' house, and selected Pádraic Ó Máille, George Nicholls, Frank Fahy, Joseph Whelehan, Liam Mellowes, Brian Cusack and Paddy Hogan for the county areas. The next thing was to collect the nomination fee of £150 for each candidate. Father Considine, the dean, told me to report to him about it and I was sent round the town collecting, but I had no list of names and was a comparative stranger. However, I did quite well and got a surprising number of £10 subscriptions and so on—in fact the money rolled in. About two weeks before the election there was a meeting with Father Dunne and some of the others in Louis O'Dea's office, and all the money which had been collected was given to me for safe keeping. It was a little short of the £1,050 required and when I told Father Considine this, he brought me into the bank and told the manager that I could use his private account for the balance. We had to withdraw the money from the bank because we might be stopped at the last minute, so I put it in an envelope and stuck it in the top of my corset in the traditional manner. I then went round with a lot of the nomination papers; we had to take precautions about asking people to sign these, shops were too easily raided and their owners ruined, so we had to ask all the others and some of them were very nervous, wanting everyone else to be asked before them. The people in the county were more courageous.

We had to plan what to do if the Tans were waiting on the steps of the court house to take the money from the men. At the last meeting to collect nomination papers, someone went to Raoul Joyce, the sheriff, and asked him would he take the money beforehand. He said that he would not take any cash, he must have a certified cheque, which made it all quite simple. Some of the men, including Seán Forde, then went to the court house with the nomination papers. I followed them with the cheque and a spare set of papers signed by women, which I had got ready in case the men were stopped. I got so many plain blank refusals among my own class that when I met Mary Malone and told her about it, she brought me down the back streets, into the small houses, where the papers were all filled up in a few minutes. There were no Black-and-Tans at the court house. There were no Redmondite candidates and some anti-nationalists had been asked to stand but did not, but until the last minute we were not sure whether they would or not. It passed off all right and the seven Sinn Féin candidates for the county and the delegates for Galway city, Tommy, Mickey Allen, Larry Sarsfield and Father Donnelly, were all elected unopposed.

At the end of May there were two things to keep our hearts up: the Custom House in Dublin was burnt by the IRA, and Brigadier General Crozier denounced the whole Black-and-Tan business.

I used to meet Liam Mellowes at intervals, usually when I was sent to Dublin on messages to him as director of purchases, and just before the Truce in July 1921 I met him on the top of the Donnybrook tram in Dublin. He had a large black moustache and I did not recognise him till he spoke to me. I asked him why no one had been sent down to help pull the Volunteer organisation in Galway together, as it had been in such a bad state all through the Terror. Liam told me that he had wanted to go to Galway, that he knew all they wanted was a leader and that the men would have followed him again, and he knew as well as I did that the people had been plundered, murdered and flogged more than if they had taken the offensive. He told me that he had asked to be allowed to go to Galway but headquarters had decided that he was too valuable where he was. I had letters from him later but never saw him again. Liam was the son of an English soldier. He was a slim, pale, boyish man with light-brown hair and a gentle manner. His most noticeable feature was his high forehead and when this was covered he was not easily recognised. He was quite fearless.

Whenever I was up in Dublin, Ma would send me around to check on the houses and any work being done in them. One of these times she sent me to No. 31 or 33 Marlborough Road to see if the work was finished. She said she had been paying for a long time. I saw that no work had been done but she did not believe me and sent me back again and this time I wrote it all down and she had to take it. She had been paying the men for a year. She sacked the lot of them and got a small contractor to do all her repairs in future.

Rory O'Connor was arrested early in 1921, about February I think, I am not quite certain, as time went slowly at times and at others, very quickly. When he was arrested he was thought to be Mick Collins in disguise. He was brought to Dublin Castle, knocked about a bit and tortured by the official torturer, Captain Hardy, until he fainted, but he managed to stay silent and answered no questions. Captain Hardy finished by turning the pressure hose on him, leaving him to lie all night on a wet floor, and he had a bad spot on his lung afterwards. His brother, Norbert, smuggled a £10 note to him in prison in the Curragh Camp and he bribed the sentry with it and walked out as part of a working party of house painters. He could not go back to the paving department of the Corporation, so he went full-time in the army under the Dáil Local Government Department.

After the Truce was announced in July of 1921, Pa, as Minister for Foreign Affairs, went to London with de Valera and Griffith and the other Treaty negotiators. Pa said that what was offered was no more than the old Home Rule Bill and he rejected it completely. Griffith, who had been willing to work with him but did not look for any more than this first offer, went back to all his old positions and rejected Pa completely. The Second Dáil had its first meeting in the Mansion House in August and Pa was made Minister for Fine Arts. The Treaty debates were nasty and seemed to be part of an insincere political game and not a genuine effort to ascertain public opinion. Griffith told Tommy that he had warned de Valera that he would not break with the English on the question of the Crown, and offered to stay in Dublin and let de Valera reject the clause himself, but de Valera insisted on him going back to London. Mick Collins seemed to be on either or both sides and drinking far too much but we all believed, and I think rightly, that Mick was a republican.

In September, de Valera held a review in Ennis and all of our Western brigade, every member who could walk, went to it. They all expected him to break off negotiations and to defy the English and start again. I think that if

Geraldine Plunkett Dillon in 1925 with her children (left to right) Eilís, Moya, Blanaid, Michael and baby Rory, who was born with hydrocephalus and died at the age of three. The youngest child, Eoin, was born in 1929.

he had done so, he would have been successful, but he relied too much on Dick Mulcahy's opinion which was that we could not fight that year. I believe that de Valera had the country behind him in any decision he made but they were deeply disappointed at his weakness. I am not criticising de Valera, he was terribly isolated. Too many men had died fighting and had left him to make the decisions. Also he was no soldier.

Pa had decided, as Minister for Fine Arts, that we should celebrate six hundred years of the poet, Dante, along with the rest of Europe, so he organised a commemorative night to be held in the Mansion House in Dublin on December 6th, 1921. It was a great success, with crowds outside in the street and the Mansion House full of visitors and dignitaries from universities, galleries and museums as well as bishops, priests, the Lord Mayor and Dáil ministers. There were readings in Irish, English and Italian, Pa gave a lecture and there was music to finish. De Valera was there introducing speakers and I saw Eamon Duggan hand him an envelope early on in the night. He did not open it then but waited till afterwards. Although there was plenty of rumour going around, we did not know what it was until later; it was word from London that the Treaty had been signed.

De Valera was completely out of control of the anti-Treaty side from the Treaty debates until the fighting actually started. Most people did not know that he was not in command of the anti-Treaty forces. I blame him for not speaking out at this time. He might have stopped the whole thing.

Rory O'Connor, Liam Mellowes and my brothers George and Jack occupied the Four Courts in April. My son Michael was born on May 5th 1922, and the general election was held in June. At one time Rory had had a very high opinion of Mick Collins; they had both been on Joe's staff before Easter 1916, and had been on the run together and even up to the last few months before the Truce, Rory spoke of Mick as the only man you could rely on to get the work done. He thought at first that Mick was doing a good deal of what he had claimed to make the Treaty a stepping stone to a republic, but then I believe that it was Mick's use of the IRB as a pro-Treaty force which made Rory think that Mick was not behaving honestly. People who did not know Rory, or the work as OC Engineering which he had been doing so quietly for years, did not understand his position when he and Liam Mellowes occupied the Four Courts, and he was misjudged accordingly, but during all the Treaty negotiations Rory had been getting more and more dissatisfied as it became plainer that there was going to be some kind of compromise, and he and a good many others believed that compromise was not necessary. To those who followed him he was the senior officer with Liam Mellowes. I think he was merely at the top of men who were going to do this thing anyway and if he was no leader, as he was not, the rest of them were even more disorganised than he.

Rory was already emotionally upset by his very frustrating love-affair with my sister, Fiona, which had now come to an end, and he thought that the ordinary man, who

Left to right: George Plunkett, Rory O'Connor and Jack Plunkett. They all took the anti-Treaty side in 1921, Jack and George following Rory in the take-over of the Four Courts in April 1922. Following his surrender in July, O'Connor was one of the first of the 77 Irregulars executed without trial from December 1922 as a reprisal measure.

had done all the work, had been let down by the leaders. He was a smallish, very dark man, dark skin, blue jaws, he had to shave twice a day and had such a deep voice that it seemed to slow his speech, yet he had great charm. My brothers, George and Jack, followed Rory blindly. Rory told my sister, Mimi, that when he had his doubts as to his being justified in continuing to occupy the Four Courts, Dick Mulcahy had said he should stay where he was. He told her this when she went to the Four Courts with some of her own cooking for him before the attack. This may have been a message from Mulcahy through someone else. Mimi could not see how it would end except in disaster for everyone, and she wanted him to leave. Liam Mellowes was, in my opinion, no longer sane and his decisions were emotional. At the end of June, the pro-Treaty forces bombarded the Four Courts and most of the occupiers were jailed.

Mick Collins was killed that August. I had watched him develop from 1915 on, and what struck me most about him was the increase in natural dignity.

Mimi Plunkett, who married the trade unionist Diarmuid O'Leary in 1918, with her son Colm in 1920. Her second son, Rory, died as a baby. Mimi died in 1926, aged forty, of tuberculosis.

His patriotism was absolutely normal and real. I think he was probably better than most men in his position would have been. As George said to me afterwards, he was a rough diamond, but a diamond, and we could not have done without him. Mick was already dead a few months when Rory O'Connor, Liam Mellowes, Dick Barrett and Joe MacKelvey were shot by the Free State government. They had been five months in jail when they were shot as a reprisal for the killing of Sean Hales, TD. They had been cut off from all control of the outside forces for that five months and could not be thought responsible for what was done elsewhere. I had heard for months before this that there was English pressure to shoot them, but could not believe it would be done. Public opinion seemed to be behind the act but no one seemed to know enough to be able to judge. Rory had been Kevin O'Higgins' best man and it was Kevin O'Higgins who ordered the killings. I never saw Rory after the Four Courts, nor did anyone I knew. Maybe his brothers did. I loved both Rory and Liam, they were very dear friends, so is Dev. In 1929, shortly after my youngest child, Eoin, was born, I went to see Desmond FitzGerald, who was Minister for Defence, to ask for permission for the soldiers of the 1st (Irish speaking) Battalion in Galway to act in the Taibhdhearc Theatre there. I had known Desmond for a long time; he had been in Gloucester jail with my husband. We talked about Rory, and Desmond said that they had to kill him because he had got hold of a land mine. This was not true but, even if it were, it was no excuse, I thought it was murder.

Mimi was joint secretary of Cumann na mBan with Min Ryan and had been working all over the place with them since she came back from New York after the Rising. In 1925 she and her husband Diarmuid stayed with us in Galway. I found her helpful and kind even though she hadn't a penny. After they went home I went up to Dublin to see her in No. 54 Marlborough Road, one of Ma's houses, where they were living. She was carrying her second child, Rory, then and looked very ill. Dr Lynn had said she had a gastric ulcer but she also had a tubercular spine and she was actually starving; she was only eating the crusts that her child, Colm, didn't eat. I told Ma that but she wouldn't help, she despised her for marrying a poor man. Her baby, Rory, died of TB and by this time she was so ill that she had to stay in the Mater Hospital for a long time. Ma paid half the Mater Hospital costs and made Diarmuid, who now had a job where he was highly thought of as transport union conciliator, pay the other half. Finally, Ma brought Mimi back to No. 40, Elgin Road where she and Pa had moved to that year (26 Fitzwilliam Street being finally sold) and nursed her. She kept looking for a miracle and would not allow Mimi's room to be disinfected, although the housekeeper, Lily MacNulty, did disinfect it eventually, against orders. Mimi was forty when she died on December 8th, 1926.

Mimi and Moya Plunkett—having fun, for once! After the convent, Moya took a teaching post in Uganda where she became very ill. She died in Port Said on her way home in 1928. She was thirty-nine.

Count and Countess Plunkett and Fiona Plunkett in No. 40 Elgin Road, where they moved in 1926. Fiona, who was firmly anti-Treaty, was Cumann na mBan OC in Kilmainham Jail in 1923. Engaged three times but never married, she lived with her parents until her mother's death. She suffered from mental illness. She died in 1976.

Meanwhile, my sister Moya had been having a bad time with the convent. They sent her off to a school in Newcastle and after a few years to the Teacher Training College in London, which she told me afterwards was much more intelligent than the other convents she had been in, but by this time eight years had gone by, it was 1922, and she had still not been professed as a nun. When she asked them why, they told her they had decided she was not fitting into life in the order. So all those years of her life had been wasted when she could have been safely occupied doing great physiotherapy work in St Vincent's Hospital. She left the Sacred Heart order and they gave her a wig and got her a job. When things did not work out she decided she would have to go and do nursing, which was really more in her line, and she qualified as a midwife and came home. By this time we had five children and, as an aftermath of the Civil War, Tommy's salary had fallen down to a basic scale of £350 a year and was completely inadequate. However, I wrote to Ma that if she could give us a very small amount of money, just what would cover Moya's food, 15s or £1 a week, that I could manage to keep Moya with me and she could claim Matriculation as a person of mature years and go to college in Galway. Ma refused and Moya went back home.

She saw no prospect whatever of being able to live here so she applied to go to Uganda as a midwife. When she got to Kampala she found that the nuns there had decided that they would not employ a lay midwife after all and they were going to do the nursing themselves. She took a teaching job in one of their small schools in the jungle but after she had been there a couple of years she got into such a frightful state of emaciation that they decided to send her home. On the way home she collapsed at Port Said, and, after an emergency operation for an obstruction, died on July 25th 1928. She was thirty-nine. Ma said that she must be brought home for burial and sent a telegram saying 'spare no expense', so they embalmed Moya in the Egyptian manner and sent her home. It cost £250 and when Ma got the bill she hit the roof. Moya had made a will leaving whatever she owned to Mimi or to me if Mimi were dead, which she was (Moya apparently had a premonition about that). Ma put Moya's will in the fire and assured the family that Moya owned nothing. Uncle Jack Cranny, who was Moya's godfather, had left her two houses on Elgin Road in his will. Ma had made Moya assign them to her before she went in to the convent and she was supposed to have paid her for them, but Moya told me herself that she had not. Moya also owned one-seventh of the residue of Uncle Jack's estate, as each of us did. None of us got any part of this inheritance until after Ma's death.

Ma got sorry afterwards for what she had done to Mimi and Moya and, she told me, tried to make up for Mimi by taking an interest in her son, Colm; as my daughter Eilis reminded her of Moya, she was also singled out for kindness.

George and Jack were still anti-Treaty and still in the IRA but after the killing of Kevin O'Higgins in July, 1927, Willie Cosgrave put a stop to the arrests of IRA men by saying that if George Plunkett said that he did not kill O'Higgins, then he did not do it. By the spring of 1932, the Cumann na Gaedheal government had outlawed the constitutional republican organisation, Saor Eire, and had put Peadar O'Donnell and George and Charlie Gilmore in Arbour Hill Detention Barracks, treating them as if they were dangerous leaders, which they were not. Desmond FitzGerald, then the Minister for Defence, told me that they were going to execute them. He showed me a file of about ten pages of names and said they were prepared to execute these men one after the other. This was because they were so convinced that any attempt to put any other party in power, however legally, would be disastrous. I asked him where did my brother George's name come and he answered, 'Oh, not till the third page!'

George and Jack continued to be active in the IRA right up to the Second World War when they were interned in the Curragh. The men there were ordered by their commanding officers to go on hunger strike to get better conditions. They started one at a time and after two men had died the hunger strike was called off. It had lasted forty days and the men were moved to Arbour Hill barracks and then to hospital. Jack would have been the next to die. When he came home ill and depressed, he found that Ma had taken over his bedroom and thrown out his stuff as though he were already dead. I had found him, at the beginning of the war, before he was interned, trying to transmit to Germany and asked why on earth he was doing it and he said he had orders and was terrified that he would be killed if he did not carry them out. I believe that this contradiction of beliefs and actions was the cause of his lifelong depression from this on.

Every time either George or Jack got a job they were arrested so that they would be sacked. This meant they had no money and Ma still hadn't made over any property to any of us. No. 40 Elgin Road was raided every other week and there was a Plunkett rule that bedrooms were to be left clean in case of a raid. This continued into the thirties, even after the government changed from Cumann na nGaedheal to Fianna Fáil. Ma gave George weekly money but he and his wife, Mary, had to go and ask her for it every time. Jack did get a job in the ESB but could never get promotion.

In 1942, at Pa's insistence, two houses each were made over to myself and George. I got 27 and 29 Marlborough Road and George got 31 and 33 Marlborough Road, and in 1943 Ballymacscanlon, a house with outbuildings and about a hundred acres of land near Dundalk in County Louth, was bought for George. He had been farming at Owenstown House in Blackrock with constant interference from Ma who brought such an odd collection of people to it that it was known in the family as 'the Sunshine Home for lousers'. George had a Grade A dairy herd, but he was not long in Ballymascanlon when he was thrown out of a cart after his horse bolted and his neck was

George Plunkett moved to Ballymascanlon House near Dundalk with his wife, Mary, and five children in 1943. A year later he was killed when the horse he was driving bolted.

broken. He died on January 21st, 1944 leaving behind Mary and his five children, Joe, Eoghan, Máire, Siobhán and Seoirse. The Liverpool Lambs turned up for his funeral in Ravensdale and very many more old comrades. My daughter Bláth cooked bacon and eggs in Ballymascanlon for three and a half hours for the lot of them after the funeral. George's comrades liked him and worked well with him. One of them told me that they knew about the rotten way he was treated by Ma and they tried to get him to resist but it was too late, he could not.*

Ma died on March 6th, 1944. Pa, who was now ninety-two, immediately gave us full authority to begin sorting out the estate. Ma used to put together all her letters and bills—often unopened—circulars and advertisements, together with a newspaper or two, perhaps the book she was reading, wrap them in a newspaper and tie them with twine. She then marked it '*Private JMP do not touch*' and put it on the rolltop desk behind her armchair. The parcels gathered over and under the desk and beside it on the floor and when they went too far the housekeeper would remove armfuls of them to the breakfast room in the Elgin Road basement. This got fuller and fuller of papers and thrown-out books and was too damp for normal use, as some kind of stream flowed under it. When I was tidying up the papers after her death, I opened thousands of these parcels and found years-old uncashed cheques, legal documents and letting agreements, as well as stacks of estate duty demands, letters, great bundles of draft wills and deeds for Uncles Jack and Gerald Cranny and her mother, Maria. Probably every letter that had been written to her or my father had been kept, as well as deed boxes containing all Gerald's and Jack's papers, and all these had to be read before being destroyed because, since the family affairs had not been put in order for a hundred years, they might contain useful information about how some things had happened.

I found the two mortgages on Uncle Jack's houses, still unpaid after forty years, demands from the building society for mortgage payments for Larkfield, which Ma never paid, the letter from the reverend mother of the convent in Kensington asking Patrick and Maria Cranny to take my mother away, and the correspondence about the settlements and payments to my parents when they were first married from Patrick Plunkett and Maria Cranny. All of this enormous amount of paper was infested with a peculiar yellow worm. I collected three lorryloads of papers and Jack did at least as much, and hundredweights of papers were burnt and still there were several tons more to be got rid of. Pa, although legally joint owner of the property, never had control over it, but straight away after Ma died he settled the houses in Belgrave Road that he got from his father on the only survivors, myself and Jack and Fiona. Ma

---

*After the funeral the Countess screamed at Blánaid, her grand-daughter, to get out of the house with her mother and never to return. They left and Gerry said to Blánaid, 'She'll be dead of bad temper in a month.' The Countess died six weeks later.

had controlled the rest, over ninety properties, more than sixty houses and the rest in ground rents. It took most of ten years, many hours with solicitors, hundreds of bills and debts to be paid, endless searches for deeds and wills and many family arguments, to settle it all between fifteen people.

Pa died on March 12th 1948, aged ninety-six. A Republican to the end, he missed the changeover from 'Free State' to Republic by nine months. I still miss him.

Great-grandfather

He leaned softly out of the bed
to the two small sisters
edging towards him
all his oldness
blotting out the bookman
the legal man
the man who opened cases
in museum rooms
allowing worshippers to hold old holy stones

discussed renaissance wonders
with any passing three-year-old
or saved the ducks from drowning
held under his coat
as flood waters
curled around his reading chair.

'Kiss me' he said
feeling death on him
and these two
ninety years away
did what they could and couldn't do.

They saw him again
after two days
lying in state
dress uniform of white and gold
a gold sword by his side
the beauty of his face candle-framed.

The two small sisters
my older sisters
wrapped it in their memory
and I was born
nine months later on his birthday.

Honor O Brolchain
January 1997

Epilogue *Honor O Brolchain*

M Y GRANDPARENTS, GERRY AND TOMMY DILLON, lived in Galway until 1952, when my grandmother came to Dublin to live with us. Galway, which she loved, gave her a real and independent life where she was willing to be involved in any venture, particularly in the Arts, and in the lives of those around her. Any visitor from Dublin was treated to an enthusiastic tour of Connemara in a hired car, and her children's university friends from Dublin and Galway gathered in the Dillons' house, which had a very open door, every holiday. She had a particular love of the small pieces of cut stone decoration, some from medieval times, here and there in the town and it was her idea to create the walk from O'Brien's Bridge to the Salmon Weir which was originally intended to have a memorial to the Volunteers. She said of Galway that, being a garrisoned town before 1922, the business people had thought they were dependent on the British police and military for survival. She said they had in fact been cheated by them and that Galway never stopped improving after independence.

She left much of herself in Galway when she moved to Dublin but her active approach to life was the same, with a propensity to adopt anyone in need, be it of education, money, a home or just encouragement. In Dublin, where she was closer to journalists and historians working in her area, she began writing her story again more extensively. She and her brother, Jack, and her sister, Fiona, were now the only survivors of her family.

Jack (Eoin or John) Plunkett was a weekly caller at our house in Dublin, and my grandmother helped him remake the houses he had inherited but his melancholia, constant since

Geraldine Plunkett Dillon in 1955. She lived avidly up to the last minute and died in September, 1986, aged 94.

322

his hunger-strike, made him difficult and she felt she could not get things right for him. He felt unable to act for himself in the sorting of the Plunkett estate and asked my mother to represent him. He did manage, thanks to my mother's persuasion, to make a statement about his 1916-1922 activities to the Bureau of Military History which is in the Military Archive. Much of his work in the War of Independence related to cars and motorbikes (there were few experts at the time) and he continued to love motorbikes all his life and to organise scrambling rallies and trials. He was an engineer in the ESB and a skilled photographer and gave us children a half-crown on every special occasion and a book every Christmas. He died in 1960 aged sixty-two. Many government representatives were at his funeral and a Guard of Honour of members of the Four Courts' Garrison, Old IRA, escorted the cortege, with the coffin draped in the tricolour, to Glasnevin Cemetery where he was buried.

Fiona Plunkett was a dedicated officer in Cumann na mBan, remained anti-Treaty all her life, and was jailed several times for her activities. She worked from time to time with the Dun Emer Guild, having a talent for fine wool work, embroidery, hand-weaving and the making of carpets, vestments and tapestry and her highly valued work was on the walls and floors of many Dublin houses. She was engaged three times but never married. On one occasion she was left by her fiancé at the church door, on another, she left her fiancé at the church door. When she was not in jail she lived at home with her parents, dependent on her mother, and from her early forties she suffered from mental instability. Her mother's death finally gave her her houses and a measure of independence, however eccentric. Fiona went to Rome with her father for the Beatification of Oliver Plunkett in May, 1920 and was there again for his Canonisation in October 1975. She died a few months later in 1976 aged eighty. A Cumann na mBan Guard of Honour escorted her coffin to Glasnevin where she is also buried.

When he retired as Professor of Chemistry in UCG in 1954, my grandfather, Tommy Dillon, followed Gerry to our house in Dublin and his colleagues ensured that he had a lab in Trinity College to continue his research into alginates, the by-products of seaweed, for which he had an international reputation. It was his belief that the development of natural Irish products was essential to the progress of the State. He was dedicated to the idea of university education.

Apart from reading Shakespeare entertainingly as bedtime stories, he had not been good as a father and had to learn to be a grandfather but once he started, he found he had a flair for it. My grandmother never quite forgave him for the various pieces of bad behaviour but they visibly re-established old comradeship, having been through things together which nobody else could have understood. On April 23rd, 1966, as the country was going into commemorative mode for the fiftieth anniversary of the 1916 Rising, they celebrated their fiftieth wedding anniversary. We all sawa how he looked at her

Thomas Dillon retired from his professorship in 1954 but continued his research in a lab in TCD and his involvement in the international world of Chemistry. He died in 1971 aged 87.

with love we hadn't seen before just as they they were leaving to dine in style in the Shelbourne Hotel, Dublin, courtesy of their son, Eoin, who was then manager there.

Tommy Dillon died in 1972 aged eighty-eight and tributes were paid to him worldwide for his contribution to chemistry. Gerry said in her obituary for him that when he had begun his professorship in Galway in 1919 the first year chemical laboratory was a room in the abandoned (and rat-infested) Model School, the rest of the faculty was one room in the main college building and there were no research students but in spite of the political turmoil going on around him Tommy managed to form a real chemical department, to get the whole Model School handed over as an independent institution, to have the most brilliant students in Ireland come to him, and finally to have his students staff chemistry departments in Ireland, England and America.

Their five children, Moya O'Donnell, doctor, and counsellor; Blanaid O Brolchain, solicitor specialising in women's issues and the sale of apartments; Eilís Dillon, novelist and writer; Michael Dillon, farmer and journalist; and Eoin Dillon, hotelier, were all larger than life and there were not many rooms in Ireland that could hold all five personalities at the same time. They all had Gerry's talent for doing a great variety of things and, since they were Dillons as well as Plunketts, a capacity to argue the hind leg off any passing donkey.

Gerry was a gourmet cook, a dressmaker, embroiderer, carpenter, plumber and electrician. She kept cows, goats, pigs, hens and ducks, could tan a hide, cure bacon and make costumes and sets. By temperament she was busy, impatient, not violent but mildly explosive and endlessly inventive. She had an extraordinarily active brain—in later years she would sit in front of the television, arguing with it, playing double Patience or Bezique and reading (at great speed) novels in French or the Book of Job, Tristram Shandy or Francis Thompson, Georgette Heyer or detective stories or the latest book by an old comrade while drinking strange concoctions—whiskey and Cinzano or wine with anything!

She moved to a nursing home when she was ninety-one and started writing her memoirs all over again! She died in 1986 aged ninety-four and is buried in Glasnevin with so many of her family. She was not perfect but she was outstandingly good. She said you needed a sense of humour to survive all that her family had been through; she had one and she did.

Sources and bibliography

1. Geraldine Plunkett Dillon

Ten handwritten copybooks of memoirs, 1950s.*

Eight folders of assorted copybooks and pages of memoirs, 1980s, National Library of Ireland.

Manuscript drafts and typescripts of seven radio talks, *The Years of Change,* broadcast on Radio Éireann, 1959.*

Manuscript and typescript for an unpublished book on 1913–1916, 1960s.*

Series of ten articles for *University Review,* 1960s.*

Statements, now in the Military Archive, to the Bureau of Military History.

Miscellaneous files from the Military Archive.

Sundry documents from her personal collection, typescripts, articles, letters, memorial cards, wills, title deeds, school reports, university results, as well as newspaper cuttings, including obituaries, from over eighty years.*

Typescript of further memoirs taped in the 1980s.*

Articles on Galway 1920–21 for the *Connacht Tribune.*

Letters between Geraldine Plunkett Dillon and Bulmer Hobson, William O'Brien, Cathal O'Shannon, Dan Nolan, Professor Desmond Williams, Giovanni Costigan, Professor William Feeney, Donagh MacDonagh, Baby Bohan, Professor Roger McHugh, Frank Robbins, Hanna Sheehy-Skeffington, Eamon Dore, Edward Shields, Aidan McCabe, Professor F. X. Martin OSA, Arthur Cox and Pádraic Colum among others.*

'The North Roscommon Election', *The Capuchin Annual* 1967.

Unedited videotape of interviews with Geraldine Plunkett Dillon and her sister, Fiona, for RTE television programme, *Portraits,* 1966 (courtesy of Kilmainham Jail Archive).

RTE Radio interviews by Donncha Ó Dulaing, courtesy of RTE Radio Archive.

Introduction to *The Poems of Joseph Mary Plunkett,* The Talbot Press, Dublin, 1916.

Obituary of Professor Thomas P. Dillon.*

*Honor O Brolchain collection

2. Other sources

RTE Radio interview with Fiona Plunkett, courtesy of RTE Radio Archive, 1970s.

Joseph Plunkett's diary of his 1915 German journey.

Joseph Plunkett's GPO diary, 1916, National Library of Ireland.

Joseph Plunkett's Court Martial proceedings, 1916.

Tomás MacDonagh's Court Martial proceedings, 1916 (British Public Records Office).

Patrick J. Plunkett's last Will and Testament, 1905.

RTE Radio interview with Moya O'Donnell by Donncha Ó Dulaing.

Short manuscript concerning her mother, Geraldine Plunkett Dillon, by Blánaid O Brolchain.

Taped interview with Blánaid O Brolchain by Honor O Brolchain, 1997.

'Joseph Plunkett' by Donagh MacDonagh, *An Cosantóir* No. 10, November 1945.

To the Stonebreakers' Yard, RTE Radio Documentary, 1999, producer: Lorelei Harris.

The diaries of Dr Kathleen Lynn, 1916, Royal College of Physicians of Ireland.

Account of 1916 events by Father Columbus, *The Irish Times*, 2006.

Reminiscences of the Easter Rising, 1916 by Dr A. D. Louis Courtenay, private publication, 1965.*

Statements, now in the Military Archive, by Jack Plunkett, Grace Gifford-Plunkett, Máire Killeen O Brolcháin, Paddy Little and Eugene Smith to the Bureau of Military History.

3. Published books and articles

An Cosantóir Defence Forces HQ, October, 1945, November 1945, 1966, 1991, 2006.

Boylan, Henry: *A Dictionary of Irish Biography*. Dublin, Gill & Macmillan, 1998.

Breatnach, Labhrás: *An Pluincéadach*. Dublin, Foilseacháin Náisiúnta Teo. 1971.

Brennan-Whitmore, W. J.: *Dublin Burning*. Dublin, Gill & Macmillan, 1996.

Cleary, Nella: *The Carsons of Dublin*. Dublin, The Rathmines, Ranelagh & Rathgar Historical Society, 1997.

Comerford, Máire: *The First Dáil*. Joe Clarke, O'Connell Street, Dublin, 1969.

Coogan, Tim Pat: *1916: The Easter Rising*. London, Cassell & Co., 2001.

Coogan, Tim Pat: *The IRA*. London, Fontana/Collins, 1971.

Coogan, Tim Pat and George Morrison: *The Irish Civil War*. London, Weidenfeld & Nicholson, 1998.

Craig, Maurice, Joseph Hone and Michael Fewer: *The New Neighbourhood of Dublin*. Dublin, A. & A. Farmar, 2002.

Cullen Owens, Rosemary: *Smashing Times:* Dublin, Attic Press, 1984.

Curtis, Joe: *Harold's Cross*. Dublin, Joseph Curtis, 1998.

Czira, Sidney: *The Years Flew By*. Dublin, Arlen House, 2000.

Daly, Mary E., Mona Hearn and Peter Pearson: *Dublin's Victorian Houses*. Dublin, A. & A. Farmar, 1998.

Devoy's Post Bag, 1871–1928 ed. W. O'Brien and D. Ryan. Dublin, C. J. Fallon, 1953.

Dillon, Eilís: *Inside Ireland* London, Hodder & Stoughton, 1982.

Dillon, Thomas P.: articles for *Cork University Review* 1945 and *University Review* 1955.

Dublin and the Sinn Féin Rising. Issued by Wilson Hartnell, 1916.

Dublin Magazine, Three Candles, Spring, 1966.

Dudley Edwards, Ruth: *James Connolly*. Dublin, Gill & Macmillan, 1981.

Feeney, William J.: *History of the Irish Theatre, Hardwicke Street*, De Paul University, Chicago, Illinois USA 1977.

Fitzhenry, Edna: *Nineteen-Sixteen: An Anthology*. Dublin, Browne and Nolan, 1935.

Gorham, Maurice: *Dublin from Old Photographs*. London, B. T. Batsford Ltd. 1972.

Griffith, Kenneth and T. O'Grady: *Curious Journey*. Cork, Mercier Press, 1998.

Hansard, British House of Commons, Oral Answers, 1921.

Harris, Nathaniel: *The Easter Rising*. London Dryad Press, 1987.

Heuston OP, John M.: *Headquarters Battalion, Easter Week 1916*. Nationalist Printers, Carlow, 1966.

Hickey, D. J. and J. E. Doherty: *A New Dictionary of Irish History from 1800*. Dublin, Gill & Macmillan, 2003.

Kelly, Deirdre: *Four Roads to Dublin*. Dublin, The O'Brien Press, 1995.

Kennedy, Tom: *Victorian Dublin*. Dublin, Albertine Kennedy/Dublin Arts Festival, 1980.

Laffan, Moira: *Count Plunkett and his Times*. Foxrock Local History Club, 1992.

Leamy, Margaret: *Parnell's Faithful Few.* London, The Macmillan Co. 1936.

Lydon, James: *The Making of Ireland.* London, Routledge, 1998.

Macardle, Dorothy: *The Irish Republic.* Dublin, The Irish Press, 1951.

MacCarthy Morrogh, Michael: *The Irish Century.* London, Weidenfeld & Nicholson, 1998.

Mac Lochlainn, Piaras F., ed. *Last Words,* Dublin, Stationary Office, 1990.

Martin OSA, F. X.: *The Irish Volunteers, 1913–1915.* Dublin, James Duffy & Co., 1963.

Moylurg Writers: *Boyle.* Roscommon Herald, 1993.

National Gallery of Ireland, *Cuimhneachán 1916.* Dublin, Dolmen Press, 1966.

Neeson, Eoin: *Birth of a Republic.* Dublin, Prestige Books, 1998.

Ní Dhomhnaill, Nuala, ed. *RTE 100 Years.* Dublin, Townhouse, 2001.

O'Brien, William: *James Connolly and Easter Week, 1916.* Dublin, At the Sign of the Three Candles, 1949.

O'Connor, John: *The 1916 Proclamation.* Dublin, Anvil Books, 1999.

O'Dwyer, Frederick: *Lost Dublin.* Dublin, Gill & Macmillan, 1981.

O'Farrell, Mick: *A Walk Through Rebel Dublin, 1916.* Cork, Mercier Press, 1999.

O'Connor, Batt: *With Michael Collins.* London, Peter Davies, Ltd. 1929.

O'Hegarty, P. S.: *The Victory of Sinn Féin.* Dublin, Talbot Press, 1924.

O'Kelly, Charles: *The Jacobite War in Ireland*, ed. Count Plunkett BL and Edmund Hogan SJ. Dublin, Sealy, Briers and Walker, 1894.

Maitiú, Séamas: *Dublin's Suburban Towns 1834–1930.* Dublin, Four Courts Press, 2003.

O'Malley, Ernie: *On Another Man's Wound.* Revised edition, Dublin, Anvil, 2002.

O'Neill, Marie: *Grace Gifford Plunkett and Irish Freedom.* Dublin, The Irish Academic Press, 2000.

O'Toole, Fintan: *The Irish Times Book of the Century*, Dublin, Gill & Macmillan, 1999.

Oidhreacht 1916–1966, Dublin, Oifig an tSoláthair, 1966.

Pearson, Peter: *The Heart Of Dublin.* Dublin, The O'Brien Press, 2000.

Pictorial Review of 1916. Dublin, Parkside Press, 1946.

Plunkett, George Noble (Count); *Sandro Botticelli.* London George Bell & Sons, 1900.

Robbins, Frank: *Under the Starry Plough.* Dublin, Academy Press, 1977.

The Royal Commission on the Rebellion in Ireland, 1916.

Ryan, Desmond: *The Rising.* Dublin, Golden Eagle Books, 1949.

Semple, Maurice: *Some Galway Memories.* Privately published, 1973.

Shaw, Henry: *Dublin Pictorial Guide and Directory, 1850,* facsimile edition Belfast, Friar's Bush Press, 1988, introduction by Kevin B. Nowlan.

Stephens, James: *The Insurrection in Dublin.* Gerrard's Cross, Colin Smythe Ltd. 1978.

The Capuchin Annual 1970, ed. Father Henry.

The Clongownian, June 1912.

The Irish Review, 1911–1914.

The Sinn Féin Rebellion Handbook, Dublin, The Irish Times, May 1917.

Thom's *Directories,* Dublin 1837–1918.

Ward, Margaret: *Hanna Sheehy-Skeffington—a Life.* Dublin, Attic Press, 1997.

Ward, Margaret: *Unmanageable Revolutionaries.* Dingle, Brandon Press, 1983.

Index of illustrations

General index

The following abbreviations have been used for the most commonly used names: GDP is the author Geraldine Plunkett Dillon; GNP is her father George Noble, Count Plunkett; JMP is her brother Joseph Mary Plunkett; TPD is her husband Thomas P. Dillon.